D1251856

"*The Jews Should Keep Quiet* is of lasting importance for the teaching and understanding of the Holocaust. Rafael Medoff's incisive examination of the complex relationship between the U.S. president and America's foremost Jewish leader shines a light on troubling aspects of American history that many would prefer to ignore. This book is must reading."

—ZSUZSANNA OZSVATH, director of Holocaust Studies,
Ackerman Center for Holocaust Studies,
University of Texas at Dallas

"*The Jews Should Keep Quiet* is a cautionary tale about the pitfalls of elite complicity with government inaction. Rabbi Stephen S. Wise regarded Franklin D. Roosevelt as a friend, even though the Roosevelt administration was unfriendly to the plight of Jewish refugees, opposed the bombing of extermination camps, and remained ambivalent toward Zionism. Meticulously researched, engagingly written, and eminently fair-minded, *The Jews Should Keep Quiet* deserves a wide audience."

—DEAN J. KOTLOWSKI, professor of history at
Salisbury University and author of *Nixon's Civil Rights* and
Paul V. McNutt and the Age of FDR

"In this important volume, Medoff shows there was a great deal Roosevelt could have done despite the political circumstances and limitations. The new material and analysis he brings to light are vital study in a field rife with apologetic, consensus historians—and dare not to be forgotten."

—ALLEN H. PODET, professor emeritus, Philosophy and Religious
Studies, Buffalo State, State University of New York

"*The Jews Should Keep Quiet* is a meticulously researched and disquieting history of the reasons behind America's failure to rescue Europe's doomed Jews. Readers may rightly conclude that if there is a Roosevelt they can admire, it is Eleanor and not Franklin."

—ALAN L. BERGER, Raddock Family Eminent Scholar Chair
in Holocaust Studies, Florida Atlantic University

THE JEWS SHOULD KEEP QUIET

University of Nebraska Press | LINCOLN

THE JEWS
SHOULD
KEEP QUIET

Franklin D. Roosevelt, Rabbi Stephen S. Wise,

and the Holocaust

RAFAEL MEDOFF

The Jewish Publication Society | PHILADELPHIA

♾

Library of Congress Cataloging-in-Publication Data
Names: Medoff, Rafael, 1959– author.
Title: The Jews should keep quiet: Franklin D.
Roosevelt, Rabbi Stephen S. Wise, and the Holocaust /
Rafael Medoff.
Description: Lincoln: University of Nebraska Press,
[2019] | "Published by the University of Nebraska
Press as a Jewish Publication Society book." | Includes
bibliographical references and index.
Identifiers: LCCN 2018052333
ISBN 9780827614703 (cloth: alk. paper)
ISBN 9780827618305 (epub)
ISBN 9780827618312 (mobi)
ISBN 9780827618329 (pdf)
Subjects: LCSH: Holocaust, Jewish (1939–1945)—
Foreign public opinion, American. | Public
opinion—United States. | World War, 1939–1945—
Jews—Rescue. | Jews—United States—Politics and
government—20th century. | Roosevelt, Franklin D.
(Franklin Delano), 1882–1945—Relations with Jews.
| Wise, Stephen S. (Stephen Samuel), 1874–1949.
| United States—Politics and government—1933–1945.
| United States—Foreign relations—1933–1945.
Classification: LCC D804.45.U55 M42 2019 |
DDC 940.53/18—dc23 LC record available at
https://lccn.loc.gov/2018052333

Set in Scala OT by Mikala R. Kolander.

In memory of David S. Wyman
scholar, teacher, friend

CONTENTS

ACKNOWLEDGMENTS

I AM GRATEFUL TO Ilya Slavutskiy and his colleagues at the American Jewish Historical Society; Simone Schliachter and her colleagues at the Central Zionist Archives; the staff members of the Franklin D. Roosevelt Presidential Library, the American Jewish Archives, the Jabotinsky Institute (Metzudat Ze'ev), the National Archives, the Library of Congress, the Public Record Office (London), and the American Friends Service Committee Archives, for their assistance and cooperation in the research for this book; and to Benyamin Korn for helping to craft the title.

As a historian, I am especially pleased to be publishing this book with the Jewish Publication Society (JPS), the nation's oldest Jewish publisher. My thanks to its director, Rabbi Barry L. Schwartz, and the JPS staff—especially to Joy Weinberg, JPS managing editor, for her superlative editing and many keen insights, from which this manuscript has benefited immensely. I am also deeply grateful to the University of Nebraska Press.

INTRODUCTION

"If Only He Would Do Something for My People!"

"JUSTINE AND SHAD HAD dinner with the Roosevelts on Saturday, including the President," Rabbi Stephen S. Wise reported to his son, with evident pride, about the honor extended to Wise's daughter and son-in-law by the First Family. And that was not all: "Justine said [President Roosevelt] sent his affectionate regards to me." But then Wise added a discordant note: "If only he would do something for my people!"[1]

The date was February 16, 1943. Two months had passed since the United States and its allies had publicly confirmed that the Germans had slaughtered "many hundreds of thousands" of Jews as part of a systematic, ongoing effort "to exterminate the Jewish people in Europe." Yet President Roosevelt and his administration insisted there was nothing they could do to aid the Jews, or interrupt the murder process, except to defeat Hitler on the battlefield. Rabbi Wise, the foremost leader of the American Jewish community in the 1930s and '40s, agonized over the slaughter of Europe's Jews and longed for some kind of U.S. intervention. Yet the very fact that he confined his critical remark about FDR to a private letter and would never express such sentiments in public illustrates both the dilemma Wise faced and the success of Roosevelt's strategy for stifling potential Jewish criticism of his refugee policy.[2]

Franklin Roosevelt has been described by many of his biographers and other scholars as "a master manipulator"—not only "of Congress, the press and the public," but also of individuals, friends and foes alike. He was "supreme in the manipulation of people," exhibiting "an almost instinctual ability" to exploit "men's ambitions, fears, and loyalties" to his advantage. Roosevelt engineered fawning press coverage by inviting select reporters to private Oval Office sessions where he would engage in "cheerful banter" and "make them feel as though they were inside participants" in the evolution of presidential decisions. He outmaneuvered subordinates by "consciously stirring rivalries among those he put in positions of power, ultimately leaving himself in control."[3]

Nowhere was Roosevelt's "passion for manipulation" on greater display than in the way he managed his relationship with Rabbi Wise. Calling Wise by his first name, extending a dinner invitation to Wise's daughter, and sending along "affectionate regards" were the kinds of gestures that touched Wise and made him feel important. A meeting in the Oval Office, however rare, made Wise feel as if he had the ear of the president. Such gestures helped ensure that Wise would keep his negative feelings about Roosevelt's refugee policy to himself. That, in turn, would help sustain the traditionally high levels of support for FDR among American Jews, who constituted a significant voting bloc in New York, the state with the largest number of electoral votes in a presidential election. Furthermore, FDR's practice of glad-handing—of making policy-related promises he had no intention of keeping—was especially effective when dealing with Jewish leaders such as Wise, who were profoundly reluctant to press Roosevelt to follow through on his unfulfilled pledges.[4]

Wise's reluctance was intertwined with how American Jews understood their own place as a small minority group—numbering five million, less than 4 percent of the national population—in a society where they were not yet fully accepted. Polls in the late 1930s and early 1940s found that more than half of the U.S. public perceived Jews as greedy and dishonest;

between one-third and one-half believed Jews had "too much power"; and about one-third regarded Jews as overly aggressive. About 15 percent of respondents said they would support "a widespread campaign against the Jews in this country" and an additional 20–25 percent indicated they would feel sympathy for such a movement; only about 30 percent said they would actively oppose it. Even on Capitol Hill, a small but vocal number of congressmen exhibited fierce xenophobia, occasionally crossing over into outright antisemitism. A 1941 diatribe by Rep. John Rankin (D-MS) accusing "international Jews" of trying to drag America into Europe's war, delivered on the floor of the U.S. House of Representatives, actually caused a Jewish congressman to suffer a fatal heart attack.[5]

These high levels of antisemitism resulted from traditional (religion-based) prejudice against Jews, compounded by insecurities and fears magnified by the hardships of economic depression. By 1940 more than one hundred antisemitic organizations were operating nationwide. More than 200,000 Americans subscribed to *Social Justice,* a weekly tabloid published by the antisemitic Catholic priest Father Charles Coughlin, and 3.5 million Americans regularly listened to his Sunday radio broadcasts; plus an additional ten million tuned in at least once each month.[6]

Antisemitism often went hand in hand with isolationism and nativism. The America First movement, which mobilized grassroots sentiment against American involvement in overseas conflicts, grew rapidly during this period. Many isolationists charged that U.S. opposition to Hitler's anti-Jewish policies could drag America into armed conflict with Germany, as aviation hero Charles Lindbergh asserted in an infamous 1941 speech. At the same time, nativists whipped up fears that immigrants would bring radical foreign ideologies with them. With the onset of the Great Depression and unemployment reaching 25 percent in the early 1930s, many Americans feared that new immigrants would take away jobs that rightfully belonged to established U.S. citizens.[7]

In this difficult environment, American Jews struggled to gain acceptance as Americans. On the one hand, Jewish organizations sought to counter anti-Jewish bigotry by enlisting prominent gentiles to denounce antisemitism and publicizing statistics to prove that many Jews had served in America's wars. At the same time, many Jewish immigrants or children of immigrants discarded their parents' religious or cultural practices, motivated not only (and sometimes not at all) by theological considerations but rather by a simple desire to fit in as Americans. Many Reform rabbis began delivering their major weekly sermon on Sunday mornings rather than the Sabbath, and a small number of Reform synagogues went so far as to officially change their Sabbath from Saturday to Sunday. The transformation of the minor holiday of Hanukkah into a major gift-giving event, paralleling Christmas, was yet another way Jews altered their religious and social behavior to advance the goal of Americanization.[8]

For the American Jewish community, the question of responding to the Nazi persecution of Jews—and how the Roosevelt administration should respond to it—became part of the broader question of how to navigate conflicts between ethnic group interests and what was deemed acceptable behavior in the American public realm. Genuine anguish over the persecution in Europe and the instinctive desire to respond as forcefully as possible sometimes clashed with fears that large or intemperate protests might somehow jeopardize the status of Jews in America. Should Jews publicly take issue with the president's refugee policy, if that meant alienating some non-Jewish Americans?

This dilemma was heightened by American Jewry's widespread and fervent support of President Roosevelt's New Deal policies. "Jewish people are not supposed to worship graven images, but my mother used to kiss this little bust of Franklin Roosevelt that was on top of the big old radio," the Broadway producer Arthur Cantor once recalled. "That was very characteristic of Eastern European Jews [in America]." Wise too was a devout supporter of the New Deal. Should Jews criticize a president whose domestic agenda they enthusiastically embraced?[9]

America's entry into World War II added a new layer to this

conflict of conscience: was it appropriate, in the midst of a world war, for Jews to request special action to aid their coreligionists alone? Wise himself had just recently opposed a colleague's proposal for a one-hour work stoppage by American Jewish laborers as a gesture of solidarity with Europe's Jews, fearing it would provoke accusations that American Jews were interfering with the war effort. Wise also had urged other Jewish leaders to refrain from calling on the Allies to threaten reprisals against the Germans, on the grounds that "Americans have not yet completely thrown themselves into this war, [so] how then could we ask the American people to take a special warlike action on behalf of the Jews?" How to respond to the plight of Europe's Jews without endangering American Jewry's own status would prove to be the most difficult challenge of Wise's life.[10]

Historians have long grappled with, yet never fully answered, many of the key questions surrounding President Roosevelt's response to the Holocaust. For example, relatively few Jewish refugees were allowed to enter the United States during the 1930s and 1940s—but why did the president go out of his way to suppress immigration far below the limits allowed by law? Why did he leave nearly two hundred thousand quota places unused, when—as refugee advocates pointed out at the time— the quotas could have been filled without new legislation or controversy? Why did he refuse pleas to let Jewish exiles stay temporarily in a U.S. territory, which would have kept them safe from the Nazis without admitting them to the American mainland? Why did he turn away the passengers of the refugee ship *St. Louis*, when the governor and legislative assembly of the U.S. Virgin Islands had just offered to open their doors to Jews fleeing the Nazis? Roosevelt abhorred Hitler and worked hard to prepare America for war with Germany in the late 1930s in the face of widespread isolationism—so why did he, at the same time, insist on maintaining cordial (sometimes even friendly) diplomatic and economic relations with Nazi Germany prior to World War II? Why did FDR repeatedly remove anti-Hitler references from a cabinet member's speeches, and send U.S. representatives to Nazi rallies in New York City and Germany? Why did he refuse to even verbally criticize the Nazi persecution of Jews throughout most of the 1930s? Why did his administration help the Nazis evade the American Jewish boycott of German goods, by allowing them to use deceptive labeling on their exports to the United States?

The Roosevelt administration claimed that rescuing Jews conflicted with the goal of winning the war—but why was it unwilling even to take steps to rescue Jews that would not have interfered with the war effort, such as using empty Liberty ships returning from Europe to carry refugees, as some Jewish advocates urged? Why did the administration refuse requests to drop bombs on the railways and bridges leading to Auschwitz, from American planes that were already flying over that area—while air-dropping supplies to Polish fighters whose revolt the administration believed would fail?

Did President Roosevelt's private attitudes toward Jews—largely overlooked by historians—play a role in shaping these and other policy decisions? Was it just a coincidence that FDR's personal opinions about Jews were strikingly similar to his view of Asians? Could there be a connection between his policy of excluding Jewish refugees and his mass internment of Japanese Americans?

Finally, how did President Roosevelt manage to prevent the American Jewish leadership, with its longstanding tradition of seeking U.S. government intervention on behalf of persecuted Jews abroad, from acting similarly during the Nazi era? How did FDR keep Rabbi Wise and other leading Jews quiet, so that his policy regarding Europe's Jews could proceed unhindered?

These are among the questions *The Jews Should Keep Quiet* will explore, not from the convenient perspective afforded by hindsight, but in the context of what was actually happening then: the harsh political and social environment of the era, the level of knowledge and belief concerning the plight of Europe's Jews, and the realistic opportunities for rescue that, if acted upon, could have saved many lives.

THE JEWS SHOULD KEEP QUIET

I

"Nothing but Indifference"

RABBI STEPHEN S. WISE was arguably the Jewish public figure best positioned to lead American Jewry in responding to the crisis of German Jewry under Nazism. A gifted orator with an imposing presence and a deep, booming voice, Wise could inspire an audience like few others, whether at a protest rally or in the pews of his Free Synagogue in Manhattan. He was the leader of, or at least a central figure in, an array of communal institutions, including two major defense groups, the American Jewish Congress (AJCongress) and the World Jewish Congress; the American Zionist movement; and a rabbinical seminary, the Jewish Institute of Religion (which later merged with Reform Judaism's Hebrew Union College). He also served as editor in chief of *Opinion*, a prominent Jewish monthly magazine.

From his earliest years in public life, Wise had established for himself a reputation as someone who was not afraid to cause controversy. In 1918 he founded the American Jewish Congress as an activist-oriented, ethnically assertive challenger to the elitist and undemocratic American Jewish Committee. He was a Reform rabbi and an outspoken Zionist during a period when most Reform rabbis were anti-Zionist or non-Zionist. If a congregant resigned in protest over something he said in a sermon, Wise remained unruffled; he liked to joke that his was "the most piously resigned Jewish congregation in our history—someone is always resigning."[1]

Born in Hungary in 1874 and brought to the United States as a toddler, Stephen Samuel Wise was the son of Rabbi Aaron Wise, one of the founders of the Jewish Theological Seminary of America and spiritual leader of Manhattan's Congregation Rodeph Sholom. Although he was raised in a strictly traditional home and received Orthodox ordination, Aaron Wise came to embrace a wide range of reforms to Jewish practice as he built his career in the New World.

His son Stephen would go much further in that direction. As a student at the City College of New York and then Columbia, Stephen excelled in Greek, Latin, and, he soon discovered, public speaking. Before long, he was receiving invitations to deliver guest sermons at local synagogues; one billed him as "Mr. Stephen S. Wise, the Great Orator of Columbia College and aspirant for the Ministry." Rather than enroll his son in an established rabbinical school, Aaron Wise sent Stephen to Vienna in 1892 to study with Adolf Jellinek, a rabbi, Judaic scholar, acclaimed preacher, and, not incidentally, an advocate of reforms in Jewish religious life. Jellinek influenced Wise in all four realms, and granted him private rabbinical ordination less than a year later.[2]

Wise's doctoral studies ended up taking a back seat to his burgeoning professional and personal obligations; he served his first pulpit, as assistant rabbi at New York City's B'nai Jeshurun, from 1893 to 1900, and was married, to the heiress and charity worker Louise Waterman, in 1900. He finally completed his PhD in semitics at Columbia in 1902, with a dissertation on the medieval Jewish sage Ibn Gabirol.[3]

Early on, Wise developed a keen interest in political and social affairs. Just before beginning his studies with Jellinek, he had attended a "summer school of the cultural sciences" run by the Social Gospel philosopher Thomas Davidson, who saw social reform as an essential component of modern Christianity. That summer's studies helped Wise hone what he called

"Liberal Judaism," a worldview that fused Jewish principles and liberal religious values with progressive social and political causes. Except for his affinity for Zionism, Wise's philosophy of Judaism closely resembled American Reform Judaism, which likewise substituted social and political concerns for the traditional religious practices it considered outdated or distasteful.

At B'nai Jeshurun, and then as rabbi of Congregation Beth Israel in Portland, Oregon (1900 to 1906), Wise stirred his share of controversy with his outspokenness on child labor and other issues of the day. Returning to New York City in 1906, he plunged into the world of public policy activism. In short order, he became a founder of the American Civil Liberties Union, a board member of the National Association for the Advancement of Colored People, and an activist for labor rights, women's suffrage, and international disarmament. He was chosen to take part in the investigation of the infamous Triangle Shirtwaist Factory fire, raised funds for striking textile workers, campaigned for the freedom of anarchists Sacco and Vanzetti, and participated in many other social justice struggles. Most American Jews shared Wise's sympathy for progressive political and social causes; hence his activism in those areas strengthened his standing as one of the most able Jewish representatives to the wider community.[4]

It was Wise's association with Franklin D. Roosevelt that would cement his status as the Jewish leader who enjoyed the most access to, and was most respected in, the halls of power. Wise's relationship with FDR did not get off to a smooth smart. He endorsed Roosevelt for governor of New York in 1928, but the two men had a falling-out in 1931 after Roosevelt refused to heed Wise's pleas to take on New York City's corrupt Tammany Hall political machine. During FDR's first campaign for the White House, in 1932, Wise shared with his close friend (and future Supreme Court justice), Harvard University law professor Felix Frankfurter, this acerbic assessment of Roosevelt: "I know him and I know how utterly untrustworthy he is the moment any problem arises, decisions or tactics touching which may adversely affect his own political fortunes. I have nothing but horror at the thought of what Roosevelt will be for four years at Washington." In another letter to Frankfurter around the same time, Wise charged that FDR had "no deep-seated convictions," and "no bed-rock . . . he is all clay and no granite." In that year's presidential election, Wise voted for the Socialist Party's nominee, Norman Thomas, rather than cast his ballot for Roosevelt.[5]

Soon after Roosevelt became president, however, Wise's attitude changed. The New Deal advanced a social justice agenda that endeared FDR to Wise, just as it endeared FDR to the overwhelming majority of American Jews. Consequently, Wise's correspondence during Roosevelt's first hundred days was filled with exuberant comments about the "magnificent beginning" to his administration and all the "big, yes wonderful things" President Roosevelt was doing.[6]

Even as he lavished praise on FDR in public, though, Wise was privately growing concerned about the president's silence as reports about the plight of German Jews multiplied. In the days following Adolf Hitler's rise to power in January 1933, Wise read increasingly harrowing reports in the Jewish Telegraphic Agency (JTA) *Daily News Bulletin* about anti-Jewish abuses in Germany. Already on the first day of the new regime, the JTA informed its readers that the new cabinet was filled with "Nazi leaders notorious for the violence of their anti-Semitic stand. . . . The entire internal policy of Germany is to be controlled by Nazis who are firm believers in violence against the Jews." By the very next day, those forebodings began to materialize. In Berlin, the windows of a Jewish bookstore were smashed, mourners in a Jewish funeral procession were assaulted, and Jewish passengers on city trains were harassed. A mob of five hundred Nazis marched onto the University of Berlin campus and drove Jewish students out of the buildings. Nazis fired shots at Jewish patrons in a Berlin cafe, ransacked a Jewish warehouse in Fridberg, assaulted Jewish passersby in Breslau and synagogue-goers in Hamburg; and stabbed a Jewish student to death in Breslau.[7]

Jewish leaders hoped a strong U.S. response would help stem the escalating crisis. In the days preceding Franklin Roosevelt's March 4, 1933, inauguration, Wise and others sought to arrange a joint statement by FDR and outgoing president Herbert Hoover condemning the mistreatment of German Jews. Lewis Strauss, a Jewish philanthropist and longtime associate of Hoover's, served as the go-between. Hoover agreed to the proposed statement; Roosevelt, however, declined. Wise then consulted with two of the president's closest Jewish confidantes, the law professor Felix Frankfurter and Supreme Court Justice Louis Brandeis, on whether they "should try to break through and see Roosevelt" about the proposal. After some discussion, they decided it was "not quite fair," in view of "[the president's] overwhelming responsibilities . . . to trouble him with our, in a sense, lesser problem," as Wise put it. Their reticence was a harbinger of the American Jewish leadership's stance concerning Roosevelt and European Jewry in the years to follow.[8]

American Jewry Divided

During the years preceding Hitler's rise to power, Rabbi Wise and his colleagues in the American Jewish leadership closely followed political developments in Germany. Nevertheless, they—like many foreign observers—were caught off-guard by Hitler's triumph. Just weeks before the November 1932 German elections that would propel the Nazi leader to power, an American Jewish Congress representative in Germany reported to Wise that all but one of the thirty prominent German Jews whom he had questioned were confident that "Hitler would never come to power." A striking indication of the initial confusion among some U.S. Jewish leaders was that nearly two weeks after Hitler was named chancellor, participants in an American Jewish Committee (AJCongress) executive committee meeting were discussing how to alleviate the problems American Jewish students were encountering in gaining admission to German universities.[9]

Wise did not doubt the veracity of the reports about discrimination and violence suffered by German Jews during Hitler's first weeks in office. "We are terribly disturbed and fearful about what is happening and going to happen in Germany," the rabbi wrote his close friend and colleague Julian Mack on March 1. Wise cited news reports that the Nazis were planning a "Teutonic" version of the sixteenth-century St. Bartholomew's Day Massacre. He was not impressed by warnings from some prominent German Jews that protests abroad would make things worse. "I do not give a penny for the counsel of the Berlin people," he wrote Mack. "They have been saying for years there is no *Gefahr* [danger] of Hitler's coming to power. They have no judgment and certainly they can have no objective judgment now."[10]

In Wise's view, the German Jewish leaders' remarks were made with the equivalent of a gun to their heads. He recalled that Rumanian Jewish leaders had once told him, "If we cable to you ten times not to take any steps, go ahead and do what you think is right. Your judgment will be better than ours." Wise pointed out to Mack that just "a year ago, Dr. Theodor Wolff of the *Berliner Tageblatt* spoke with utmost assurance with respect to the future of the Jews in Germany [and] today . . . he is in hiding." Wise generally assumed that the situation under Hitler was worse than what was known; in one letter to a friend later that year, he wrote that "we know 10% of the truth of what is happening in Germany."[11]

On February 22, Wise met with leaders of the two other largest U.S. Jewish defense groups, the American Jewish Committee and B'nai B'rith, to discuss possible responses to the crisis. These two groups were dominated by well-to-do German-born Jews who opposed public Jewish protests. "Hot-headed Jews should be suppressed," New York appellate judge Irving Lehman, a leading AJ committee member, advised. Rabbi Wise privately characterized such Jewish advocates of caution as "the old Temple Emanuel-Harmonie Club crowd" (referring to the synagogue and the Manhattan social club they frequented), who were "dumb, paralyzed by the fear of the *Centralverein* [the cautious central Jewish organization in Germany] crowd or else shamefully silent because of their assimilationism." On another occasion, he privately derided "the cowardice of these Jewish invertebrates, always ready to sacrifice Jewish honor for the sake of fancied Jewish security." Perhaps not surprisingly, a number of Wise's interlocutors found his criticism of fellow Jews more than a little off-putting. James G. McDonald, the League of Nations High Commissioner for Refugees Coming from Germany, took note in his diary of Wise's scathing remarks to him about some of the rabbi's rivals in the Jewish community. McDonald commented: "And it was in this same conversation that Rabbi Wise deplored at length the divisive tendencies among the Jews!"[12]

For all his heated rhetoric about the AJcommittee–B'nai B'rith crowd, Wise too was not yet convinced that a public outcry would be the most appropriate response. The February 22 conferees agreed that in view of the uncertainty regarding forthcoming policies of the Hitler government, and the possibility that foreign protests might result in repercussions against German Jews, a cautious approach was advisable. They decided to create a Joint Consultative Committee to "keep a close watch" on the situation in Germany, but not to protest openly, because "for the present, public agitation would not serve the cause of Reich Jewry."[13]

Even as Rabbi Wise agreed to that approach, he faced hurdles his Joint Consultative Committee colleagues did not. The AJcommittee was an elitist rather than a mass membership organization, and B'nai B'rith was a fraternal order and social service organization; hence neither of them were subject to significant grassroots pressure on political issues. Wise, by contrast, regarded the leadership of the AJcommittee and B'nai B'rith as "Hof-Juden," or court Jews, a reference to the traditional role of Jewish leaders in Europe, who had acted through private intercession with the local rulers. Wise and the other founders of the AJcongress, by contrast, proclaimed themselves the authentic representative of the Jewish masses and sought to replace the old power structure with "Jewish self-determination." Thus

Wise could not easily ignore the new groundswell of demands from his membership for action. While the AJ committee and B'nai B'rith denounced the idea of public demonstrations as "an ineffectual channel for the release of emotion," Wise concluded that his constituents needed an outlet for their anti-Nazi sentiment. "You cannot imagine the feeling that rages throughout the country," he confided to one colleague. "There are all sorts of things being spoken of, such as boycotts of [German] goods." To another associate, he wrote: "You cannot imagine what I am doing to resist the masses. They want organized boycotts. They want tremendous street scenes."[14]

In addition to feeling pressured by the AJ congress rank and file, Wise was shocked and moved by first-hand reports about anti-Jewish violence in Germany. Letters smuggled from the Reich "told me of tortures, the cutting of *Hackenkreuze* [swastikas] into the flesh of Jews, imprisonment, death, night visits and night rides [a term usually associated with Ku Klux Klan violence in the American South] from which Jews never returned—as well as of the economic and social outlawing of Jews from the professions, business, and all ordinary contact with non-Jewish neighbors," he later recalled. "From one who had temporarily crossed the border into France I got the message: 'Do not believe the denials. Nor the Jewish denials.'" Such reports contradicted State Department officials' private remarks to Wise suggesting that anti-Jewish violence in Germany was subsiding. Furthermore, according to one of Wise's European interlocutors, a number of American Jews in Germany had been "beaten senseless and left out in the woods" by Nazis, but local U.S. diplomats had "toned down" information about the assaults prior to transmission to the State Department "in order that [the administration] may have something to show to representatives of Jewish societies who complained to the Department 'that will pacify them instead of alarming them,' as one [embassy staffer] put it."[15]

Wise attempted to elicit a public statement of sympathy from the Roosevelt administration, but made no headway. After a meeting between Undersecretary of State William Phillips and an AJCongress delegation headed by Wise on March 21, Phillips said the administration would not protest German government actions "unless Americans were involved." If the victims were German citizens, he said, "the sympathy of our citizens" was outweighed by the conventional standards of non-intervention prevailing among "the community of nations." Wise had hoped that he or the delegation could speak with President Roosevelt directly, but FDR's de facto chief of staff Louis McHenry Howe rebuffed the request, telling Wise it would be "a mistake" to raise the issue with the president.[16]

There was ample precedent for a U.S. diplomatic protest against a foreign government that was persecuting its citizens. At the request of American Jewish leaders, the Van Buren, Buchanan, and Grant administrations, respectively, protested the mistreatment of Jews in Syria, Switzerland, and Rumania. Theodore Roosevelt protested the persecution of Jews in Rumania (1902). The U.S. government, under President William Howard Taft, canceled a Russo-American treaty to protest Russia's oppression of Jews (1911). President Woodrow Wilson inserted clauses protecting minorities in agreements reached at the Paris Peace Conference (1919), and Germany had pledged to abide by those clauses. Nevertheless, President Roosevelt declined to say anything that conceivably might irritate U.S.-German relations.[17]

Meanwhile, despite Wise's agreement with his Joint Consultative Committee partners to refrain from "public agitation," pressure from his AJCongress colleagues was forcing him to change course. Over Wise's private objections, the AJCongress held an emergency conference of Jewish organizations on March 19 for the purpose of planning anti-Hitler protests. Some fifteen hundred representatives of American Jewish organizations attended. In his opening remarks, AJCongress president Bernard Deutsch made clear what was driving the campaign: "The offices of the American Jewish Congress are being flooded with messages from all over the country demanding protest action," he said. "We are met here to translate this popular mandate into responsible, vigorous, orderly and effective action." The delegates decided to hold a "Stop Hitler Now" protest rally at Madison Square Garden on March 27.[18]

The AJcommittee recoiled at these developments. To a significant extent, the Committee's establishment back in 1906 had been intended to prevent the then mostly eastern European immigrant masses from influencing the American Jewish leadership's positions in its contacts with the non-Jewish world. By contrast, Rabbi Wise had established the AJcongress in 1918 precisely to give the immigrant generation a greater say in communal affairs. Cyrus Adler, AJcommittee president from 1929 to 1940, was not far off the mark when he remarked that the AJcongress "was created with the intention of destroying the American Jewish Committee."[19]

AJcommittee leaders rejected the AJcongress's plan to hold protest rallies, fearing such protests might provoke not only harsher German treatment of Jews, but antisemitism at home. "The noise of mass meetings, parades, boycotts has only served to generate more antisemitism in this and other countries," AJcommittee executive vice president Morris Waldman advised a colleague in 1933. "[G]reat numbers of inarticulate and 'average' Americans are becoming a bit irritated by this struggle within their borders, yet alien to them," he subsequently reported to the 1934 Rabbinical Assembly conference. "It may be that some Jewish groups have too many times protested against Hitlerism."[20]

Wise was of two minds. On the one hand, he did not entirely disagree with the AJcommittee's concerns. He, too, worried that overly boisterous Jewish behavior, such as rallies featuring militant criticism of the Roosevelt administration, would be going too far, and might provoke antisemitism. At the same time, however, he believed the American public would accept more restrained Jewish protests, so long as they were conducted in a "reserved dignified style," included "some outstanding Gentiles" among the speakers, and refrained from adopting "demagogical hysterical resolutions."[21]

In the days leading up to the March 27 rally, Wise began to find his footing. "Silence is acquiescence," and it had never been his style to remain silent in the face of injustice, he wrote to one friend. "The time for caution and prudence is past. . . . We must speak up like men." In another letter, he compared his refusal to cancel the rally to the biblical Mordechai refusing to bow down before "Haman, the Hitler of an earlier Persian day." There was "hideous pressure" on him "from all over the world to call off the meeting, to which pressure I was at moments tempted to yield," Wise later recalled. "I am going through days and nights of hell," because "timid and fearful German Jews both in Germany and America are at my heels to desist."[22]

Shortly before the event, both the German Foreign Office and the German Embassy in Washington contacted Wise, offering "some moderating of anti-Jewish measures" if the rally was canceled. Uncertain whether to trust such assurances, and "hesitating and fearful" in the face of the various pressures, Wise consulted Brandeis. The Supreme Court justice advised: "Go ahead and make the protest as good as you can."[23]

The rally went forward as planned. Twenty thousand people filled Madison Square Garden for the event, and another thirty-five thousand listened from loudspeakers in the surrounding streets as a long list of political figures, Jewish leaders, and prominent Christians denounced the mistreatment of German Jewry. Wise was the final speaker. Afterward, he recalled with pride how he spoke with "absolute self-restraint," in "prudent and cautious" language, and had been careful to avoid using "the term 'boycott' or 'reprisal,'" even though "the easiest thing in the world would have been to rouse that audience . . . to murderous rage." Like the other speakers, Wise emphasized in his remarks that the rally "is not against the German people whom we honor and revere and cherish," and "is not against the political program of Germany, for Germany is master within her own household, but solely against the present anti-Jewish policy of the Nazi government." The speakers appealed generally to "the civilized nations" to oppose Nazi

antisemitism, but there were no calls on the Roosevelt administration, or any other specific government, to take action. The
only attention given to the U.S. government's position was a
mention in the *New York Times* that Bishop John Dunn of the
Catholic Archdiocese of New York had canceled his planned
address to the rally after Secretary of State Cordell Hull sent
a cable to the AJCongress, AJCommittee, and B'nai B'rith earlier that week asserting that violence against Jews in Germany
"may be considered virtually terminated." Wise had done his
best to perform a complex balancing act. Proceeding with the
rally satisfied his constituents. Imposing a cautious tone on
the event and carefully choreographing the choice of speakers
would, he hoped, appease the AJCommittee and other opponents of public Jewish clamor. Avoiding any criticism of the
Roosevelt administration would protect his access to government officials and head off any Jewish clash with a president
whose policies he strongly favored.[24]

Christian Responses

The prominent role of Christian speakers at the March 27 rally
was crucially important to Wise, because their participation
demonstrated that Nazi antisemitism was a matter of concern
not only to Jews, but to non-Jews as well. When asked by NBC
Radio to choose a limited number of the speeches to be nation-
ally broadcast that evening, "we put only Christian speakers on
the air," Wise noted. He wanted the American public to see the
protest not as an instance of Jews engaged in narrow special
pleading, but rather as representing a legitimate cause whose
supporters reached well beyond the Jewish community.[25]

From his earliest days as a rabbi, Wise placed a premium
on interfaith relations. The very first line-up of guest speakers whom Wise invited to share his pulpit at New York City's
Free Synagogue in the autumn of 1907 included the Unitarian minister and author Edward Everett Hale and the Bap-
tist pastor and social justice advocate Walter Rauschenbusch.
Likewise, at Wise's rabbinical seminary, the Jewish Institute of

Religion, students were often treated to guest lectures by such Christian progressive luminaries as peace activist Rev. Henry Atkinson, Catholic reform crusader Father John A. Ryan, and the leftwing political activist Rev. Henry F. Ward. In addition, one of Wise's lifelong friends was Rev. John Haynes Holmes, a prominent Unitarian minister with whom he collaborated on numerous causes and frequently exchanged or shared pulpits on Sundays.[26]

It was no coincidence that Wise's Christian friends and colleagues could often be found on the politically and theologically liberal wings of their denominations. These were the men whose temperament, political and cultural preferences, and general outlook most closely resembled his own, and with whom he felt socially and intellectually at ease. Wise's unconventional view of Jesus, as a sagacious rabbi from whom Jews could learn important ethical lessons, differed only to a small degree from the view of Jesus among Unitarians such as Rev. Holmes—but substantially differed from the views held by fundamentalist or evangelical denominations, which were strong in America's South and Midwest.[27]

Wise, along with many Jews of his generation, harbored a strong suspicion of the more conservative political and religious regions in the United States. That attitude was reflected in a 1934 remark by the executive secretary of the AJ committee, Morris Waldman, that "inarticulate and 'average' Americans" were easily stirred to anti-Jewish sentiment. Occasionally, Rabbi Wise would use geographic references as shorthand for the type of American whom he perceived as ignorant, backward, and probably antisemitic. In one instance, for example, he revamped plans for an American Jewish Congress–sponsored referendum out of fear that "people in Des Moines and Texas" would misunderstand and resent it. On another occasion, he fretted about some recent remarks in the Nazi press that he thought "may make some impact upon Oklahoma and Arizona!"[28]

In Wise's view, there existed a large, unwashed mass of xenophobes with whom he would never have contact, whose worldview was completely different than his, and whom he could never hope to win over to his point of view on any issue of significance. This perspective added to the thick layer of fears of antisemitic reaction that colored Wise's perception of what constituted appropriate Jewish public behavior and dimmed his sense of what American Jews were capable of achieving in the public arena.

This perception would reduce Wise's leverage in the halls of power. Cultivating relations with only one segment of the Christian clergy and public, like cultivating relations with only one of the major political parties, would put Wise at a disadvantage in the political arena. It would leave him dependent on the good will of one side, with little to no leverage, because there was no reason for liberal Christians to fear that he would then turn to conservative or evangelical Christians or their political allies. Wise's tendency to embrace the likeminded and exclude those with whom he felt politically or religiously uncomfortable ultimately weakened his hand as a national Jewish leader.[29]

Political outreach to the larger Christian community had the potential to yield significant results. A substantial public outcry by Christian clergy would have demonstrated to the Roosevelt administration and Congress that the plight of Germany's Jews was a matter of concern to a significant segment of the American public, not just the Jewish community. This would have increased pressure on the president to take actions such as filing a diplomatic protest or making a public statement, which in turn might have caused the Nazi leadership to more seriously consider the risks of harming their relations with the United States. Alternatively, a Christian outcry might have prompted President Roosevelt to at least permit the quota of immigrants from Germany to be filled to the legal limit, a step that would have resulted in haven for tens of thousands of German Jews in 1933–1934 alone (see chapter 2). For such an outreach effort to have succeeded, however, Rabbi Wise and his colleagues would have needed to seek the support of clergy from across the religious and political spectrum. This is not to say that all evangelical or conservative Christians necessarily would have been responsive to such appeals, but it is likely that Wise would have found at least some support among those fundamentalists who regarded the rescue of the Jews, and especially the prospect of Jews being ingathered to the Holy Land, as precursors of the messianic age.

Instead, Wise quickly discovered that while the Christian colleagues he did solicit found common cause with him on many political and social causes, they repeatedly disappointed him on issues of Jewish concern—including his early efforts to mobilize them in response to the rise of Hitler. Meeting with twenty liberal Christian ministers in the Manhattan apartment of the Rev. Harry Emerson Fosdick in the autumn of 1933, Wise described the persecution of German Jews at the hands of "the modern Haman"; many of the attendees dismissed his report as "unbalanced" and "intemperate." Even more alarming was the position taken by the socialist Rev. Dr. Charles Clayton Morrison, editor in chief of America's leading liberal Protestant journal, *Christian Century*. In an editorial commenting on an April 1933 AJ congress meeting on the plight of German Jewry, Morrison blamed German Jews for what the Nazis were doing to them. "May we ask if Hitler's attitude may be somewhat governed by the fact that too many Jews, at least in Germany, are radical, too many are communists?" Morrison wrote. "May that have any bearing on the situation? There must be some reason other than race or creed—just what is that reason?"[30]

Rabbi Wise's Quaker friends proved particularly resistant to his pleas concerning German Jewry. His longtime acquaintance Clarence Pickett, executive director of the Philadelphia-based American Friends Service Committee, the foreign policy arm of the Quakers, wrote to colleagues just after the March 1933 Madison Square Garden rally that any support by the Friends for such protests would put the movement's German branch in "disfavor with the [Hitler] government." Besides, Pickett argued, "the persecutions which are endured by Jews in Germany are probably slight as compared with the persecutions of minorities in a good many countries that have been going on for a long time in Europe and we have made little protest."[31]

Wise reeled in disbelief at the attitude expressed by the liberal Presbyterian minister Everett Clinchy, his longstanding Christian partner in the interfaith relations movement and co-founder of the National Conference of Christians and Jews. In a 1934 letter, Clinchy berated Wise over the AJCongress's plan to hold a public program to counter a New York City rally by pro-Nazi German Americans. "The situation is now like a tense quarrel between husband and wife in a family," Pickett counseled, "and when such a quarrel is at its height, the intelligent thing to do is to stop yelling at each other and wait a bit until the emotion of the situation is moderated." The advice was barbed, and the analogy incomprehensible. "I really do not understand you, Everett," the shocked and exasperated rabbi wrote back. "There [is no] parity between domestic quarrels and the bloodthirsty attempts at destruction of the Jewish people by the Nazi government."[32]

Years later, in the section of his 1949 autobiography dealing with the Holocaust, Wise would reserve his strongest language for the Christian religious leaders in whom he had placed his friendship and trust. "It is because of my deep disappointment over the failure of American Christendom to bestir itself and to arise against the brutal foes and destroyers of the people of its Christ that my interest in the so-called interracial and interreligious goodwill movement has become attenuated," Wise wrote. "It failed, deliberately chose to fail, in the hour of our greatest need."[33]

Without diminishing the moral responsibility of American Christian leaders with regard to the slaughter of Europe's Jews, their failure to speak out also reflected a failure of Rabbi Wise's judgment. He chose to rely on one particular segment of Christian leadership, those with whom he felt personally comfortable. Even when his expectation that they would respond proved unfounded, he did not adjust his strategy and reach out to other segments of the American clergy.

"Not the Faintest Interest"

Two days after the March 27, 1933, Madison Square Garden rally, Hitler announced that his government would sponsor a one-day nationwide boycott of all German Jewish businesses on April 1, to be resumed three days later if international protests against Nazi Germany did not cease. Wise, accompanied by Bernard Deutsch, hurried back to the State Department for meetings on March 30 and 31 with Undersecretary Phillips.

Phillips rebuffed the Jewish leaders' appeal for a public statement by the administration against Hitler's announcement; he would go no further than telephone the U.S. embassy in Berlin to assess the situation. For his part, Wise agreed to Phillips's request on April 2 (the day after the boycott) to "not say anything [about the German situation] for a few days." Wise told a friend that Secretary Hull himself "begged us not to say anything for a few days." As a result, a meeting of the AJCongress executive committee later that day concluded with the statement, "We refrain from comment on the tragic situation of the Jews in Germany." Fearing that grassroots AJCongress members would be surprised and disappointed by that stance, Wise hoped "that the use of the term 'tragic situation,' used the day after the boycott, was enough to indicate that there was no lessening of our concern over the whole situation." Wise honored the pledge of silence until April 6, at which point he felt no longer "able to keep the [AJ]Congress from making a statement" about the situation of German Jewry, which, he wrote to a friend that day, "is as grievous as it can be."[34]

American Jewish groups that had opposed the March 27 Madison Square Garden rally viewed the Nazis' boycott announcement as confirmation of their warnings of a backlash against foreign Jewish protests. Wise disagreed. He was convinced the Nazis' boycott plan was "nothing more than the overt commission of acts that would have been covertly performed, protest or no protest." The claim that the German boycott came in response to the rally was implausible, he asserted, citing a letter from one of his colleagues in Berlin that pointed out: "It was prepared months ago. . . . Could any country in 48 hours have a complete list of every Jewish shop in Germany? This, mind you, included seamstresses, little shopkeepers, tiny shops in basements that sell vegetables, and all this in the smallest hamlets and towns. You have no idea how all this was organized to the nth degree." A second letter, this one from "a Berlin lawyer in Zurich," informed Wise: "It was only foreign protests, especially that of America, which prevented even more happenings, a greater number of kidnappings and bloody beatings and possibly one big general pogrom."[35]

Wise's correspondence in the weeks to follow was a veritable portrait in both anguish and indecision. Wise wrote to one friend that Hitler was "waging a war of extermination" against the Jews (referring to economic devastation and the destruction of communal life), while writing to another that he was reluctant to call for a boycott of German goods without "the sanction of our government."[36] He asserted hopefully that because FDR was "acting with such independence of spirit and such extraordinary courage in many ways [related to the New Deal]," perhaps "he might in this case, too, show something of the same spirit." Yet in the very same letter, Wise predicted that the AJ congress might "have to do the very, very lamentable thing of crying out against the President who has not by a single word or act intimated the faintest interest in what is going on [concerning German Jewry]."[37] Wise was exuberant to receive Frankfurter's reassurance that he had "seen General Headquarters" (Roosevelt) and "I feel sure that he is watching the thing with understanding and sympathy." But just five days later, Wise was "horrified" by a report that Roosevelt intended to receive a German envoy at the White House and "make a speech about friendly relations, etc." Several weeks later, FDR met with Hjalmar Schacht, who had been appointed by Hitler to head the Reichsbank. "The president greeted this emissary with full fanfare and ostentatious friendliness," the historian Manfred Jonas notes. Schacht reported back to Hitler that the

American president exhibited "doubtless sympathy for the personality of the Chancellor." Roosevelt told Schacht that the question of Germany's Jews could affect German-American relations; according to Schacht, FDR did not seem particularly sympathetic to the Jews but was speaking "out of the old Anglo-Saxon sense of chivalry toward the weaker."[38]

Meanwhile, the news from Germany was increasingly bleak. "The letters I have seen and the people who have escaped and whom I am beginning to meet tell me stories which make it certain that the half, nay not even a tithe has been told," Rabbi Wise wrote a colleague on April 17. "It is hell, truly worse than hell. Only Dante could have pictured the hell which Germany is become." Moreover, it was not some aberration but rather the inevitable culmination of a long process: "Germany has been preparing for this day by a thousand years and more of anti-Jewish feeling and conduct."[39]

A conversation in early May with James G. McDonald gave Wise further reason for concern. Based on his contacts in Berlin and Washington, McDonald warned the rabbi that reports in the U.S. press about the abuse of German Jews were "understated," and "at any moment, a worse situation might be created in Germany for the Jews, with a general massacre in which many thousands would be slain." Despite that grim prospect, "the Administration would do nothing" about the situation, McDonald reported. President Roosevelt was "much concerned," but he had "larger fish to fry in Germany," and therefore did not intend to "make any public statement" about the Jews.[40]

Nonetheless, protecting the administration from Jewish criticism remained a priority for Wise. He "sent word to the White House" through intermediaries in early April that he was "trying desperately to avert bitter criticism of the administration" over reports that Hitler would be invited to attend an international economic conference in the United States. "We know that it is inevitable and that he cannot be treated as an outlaw quite yet, seeing that we are in friendly relations with Germany, one of our debtor nations," Wise conceded, while alerting U.S.

officials that some "embittered" American Jews might start demanding some statement from the administration. A few days later, Wise wrote to Frankfurter: "I am having an awfully hard time of it with the Jewish masses, who cannot be expected to understand why no word has come from the Administration in all these weeks."[41]

A stark example of that bitterness was displayed at a May 10 anti-Nazi march and rally in New York City, when speaker Isadore Apfel, leader of the Independent Order of Brith Abraham, a prominent union of Jewish fraternal lodges, declared: "Are we to believe that new deal will mean raw deal for our people? I call upon our president . . . to stay the hand of the Angel of Destruction. . . . Let the voice of official America be heard. England has done it! France has done it! Why can't Free America do it?"[42]

In a note to Frankfurter a few days later, Wise acknowledged that President Roosevelt had not "yet lifted a finger to save the Jews of Germany from Hitler." The rabbi told Frankfurter he would be able to "*beruhigt* [silence] my own following" if Roosevelt's apparent delay in appointing a new ambassador to Germany was intended as a protest against the mistreatment of German Jewry. Likewise, Wise asserted at a conference of Jewish groups in New York City on April 19 that they should be satisfied "that no American ambassador has been sent to Berlin."[43]

Actually, FDR had intended no such protest. Six weeks later he named University of Chicago history professor William E. Dodd as the new envoy. The president informed Dodd that the persecution of German Jewry was "not a [U.S.] governmental affair" and therefore he should employ only "unofficial and personal influence" in that regard, unless it involved the handful of U.S. citizens residing in Germany. Roosevelt thus in effect reversed outgoing president Herbert Hoover's directive to the then-U.S. ambassador in Germany, Frederic Sackett, "to exert every influence of our government" on the Hitler regime to halt the persecution of German Jews, not just American residents of Germany.[44]

Wise was not privy to what Roosevelt told Dodd, but a conversation with the new ambassador that summer gave him a glimpse of the new administration's thinking on Germany. Setting out for Europe in July (for meetings to plan the establishment of the World Jewish Congress, and to survey the political situation in countries adjacent to Nazi Germany), Wise chanced to find himself on the same ship that was bringing Dodd to his new post in Berlin. In a subsequent report to the AJCongress executive committee, the rabbi recounted his "disturbing" conversation with the new ambassador. Dodd, who had authored a biography of Thomas Jefferson, remarked to Wise: "One cannot write the whole truth about Jefferson and Washington—people are not ready and must be prepared for it." Wise wondered: "If people must be prepared for the truth about Jefferson and Washington, what will he do with the truth when he learns it about Hitler, in view of his official post?"[45]

It did not take long for Wise's fears to be confirmed. The new ambassador ignored his suggestion that he meet with a German Jewish associate of Wise's to hear first-hand about Nazi atrocities. In fact, the only time Wise heard from the ambassador that summer was in a letter from Dodd claiming that "things are improving" for Germany's Jews. The rabbi was "shocked and perplexed by that because just about that very time ... things were almost at their worst." Stunned by Dodd's note, Wise offered to come to Berlin (from Switzerland) to speak with the ambassador about the situation, despite warnings from local friends that it would be dangerous for him to enter Nazi Germany. "But he never answered my suggestion," Wise reported to colleagues.[46]

The Boycott Dilemma

Even before the tumult over the March 27 rally fully subsided, vigorous disagreements emerged among American Jews over whether to boycott German goods. Spontaneous boycott activity had begun in the Jewish community almost immediately upon Hitler's rise to power. At the aforementioned March 19 emergency conference of Jewish groups called by the AJ congress, J. George Fredman of the Jewish War Veterans and Mordecai Danzis of the nationalist Revisionist Zionists introduced a resolution calling for an organized boycott of German products. Leading the opposition, Joseph Proskauer of the AJ committee argued that a boycott would "kill the Jews in Germany." Wise sided with the opponents and blocked Fredman's resolution.

Nonetheless, the war veterans group announced its support for the boycott and, four days later, staged a march through Manhattan to promote it. Four thousand veterans took part. Soon afterward, New York City mayor Fiorello La Guardia endorsed the boycott, and the newly established American League for the Defense of Jewish Rights, taking over leadership of the boycott movement from the war veterans, recruited the prominent attorney and Zionist activist Samuel Untermyer to chair the campaign. Later, to broaden the group's appeal beyond the Jewish community, the League changed its name to the Non-Sectarian Anti-Nazi League to Champion Human Rights.[47]

Several major Jewish organizations opposed boycotting. American Jewish Committee officials warned that a boycott would "stimulate anti-Semitic activity" by spreading the notion "that the Jews exert a so-called 'world economic influence.'" Committee president Joseph Proskauer argued that a boycott would be "a doctrine of destruction for American Jewry" because it would "imperil the foreign relations of my country— which is America—with a government with whom we are at peace," thereby breeding resentment against American Jews. B'nai B'rith's journal, *National Jewish Monthly*, characterized the boycott as "little short of madness." Such an effort "might undermine to some extent German commerce and might even force Germany to give up some of its export trade," the journal noted, "but in doing so would give the enemies of the German Jew a greater provocation to continue the outrages" perpetrated against the Jews. The only solution to the crisis, according to the B'nai B'rith organ, was "a dignified silence, silence with suffering, [which] may become more potent than emotion."[48]

Mail to the AJCongress office was running heavily in favor of the boycott, and at a chaotic AJCongress executive committee meeting on April 13, Wise encountered mounting pressure to endorse the boycotters. "The meeting was another noisy and confused affair with a lot of heated and aimless talk," one AJCongress official reported to a colleague. Wise was able to push off the boycott demands by agreeing to hold a conference of Jewish organizations on April 19 to plan further protests. "I do not think we can stand out against a formal and organized boycott," Wise confided to Frankfurter two days later. "I would be willing to stand out against it to the end, and I might prevail if I had a word from Headquarters [the White House] that would strengthen my position." Wise evidently believed that if the president would only make a statement challenging Hitler's treatment of the Jews, he would be able to persuade his Jewish colleagues to postpone endorsing the boycott. Instead, not only did Roosevelt refrain from criticizing the Nazis, but the administration explicitly opposed the boycott. Secretary of State Cordell Hull declared that "a racial or political boycott" of Germany would be damaging to American interests because it would harm U.S. exports. The administration even sought to undermine the boycott movement by permitting German goods to be labeled as having been made in a particular city or province, so they could be stamped with a local (and thus generally unrecognizable) name rather than "Made in Germany."[49]

Wise nonetheless did his best to hold out against the rising tide of grassroots Jewish pressure. Addressing one thousand delegates from six hundred Jewish organizations at an April 19 conference, the rabbi urged a cautious approach: "We can't expect our government to act towards Germany as if we were in a state of war. We do not want to go to war with any people in the world." In response to shouts from the audience calling for a boycott, Wise replied that "the time has not yet come for an official boycott—we still have other weapons." At the same time, Wise privately assured Undersecretary Phillips that "responsible" Jewish organizations opposed the boycott. In a note to President Roosevelt in April, Wise pointed to his own efforts at "averting an organized boycott of German goods by American Jews." Behind the scenes, however, Wise agonized over defending the administration in the face of congressional efforts and his own increasingly restless constituency. "I think I have been a little guilty in restraining [protest] action up to this time," he confided to Mack on May 4. "I dare not do it any longer. I have no right."[50]

Wise's attitude toward the boycott was further influenced by eyewitness accounts of Nazi atrocities. He met many exiled German Jews in London, Paris, Geneva, and Prague that summer. "We go to bed wondering what hour in the night the police will pull us out of bed," one young German Jew told him in Prague. "We arise wondering what the day will bring forth." On a train from Geneva to Paris, a teenage Jewish refugee recounted how the German police had burst into the apartment of her twenty-six-year-old brother and three of his friends. "The next day, four coffins were delivered to the families with instructions that the boxes were not to be opened. All were tagged *Erschossen in Flucht*—'shot in flight.'" Ignoring the instructions, she opened her brother's coffin. "My brother's face had been shot away while he was 'in flight.'"[51]

Wise later wrote: "Everywhere I went [in Czechoslovakia, Austria, Switzerland, and France], I visited the asylums or shelters for German Jewish refugees, and through their eyes looked into the depths of hell. When I spoke to one man who became hysterical, I turned to his wife, asking if she could not control him so I could understand. She replied, 'If you knew what my husband has lived through, what he has seen and heard and experienced—you would not ask that question.'"[52]

Wise also found the German Jewish refugees "almost unanimous" in the view "that our great protest in America had the largest part in saving German Jewry from the direst things." He felt vindicated that the Madison Square Garden rally had "performed a very great service for German Jewry, for world Jewry, for civilization." The fact that the Nazi boycott was confined to one day, and not renewed as Hitler initially threatened, indicated to him that the Fuhrer was keenly concerned about foreign protests.[53]

These experiences played an important role in persuading Rabbi Wise to rethink his position regarding the boycott of German goods. Hearing first-hand about Nazi atrocities underlined the urgency of American Jewish action. The evidence that German Jews themselves felt the March rally was necessary and effective encouraged Wise to believe additional protest activity should be undertaken, although he remained conflicted. Soon there was a noticeable change in the tone of at least some of his public comments regarding the boycott. The *New York Times* quoted him in mid-August as telling an audience in Prague that "decent self-respecting Jews cannot deal with Germany in any way, buy or sell or maintain any manner of commerce with Germany or travel on German boats."[54]

While Rabbi Wise was still abroad, the AJCongress administrative committee met on August 17 to consider what its members called "the enormous public pressure in America" in support of the boycott movement. Still not quite ready to publicly embrace the boycott, Wise sent a cable to his AJCongress colleagues asking for postponement of any vote on the issue. The telegram was read aloud at the meeting. Nonetheless, the attendees voted in favor of recommending to the organization's executive committee that it endorse the boycott at its next session, and three days later, the executive committee did just that. Wise returned from Europe to a fait accompli.[55]

With eyewitness accounts of German atrocities fresh in his mind and the overwhelming pro-boycott sentiment among his constituents, it was not difficult for Rabbi Wise to make the adjustment. It helped that Justice Brandeis, whom Wise idolized, sent an encouraging word. Upon his return, the rabbi found a note waiting for him from the esteemed jurist and Zionist elder statesman reminding Wise of "the part played in America's struggle for independence by the boycott of British goods," complete with citations about the matter from a new biography of Thomas Jefferson. "I cannot tell you how grateful I am to you for the hint that you give me about the boycott of British goods," Wise replied. "I shall at once look up the references to which you allude."[56]

The AJCongress quickly took the helm of the boycott movement. Its stature and resources enabled a significant expansion of boycotting activity, transforming a loose and unorganized effort into a sophisticated and effective campaign. The AJCongress's national headquarters, chapters around the country, and especially its Women's Division threw themselves into the work of pinpointing importers of German goods, alerting consumers about the offenders, and organizing picket lines. "Vigilance Committees" personally visited stores to determine the origins of suspected goods; "Drug Squads" contacted local doctors and pharmacists to inform them of non-German alternatives to German-made medicines.[57]

Yet even as the AJCongress threw itself full-throttle into the business of boycotting, Wise remained deeply apprehensive about the perception that he, or American Jews in general, were acting contrary to the wishes of the Roosevelt administration. In October, Wise learned "from an authoritative source" that presidential secretary Marvin McIntyre had "called at the offices of the A[merican] F[ederation] of L[abor], asking them not to adopt the boycott resolution because it would embarrass the United States government." Even if the information was confirmed beyond doubt, "I am not at all sure that we could afford to take the case into the open," Wise reported to Brandeis. "I feel very deeply about it." Publicizing the administration's stance would draw attention to the contrary position of the AJCongress, potentially casting aspersions on the patriotism of American Jewry.[58]

Confronting Congress

Even as he wrestled with the boycott controversy, Wise labored to keep Congress from embarrassing the president over the Nazi issue. When Wise learned, in April, that Senator William

King (D-UT) intended to introduce a resolution expressing sympathy with German Jewry, the rabbi "begged members of the Senate to say nothing" because "any congressional utterances now would seem to be a deviation from the silence of the Administration" and therefore would "seriously embarrass the White House." Wise let the president know of his role in "postponing discussion in the Senate of the proposed Hitler war of extermination against Jews."[59]

Remarkably, even as Wise worked to dissuade non-Jewish members of Congress from acting on the issue, he privately berated Jewish congress members for their reluctance to do just that. In May, Wise and three AJcongress colleagues met in Washington with seven of the eleven sitting Jewish members of the U.S. House of Representatives. Wise's report of the meeting to several close colleagues dripped with contempt. William Sirovich (D-NY) was "a super-articulate charlatan," he wrote. Emanuel Celler (D-NY) was "blatant but insignificant." Samuel Dickstein (D-NY) "can best be characterized as Dickstein" (presumably a play on the fact that *dicke stein* in German means "dense stone"). Florence Kahn (R-CA) was "probably the best of the whole crowd—though that does not mean very much." All except Kahn, Wise complained, were "eager to [support] the administration rather than do the thing that is obviously needed in the Jewish interest,"—that is, to speak out on behalf of Germany's Jews. They feared raising their voices would provoke "pro-German and anti-Jewish speeches in the House." The rabbi was not impressed by the danger. "[M]uch of what they imagine to be anti-Semitism in general is nothing more than contempt and loathing for them personally, which of course they rationalize away in the self-protective terms of anti-Semitism," Wise asserted.[60]

According to Wise, the congress members also connected their reticence to the division of opinion among Jewish organizations. Rep. Henry Ellenbogen (D-PA) reported that President Roosevelt had recently said to him, "There are two kinds of Jews—those who want me to spread-eagle and those who want me to be silent." Adolph Sabath (D-IL) and Sol Bloom (D-NY) "were constantly harping on the lack of unity which the President knows, of the quarrels between the two factions, etc., etc." Sabath in particular "was almost violent in his defense of the President, playing the part of statesman and telling us that we did not know how much the President was doing" behind the scenes about the German situation. Sabath and Bloom "justify every manner of inaction [and,] like true underlings and *Staatlanim* [that is, *shtadlanim*—court Jews], they go further than their Christian master." After two hours with "this poor, incoherent, uncomprehending little group," Wise concluded: "I am afraid that if my acquaintance with Jews and the Jewish question were limited to my acquaintance with these Jewish representatives, I would not be passionately Philo-Semitic."[61]

Wise was not mistaken in his assessment. Many Jewish congress members, including Bloom, Sabath, Sirovich, Ellenbogen, and Kahn, were reluctant to take an interest in Jewish concerns. In particular, Bloom, as chairman of the House Foreign Affairs Committee, would become a significant obstacle to Jewish organizational efforts to influence U.S. refugee policy in the years to follow.

Celler and Dickstein, however, exhibited a different mindset. In fact, just two months earlier, Rep. Dickstein had used his position as chairman of the House Immigration and Naturalization Committee to promote a measure to liberalize the entry of German Jews to the United States. Celler, for his part, would soon emerge as the most outspoken voice on Capitol Hill challenging the Roosevelt administration's Jewish refugee policy. It was their blunt criticism of the administration, not the excessive caution described by Wise in his May 1933 report, that would most discomfit the rabbi.[62]

Just eight days after sending Frankfurter, Brandeis, and Mack that caustic report accusing Jewish congress members of being insufficiently outspoken, Wise wrote to Frankfurter to express his fear that the Jews in Congress would be too outspoken. The rabbi explained that he and his colleagues in the Joint

Consultative Committee (the AJ committee and B'nai B'rith) opposed holding any hearings in the House regarding Germany's Jews, for two reasons. First, the antisemitic Pennsylvania congressman, Louis McFadden, might "utilize the occasion to make another *Protocols of the Elders of Zion* speech"—exactly the fear for which Wise had derided the Jewish members of Congress in his earlier memo. Second, "we are fearful of the super-intervention of the Jewish members of the House of Representatives," because they might be too forceful in their remarks. Only "the wiser heads among them," such as Sabath, "share our fears," Wise wrote. Therefore, he intended to speak directly with Sabath, "telling him that we feel the thing must be left to the Senate, where there is less likelihood of any explosion against us." The senate, Wise reported, "is the more easily controlled," because Senate majority leader Joseph Robinson would not permit any debate concerning German Jewry "until General Headquarters [the White House] assents—and I hardly believe General Headquarters will assent."[63]

The Nazi Olympics

One of the early targets of the boycott movement was the Olympics. In 1931, two years before the Nazis rose to power, the International Olympic Committee had selected Berlin as the site of the 1936 games. American Jews seeking to have the Nazis branded as international pariahs were faced with the specter of their own government participating in an event that Hitler hoped would secure international legitimacy for his regime.

Already in 1933, three years before the games were scheduled to take place, Wise and the AJ congress publicly called for a U.S. boycott of the games. In a series of petitions to the American Olympic Committee (AOC), Wise and his colleagues argued that the German government's refusal to permit German Jewish athletes equal access to training facilities or to give them serious consideration for inclusion on the German team constituted violations of the Olympics' spirit of fair play. The AJ congress also maintained that Jewish athletes from other countries who took part in the games might become targets of harassment or even violence, given the severe antisemitic atmosphere in Nazi Germany.[64]

The AOC's president, Avery Brundage, strongly supported U.S. participation in the Berlin games. To counter the AJ congress's campaign, he announced that he would visit Germany in 1934 to personally assess the situation. The Nazi authorities played along, announcing—on the eve of Brundage's visit—the names of five Jewish athletes who supposedly were considered candidates to make the team. After returning to the United States, Brundage announced: "I honestly believe that Germany will live up to her pledges. . . . We have received unqualified assurances of non-discrimination." Meanwhile, Brundage's AOC colleague, Brigadier General Charles Sherrill, publicly warned boycott advocates that if they continued their protests, "we are almost certain to have a wave of anti-Semitism." The boycott campaign was "overplaying the Jewish hand in America as it was overplayed in Germany before the present suppression and expulsion of the Jews were undertaken."[65]

Unable to make headway with the AOC leadership, the AJ congress sought to broaden support for the boycott by establishing the nonsectarian Committee on Fair Play in Sports and recruiting prominent non-Jewish allies. Endorsers included the governors of Massachusetts and Pennsylvania, the NAACP, the Catholic War Veterans, and a number of well-known Christian clergymen. The AJ congress also reached out to individual athletes and local athletic associations throughout the country, urging them to boycott the games. Only a handful of athletes did so; one, the star sprinter Herman Neugass of Tulane University, attributed his decision to a letter he received from Rabbi Wise.[66]

Meanwhile, Ambassador Dodd warned Washington that the Nazis intended to use the Olympics "to rehabilitate and enhance the reputation of the 'New Germany.'" Foreigners will "have only the usual tourist contacts" and are likely to come away doubting the veracity of "the Jewish persecution which they have previously read in their home papers," he predicted. The corps of two thousand translators hired by the government were also being trained at "parrying embarrassing questions and insinuating praise of National Socialism in their small talk." The American consul general in Berlin, George Messersmith, sent numerous reports to the State Department warning that the Nazis would exploit the Olympics to deceive the international community about the actual situation in Germany. It was all to no avail; the Roosevelt administration rejected the boycott as undue interference in American-German relations.[67]

As Dodd expected, antisemitic literature was taken off the newsstands in Berlin shortly before foreign visitors began arriving in the summer of 1936. Physical assaults on Jews were kept to a minimum during the games. Visiting journalists were duly impressed. The *New York Times* praised the German government for its "flawless hospitality." A *Los Angeles Times* correspondent wrote: "Zeus, in his golden days, never witnessed a show as grand as this." An editorial in that newspaper even predicted that the "spirit of the Olympiads" would "save the world from another purge of blood."[68]

Even President Roosevelt was taken in, or perhaps was looking for a way to justify America's participation, when Rabbi Wise visited the White House shortly after the games. The president told Wise he had learned from two tourists who had attended the games "that the synagogues are crowded and apparently there is nothing very wrong in the situation [of Germany's Jews] at present." Horrified, Wise tried to "explain to him how grave conditions were," as Wise recounted to Brandeis. "[I] told him of some recent happenings in Germany. . . . Cited other examples of the ruthless and continuing oppression of the Jews. He listened carefully; but I could see that the tourists (whoever they were, the Lord bless them not) had made an impression upon him."[69]

FDR and the Nazis

Despite the escalating abuse of German Jews throughout 1933, FDR continued to refrain from making any public statement about their plight. The events of the spring and summer months in Germany had included, among other things, the nationwide burning of books authored by Jews; the enactment of legislation barring Jews from the civil service and an array of medical and judicial professions; the expulsion of most Jewish faculty members from universities and the imposition of a 1.5 percent quota on the admission of Jewish students; and prohibitions on Jews working in journalism and entertainment. That the White House remained silent in the face of such abuses was a source of growing frustration for Rabbi Wise. "We have had nothing but indifference and unconcern up to this time," Wise wrote to Mack in October. The following month, the rabbi lamented to another friend that with regard to German Jewry, FDR was "immovable, incurable and even inaccessible except to those of his Jewish friends whom he can safely trust not to trouble him with any Jewish problems."[70]

A number of "Jewish friends" served in positions close to the president. Samuel Rosenman, a senior adviser and speechwriter for FDR during his gubernatorial years, played a similar role in the Roosevelt White House, initially behind the scenes and eventually as the first presidential general counsel. Henry Morgenthau Jr., Roosevelt's friend and neighbor in Hyde Park, New York, was appointed secretary of the treasury in 1934. Supreme Court justice Louis Brandeis was a behind-the-scenes adviser to the president, as was Harvard University law professor Felix Frankfurter, who would join Brandeis on the Court in 1939. Ben Cohen, a protégé of Frankfurter's, played a key role in drafting New Deal legislation, starting in 1933. That same year, Roosevelt chose Isador Lubin to head the Bureau of Labor Statistics. Starting in 1936, David Niles would serve in a number of positions in the Roosevelt administration, including adviser on ethnic issues and unofficial liaison to the Jewish community.

For some American Jews, the unprecedented number of their coreligionists in such positions demonstrated that the Jewish community had a genuine friend in the Oval Office. Yet FDR's Jewish advisers generally were reluctant to raise Jewish concerns with the president. "I don't feel that I should push myself into Jewish matters where the skipper does not ask my advice," Cohen wrote to a friend in 1940—a sentiment shared by the other Jews in FDR's inner circle.[71]

Besides Wise, several other American Jews of prominence sought, but failed, to interest Roosevelt in the crisis of German Jewry. Professor Frankfurter's letters to FDR in 1933–34 covered a number of subjects, including the plight of German Jews. Roosevelt typically responded at length, addressing every topic Frankfurter raised—except the plight of the Jews. During a visit to the White House in September 1933, Henry Morgenthau Jr. and New York judge Irving Lehman requested a presidential statement about the persecution of German Jewry; FDR told them he preferred to say something about human rights abuses in Germany in general, rather than focus on the Jews. In the end, however, he did not do even that. In the eighty-two press conferences Roosevelt held in 1933, the subject of the persecution of the Jews arose just once, and not at the president's initiative. It would be five years, and another 348 presidential press conferences, before he would again mention anything about Europe's Jews. Roosevelt was not willing to risk even mildly straining American-German relations by publicly taking issue with Hitler's human rights abuses. As State Department official Herbert Feis later noted, the U.S. policy of not criticizing Hitler's persecution of the Jews in the 1930s was based on the administration's concern about "hurt[ing] our chances of securing the cooperation of the Nazi regime in international economic and political affairs and disarmament by interfering to protect the Jewish and other minorities in Germany." This mindset led to a series of incidents in which the administration tried to suppress Jewish criticism of the Nazis or in other ways went out of its way to show friendliness to the Hitler government.[72]

The Roosevelt administration's attitude toward the new German regime was tested in December 1933, when a German American group, the Steuben Society, organized a rally at Madison Square Garden. Although the ostensible purpose of the gathering was merely to commemorate the 250th anniversary of the first German settlement in North America, there were significant contemporary overtones, including the fact that Hitler's ambassador to Washington, Hans Luther, would be the featured speaker; the swastika flag would be prominently displayed; and the openly pro-Nazi League of Friends of the New Germany was playing a major role in organizing the event. Nonetheless, the White House sent Secretary of Commerce Daniel C. Roper to address the gathering. "I am not happy to think that the first word [by the administration] since Hitler came into power should be spoken by a member of the Cabinet at a Hitler-Day celebration," Wise wrote to Brandeis. He did not comment on the matter publicly, however.[73]

Roper extended greetings from President Roosevelt, then spoke about German contributions to America before launching into a lengthy defense of the administration's economic policies. The commerce secretary made no allusion to the Hitler regime, but the mere fact of a cabinet member's presence constituted a declaration of the administration's interest in friendly relations with the new Germany. Wise's caustic characterization of the event as a "Hitler-Day celebration" indicates that he understood the implications of Roper's participation.[74]

Ambassador Dodd figured in several incidents of American expressions of friendliness toward the Hitler regime. After several American citizens in Germany were assaulted in 1933 for failing to give the Hitler salute during parades, Dodd reported to Foreign Minister Konstantin von Neurath that on several occasions, he had managed to keep news about the incidents "out of the [American] press reports and otherwise tried to prevent unfriendly demonstrations." On a number of other occasions, Dodd advised top Nazi officials that criticism of Germany was growing in the United States and asked them for "explanations and promises which I might wire to Washington in the hope of easing off the excitement." In an attempt to head off American Jewish criticism of the German government, Dodd assured Jewish acquaintances in Chicago that Hitler's anti-Jewish policies appeared to be softening, citing the reported closure of "Berlin's worst prison" and "the re-establishment of a warrant system in making arrests."[75]

On March 5, 1934, Ambassador Dodd was summoned to the German Foreign Office, where Foreign Minister von Neurath harangued him about the AJ congress's plan to stage a mock trial of Hitler before "the High Court of Humanity" at Madison Square Garden later that week. Von Neurath pressed Dodd to ask "the President or Secretary [of State Cordell] Hull [to] intervene and stop the trial." Dodd's reply, which he recorded in his diary, is revealing. At first, Dodd said that "nobody in the United States could suppress a private or public meeting . . . without violating the constitutions of the nation and of the several states." Compelling the Jews, or any U.S. citizens, to keep quiet would "violate fundamental American principles." But when von Neurath persisted, Dodd cast aside all the talk about principles. "I said that if [the German ambassador to the United States, Hans] Luther had cabled the news [of the plans for a mock trial] before the publicity of the plan had been given out, it might have been possible for Roosevelt to dissuade the leaders from such a demonstration on the ground[s] of hurting relations between our two countries." Dodd seemed to be saying that the problem was not principles, but optics; if the president could have silenced Hitler's Jewish critics without the public finding out, he would have been willing to do so.[76]

Two days later, Dodd met with Hitler. Although the two did not discuss the mock trial—which took place that same day— the subject of the Jews occupied a significant part of their conversation. When Dodd raised the issue of the Nazi regime distributing brochures to German Americans urging them to swear "allegiance to the fatherland," Hitler "broke in frequently with such expressions as 'Damn the Jews,'" and insisted that Jews were to blame for "all of the ill feeling in the United States towards Germany." Dodd responded by offering what was, in effect, friendly advice on how the Nazis could address the "problem" of Jewish overrepresentation without harming Germany's image in the United States:

> I then argued a bit with him about the effects of violent treatment in the United States, and said: "You know a number of high positions in our country are at present occupied by Jews, both in New York and Illinois," naming some of the eminent fair-minded Hebrews like Henry Morgenthau, senior. I explained to him that where a question of over-activity of Jews in university or official life made trouble, we had managed to redistribute the offices in such a way as not to give great offense, and that wealthy Jews continued to support institutions which had limited the number of Jews who held high positions. . . . My idea was to suggest a different procedure from that which has been followed here—of course never giving pointed advice.[77]

It was indeed advice, albeit couched in diplomatic rather than pointed terms.

Dodd's attempt to coach the German dictator on more effective ways to restrict Jewish participation in German society (potentially even with the support of some "wealthy Jews") reflected the attitudes among some senior Roosevelt administration officials—including, as will become apparent, the president himself. From their perspective, the presence of a significant number of Jews in certain professions or public positions was undesirable; quietly limiting their numbers was feasible; and "fair-minded Hebrews" such as Henry Morgenthau Sr. were tolerable. Ambassador Dodd's mention of Morgenthau probably alluded to the fact that he was assimilated, anti-Zionist, and seldom mentioned Jewish concerns. Dodd's reference to "wealthy Jews" acquiescing in discrimination against other Jews alluded to the phenomenon of successful, usually German-born, American Jews who feared that Jewish visibility might endanger their own status as Americans. FDR himself would later claim that Morgenthau Sr. endorsed the decision by Roosevelt and other members of the Harvard University board of trustees to limit the number of Jewish students admitted to the school.[78]

The mock trial, billed as "The Case of Civilization Against Hitlerism," featured an array of high-profile participants. Former Secretary of State Bainbridge Colby served as presiding judge. Prominent individuals from various walks of life appeared as prosecution witnesses, each making a brief presentation summarizing Hitler's offenses in a particular area or against a particular group. New York University president Harry Woodburn Chase, for example, speaking on behalf of the academic community, decried the Nazification of German institutions of higher learning, while Michael Williams, editor of the Catholic magazine *Commonweal*, challenged Hitler's mistreatment of German Catholic clergy. New York City mayor Fiorello La Guardia and U.S. senator Millard Tydings (D-MD), appearing on behalf of "American public opinion," declared Nazi Germany guilty of having "turned its face against historic progress and the positive blessings and achievements of modern civilization." The proceedings were broadcast live on leading New York City radio stations and reported widely in the American press, including on the front page of the *New York Times*.[79]

Learning of plans for a second mock trial, to be held in Chicago, Dodd decided to intervene. During a visit to the United States in late March, he turned to an old friend, presidential adviser Colonel Edward M. House, to help undermine the second trial. In a letter to House on March 24, Dodd argued that "these Jewish demonstrations [against Nazism] are creating a race issue here and even winning Nazi support." (It is not clear if the ambassador actually believed Jewish protests drove other Americans to sympathize with the Nazis, or, more likely, that they were undesirable in general because they stirred controversies that could harm U.S.-German relations.) Dodd also told House he had personally assured Hitler "that Chicago Jews were not so wild," so cancelation of the mock trial was important to maintain Dodd's own credibility. Moreover, Dodd asserted, Hitler had recently agreed to "ease up on the Jews" by "closing the Nazi prisons where Jews were maltreated" and banning unauthorized arrests, which Dodd believed was the outcome of his meeting with the Nazi leader. "Everybody in [the] diplomatic corps in Berlin agreed that I had brought the chancellor to do an excellent thing," Dodd wrote.[80]

Dodd therefore proposed to House that the two of them try to arrange the withdrawal of one of the planned Chicago keynote speakers: former judge James Gerard, who had served as U.S. ambassador in Berlin during World War I. Dodd asked House to "find a way to influence Judge Gerard to decline the invitation," such as persuading Gerard of "the discredit to his own fame" that would ensue if he publicly criticized Hitler despite the new, moderate position the chancellor supposedly had adopted. On March 31, House reported back with good news: "The Judge will not go to Chicago." Dodd, meanwhile, enlisted the assistance of Leo Wormser, director of the Jewish Charities of Chicago, and Max Epstein, a prominent Chicago Jewish philanthropist, to pressure the organizers to cancel the proposed event. The withdrawal of Gerard and the intervention of Wormser and Epstein appear to have played a major role in the cancelation of the second mock trial. Dodd subsequently noted in his diary that President Roosevelt personally "thanked me for checking the Chicago agitation."[81]

Even as Dodd and House were working to silence Wise's "agitation," Wise was trying to silence a new group of Jewish dissidents known as "Brooklyn Jewish Democracy," which pledged "militant leadership for the Jewish people." The same week the first mock trial was held, an audience of 4,500 attended the organization's launch event. The driving force behind the group was Louis Gross, a Reform rabbi and editor in chief of the *Brooklyn Jewish Examiner;* other key figures were Samuel Liebowitz, an attorney best known for his role in the defense of the Scottsboro Boys, and Queens rabbi Joshua Goldberg, whom Wise had ordained. Their platform called for uniting

Jews "in a solid and formidable phalanx" to assert Jewish rights and combat antisemitism "through educational activities and by means of the ballot." They spoke unabashedly of mobilizing a "Jewish vote" to defeat candidates whose positions they regarded as inimical to Jewish interests.[82]

Not surprisingly, the established Jewish organizations were appalled by such bold expressions of Jewish political militancy, which they feared would arouse antisemitic accusations that Jews put Jewish concerns ahead of all else. B'nai B'rith president Alfred Cohen urged the New York state authorities to revoke the group's articles of incorporation on the grounds that "listing Jews as a distinct political entity" was "un-American to the core." When American Jewish Committee leaders learned Rabbi Gross was writing "private letters to prominent personalities" suggesting a liberalization of immigration restrictions so that more Jewish refugees could enter the United States, an AJcommittee staff member visited the rabbi and succeeded in "persuading him to discontinue his agitation."[83]

Rabbi Wise was especially vehement in his denunciations of Brooklyn Jewish Democracy, evidently because it posed multiple dangers. First, it threatened to draw members away from his American Jewish Congress by positioning itself as the activist alternative to the AJcommittee and B'nai B'rith, a mantle that Wise wanted to maintain for his own organization. Second, the Jewish Democracy group's success in persuading two United States senators, both Democrats, to speak at its founding conference jeopardized Wise's position as the primary Jewish communal spokesman in Washington. Finally, the group's promotion of the concept of a "Jewish vote" horrified Wise as an invitation to antisemitism. Wise angrily rebuffed a suggestion from his former student, Rabbi Goldberg, to discuss the new group. The organization, Wise declared, was the work of "racketeering gentlemen who hope to boost themselves into places which they are unfit to occupy and their occupancy of which would bring infinite hurt to the Jewish people." So great were the "perils" posed by Brooklyn Jewish Democracy, Wise wrote Goldberg, "that I cannot bring myself even to discuss it with you or anyone else."[84]

Yet the very same day Wise said he could not bring himself to discuss the new organization, he harshly denounced it from the pulpit of his Free Synagogue. The leaders of Brooklyn Jewish Democracy were "vile," "our foremost enemies," and "racketeers and gangsters" who had banded together for their "own filthy gain," he declared. Their political strategy was downright dangerous; "anyone who dares link the name of 'Jew' with any political organization ought to be scourged and excommunicated." Even excommunication would not be sufficient punishment, Wise asserted: "I would organize a vigilance committee to visit every judge in the city, urging that they punish these men to the full extent of the law."[85]

Although no such committee was established, Wise appears to have acted as something of a one-man vigilance squad. He lobbied Mayor La Guardia to refrain from reappointing Gross to the Board of Higher Education, deriding him as "the head of that racketeering crew calling itself the Brooklyn Jewish Democracy, which is nothing but a job-hunting conspiracy against the public welfare." Wise also spread the word among colleagues that Gross's brother was a "foul renegade" who "has been expelled from a number of congregations," as if that somehow reflected on Gross. Even ten years later, when Gross and Brooklyn Jewish Democracy had long since faded from public view, Wise was still railing in his private correspondence against Gross as an "awful" person who was surrounded by "a lot of cheap nobodies."[86]

That Gross's activities triggered such a vehement response from Rabbi Wise was indicative of Wise's extreme sensitivity to what he imagined were potential threats to his leadership. These turned out not to be actual threats. Although the large turnout at its founding event suggested Brooklyn Jewish Democracy had the potential to marshal a substantial pool of grassroots anxiety over antisemitism at home and abroad, it never developed into a full-fledged organization or genuinely challenged Wise's power. Not until the 1940s did significant groups of dissidents emerge, both outside Wise's organizations (see chapter 4) and within them (see chapter 6). To thwart them, he would use many similar tactics to those he now employed against Brooklyn Jewish Democracy: urging non-Jewish political figures to stay away from them, spreading rumors impugning their personal reputations, and denouncing them, too, as "racketeers" and "gangsters."

Apologizing to the Nazis

Ambassador Dodd soon came to realize just how mistaken his hopeful assessment had been, and explained as much in a report to President Roosevelt in August. "On the assumption that [Hitler's] promises [to close prisons and otherwise ease up on the Jews] would be kept, I managed to prevent a Hitler mock-trial in Chicago and otherwise persuaded American Jews to restrain themselves," he wrote. But already on the ship steaming back to Germany, he read "a speech of [Nazi Propaganda Minister Joseph] Goebbels which declared that 'Jews were the syphilis of all European peoples.' . . . I was put in the position of being humbugged, as indeed I was." Throughout the remaining three years of his tenure in Berlin, Dodd would provide Washington with a steady stream of reports about German military rearmament in violation of the Versailles Treaty, the persecution of German Jewry, and the general untrustworthiness of the Hitler regime.[87]

Despite that information, Roosevelt's attitude toward U.S.-German relations remained unchanged, as a controversy in 1935 illustrated. On July 26, 1935, a German ocean liner, the SS *Bremen*, cruised into New York's harbor, flying the swastika flag from its mast. Crowds of anti-Nazi protesters had gathered on shore. Some of them burst past the police lines, tore down the Nazi flag, and hurled it into the water. Six of the demonstrators were arrested. When the protesters were arraigned before New York City magistrate Louis Brodsky on September 6, Brodsky dismissed the charges on the grounds that tear-ing down the Nazi flag was justified. It was the ss *Bremen* that was guilty, the judge declared; it had engaged in "gratuitously brazen flaunting of an emblem which symbolizes all that is antithetical to American ideals." Hitler's ship, he ruled, was the equivalent of "a pirate ship with the black flag of piracy proudly flying aloft."[88]

The German government was furious. Goebbels's newspaper, *Der Angriff,* called Judge Brodsky "an Eastern Jew" who promoted "Jewish-communistic agitation." The Berlin newspaper *Boersen Zeitung* accused Brodsky of "incomparable impudence and brazen-faced provocation of the honor of the German people." The *Deutsche Allgemeine Zeitung* blasted Brodsky's decision as "an unheard-of insult to Germany." Hitler's ambassador in Washington, Hans Luther, demanded an official U.S. government apology, and he got one: Secretary of State Cordell Hull sent the Hitler regime a note expressing "regret" at Judge Brodsky's ruling.[89]

Shocked and dismayed by this turn of events, Rabbi Wise publicly challenged FDR's policy concerning the Nazis for the first time. In his Rosh Hashanah sermon at the Free Synagogue, Wise said the "horror" of the Nazis' recent enactment of anti-Jewish laws "was made more full of horror by the act of our own government in apologizing with exaggerated profuseness and abjectness to the Nazi regime for a word of disrespect and contempt for that regime, uttered in the course of a judicial decision from the bench of the lower criminal court of our city. Such apology would have come more fitly if our government had ever uttered one brave word in condemnation of the program and the practices of the Nazi regime."[90]

Secretary Hull apologized to the Nazis twice more, in 1937, when New York City mayor Fiorello La Guardia said the upcoming World's Fair should include a "Chamber of Horrors" featuring "that brown-shirted fanatic who is threatening the peace of the world." The German government-controlled press called La Guardia a "dirty Talmud Jew" as well as a "pervert" and a "pimp" (terms characterized as "language for the most part unprintable in American newspapers" by the Jewish Telegraphic Agency, which itself allowed only that the Nazis accused the mayor of "immorality"). The use of "pimp" referred to the fact that La Guardia had made his remarks at a luncheon of the American Jewish Congress Women's Division, headed by Wise's wife, Louise Waterman Wise; the Nazi press characterized the audience as "women of the streets."[91]

Initially Secretary Hull had issued only a general expression of "regret" over "utterances calculated to be offensive to a foreign government." When that proved insufficient to satisfy the Hitler regime, James C. Dunn, chief of the State Department's Division of Western European Affairs, officially informed the German Embassy that "I very earnestly deprecate the utterances which have thus given offense to the German Government. They do not represent the attitude of this Government toward the German Government." For his part, Rabbi Wise publicly defended La Guardia, while adding that it "may be technically necessary for the State Department to disavow the utterance of the Mayor." Wise's attempt to straddle the issue contrasted with his wife's demand that the Roosevelt administration seek an apology from the German government for its slur against the AJ Congress women. Ambassador Dodd delivered an official note of protest to the German Foreign Ministry, but Berlin refused to apologize.[92]

Meanwhile, the anti-Nazi activist Samuel Untermyer publicly condemned the State Department's apology, asserting that in view of "the unspeakable libels daily heaped upon Americans and American institutions, including our president, in the German-owned press," Secretary Hull should have "held his peace" rather than give in to the Germans' demand. Mayor La Guardia called the U.S. apology "embarrassing," and an editorial in the *New York Post* urged Roosevelt administration officials to "stop reading their Emily Post [rules of etiquette]" and try "less bowing and scraping" in response to Nazi complaints. When the Germans protested a new anti-Hitler remark by La Guardia the following week, Secretary Hull reiterated his previous apology and suggested that the mayor and the Nazis were equally to blame. "I am personally hopeful that all who are participating in the present controversy, which is marked by bitter and vituperative utterances in this country and in Germany, may soon reach the conclusion that it would be to the best interests of both countries for them to find other subjects which can be discussed more temperately."[93]

Ostensibly in furtherance of the goal of maintaining a "temperate" climate of relations between the United States and Nazi Germany, President Roosevelt compelled Secretary of the Interior Harold Ickes to remove critical references to Hitler from his speeches on at least three occasions. In May 1935, Ickes sent the White House remarks he intended to make at the University of Alabama's commencement exercises later that month. His draft described universities in Nazi Germany as "mere bond slaves to a strutting and vainglorious Nazism," and those in Fascist Italy as "permitted to teach only what the government permits them to teach." A reply from presidential aide Stephen Early informed Ickes's staff that "it is the President's request that the references to the foreign countries be entirely eliminated."[94]

A similar episode occurred in the spring of 1938, when Ickes was invited to speak at an anniversary dinner of a Chicago Jewish newspaper. "The only reason I accepted this engagement," Ickes wrote in his diary, "was because I could get a national [radio] hookup which would give me an opportunity to say something to the country about recent developments of fascism, particularly with reference to the persecution of the Jews in fascist countries in Europe. I have been promised one-half hour's time on the Columbia Broadcasting System. . . . I have been told that I am to have the full 110 stations of Columbia." Ickes showed his draft to President Roosevelt, who told him to "cut out the references that I had made to Naziism [sic] as well as references I had to current dictators." FDR said "it was all right to discuss fascism in a critical vein," but only in a general way. Three days later, Secretary of State Hull pressed Ickes to water down the speech even further. Hull insisted that the word "fascist" be removed in "three or four places," and that "a different turn of expression" be employed in an additional sentence, lest those references be seen as implicitly referring to Mussolini and thereby harm U.S.-Italian relations.[95]

This sequence of events was repeated in November 1938, when Ickes was invited to participate in a CBS radio broadcast of speeches by public figures responding to the Kristallnacht pogrom. In that night-long orgy of government-orchestrated violence in Nazi Germany, nearly one hundred Jews were murdered, hundreds were beaten in the streets, and thirty thousand more were hauled away to concentration camps. In addition, some seven thousand Jewish businesses were ransacked, and several hundred synagogues were burned down. Ickes, working with White House adviser Ben Cohen, presented a draft of his remarks to the White House and State Department. "The draft as submitted was approved," Ickes noted in his diary, "except that the President wanted us to cut out all references to Germany by name as well as references to Hitler, Goebbels, and others by name." Ickes complied.[96]

The president likewise was studiously circumspect in his own public remarks concerning the Nazi regime. For example, when he was pressed by reporters about Franco-German relations during a September 1934 press conference, FDR cited an anecdote about Germany preparing its schoolchildren for war. But he twice emphasized that the remark was "entirely off the record" because "I cannot talk foreign affairs about so-called friendly nations." The president said nothing when Germany revealed in 1935 that it had created an air force (in violation of the Versailles Treaty), or when German troops occupied the Rhineland in 1936. Roosevelt's famous 1937 speech urging the international community to "quarantine" aggressive regimes did not mention Nazi Germany or any other countries by name, and Undersecretary of State Sumner Welles quickly assured the German ambassador that the president mainly had Japan and Italy in mind. At a March 1939 press conference, President Roosevelt noted that "many people" were worried that Germany might have expansionist intentions. But he prefaced that remark by cautioning the reporters that his statement was "a background story without attribution. . . . In other words, do not bring me into it."[97]

Ickes, for his part, did manage to emerge victorious in one struggle with FDR over U.S. policy toward Nazi Germany. In late 1937, the president approved the sale of helium to power Germany's Zeppelin airships, telling Congress it was "sound national policy" for the United States to be "a good neighbor" to Germany. After initially supporting the sale, Ickes reversed himself in the wake of Hitler's annexation of Austria in March 1938, arguing it would be dangerous to provide the Nazis with a gas that was "of military importance." News of the dispute leaked to the press. A number of congress members then publicly opposed the sale, and mail to the White House ran heavily against it as well. At a White House conference between Roosevelt, Ickes, and the administration's legal experts in May, the solicitor general informed the president that the sale could not go forward without the interior secretary's approval. FDR refused to give up. At a cabinet session two days later, the president again pressed Ickes to support the sale; Roosevelt was backed by all but two of the cabinet members (Perkins and Morgenthau said nothing). FDR suggested he could alleviate Ickes of responsibility by giving him a letter stating it was his "judgment, as Commander in Chief of the Army and Navy, that this helium was not of military importance." Ickes refused to budge. In his diary, Ickes expressed surprise that "the President is ignoring entirely the public sentiment . . . which is overwhelming—I would say well over ninety per cent of those heard from." In fact, Roosevelt had demonstrated on other occasions, such as in the fight over his Supreme Court restructuring proposal, that he was willing to take on unpopular causes in which he deeply believed. In this case, there was a political consideration, as well. When talk of the helium sale resurfaced in July, senior presidential adviser Thomas Corcoran confided to Ickes that (according to Ickes's diary) "the President won't try to force my hand. He believes that the politics of the situation are with me. If we now ship helium to Germany, it would offend the Jewish vote." Evidently the White House was uneasy about the prospect of Jewish voters supporting Republican candidates in the upcoming midterm congressional elections.[98]

The administration's cordiality toward the Hitler regime in the 1930s extended to receiving Nazi warships in American ports. Two German navy cruisers, the *Karlsruhe* and the *Emden*, were sent to visit the United States on multiple occasions between 1934 and 1936, in order, as the captain of the *Karlsruhe* put it, to "carry into the outside world something of the spirit of the New Germany." The *Karlsruhe* even brought along two thousand copies of Hitler's *Mein Kampf,* most of which it distributed in the United States. The Nazis hoped these friendly naval visits would "end once [and] for all the rumors and propaganda which had been spread abroad" concerning the persecution of German Jewry. The Hitler regime also believed forging relationships with U.S. military officers and other Americans of prominence might later help undermine America's interest in intervening against German aggression in Europe.[99]

The Roosevelt administration not only approved, but actively cooperated with, the visits of the warships. When the *Karlsruhe* docked in Honolulu, for example, the Nazi officers were taken on a tour of U.S. army and navy stations. On the *Karlsruhe*'s return visit to the West Coast the following year, U.S. navy vessels provided boats, personnel, and equipment to assist it in carrying out military exercises off the Los Angeles coast. When longshoremen in San Francisco called a strike to protest the *Karlsruhe*'s visit to their city, the State Department authorized the crew members to carry pistols as they walked around town. The *Emden* likewise enjoyed a warm reception. Its visit to Baltimore included a tour of the U.S. Naval Academy for 150 of the Nazi sailors. When the *Emden* docked in Honolulu, 1,200 U.S. troops staged a parade to honor its arrival. At almost every port of call, the Nazi warships were greeted by senior U.S. military and naval officers—sometimes the Coast Guard as well—and were often accompanied by a twenty-one-gun salute.[100]

An episode in the early fall of 1937 put the administration's cordial relationship with Nazi Germany in the spotlight once again. While Ambassador Dodd, exhausted and ailing, was visiting the United States for recuperation and medical appointments, his temporary stand-in at the Berlin embassy, charge d'affaires Prentiss Gilbert, attended the annual weeklong Nazi Party rally in Nuremberg as America's official representative. Dodd was appalled that the United States was, in effect, giving a stamp of legitimacy to a "Nazi propaganda performance" whose purpose was to "scare Europe" and "ridicule democracies." American Jewish organizations were likewise outraged.

The Joint Boycott Council, a coalition of the American Jewish Congress and the Jewish Labor Committee (representing Jews in the labor movement), publicly protested the U.S. action— the only instance in which the AJCongress would ever publicly criticize the Roosevelt administration on a Jewish issue. Rabbi Wise, for his part, sent a private telegram to the president, declaring himself "sick at heart" over the plan to attend the Nuremberg event and pleading that he "act with Rooseveltian decisiveness" by "order[ing] the recall of our American representative to Nuremberg." The president was not moved.[101]

The episode pushed Dodd closer to the end of his rope. State Department officials were already irritated by Dodd's inability to secure repayment of Germany's wartime debt to the United States. Dodd believed Germany's economic condition was so fragile as to make timely repayment impossible and therefore not worth aggressively seeking; Secretary Hull and his colleagues believed the fault lay with Dodd, who, because of his bookish demeanor, "put up very little fight" in his discussions with Nazi officials regarding the debt and was insufficiently concerned with the interests of what Hull called "the estimated 60,000 innocent holders [of German bonds] in this country."[102]

But there was also an important political dimension to the gulf between State and Dodd: some U.S. officials blamed the debt repayment problem on Dodd disliking the Nazis too much and not falling in line with the administration's efforts to foster friendly relations with Hitler. "[Dodd] hates the Nazis too much to be able to do anything with them or get anything out of them," the American ambassador in Paris, William C. Bullitt, wrote the president. "We need in Berlin someone who can at least be civil to the Nazis and speaks German perfectly."[103]

Dodd's opposition to U.S. representation at the Nuremberg rally further exacerbated his increasingly testy relationship with State. Meeting with President Roosevelt in October, Dodd signaled his intention to resign, but asked that he be kept on until the spring of 1938; he did not want it to appear that his departure was caused by Germany's complaints following press reports of his view of the Nuremberg episode. The president indicated his assent to that timetable, but less than a month after his return to Germany, Dodd received a blunt notice from the secretary of state that he was being replaced. The new ambassador, Hugh Wilson, was far gentler in his assessment of the Hitler regime and considerably more amenable to friendly U.S.-German relations.[104]

The president's prewar policy toward Nazi Germany should not be misunderstood as reflecting any kind of sympathy on his part for the policies or ideology of the Hitler regime. On the contrary, in numerous private conversations and cabinet discussions throughout the 1930s, President Roosevelt made it clear that he abhorred Nazism and regarded Hitler as a potential threat to world peace. In 1933 he told the French ambassador to the United States, "Hitler is a madman and his counsellors, some of whom I personally know, are even madder than he is." During a meeting with interfaith leaders on the refugee question in 1938, FDR referred to Hitler as "a maniac with a mission." In a cabinet discussion in early 1940 concerning German actions in occupied Poland, Roosevelt said "probably nothing in all history exceeds the[ir] sadistic cruelty."[105]

Anticipating war with Germany, President Roosevelt did what he could to gradually prepare the nation for that eventuality, including doubling the size of the navy, instituting the first peacetime military draft, securing repeal of neutrality legislation that would have blocked aid to U.S. allies, and pushing through the Lend-Lease bill to provide military assistance to the British. Those were no mean feats in the face of widespread isolationist sentiment. Polls consistently showed overwhelming public opposition to U.S. involvement in overseas conflicts, a sentiment no politician could afford to ignore. And at the end of 1940, following the German conquest of much of western Europe and the establishment of the German-Italian-Japanese Axis, Roosevelt delivered his famous "arsenal of democracy" speech. At last abandoning his longstanding taboo on publicly criticizing the Hitler regime, FDR explicitly warned that "the Nazi masters of Germany intend . . . to enslave the whole of Europe and then to use the resources of Europe to dominate the rest of the world."[106]

President Roosevelt's decision to maintain cordial—sometimes friendly—relations with Nazi Germany prior to America's entry into World War II reflected both his view that such relations were more important to U.S. interests than any human rights considerations, and his calculation that public opinion would frown upon any tensions between America and Germany.

Yet even after the "arsenal of democracy" speech, the longtime U.S. policy of cordiality toward Nazi Germany was not abandoned. The Roosevelt administration's failure to respond to the euthanizing of disabled Germans reflected the old mindset. During 1940–1941, Jacob Beam, third secretary at the U.S. embassy in Berlin, sent the State Department at least ten reports about the Hitler regime's execution of tens of thousands of Germans with physical or mental disabilities. Altogether, an estimated two hundred thousand "unfit" individuals were gassed as part of the Aktion T-4 program, which would serve as a prototype for the mass-murder techniques of the Holocaust. The administration's refusal to make any kind of statement in response to the murders evidently prompted Beam to leak the information to journalist William Shirer, who wrote about it in *Life* and *Reader's Digest* in early 1941.[107]

President Roosevelt's insistence on preserving good relations with Nazi Germany in the 1930s was a source of genuine anguish for Jewish leaders such as Rabbi Wise, who wished the president would lead public opinion rather than follow it. Nevertheless, with the exceptions of his Rosh Hashanah sermon concerning the *Bremen* affair apology and the American Jewish Congress protest against U.S. representation at the Nuremberg rally, Wise and the organizations he headed refrained from publicly taking issue with FDR's approach. This reluctance to challenge a policy that clearly discomfited him reflected two considerations: Wise's fear of provoking public suspicions that Jews were trying to drag America into a conflict with Germany, and his desire to protect the reputation of a president whom he passionately supported on other issues. By keeping quiet, Wise believed he was helping to ensure the U.S. administration's continued high levels of support from American Jewry, while preempting any potential public controversy over the president's stance regarding Nazi Germany. That he was able to sustain his own image as an outspoken critic of Hitler, while simultaneously shielding FDR from criticism over his refusal even to verbally confront the Nazi regime, is testimony to Rabbi Wise's impressive public relations skills.[108]

Reconciliation and Its Consequences

Rabbi Wise did not enjoy access to the president during Roosevelt's first three years in office. Several senior presidential advisers, most notably the de facto chief of staff Louis Howe, still resented Wise because of the dispute with FDR during the gubernatorial period, and initially blocked him from visiting the White House. Then Howe's declining health in late 1935 removed him from Roosevelt's inner circle and cleared the path for a Wise-Roosevelt reconciliation. A desire to cement Jewish electoral support for his upcoming reelection campaign also may have been one of Roosevelt's considerations.

As much as Wise longed for a rapprochement, when he heard from intermediaries in October that FDR had expressed an interest in seeing him, the rabbi replied that a "verbal, second-hand invitation" from the president was not good enough. The following month, Wise wrote presidential adviser David Niles that he "had better quit" his efforts to arrange a meeting with the president, because Wise had decided "I do not want to go to him," even if an invitation was extended. "I do not feel like it anymore," he asserted. Later in the letter, the rabbi groused about those Jews who had been to the White House while Wise was excluded: "When I think of the cheap little shyster bums like Gus Rogers, the lawyer of New York, being admitted to and welcomed at the White House, and the Sam Rosenmans, and the fact that I, as much at least as any man leader of four million Jews in America, have been denied admittance to the White House for two and one-half years, I really feel it is now too late." This exchange, which may have been an exercise in reverse psychology on Wise's part, evidently galvanized Niles to redouble, rather than cease, his efforts. Finally, in early 1936, a formal invitation was proffered by the president to the rabbi.[109]

The pent-up resentments about "Gus Rogers types" now behind him, Wise visited the White House on January 11, 1936. The meeting did not go exactly as Wise had hoped, however. "As I began to deal with the German Jewish question," the rabbi reported to Brandeis, "[the president] threw up his hands as it were and said, 'Well, Max (Warburg) wrote to me a month ago and said things are so bad in Germany there is nothing that can be done.'" Max, and his brothers Paul and Felix, were central figures among the German-born Jewish leaders whom Wise considered his archrivals. They favored extreme caution in responding to Nazi persecution. It was convenient for the president to cite Warburg's alleged statement as his reason for concluding that "nothing can be done," but as Wise knew, there was much FDR could do, such as quietly allowing the annual immigration quota from Germany to be fully utilized; the previous year, only 20 percent of those 25,957 places had been filled. Wise nonetheless chose to hold his tongue. (For a fuller examination of the immigration issue, see chapter 2.) For many years afterward, the rabbi would blame the Warburgs' alleged influence for Roosevelt's reluctance to do anything for German Jewry in the 1930s. Castigating his old foes was a more natural response for Wise than holding the president responsible for his policy decisions regarding Nazi Germany.[110]

Seeking another way to encourage the president to say something sympathetic regarding German Jewish refugees, Wise suggested at the meeting that FDR "write a word in appreciation of [James] MacDonald's [sic] work and his proposals" during his term as League of Nations High Commissioner for Refugees Coming from Germany. McDonald's efforts to persuade various governments to help fund Jewish emigration had consistently met with frustration. Rabbi Wise did not know that Roosevelt had just recently failed to fulfill a pledge to provide token U.S. financial support for McDonald's efforts. Meeting with the president at the White House on December 17, 1934, McDonald asked for "a symbolic contribution" of $10,000. This small gesture, McDonald said, would have "great moral value," because "if the United States as a great power would be willing to go along, there would be a great chance of inducing Great Britain, France, and perhaps Italy to follow." FDR replied, "All right," and then turned to his secretary, Missy LeHand, instructing her "to speak to me tomorrow about the matter at the budget conference." However, every subsequent time McDonald raised the matter with administration officials, he was given excuses and a runaround. Finally, a dejected McDonald concluded that FDR had "forgotten that he had promised to take the initiative" and withdrew the request. Nonetheless, in July, McDonald sent First Lady Eleanor Roosevelt a detailed update on the travails of German Jewry, asking "whether the time has not come when, in harmony with other precedents in American history, the American Government should take the initiative in protesting against the prevailing violations of the elementary civil and religious rights in Germany." Mrs. Roosevelt gave the letter to the president; he did not reply. Later that year, McDonald resigned in protest from the League of Nations refugees commission over the international community's failure to pay anything but "lip service" to the plight of Jews fleeing Hitler.[111]

Wise's other proposal at the January 1936 White House meeting was for the president to send greetings to the following month's national conference of the United Palestine Appeal (UPA). Established in 1925, the UPA served as the established Jewish leadership's primary channel for raising funds to develop a Jewish homeland in British Mandatory Palestine. FDR was responsive to Wise's request, but he used boilerplate language, expressing America's "sympathy with the great purpose of a national Jewish home in Palestine." The conference delegates did not know that Roosevelt had omitted two key sentences from Wise's draft of the statement: the first expressing hope that last year's "notable" record of sixty-one thousand Jewish refugees admitted to Palestine "would be surpassed in the present year," and the second calling for "opening wide the doors of Palestine to the largest number of homeless Jews, especially from lands of religious persecution and racial oppression." This was the first in what would be a number of instances in which Roosevelt would significantly dilute a proposed statement by Wise about Palestine; and Wise would subsequently conceal that information from fellow Jewish leaders and the Jewish public.[112]

Unaware that the president would significantly dilute his draft, Wise emerged buoyant from his meeting with Roosevelt. "The friendliest of relations have been restored between the President and myself," the rabbi reported to World Zionist Organization president Chaim Weizmann. "I now have, as in the old days, direct and immediate access to FDR." But would access equal influence?[113]

Not long after that first White House meeting, Wise conceived what he thought would be an effective way for the president to express anti-Nazi sentiment, and thereby prevent the Republican Party from "making capital," in that year's presidential campaign, of what they "will hold to have been FDR's inaction re Nazism." Through Frankfurter, the rabbi suggested that Roosevelt, "the most distinguished Alumnus of Harvard University," write a letter to Harvard president James Conant, "approving of what he expects will be President Conant's fine attitude in declining or rejecting the invitation of Heidelberg." Like other German universities, the University of Heidelberg had been purged of Jewish faculty and students, and now adhered to a strictly Nazified curriculum. It had recently extended invitations to major American universities to send representatives to participate in its upcoming 550th anniversary celebration. Evidently Wise's sources of information regarding Conant were less than reliable, for on the very day he sent his proposal to Frankfurter, Conant announced his acceptance of the Heidelberg invitation. Even had Conant rejected Heidelberg, it was highly unlikely that President Roosevelt would have applauded such a decision, because doing so would have been entirely at odds with his policy of maintaining cordial relations with Germany.[114]

Two White House messages, issued at about the same time, provided additional evidence of the president's determination to refrain from publicly criticizing Nazi Germany's persecution of the Jews. The Mizrachi Religious Zionist movement and Conservative Judaism's United Synagogue of America had requested greetings from the president to be read aloud at their upcoming national conferences, in February and March 1936, respectively. White House press secretary and senior presidential adviser Stephen Early instructed U.S. Commissioner of Education John W. Studebaker, who had been tasked with drafting the messages, to focus on "the cultural aspects of Judaism." Cautioning Studebaker that "the Nazi question" was "quite likely . . . to come up for discussion at either or both of these conventions," Early stressed that it was important to ensure that the president's words "cannot be misconstrued or misunderstood"—that is, misunderstood as criticism of the Hitler regime, which he did not intend. The message to Mizrachi spoke blandly of the role of religion in civilization through the ages; at the United Synagogue event, Interior Secretary Harold Ickes delivered an inoffensive address about the New Deal, comparing the wandering of the ancient Israelites in the desert to what he called the wandering of contemporary Americans in "the social desert" without appropriate government safeguards.[115]

Wise's relationship with the president during the next several years did occasionally create opportunities for the rabbi to advance Jewish concerns. The only one in which Wise was able to achieve meaningful results occurred in the autumn of 1936. Wise learned that the British, responding to a wave of Palestinian Arab violence, were poised to severely restrict Jewish immigration to the Holy Land. Acting at the request of Wise and other American Zionist leaders, FDR persuaded the British government to postpone the planned restrictions. Wise's access to the White House also resulted in occasions of significant personal gratification, such as the inclusion in the president's 1937 inaugural address of a sentence the rabbi suggested (see chapter 2).[116]

At the same time, the president did not hesitate to leverage his relationship with Wise to suppress Jewish protests that might prove politically inconvenient for him. In May 1936, the British government announced the appointment of a Royal Commission to investigate the causes of recent Palestinian Arab violence. Wise and other Zionist leaders were deeply distrustful of London's intentions, recalling that the last such commission, seven years earlier, blamed Jewish development for "provoking" Arab violence and recommended restrictions on Jewish immigration and land purchases. Acting to preempt Jewish agitation over the new commission, Felix Frankfurter, conveying the president's sentiments, "warned us that we were not to make any outcry against the Royal Commission," Wise reported to Chaim Weizmann. The White House did not want Zionist protests irritating U.S.-British relations and dragging the president into the latest round of the Palestine dispute.[117]

Later that year, FDR used Jewish fears of antisemitism to try to intimidate Rabbi Wise into keeping quiet on matters of Jewish concern. Wise confided to presidential aide David Niles in October: "The Chief said something to me the other day at Hyde Park about the necessity for a time of Jews lying low. He was speaking of the appalling growth of anti-Semitism in America." In the years to follow, there would be a number of instances in which the president would try to quiet American Jewish voices by paternalistically assuring them he was just looking out for their own welfare.[118]

In 1938, for example, Roosevelt objected when the AJCongress initiated plans to hold a plebiscite among American Jews. Hoping to bolster his standing as America's preeminent Jewish leader, Rabbi Wise calculated he could secure an overwhelmingly affirmative response to ballot questions on issues such as fighting antisemitism, creating a Palestine homeland, and fostering Jewish unity. Word soon reached Wise, via Brandeis, that Assistant Secretary of State Messersmith "was greatly disturbed" by the plebiscite plan, "which he thought might have serious results." Then, to Wise's chagrin, presidential speechwriter Samuel Rosenman and four other AJcommittee leaders issued a public statement decrying the planned plebiscite as an "undemocratic attempt to make of Americans who are Jews a distinct political unit." Making matters much worse, Rosenman then brought the plebiscite to the attention of President Roosevelt, who had not previously heard of it. Rosenman reported back to Wise that FDR was "filled with horror" and had warned that "the whole thing is 'loaded with dynamite.' The president asked, 'Won't this enable Americans to say that the fellows who wrote the *Protocols of the Elders of Zion* had some justification?'" The president was also said to have pointed out that "good Orthodox Christians" would be offended that the plebiscite was scheduled to take place on a Sunday. Rosenman then spent an hour trying to persuade Wise of "the unwisdom and danger at this time of having a Jewish election." Part of the problem, Wise explained to an associate, was that "even if the *Times* gives it straight, the *Des Moines Register* will not and the people in Des Moines and Texas will read [about] a Jewish election for Congress." Irritated that Rosenman had FDR's ear ("I am sure that Jewishly his influence is all to the bad," Wise confided to a colleague), but unwilling to defy the president, Wise found a face-saving way to cancel the plebiscite. He announced that the vote was no longer necessary in view of the pending creation of the General Jewish Council, a revival of the old Joint Consultative Committee, which had lapsed into inactivity years earlier.[119]

2

In Search of Havens

The Jews must leave Germany.

—Justice Louis Brandeis to Rabbi Stephen Wise

Justice Brandeis's blunt words to Stephen Wise, just days after Hitler became chancellor, caught the rabbi by surprise. Wise's instinctive reaction to the rise of the Nazis was to seek ways of pressuring Hitler to moderate his treatment of the Jews, not to organize mass Jewish emigration from Germany.

As the months wore on and the reports of violence and discrimination mounted, however, Wise began to reconsider. Especially jarring was a conversation he had in June 1933 with several exiled German Jewish scientists, who told Wise that Jews had no future in Germany. He reported to Mack: "I really felt as though I had been struck a blow between the eyes to hear two distinguished German Jews . . . speak in these terms. Again and again, they said, '*Nur heraus*' [only emigration]. I confess to you that when Brandeis said that two months ago, I could hardly believe my ears; and I could hardly believe that he was sane. A people to migrate!"[1]

Three months and numerous atrocity reports later, Wise told Brandeis he had come around to his point of view. "I have met no one from Germany, including Germans who came expressly from Berlin to confer with me, who failed to agree with you [that the Jews must leave]," Wise wrote. "The Jews must leave Germany, apart from Germany's resolve that they shall."[2]

Some six hundred thousand Jews then lived in Germany. Where would they go?

Unfilled Quotas

The United States was a potential haven, but only within the limitations imposed by America's 1921 and 1924 immigration legislation. The quotas these laws established had reversed the nation's tradition of welcoming the downtrodden from around the world.

The new system, based on national origins, drew upon the theories of late-nineteenth and early twentieth-century anthropologists and eugenicists who regarded Anglo-Saxons as biologically superior to other peoples. This race-dominated view of human society had gained prominence in the years following World War I, as the American public's anxiety about Communism mounted following the Soviet revolution in Russia. A combination of racism, fear of Communism, and general resentment of foreigners had bolstered public support for immigration restriction.

The 1921 law, known as the Johnson-Reed Immigration Act, stipulated that the number of immigrants from any single country during a given year could not exceed 3 percent of the number of immigrants from that country who were living in the United States at the time of the 1910 national census. In 1924 Congress tightened the regulations even further: the percentage dropped from 3 percent to 2 percent, and the quota numbers were henceforth based on the 1890 rather than the 1910 census. The purpose of the changes was to reduce the number of Jews and Italians entering the country, considering the bulk of Jewish and Italian immigrants living in the United States had arrived after 1890. Indeed, the original version of the Johnson-Reed Act had been submitted to Congress together with a report by Wilbur Carr, the chief of the United States

Consular Service (who would oversee immigration as assistant secretary of state under FDR from 1933 to 1937), which characterized would-be Jewish immigrants from Poland as "filthy, un-American, and often dangerous in their habits . . . lacking any conception of patriotism or national spirit." The immigration system contained no special provision for refugees. Those who were fleeing racial or religious persecution competed for the same visas as individuals seeking to enter the United States for less urgent reasons.[3]

More than two million Jews from eastern Europe, primarily Russia, immigrated to the United States between 1880 and 1920, driven out by pogroms and severe economic discrimination. The ban on emigration enforced by the new Soviet regime in Russia (as of 1918), combined with the minuscule quotas for other eastern European countries with large Jewish populations, ensured that the purpose behind the restrictive new immigration system would be fulfilled. Poland's quota was 6,524 annually; Czechoslovakia's was 2,874; Hungary's, 869; Rumania's, 377. The German quota of 25,957 (which increased to 27,370 when Hitler annexed Austria in 1938) was the largest for any European country with a large and distressed Jewish community.

The size of each nation's quotas, however, was only one of the obstacles to significant Jewish immigration to the United States in the 1930s. A more immediate impediment was the way in which the government administered the quota system. In 1930, in response to the onset of the Great Depression, the Hoover administration tightened the requirements for approval of an immigration visa so that applicants considered "likely to become a public charge" (that is, dependent upon government assistance) were excluded. The final decision on visa applications rested in the hands of individual consular officials abroad, who acted on the instructions of the State Department, which, in turn, reflected the wishes of the White House.

The Roosevelt administration took a harsh system and made it worse. Assistant Secretary of State Breckinridge Long would later explicitly recommend using "various administrative devices" to "postpone and postpone and postpone the granting of the visas." One U.S. consul in Europe assured the chief of the visa division at the State Department, John Farr Simmons, in 1938 that he understood it was "the Department's desire to keep immigration to a minimum." Simmons himself acknowledged that "the drastic reduction in immigration [during the 1930s] was merely an obvious and predictable result of administrative practices."[4]

To begin the process, a person applying for a visa to enter the United States was required to fill out a four-foot-long application form and present more than fifty pages of documents proving that he or she had no criminal record and no significant health problems, along with a detailed financial statement from someone in the United States who would guarantee that the immigrant would not become a "public charge." Yet, even applicants who qualified in all other respects and were able to secure such sponsors sometimes found the sponsorship was insufficient to satisfy the consuls. President Roosevelt himself remarked unhelpfully in 1936 that a distant relative might feel "no legal or moral obligation to support the applicant," the way a closer relative might.[5]

Many consuls searched high and low for grounds to reject an application, no matter how flimsy or arbitrary. In the case of nineteen-year-old Hermann Kilsheimer, for instance, three relatives did not suffice. He presented the American consulate in Stuttgart with affidavits from his brother-in-law and two cousins, all gainfully employed American citizens, pledging to support him. The cousins' affidavits were rejected on the grounds that they were not close enough relatives, and the consul decided that Hermann's brother-in-law earned too little to both support his own family and pay for Hermann's tuition if he chose to attend college.[6]

U.S. immigration law contained several important exceptions that could have been used to increase the number of refugees admitted: "ministers" (rabbis and cantors) and their families, professors and their families, and students at least fifteen years old were all permitted by law to enter the United States outside the quotas. The Roosevelt administration, however, often seemed to go out of its way to find grounds to reject applicants for such visas. Numerous German Jewish refugee students, for example, gained admission to American universities but were prevented from entering the United States. As Raymond Geist of the U.S. consulate in Berlin explained in turning down a student who had been accepted by Dropsie College, "He is a potential refugee from Germany and hence is unable to submit proof that he will be in a position to leave the United States upon the completion of his schooling."[7] Faculty members at accredited European universities who were offered positions at American universities were eligible for non-quota visas. However, when Hebrew Union College, in Cincinnati, established a college-in-exile and began inviting European Jewish scholars to its faculty, the Roosevelt administration threw up an array of roadblocks. One distinguished German Jewish scholar was disqualified on the grounds that he was primarily a librarian rather than a full-time professor. The State Department also accepted the Nazi regime's downgrading of the Higher Institute for Jewish Studies, the *Hochschule fur die Wissenschaft des Judentums*, from "Hochshule" (an institute of higher learning, or college) to "Lehranstalt" (a lower-level institution of learning, or an academy). Once the institution was no longer considered to be at the university level, its faculty members were no longer eligible for non-quota visas.[8]

The reasons given for rejections ranged from absurd to maddening. Some visa applicants at the U.S. consulate in Stuttgart presented affidavits of support from the multimillionaire Hollywood mogul Carl Laemmle, but the consul-general rejected them on the grounds that Laemmle was seventy-one years old, and therefore might not live long enough to assist the refugees whom he was promising to help.[9] When the world-famous German Jewish chemist Fritz Haber approached the U.S. ambassador to Germany, William Dodd, in July 1933 to ask about "the possibilities in America for emigrants with distinguished records here in science," Dodd told him (according to Dodd's diary) "that the law allowed none now, the quota being filled." In fact, the German quota was 95 percent unfilled that year.[10]

Ten-year-old Herbert Friedman was denied permission to accompany his mother and brother to the United States in 1936 after an examining physician at the Stuttgart consulate claimed he had tuberculosis. The tests all proved negative, and an array of German and American specialists who reviewed his x-rays likewise concluded that he did not have the disease. Yet the consulate would not budge. The family eventually managed to enlist Albert Einstein, who reported on the case in a letter to the surgeon general: "I have spoken to a reliable young man who recently emigrated from Germany; when I told him about the Stuttgart Consulate's refusal to issue the visa for the child, without giving the young man the reason for the refusal [that is, Einstein did not tell him about the claim of tuberculosis], he immediately said, 'That is an old story. Tuberculosis!' This shows clearly that this case is not an isolated case but that it is becoming a dangerous practice."[11]

Some applicants in Germany ran into trouble when they presented a *ketubah*, the traditional Jewish religious wedding certificate, as evidence of their marital status. These Jews had been married in a religious ceremony only, and not according to civil law; or they found it impossible to obtain evidence of their marital status from a Nazi government office; or they had been married in Russia before the Soviet takeover and could not enter the USSR to retrieve the necessary documentation. U.S. consular officials refused to recognize a *ketubah* as proof of marriage and therefore deemed the applicants' children "illegitimate" and rejected them on the grounds of low moral character.[12]

As a result of the administration's methods, the quota for Germany was underfilled almost every year. The unused places were not rolled over into the next year; they simply were canceled. Just 1,375 places—barely 5 percent of the German quota—were used in 1933, Hitler's first year in power. The following year, 3,556 places—fewer than 14 percent—were utilized. In eleven of Roosevelt's twelve years in office (1933–45), the German quota was not filled. The only exception was 1939, when FDR permitted it to be filled as a result of the strong public outcry over the antisemitic brutality accompanying the German annexation of Austria, and the nationwide *Kristallnacht* pogrom (see below).

Starting in late 1936, there was a modest increase in the number of German nationals admitted to the United States as a result of a report submitted by U.S. Foreign Service inspector Jerome Klahr Huddle. Some American consuls in Germany had complained of being short-staffed, so Huddle went to Germany to assess the situation. In his report, Huddle recommended that more-distant relatives of visa applicants could be relied upon to provide support, because they undoubtedly felt genuine sympathy for their persecuted family members. Eliot Coulter of the Visa Division agreed, in an internal memorandum, that "the Jewish people often have a high sense of responsibility toward their relatives, including distant relatives whom they may not have seen." As a result, German immigration increased from 6,307 in 1936 to 11,127 in 1937. Still, the total for 1937 represented just 42 percent of the available spaces that year; the majority of the German quota remained unfilled.[13]

After the exceptional period in 1939 when the quota was briefly filled, the usual practice of suppressing German immigration below the legal limit was resumed. Beginning in 1940, the administration of the immigration system fell to a newly appointed assistant secretary of state, Breckinridge Long, a long-time Roosevelt friend and donor who had recently served as U.S. ambassador to Italy. Long became responsible for twenty-three of the State Department's forty-two divisions, including the visa section. Soon after assuming his new position, Long outlined to his colleagues his strategy to "delay and effectively stop for a temporary period of indefinite length the number of immigrants into the United States." The key, Long explained, was "to put every obstacle in the way and to require additional evidence and to resort to various administrative devices which would postpone and postpone and postpone the granting of the visas." In that same spirit, the U.S. consul general in Berlin that year encouraged his deputies to reject German (Jewish) visa applicants on the grounds that their opposition to the current German government was only temporary and did not necessarily supersede their loyalty to Germany. Long helped craft a stringent new policy, approved by FDR and adopted in June 1941, of rejecting all visa applicants who had close relatives in German-occupied territory, on the grounds that the Germans might take the relatives hostage to pressure the refugee to become a Nazi spy. Needless to say, an extremely large number of applicants had such relatives. No evidence of refugees becoming spies was ever found, and only one case was ever discovered in which a German spy posed as a Jewish refugee immigrant. The man got only so far as Cuba; he was captured there and executed.[14]

After Pearl Harbor, Jews born in countries at war with the United States were automatically branded "enemy aliens," which further lengthened and complicated the immigration application process. In addition, refugees who had escaped to neutral countries such as Portugal or Spain sometimes were denied visas because local U.S. consular officials deemed them to be "not in acute danger." Furthermore, once the United States entered the war, there were no American consulates functioning in the Axis-occupied countries where refugees might have been considered "in acute danger." To make matters worse, new U.S. government interdepartmental review committees grilled the sponsors of would-be immigrants, focusing on possible Communist connections or searching for other reasons to reject applicants. Refugee advocate Dorothy Detzer cited the questioning of a woman whose daughter was trapped in Vichy France and whose son-in-law, a soldier in the British army, was among the British troops evacuated en masse from Dunkirk. A member of the review committee asked her, "Well, when your son-in-law left Dunkirk with the English, why didn't he get his wife to come up from southern France to go with him?"[15]

The Roosevelt administration's overall approach to immigration, compounded by specific measures such as the close relatives edict, ensured that the admission of German and other European Jews to the United States during the Hitler era was far below what the law permitted. Altogether, during the period of the Nazi mass murder, from late 1941 and until early 1945, only 10 percent of the quotas from Axis-controlled European countries were actually used. Nearly 190,000 quota places remained vacant. For all of Franklin Roosevelt's efforts to portray himself as a caring humanitarian by contrast with the (supposedly) cold-hearted Republican, Herbert Hoover, immigration was one area in which Presidents Roosevelt and Hoover were in accord. The immigration numbers from countries with large Jewish populations in Hoover's final year, 1932, were similar to those in FDR's first year as president, 1933. Immigration from Germany totaled 2,086 in 1932 and 1,324 in 1933. The United States welcomed 917 immigrants from Poland in 1932 and 961 in 1933; from Czechoslovakia, 304 and then 171; from Hungary, 329 and then 187; and from Rumania, 318 and then 236. The important difference between the two presidents was that Hoover was closing the doors at a time when no large European Jewish population was seeking haven in the United States, while Roosevelt closed the doors even further precisely at the time when large numbers of Jews desperately needed shelter from persecution. Ironically, Hoover, in his post-presidential years, would become a public advocate of steps such as granting haven to German Jewish children outside the quota system, while Roosevelt's position remained inflexible.[16]

That FDR was aware of the unfilled quotas on his watch is evident from a number of sources. Assistant Secretary Long, for one, periodically briefed the president on immigration matters. In one diary entry from 1940, Long reported that in a discussion at the White House on ways to curtail immigration, he "found that [FDR] was 100% in accord with my ideas. The President expressed himself as in entire accord with the policy which would exclude persons about whom there was any suspicion that they would be inimical to the welfare of the United States no matter who had vouchsafed for them. I left him with the satisfactory thought that he was wholeheartedly in support of the policy which would resolve in favor of the United States any doubts about admissibility of any individual."[17]

The president's awareness that the German quota was under-filled is also evident from a letter he sent in reply to a 1935 plea from New York governor Herbert Lehman for a more lenient approach to visa applicants from Germany. "I am informed that nearly all immigration quotas have been considerably under-issued during the past four years," FDR wrote. He even cited the statistics for visas granted to German nationals in each of those years.[18]

American Jewish leaders likewise were aware that the quotas were under-filled. Rabbi Wise, for one, alluded to the problem in his September 23, 1933, report to the AJ Congress adminis-trative committee about his recent visit to Europe:

> Is it an under-statement on my part to say that under 5,000 Ger-man Jewish refugees have been admitted in America? France, a small country, admitted 25,000. Europe cannot understand America not being even as hospitable as is England in its lim-ited hospitality. Czechoslovakia has 6 to 8,000; Switzerland a few thousand; Holland and Belgium probably have 4 to 7,000; Egypt is accepting some. Europe cannot understand the ineffec-tiveness of Jewish opinion in America in the matter of moving the President of the United States or the Congress, or who-ever are the authorities to be reached at least to admit some thousands of the refugees from Europe. They know all about the labour laws and the economic conditions are no worse in America than in Czechoslovakia. The misery, the beggary, the destitution that prevail in a country such as Czechoslovakia are indescribable.[19]

In the years to follow, the fact that the quotas from Ger-many and other European countries were almost never filled continued to be a matter of common knowledge. The matter

received mention on various occasions in newspapers rang-
ing from the *New York Times* to the liberal political weekly the
New Republic to the Communist periodical the *Militant*, not
to mention Jewish publications such as the AJCongress's *Congress Weekly* and the U.S. Labor Zionists' *Jewish Frontier*. It was
publicly cited by officials of Jewish organizations such as the
World Jewish Congress, the American Jewish Conference, and
the Hebrew Immigrant Aid Society, as well as by literary figures, such as the investigative journalist I. F. Stone and the
author Laura Z. Hobson.[20]

Stymied by the Roosevelt administration's restrictive practices, as well as strong congressional and public opposition to
immigration, Wise and other American Jewish leaders looked
for ways to increase the level of German Jewish immigration
closer to the maximum the quotas permitted. They believed
this would be a more realistic strategy than challenging the
quota laws themselves. At a House Immigration Committee
hearing on March 22, 1933, chairman Rep. Samuel Dickstein
(D-NY) suggested waiving the "public charge" stipulation in
cases of German Jewish relatives of American citizens. Wise
worried that such a measure would fail if it appeared to be an
attempt to flood the country with German Jewish refugees.
He testified that he would prefer if the waiving of the require-
ment were to apply to all foreign relatives of Americans seeking visas, not just Jews fleeing persecution. Wise's approach,
however, would have resulted in even more immigration from
a number of countries (rather than just Germany). That was
not likely to gain traction on Capitol Hill at a time of economic
depression and an unemployment rate of nearly 25 percent.[21]

Congressman Dickstein ultimately proposed a more limited resolution. It would direct consuls abroad to disregard
the public charge provision in cases of "children and aged and
infirm relatives"—rather than all relatives—of U.S. citizens;
and it did not specify Germany. But even that watered-down
version failed to make it out of committee. Two months later,
Dickstein suggested allowing American relatives of rejected

visa applicants from Germany to appeal the rejections to the secretary of labor. That proposal never went forward, either.[22]

A different strategy for easing the admission of German Jewish refugees originated in the Department of Labor. Acting on a suggestion from Julian Mack, Secretary of Labor Frances Perkins proposed permitting American citizens to post a bond in place of other financial guarantees for would-be immigrants. The State Department opposed the plan. President Roosevelt sided with State, even though the attorney general issued an opinion in favor of Perkins. The consuls in Europe continued following the existing procedures.[23]

Zionism and Refugees

Even as America's doors were closing, Palestine's were opening. On the eve of Britain's liberation of the Holy Land from the Turks in 1917, London issued a policy statement, known as the Balfour Declaration, pledging to facilitate the revival of a "national home for the Jewish people" in Palestine. In 1920 the League of Nations assigned Great Britain the mandate for Palestine; Jewish immigration and development of the country soon proceeded in earnest.

Rising antisemitism in Germany led to a significant increase in the number of German Jews immigrating to Palestine. German Jewish immigration to the Holy Land rose from fewer than five thousand in 1930 and 1931 to 12,533 in 1932, 37,337 in 1933, and 45,267 in 1934. For American Zionists such as Rabbi Wise, this trend facilitated the desired goal of building up the Jewish homeland, while at the same time helpfully relieving some of the pressure to bring more refugees to the United States.

Wise's boyhood home was permeated with Zionism. His father, Rabbi Aaron Wise, was one of the earliest Zionist activists in the United States, and his maternal grandmother, who lived out her final years in Turkish-ruled Palestine, was buried on Jerusalem's Mount of Olives. Wise himself cofounded the first national U.S. Zionist organization, the Federation of American Zionists, in 1898. He traveled to Basel that year to attend the Second Zionist Congress, where he met the world Zionist movement's legendary founder, Theodor Herzl. The inspiration he derived from his encounter with Herzl would undergird his lifelong commitment to the Zionist cause. For Wise, Zionism represented the rebirth of a great national culture; a healthy restoration of Jewish pride and self-sufficiency after centuries of weakness and submission; and, above all, a haven for Jews in distress.

Like most American Zionists, Wise thought of Palestine as a refuge for other Jews, not for himself, although at brief moments he seemed tempted by the idea of settling there. Pronouncing himself "miserable about the Jewish situation [in Europe]" and fed up "with my fellow-Jews in America, who today are wasting more money in two winter months in Florida than they have put into Palestine in twenty-five years," Wise wrote his colleague Emanuel Neumann in Tel Aviv in early 1938 that "this generation [of American Jews] is not worth saving" and "I am almost prepared to swim over and live in a hut with my fellow-Jews." He asked Neumann to help him find "a little orange plantation" somewhere in Palestine to purchase, but then added, "of course, without a home." At around the same time, he wrote to another colleague, "Louise and I want to get some land in Palestine—perhaps just enough for graves."[24]

The Doors Begin to Close

In 1936, the British began restricting Jewish immigration to Palestine in response to Arab rioting there. By the end of that year, the total number of arrivals was down to 29,595, fewer than half of the previous year's total.

The turmoil in Palestine coincided with a surge of antisemitism throughout Europe. The Nazis' consolidation of power in Germany strengthened pro-Nazi movements elsewhere on the continent in the mid-1930s, and encouraged other governments to enact antisemitic legislation and tolerate attacks on their Jewish citizens. Now Germany's Jews were no longer the only European Jewish community under assault and in need of refuge.

In Rumania, the two largest antisemitic political factions, the National Peasants Party and the League of National Christian Defense, united in 1937 and established a coalition government. Although the new regime was short-lived, it held the reins of power long enough to enact legislation stripping one-third of Rumania's 750,000 Jews of their civil rights. That action paved the way for additional anti-Jewish discrimination and legislation by subsequent Rumanian governments and further encouraged the rising tide of popular antisemitism in the country.

Benito Mussolini and his Fascist Party, the rulers in Italy since 1922, did not mistreat the country's small Jewish population during their first years in power. In the mid-1930s, however, Mussolini drew increasingly close to Hitler and began turning against Italy's forty-eight thousand Jews. In the autumn of 1938, he issued a series of racial laws that stripped Jews of their civil rights, prohibited them from teaching or studying in public schools, banned marriages between Jews and non-Jews, ejected Jews from a wide range of professions, and expelled thousands of foreign-born Jews from the country altogether.

Extreme rightist Karlis Ulmanis came to power in a 1934 coup in Lithuania. His brand of strident Lithuanian nationalism led to a harsh deterioration in the economic lives of 155,000 Jewish citizens. In the name of "Lithuaniazation," the regime severely reduced the number of Jews in government jobs, helped push Jews out of various private industries, and facilitated an environment of economic pressure that significantly decreased the number of Jewish students enrolled in Lithuanian universities. Sporadic instances of local anti-Jewish violence made life even more tenuous for many Jews in interwar Lithuania.

In 1930s Poland, longstanding grassroots antisemitism, combined with the disastrous impact of the worldwide depression, made life increasingly intolerable for the country's three million Jews. Although in the wake of World War I Poland had signed "minorities treaties" that were supposed to protect Jews as well as other ethnic minorities, antisemitic discrimination and occasional outbursts of anti-Jewish violence became the norm in the years leading up to World War II. Local anti-Jewish boycotts also were common. Gangs of antisemitic thugs pressured Christian landlords, artisans, and shopkeepers to refrain from doing business with Jews. Those who cooperated with the boycott were given signs to place in their windows announcing that they dealt only with "Aryans." Those who refused had their names published in extreme nationalist Polish newspapers. The boycott enforcers also frequently carried out physical assaults on Jewish businesses, demanding that they close down, and the attacks sometimes escalated into all-out pogroms. A study of Jewish-owned stores in eleven towns in Poland's Bialystok region calculated that from 1932 to 1937, the number of Jewish shops decreased by more than one-third. The Polish government, for its part, endorsed anti-Jewish boycotts as necessary to realize the "Polonization" of the nation's economy, which Polish authorities claimed was under Jewish domination.

During the mid-1930s, Rabbi Wise's meetings with U.S. government officials concerning Jews in Europe focused almost exclusively on matters related to German Jewry. When Wise stepped into the Oval Office on January 22, 1938, however, he had a different agenda. He spoke to President Roosevelt about "the troubled Jewish position in Rumania," the danger that "[Y]ugoslavia [is] threatening to go the same way," and recent reports that "Poland demands that Jews, who lived there six to nine hundred years, leave at once." To Wise's shock and dismay, FDR responded by relaying an anecdote that suggested antisemitism in Poland was simply a response to the fact that "the Jewish grain dealer and the Jewish shoe dealer and the Jewish shopkeeper" were controlling the Polish economy. Wise protested: "But, Chief, this is pure Fascist talk. They must find scapegoats to whom to point in order to satisfy the landless and unfed peasantry, and the Jew is the convenient and traditional and historical scapegoat." Wise's plea was to no avail. Roosevelt evidently "assented to every word" he had heard about Jews and

the Polish economy. Wise suspected the allegations had originated with the Polish ambassador in Washington, Count Jerzy
Potocki. "It was," Wise wrote in a private account of the conversation, "like a blow in the face to have F.D.R. swallow and
regurgitate this stuff of Potocki, himself of the landed gentry."[25]

The deteriorating situation for Jews in Poland created a
dilemma for Wise and other American Jewish leaders. It was
difficult to deny that the severe antisemitism and anti-Jewish
discrimination there meant emigration would be the best solution for at least some Polish Jews. At the same time, however,
the Polish government's unabashed expressions of interest in
effecting the emigration of large numbers of Polish Jews conflicted with the principle of equality for all citizens—a principle that American Jews cherished.[26] Thus, when Polish foreign
minister Jozef Beck referred to Poland's Jews as "superfluous,"
Wise responded with a stern telegram admonishing Beck that
"the solution of the problem of Jewish relations can be found
only on the soil of Poland." Though Wise did not object to individual Jews emigrating from Poland—in general, he viewed
eastern European rather than American Jews as the future residents of a Jewish homeland in Palestine—even more important in his view was the possibility that a dangerous precedent
would be set if the Polish regime pressured Jews to leave and
the international community failed to object. If Poland's leaders were to systematically push out its Jewish citizens, that
"might well become the *locus classics* [accepted standard] for
all groups in all lands, seeking to rid themselves of their Jewish populations," Wise wrote in a lead editorial in his magazine, *Opinion*. "France, Czecho-Slovakia, or England might
conceivably propose a conference on Jewish emigrants and refugee, without exciting suspicion with respect to their purpose."
Although he named three European countries rather than the
United States, Wise likely was thinking, too, of the possibility that the Polish precedent might inspire some of his fellow-
Americans to advocate similar action against American Jews.
Wise's close colleague Louis Lipsky said so explicitly when the

two of them met with the Polish ambassador in Washington some months later. The translation of their conversation by the ambassador's staff is somewhat stilted, but Lipsky's point was clear: "The American people should not imagine that the Jews in Poland should not be welcome, [lest] this attitude will eventually perpetrate [sic] into the minds of the Americans."[27]

"An Orgy of Sadism"

On March 12, 1938, German troops marched across the Austrian border as Hitler proclaimed the *Anschluss* (unification) of Germany with his land of birth. Huge, cheering crowds of Austrians greeted the conquering army.

The celebrations unleashed a wave of violent antisemitism that CBS Radio broadcaster William L. Shirer described as "an orgy of sadism" targeting Austria's 190,000 Jewish citizens. "Day after day large numbers of Jewish men and women could be seen scrubbing . . . the sidewalk and cleaning the gutters. While they worked on their hands and knees with jeering storm troopers standing over them, crowds gathered to taunt them. Hundreds of Jews, men and women, were picked off the streets and put to work cleaning public latrines and the toilets of the barracks where [Nazi secret police officers] were quartered. Tens of thousands more were jailed. Their worldly possessions were confiscated or stolen." The suicide rate among Vienna Jews skyrocketed in the weeks to follow, while lines outside the United States consulate in Vienna stretched for blocks, as tens of thousands of Austrian Jews sought permission to immigrate to America. The brutal expulsions of thousands of Jews from eastern Austria across the nearby borders with Czechoslovakia and Hungary were detailed in harrowing front-page stories in major U.S. newspapers, including the *New York Times*. Over the course of several days in April, *Times* readers followed the travails of one group of fifty-one Jews who were "stripped of all their possessions" and left stranded on "a narrow breakwater well out in the Danube [River]." They included an eighty-two-year-old rabbi "and his sick wife and many other women and children." Responding to "feeble cries in the semi-darkness," a Czech border patrol found the refugees "crouched together on rough stones barely emerging from the swollen river." The Czechs cared for them overnight, then forced them across the border into Hungary. The Hungarians, in turn, drove them back into Austria. Thirty-five were jailed; the others "are hiding helpless and homeless" in a Hungarian forest.[28] With some prominent journalists and members of Congress calling for U.S. intervention to aid Austria's Jews, State Department officials decided to "get out in front and attempt to guide" the pressure before it got out of hand by recommending two gestures, both of which the president accepted. The first measure was to combine the German immigration quota of 25,957 and the Austrian allotment of 1,143. Had there been an insufficient number of qualified German applicants, this step would have represented some slight relief for the suddenly beleaguered Austrian Jewish community. In practice, however, the number of Germans seeking refuge in the United States far exceeded the available quota spaces, so the combination of the two quotas made little real difference.[29]

The second gesture was the president's announcement, on March 24, that the United States was inviting thirty-three countries to send representatives to a conference on the refugee problem, to be held in the French resort town of Evian. At the same time, a State Department memorandum explained that U.S. immigration policy would not change, because refugees would take jobs from Americans or become public charges; because no U.S. government aid was available to assist with refugee resettlement; and because taking special action for refugees from Germany or Austria would mean discriminating against refugees from other countries. After making the announcement, the president took little interest in the conference. Asked by reporters on the eve of the Evian assembly whether the U.S. delegation would present "any definite plan to the Refugee Conference," Roosevelt replied: "I do not know; I cannot answer. You had better ask the State Department."[30]

On the same day as the president's announcement, Representatives Celler and Dickstein unveiled proposals to increase
Jewish refugee immigration to the United States. Celler said
he would introduce a resolution calling for the admission of
all victims of political or religious persecution; Dickstein proposed giving refugees previously unused quota places. Senior
officials of major Jewish organizations and refugee advocates,
led by the AJcongress and AJcommittee, meeting on April
4, resolved to inform Celler and Dickstein that the proposed
bills were "inadvisable" because they "may interfere with the
government's plans in connection with the international conference." They also privately assured the State Department of
their "misgivings" regarding the Celler and Dickstein initiatives. The congressmen withdrew their bills.[31]

In an additional response to the widening refugee crisis,
that April, Roosevelt created a nine-member President's Advisory Committee on Political Refugees (PACPR). At the belated
suggestion of Secretary Ickes, Rabbi Wise was included in the
committee, albeit too late to participate in its founding session at the White House. Wise was pleased that the president
finally seemed to be showing interest in the plight of Jewish
refugees, and further encouraged by being appointed (along
with Paul Baerwald of the American Jewish Joint Distribution
Committee) as one of two Jewish representatives in the advisory group. At the same time, the fact that Wise was included
as an afterthought suggests his relationship with the president
was not nearly as close as he hoped or imagined.[32]

The president envisioned the PACPR primarily as a liaison
between whatever refugee resettlement mechanism would
emerge from the Evian conference and the American organization that Roosevelt hoped would finance resettlement efforts.
A major function of the committee was to study potential refugee colonization sites around the world. Over the course of
the next five years, the PACPR sent experts to dozens of locales
throughout the globe to canvass settlement possibilities and
report their findings to the White House.

Despite the high hopes accompanying the PACPR's establishment, in practice President Roosevelt almost never consulted with the committee or took its advice. When the PACPR
clashed with the State Department—for example, over allocat-
ing emergency visas to a small number of refugee intellectuals
in 1940—Roosevelt sided with State. The president caustically
warned PACPR chairman James McDonald not to give him "any
sob stuff" about the immigration of downtrodden intellectuals being impeded by heartless diplomats.[33]

Pleasure Cruises

Rabbi Wise and other Jewish leaders were heartened by Roosevelt's gestures of combining the German and Austrian quotas, creating the advisory committee, and announcing the Evian
conference. The central obstacle they still faced, however, was
FDR's rejection of the idea that the United States bore any
humanitarian responsibility to make more than a meager contribution to resolving the refugee crisis. This problem was
compounded by the Roosevelt administration's promise to the
British to exclude Mandatory Palestine from discussions of possible refuge sites at the Evian conference. In fact, at the first
PACPR session, the guest speaker, Assistant Secretary of State
George Messersmith, warned the committee members to refrain
from trying "to move Great Britain to open more widely the
doors to Palestine." The Palestine issue "should be very carefully avoided" both at Evian and beyond, Messersmith said,
swatting aside complaints by Rabbi Wise and James McDonald. London feared that increased Jewish immigration to the
Holy Land would provoke Palestinian Arab violence and the
Roosevelt administration did not want to instigate any conflicts with its British ally.[34]

Wise initially considered attending the Evian conference as
an observer but ultimately decided against doing so, for reasons
which foreshadowed some of the factors that would handicap
his response to the European Jewish crisis in the years to follow. First, his PACPR colleagues felt the attendance of promi-

nent Jewish leaders would call too much attention to the Jewish nature of the refugee problem. They believed downplaying the Jewish identity of the refugees would make their admission to various countries more palatable. Indeed, the PACPR's very name—"political" rather than "Jewish" refugees—reflected this approach. In practice, however, obscuring the victims' Jewishness served to undermine public awareness of their plight and undercut the pressures to aid them.[35]

Second, Wise had a prior commitment to participate in a Zionist convention in Detroit that weekend. Wise's wide-ranging interests and involvement in a long list of Jewish and secular organizations sometimes distracted him from focusing on the plight of European Jewry. He occasionally acknowledged—in private—that it was "foolish" for him to play leadership roles in multiple institutions. Yet he never could quite bring himself to do otherwise.[36]

The third consideration affecting Wise's decision not to attend Evian was his deteriorating health. In June 1938, the sixty-four-year-old rabbi began x-ray treatments for an enlarged spleen, one of numerous ailments that slowed him down. While in hindsight Wise's attendance almost certainly would not have affected the outcome of the Evian conference, he had no way of knowing that. Thus, the fact that his deteriorating health was part of the reason he could not attend what appeared to be a critical international gathering on the refugee issue raised questions about his fitness for leadership in Jewry's darkest hour.[37]

The Evian conference opened on July 6, 1938, at the luxurious Hotel Royal. Although the delegates arrived on time, some of the early sessions were sparsely attended. "It is difficult to sit indoors hearing speeches when all the pleasures that Evian offers are outside," the hotel's chief concierge recalled. The delegates "took pleasure cruises on the lake," gambled at night at the casino, and "took mineral baths and massages," among other amenities enjoyed.[38]

When the delegates finally got around to the conference agenda, they had little to offer. The chairman of the U.S. delegation appealed to the attendees "to act promptly" in addressing the refugee problem, but, as *Newsweek* noted, "Most governments represented acted promptly by slamming their doors against Jewish refugees." Speaker after speaker reaffirmed their countries' unwillingness to accept more Jewish refugees. Typical was the Australian delegate, who asserted that "as we have no real racial problem, we are not desirous of importing one." The lone exception was the tiny Dominican Republic, whose leaders offered to accept as many as a hundred thousand Jewish refugees. (That project never materialized, for reasons to be discussed below.) The gathering concluded by creating an Intergovernmental Committee on Refugees, but the committee quickly proved ineffective, as the governments whose actions it was supposed to coordinate proved unwilling to tackle the refugee crisis. The Intergovernmental Committee's chair, George Rublee, later remarked that if he had realized FDR's true intentions in calling the conference and creating the committee, he never would have taken the job, because it was now obvious to him that the committee was established not to rescue the refugees but merely "to assuage the indignation excited by the persecution of the Jews."[39]

Commentators saw few reasons to cheer. *Time* reported that Evian was known as the source of "still and unexciting table water [and] after a week of many warm words of idealism [and] few practical suggestions," the conference "took on some of the same characteristics." Many Jewish commentators were equally critical. Palestine Labor Zionist leader (and future Israeli prime minister) Golda Meir, who attended Evian as an observer, remarked at a press conference afterward that "nothing was accomplished at Evian except phraseology. . . . There is only one thing I hope to see before I die, and that is that my people should not need expressions of sympathy any more." By contrast, Rabbi Wise, writing in his journal *Opinion*, characterized Evian as an example of "American generosity and British caution." He contended that "the appalling disappointment of Evian" was "the failure of the British Government to rise to a great occasion," but could not bring himself to acknowledge the failure of the American government to rise to it, either.[40]

Diminishing Enthusiasm

At President Roosevelt's request, the PACPR prepared numerous colonization reports during the years to follow. The renowned geographer Isaiah Bowman, who served as the president's adviser on population resettlement issues, undertook many additional refugee resettlement studies. But the White House never mustered a meaningful or sustained interest in any of the potential havens. "Roosevelt's enthusiasm [for refugee resettlement plans] appeared to grow the further away such projects were from the Western hemisphere," the historian Henry Feingold noted.[41]

One of the most promising possibilities, the plan to bring Jewish refugees to the Dominican Republic, foundered chiefly because of obstructionism by Roosevelt administration officials who feared the refugees would use the Caribbean island as a steppingstone to sneak onto the nearby American mainland. At one point, the FBI was informed by "confidential and reliable" Cuban police sources that the handful of Jewish refugees in the republic's Sosua region were carrying out Axis espionage through "shore-to-sea signals, supplying of enemy submarines, and short-wave signals." An investigation found the lights seen on the shore were actually beams from flashlights carried by refugees as they went about their evening chores.[42]

On the night of November 9–10, 1938, mobs of Nazi storm troopers unleashed an all-night hurricane of violence and destruction upon Germany's Jews, a pogrom known as Kristallnacht, or the "Night of Glass," because of the enormous number of Jewish homes and stores whose windows were smashed. President Roosevelt initially seemed less than eager to comment on the pogrom. At his first press conference following the pogrom, on November 11, Roosevelt was asked if he had "anything to say about the Nazi Government's extended campaign against the Jews." He replied: "No, I think not, Fred; you better handle that through the State Department." At his next press conference, four days later, amid mounting public outrage and international front-page news coverage, FDR read a prepared four-sentence statement about "the news from Germany," saying he "could scarcely believe that such things could occur in a twentieth-century civilization." He did not mention that the victims were Jews. He did announce that the U.S. ambassador in Germany was being instructed "to return at once for report and consultation," thereby heeding the suggestion by Assistant Secretary of State George Messersmith, who was concerned that without such action, "we shall be much behind our public opinion in this country." A Gallup poll that month found 88 percent of Americans "disapproved" of the anti-Jewish violence in Germany.[43]

Seeking clarification regarding the return of the ambassador, a reporter asked Roosevelt, "Would you elaborate on that, sir?" to which FDR responded that his statement "speaks for itself." To another reporter's query, "Have you made any protest to Germany?" the president replied, "Nothing has gone that I know of." Asked whether he would "recommend a relaxation of immigration restrictions so that the Jewish refugees could be received in this country," Roosevelt replied: "That is not in contemplation; we have the quota system."[44]

Three days later, at his next press conference, the president unveiled the one practical step he would take to assist German Jewish refugees in the wake of Kristallnacht. It concerned German citizens who were then in the United States on visitor's visas. Such visas, which had a maximum length of six months, were issued to tourists. Secretary of Labor Frances Perkins, the lone voice within the cabinet for admitting significantly larger numbers of refugees, had urged the State Department to be more flexible in granting such visas to applicants who did not qualify for regular visas. Calling the Perkins proposal "a loophole in the law [that] would be contrary to the spirit of our immigration laws," Assistant Secretary Messersmith contended that it "would have the effect of breaking down our whole immigration practice." In the immediate aftermath of Kristallnacht, as pressure mounted for a U.S. response, Messersmith became increasingly concerned that Perkins's "hysterical" proposal, as he characterized it, might gain traction.[45]

President Roosevelt was not willing to go so far as to adopt Perkins's plan of wide-scale use of visitor's visas, but he saw merit in her alternative and much more modest suggestion: to unilaterally extend the visitor's visas of those German Jews who were already in the United States. That step was acceptable to the president because it did not involve admitting any additional refugees. Furthermore, the visa extensions addressed the otherwise problematic situation caused by the German government's recent announcement that it was canceling the passports of German Jews currently in the United States as visitors. If the visas were not extended, the administration would find itself in the unpalatable position of having to forcibly deport thousands of stateless Jews to Nazi Germany. Thus at his November 14 press conference, the president announced that he was taking action in relation to the "large number . . . [of] refugees from, principally, Germany and Austria—what was Austria—who are in this country on what is called 'Visitors' Permits,' I think that is [the] word." Emphasizing that the German citizens in question "are not all Jews by any means," FDR said that it would be "cruel and inhuman" to send them back to "concentration camps, et cetera and so on," and therefore he would authorize the secretary of labor to grant them six-month extensions of their visitor's visas. (Owing to the worsening situation in Europe, and then the outbreak of war, they would receive additional six-month extensions, until they eventually applied for permanent residence via the regular immigration channels.) Roosevelt acknowledged he was not certain of the number of refugees involved: "I think you had better check these figures through the Secretary of Labor but I am inclined to think that they run as high as twelve to fifteen thousand."[46]

That figure was widely reported at the time, and repeated in many subsequent histories of the period as evidence of Roosevelt's determination to find ways to assist Jewish refugees despite legal restrictions. The gesture was less magnanimous than it seemed, however; the commissioner of immigration and naturalization, James Houghteling, soon afterward reported that the actual number of German citizens who received extensions on their tourist visas was no more than five thousand. How many of them were ordinary German tourists who intended to return anyway, and how many were German Jews posing as tourists in order to escape Nazi Germany, remains unknown.[47]

Roosevelt's response to Kristallnacht was far less generous than that of Great Britain, which, despite being less than one-fortieth the size of the United States and directly threatened by Nazi Germany, admitted ten thousand German Jewish children on the *Kindertransport* program. It also took in fifteen thousand young German Jewish women as nannies and housekeepers.[48]

No other presidential responses to the pogrom were forthcoming. The Roosevelt administration rejected Great Britain's offer to have the unused places from the British quota transferred to German Jews. The British quota was 65,721—more than twice the size of the German quota—and only 3,365 of those places had been used in 1938.

Meanwhile, Rabbi Wise proposed, via David Niles, that the president "write a letter to some Jewish friend, for publication," concerning the German situation; and that he summon the German ambassador to the White House to tell him, "This cannot go on, and have anything like decent relations with our country." Wise's request was ignored. Despite Kristallnacht, Roosevelt remained committed to maintaining diplomatic and trade relations with Nazi Germany.[49]

In early 1939, U.S. senator Robert Wagner (D-NY) and Rep. Edith Rogers (R-MA) introduced legislation to admit twenty thousand German—presumably Jewish—children to the United States, outside the quota system. The Wagner-Rogers bill was supported by a wide range of clergymen, labor leaders, university presidents, actors such as Henry Fonda and

Helen Hayes, and prominent political figures, including former president Herbert Hoover, 1936 Republican presidential nominee Alf Landon, and his running mate, Frank Knox. Former First Lady Grace Coolidge announced she and her neighbors in Northampton, Massachusetts would personally care for twenty-five of the children.

Numerous patriotic and anti-foreigner groups, including the American Legion and the Daughters of the American Revolution, mobilized against Wagner-Rogers. Laura Delano Houghteling, a cousin of President Roosevelt and wife of the U.S. Commissioner of Immigration, summarized the opposition's sentiment when she remarked at a dinner party that "20,000 charming children would all too soon grow up into 20,000 ugly adults."[50]

Eleanor Roosevelt let it be known that she sympathized with Wagner-Rogers, but the president took no position on the bill. An inquiry by a congresswoman as to the president's stance was returned by Roosevelt to his secretary, marked "File No action FDR." Mindful of polls showing most Americans opposed more immigration—a Gallup survey taken when it was thought that only ten thousand children would be admitted found 66 percent of Americans opposed to the proposal—Roosevelt chose to "follow public opinion rather than to form it and lead it," as Winston Churchill described one of FDR's traits. Congresswoman Clare Booth Luce once quipped that international leaders often were known by a typical gesture. Hitler had the upraised arm, Churchill the V sign; for Roosevelt, she wet her index finger and held it up."[51]

In April 1939, a joint Senate-House committee held four days of hearings on Wagner-Rogers. Sympathetic witnesses offered moving humanitarian pleas. They also stressed that children would not compete with American citizens for jobs. Nativist opponents presented standard anti-immigration claims as well as innovative assertions. They claimed the wording of the bill could enable twenty thousand Nazi children to come to the U.S., and therefore it would tear German families apart.

Both the Senate and House subcommittees voted unanimously in favor of Wagner-Rogers. The legislation moved on to the full House Immigration Committee for its consideration. Opponents then mounted a vigorous behind-the-scenes attack. This, together with the absence of White House support, resulted in the committee voting to require the twenty thousand child immigrants to be charged against the existing German quota. This maneuver nullified the original purpose of the legislation. Wagner-Rogers was, in effect, killed. Ironically, a year later, when British children were endangered by German bombing raids, President Roosevelt and Congress joined hands to rush through legislation enabling thousands of those children to come to the United States.[52]

Island Refuge

The possibility of using the U.S. Virgin Islands as a refuge was widely discussed in the aftermath of Kristallnacht. As a U.S. territory, the islands were subject to the same immigration quotas as the mainland United States with regard to permanent immigrants; however, the governor of the Virgin Islands had the authority to admit as many "temporary visitors" as he chose.

On November 18, 1938, at Governor Lawrence Cramer's urging, the Legislative Assembly of the Virgin Islands adopted a resolution offering to open its borders to refugees. Interior Secretary Ickes and the Labor Department strongly supported the idea of bringing European Jews to the islands. The State Department, however, regarded the plan as an attempt to sneak refugees into the mainland United States through a back door. By 1940, when Breckinridge Long became assistant secretary of state, the idea of using the Virgin Islands as a refugee haven was still being discussed in government circles, and Long quickly became one of its most vigorous opponents. He characterized the Virgin Islands' offer of haven as an attempt "to siphon refugees out of [Europe] into the United States without the precautionary steps of investigation and checking." In his diary, Long attributed the Legislative Assembly's proposal to pressure from "persons largely concentrated along the Atlantic Seaboard, and principally New York" (that is, Jewish organizations, journalists, and members of Congress).[53]

Secretary of the Treasury Henry Morgenthau Jr. discussed with Secretary of State Hull the possibility of using the Virgin Islands as a refuge for the 907 German Jewish passengers on the refugee ship *St. Louis* after they were turned away from Cuba at the end of May 1939. Hull dismissed the proposal on a technicality. Because the German quota was at that moment full—1939 was the only year in the Roosevelt administration's twelve years that it was filled—the only way to admit them to the Virgin Islands would be as tourists. But to qualify for a six-month visitor's visa, Hull told Morgenthau, the passengers would need to prove that they had "a definite home where they were coming from and in a situation to return to it" when the six months elapsed. Given the state of affairs in Germany, it could not be assumed that it would be safe for them to return; therefore they could not qualify for visitor's visas. In other words, the passengers had fled because it was not safe for them to live in Germany, and now they were being denied haven elsewhere because it was not safe for them to live in Germany. Actually, the Roosevelt administration had more leeway on the visitor's visa issue than it had acknowledged. Because the passengers had been required to pay a return fare of $81 in advance, in case they were turned away from Cuba, the administration could have chosen to consider their prepayment as evidence that they could return somewhere. Or—as he had done after *Kristallnacht*—the president could have declared that it was unsafe for them to return to Nazi Germany, and therefore he was waiving the "return address" requirement.[54]

The *St. Louis*, which the *New York Times* dubbed "the saddest ship afloat," hovered off the Florida coast for three days. The passengers sent a telegram to the White House, pleading for mercy and emphasizing that "more than 400 [of the refugees] are women and children." The administration's reply came in the form of a Coast Guard cutter, which trailed the *St.*

Louis to ensure it did not come closer to America's shore. The ship was forced to return to Europe. When he decided to rebuff the *St. Louis*, President Roosevelt had no reason to believe the ship would be going anywhere except back to Nazi Germany. As it turned out, England, France, Belgium, and Holland each agreed to admit a portion of the passengers. The latter three countries, however, were overrun by the Germans the following year, and many of the passengers were murdered in the Holocaust.[55]

Rabbi Wise and other American Jewish leaders said nothing in public about the ship. This was partly in deference to the behind-the-scenes efforts by the American Jewish Joint Distribution Committee—the community's primary agency for overseas philanthropy—to negotiate the refugees' entry to Cuba or other countries. It also reflected Wise's profound aversion to saying anything that would embarrass President Roosevelt.

Two peculiar essays in the official weekly publication of Wise's AJCongress, *Congress Bulletin*, gave expression to the defensiveness and incoherence of the mainstream American Jewish leadership in the wake of the Roosevelt administration's rebuff of the *St. Louis*. While acknowledging that the episode "has raised in many minds the question of the effectiveness of the Jewish leadership," an unsigned editorial in the June 9 issue insisted the blame lay elsewhere. Part of the problem, it argued, was the recently proclaimed British White Paper restricting Jewish immigration to Palestine, "for which no Jew can be held responsible." The other source of blame, it contended, was those Jewish groups who were trying to "solve the problem of migration by widening the dispersion." This was a reference to Wise's non-Zionist rivals, such as the AJcommittee and the Joint Distribution Committee, which had sought havens for Jewish refugees in various parts of the world other than Palestine. The author of the editorial seemed oblivious to the contradiction between blaming the closure of Palestine and simultaneously blaming those who sought refuge for European Jews elsewhere.[56]

The next edition of *Congress Bulletin* included an essay by World Jewish Congress staff member Jacob Lestschinsky featuring this remarkable passage: "It did not even occur to Jews to appeal to the American government to find a way of saving the hapless passengers of the *St. Louis*. . . . This was not because the Roosevelt administration is any less friendly to Jews [but because] the government was simply afraid of the demagogic political agitation of the fascists." The implication was clear: American Jews had no choice but to remain quiet and accept the administration's position.[57]

Several other refugee ships also tried to reach the Western hemisphere in 1939–40. The ss *Orduna*, a British ship, arrived at Havana on May 27, carrying 120 German, Czech, and Austrian Jewish refugees. The Cuban government allowed forty-eight of the passengers to disembark. Almost all of the others had registration numbers or affidavits to immigrate to the United States, so Cuban officials sent a telegram to President Roosevelt for help; they received no reply. The ship traveled to various South American ports, staying in each for several days. Finally, the Joint Distribution Committee arranged for the majority of the passengers to be transferred temporarily to the Panama Canal Zone. The following year, they were included among the immigrants admitted to the United States under the quotas.

The ss *Flandre*, a French ship with 104 German, Austrian, and Czech Jewish passengers, reached Havana in late May. Refused entry to Cuba, the ship docked at several Mexican ports, but at each port the passengers were denied entry. The *Flandre* returned to France and the refugees were put in internment camps, ultimately to face the same fate as the Jews of France under Nazi occupation.

The ss *Orinoco*, a German ship with two hundred Jewish passengers, left Hamburg in May 1939, intending to sail for Cuba. Then, learning by radio that they were likely to be turned away, the *Orinoco* waited off the coast of southern France while American diplomats sought a promise from the German government that the refugees would not be persecuted. Based on that German assurance, the ship returned to Germany in June 1939. The passengers' fate has not been traced.

Finally, the Portuguese ship *Quanza* docked in New York on August 19, 1940. Of its 317 passengers, 196 had the necessary papers and disembarked. The other 121, including nearly all of the Jewish passengers, remained on board as the *Quanza* sailed to Mexico. Upon its arrival on August 30, thirty-five passengers were admitted, leaving eighty-six, most of them Belgian Jews. As the *Quanza* began heading back to Europe, it stopped briefly for coal in Norfolk, Virginia. A local attorney, hearing of the Jews' plight, filed a federal lawsuit that kept the ship in port for six days. One passenger jumped overboard and reached shore but was caught and taken back to the ship. Jewish groups lobbied Eleanor Roosevelt to allow the passengers to stay; she appealed to the president, and for once, FDR agreed to admit additional Jewish refugees. Eighty of the eighty-six settled in America. The other six chose to return to Europe. Although the president left no record of the reasons behind his decision, most likely it was because the number of refugees to be admitted was so small, and admitting them could help cement Jewish electoral support in the November 1940 presidential election. It was an exception that proved the rule.[58]

The First Lady

Those who knew Eleanor Roosevelt as a young adult might have been surprised by her sympathy for the Wagner-Rogers legislation and intervention on behalf of the *Quanza* refugees. Like many members of her extended family, Mrs. Roosevelt was known to have made antisemitic remarks in her early years. For example, after a party in 1918 for financier Bernard Baruch, she wrote to her mother-in-law that "the Jew party [was] appalling" because the attendees were "mostly Jews." However, as a result of her increased social relationships with Jews, including Baruch and Henry and Elinor Morgenthau, Mrs. Roosevelt gradually shed such prejudices. She even resigned from New York's Colony Club after it refused to admit Mrs. Morgenthau.[59]

On a number of occasions, Mrs. Roosevelt expressed sympathy for the plight of the Jews in Nazi Germany. Some of the First Lady's information about the persecution of Jews came from her friend Dr. Alice Hamilton, who spent ten weeks in Germany in 1933. Mrs. Roosevelt brought Hamilton to Hyde Park to brief the president on life under the Hitler regime. But the First Lady was not consistent in her handling of such information. The Quaker activists Clarence and Lilly Pickett, visiting Germany in 1934, sent her harrowing accounts of Jewish suffering, yet in the newspaper column she wrote about the Picketts' journey, she made no mention of the anti-Jewish atrocities they witnessed. She evidently understood that entreaties to the president on these issues were unwelcome. In response to the sinking of the refugee ship *Struma* in February 1942, resulting in the deaths of 768 passengers, Mrs. Roosevelt wrote to the State Department that the British refusal to let the *Struma* reach Palestine was "cruel beyond words," but as far as is known, she did not raise the issue with the president. When she complained to FDR that the notoriously anti-refugee Breckinridge Long was "a fascist," the president reportedly snapped in response, "I've told you, Eleanor, you must not say that."[60]

Yet for all her heartfelt sympathy for Jewish refugees, Mrs. Roosevelt was unable to shed one conviction about Jews that she shared with her husband: the notion that it was the Jews' own untoward behavior that caused antisemitism, and if only the Jews would keep quiet, their lot would improve. When, in the wake of Kristallnacht, a letter-writer asked how to eliminate antisemitism, the First Lady replied: "I think it is important in this country that the Jews as Jews remain unaggressive and stress the fact that they are Americans first and above everything else . . . and, as far as possible, wipe out in their own consciousness any feeling of difference by joining in all that is being done by Americans."[61] Apparently her views had not progressed very much since 1929, when she was interviewed about the number of Jewish children attending the Todhunter School, which she co-owned and where she had taught. She acknowledged and defended the school's unofficial quota for Jews: "I'm sorry— I'm very sorry—but I'm afraid there's a feeling—even, I think among the Jews themselves—that the spirit of the school, and the school itself, would be different if we had too large a proportion of Jewish children." The interviewer asked if the Jews would ever be accepted as equal Americans. Mrs. Roosevelt replied:

> That is the American tradition. . . . The difficulty is that the country is still full of immigrant Jews, very unlike ourselves. I don't blame them for being as they are. I know what they've been through in other lands, and I'm glad they have freedom at last, and I hope they'll have the chance, among us, to develop all there is in them. But it takes a little time for Americans to be made. And, meanwhile, the old stock can't feel they're Americans, and unfortunately they also class real Americans who are Jews together with them. Well, one day, I hope, we'll all be Americans together.[62]

"Undesirables and Spies"

On September 1, 1939, Germany invaded Poland, triggering World War II. More than 3.3 million Polish Jews, the largest Jewish community outside the United States, lay in the path of the advancing German armies.

Information about the suffering of Poland's Jews soon reached the American Jewish press. In addition to the expected news of Jewish communities hit by German bombardments or other war-related damage, there were soon reports of atrocities targeting Jewish civilians. The Gestapo reportedly "arrested thousands of Jews in Lodz and executed hundreds of them." In Warsaw, sixteen Jewish religious leaders, including the chief rabbi of the city, were said to have been rounded up and massacred. Along the Polish-Lithuanian border, the Germans "imposed conditions akin to slavery." The Nazi newspaper *Der Sturmer* published letters from German soldiers in Poland who boasted of executing Jews after compelling them to sign confessions that

they "poisoned wells." Polish Jewish refugees reached Rumania with photographs of hundreds of elderly Jews being massacred by German troops in a forest.[63]

"All of us are aghast over what has happened in Poland,"
Rabbi Wise wrote to a colleague in late September. "We face
a relief problem and a refugee problem which are beyond calculation and even belief." At the same time, however, "everything is complicated for us because [the United States is] not
yet in the war and because Jews are or feel they must be tre-
bly careful lest they seem to be guilty of war-mongering." To
another associate, Wise wrote: "We Jews are in a peculiarly difficult position. . . . We do not want to give anyone, even the bit-
terest and most mendacious of our foes, the right to charge us
with war-mongering. We Jews must not give the appearance
of seeking to rush America into war."[64]

Soon the U.S. press was filled with sensationalist stories
about Nazi spies seeking to penetrate America's borders. Such
warnings resonated with the public. To many Americans, the
speed with which Denmark, Norway, France, Belgium, and the
Netherlands were conquered in early 1940 seemed inexplica-
ble without the involvement of a traitorous fifth column bor-
ing from within the targeted countries.

President Roosevelt used the Nazi spy hysteria to whip up
public fears about Jewish refugees. Speaking at a press conference on June 5, 1940, he declared: "Now, of course, the refugee
has got to be checked because, unfortunately, among the refugees there are some spies, as has been found in other countries.
And not all of them are voluntary spies—it is rather a horrible
story but in some of the other countries that refugees out of
Germany have gone to, especially Jewish refugees, they found
a number of definitely proven spies." In fact, not a single case
of a Nazi spy disguised as a refugee entering the United States
was ever uncovered. But the president's assertion helped intimidate American Jewish leaders. Advocacy for the admission of
refugees now carried the taint of risking national security.[65]

For Wise, there was also a political factor. Shortly before

the 1940 presidential election, he wrote to a colleague that the admission of refugees to the Virgin Islands "might be used effectively against [Roosevelt] in the campaign." Therefore, the rabbi explained, "Cruel as I may seem, as I have said to you before, his re-election is much more important for everything that is worthwhile and that counts than the admission of a few people, however imminent be their peril."[66]

Shortly after the election, Breckinridge Long acted to permanently block Secretary Ickes's promotion of the Virgin Islands as a refuge. Long asked the chief of Naval Intelligence, Admiral Alan T. Kirk, to declare the area a "closed naval zone." The action was necessary to prevent "all kinds of undesirables and spies" from entering the islands disguised as refugees, Long told the president. Not that FDR needed much convincing. On December 18, the president asserted in a memo to Secretary Ickes that the Virgin Islands already had its own "social and economic problem[s]," and bringing in refugees would only make matters worse. "I cannot do anything which would conceivably hurt the future of present American citizens," FDR wrote.[67]

Another U.S. territory widely discussed as a possible refuge in the aftermath of Kristallnacht was Alaska. Rich in natural resources but severely underpopulated, the vast northern territory had been purchased by the United States from Russia in 1867. In the 1930s, Japanese aggression against China and the likelihood of war in Europe intensified American concerns about Alaska's strategic value, as well as its vulnerability. Senator William King (D-UT) argued that refugees from Hitler would not be dissuaded by the hardships of Alaskan frontier life, because they "would not be thinking of the comforts of life in the States that they had sacrificed, but in terms of the savagery and hopelessness of the conditions abroad from which they had been rescued."[68] At a press conference two weeks after Kristallnacht, Ickes formally proposed Alaska as "a haven for Jewish refugees from Germany and other areas in Europe where the Jews are subjected to oppressive restrictions." Alaska was "the one possession of the United States that is not fully devel-

oped," he pointed out. Ickes noted that two hundred impover-
ished families had recently relocated from the dust bowls of
the American West to the twenty-three-thousand-square-mile
Matanuska Valley in south central Alaska; he predicted their pio-
neering efforts would "open up opportunities in the industrial
and professional fields now closed to the Jews in Germany."[69]

The Interior Department prepared a full report explaining
the vast economic potential of Alaska, the military risks of leaving the area unpopulated, and the logic of bringing in "hundreds of thousands of pioneers" from other countries. Based
on the report, Senator King and Rep. Franck Havenner (D-
CA) introduced legislation to allow refugees to settle in Alaska.

Refugee advocates created a National Committee for Alaskan
Development, which built an ecumenical coalition of VIPs to
back the legislation. Endorsers included the Academy Award–
winning actors Luise Rainer and Paul Muni, the theologian
Paul Tillich, the American Friends Service Committee, and
the Federal Council of Churches.

Jewish supporters, however, were few and far between.
Rabbi Wise declined to endorse the Alaska plan because he
feared it "makes a wrong and hurtful impression . . . that Jews
are taking over some part of the country for settlement." He
believed that "just because small numbers of Jews might settle there" was not sufficient reason to support the proposal.
Zionist Organization of America (ZOA) president Solomon
Goldman feared "the cause of Palestine will be harmed" if refugees were systematically settled in territories other than Palestine. The only U.S. Jewish organization to publicly endorse
the King-Havenner bill was the Labor Zionists of America.
When Rep. Samuel Dickstein introduced a bill to use unfilled
quota places to admit refugees to develop Alaska, the Labor
Zionists of America again was the only American Jewish organization to endorse the measure.[70]

Nativist and patriotic groups rallied against the King-
Havenner legislation. According to one critic, it would open
America to "Trojan horses," including Jews who believed in

"the Marxian philosophy." The State Department vigorously opposed the initiative as well. For his part, President Roosevelt refrained from saying anything publicly about refuge in Alaska. FDR told Secretary Ickes he would support the admission of only ten thousand settlers per year for five years, and of that number "not more than ten percent would be Jews [so] we would be able to avoid the undoubted criticism that we would be subjected to if there were an undue proportion of Jews." The White House also compelled Ickes to water down a December 1938 address in which he had planned to gently suggest that "in time," the United States might yet "return to its former noble historic policy" regarding immigration. As for the King-Havenner bill, it was the subject of hearings before a Senate subcommittee in May 1940, gained no traction, and was quietly buried.[71]

3

Silence and Its Consequences

NAZI ANTI-JEWISH PERSECUTION IN the early and mid-1930s—characterized by discrimination, disenfranchisement, and sporadic outbursts of local violence—paved the way for the organized nationwide *Kristallnacht* pogrom in November 1938. The German occupation of Poland in September 1939 was followed by ghettoization of Polish Jewry and induced starvation. The mass murder process began in June 1941. Mobile deaths squads known as the *Einsatzgruppen*, accompanying the German invasion of the Soviet Union, carried out massacres of thousands, then tens of thousands, of Jews at a time, ultimately slaughtering an estimated 1.5 million in total. By the end of 1941, a number of concentration camps were transformed into organized death camps with the introduction of mobile vans for group executions by poison gas. Early 1942 saw the construction of huge stationary gas chambers and crematoria in camps such as Auschwitz, Treblinka, and others. How much did the American public know about the mass killings, and when? What did Rabbi Wise know, and when? What did he do with the information?

Wise's first and most important source of information at the breakfast table each morning was the *New York Times*. Another was the Jewish Telegraphic Agency (JTA), a news service with staff correspondents around the world whose four-page *Daily News Bulletin* was read by Jewish leaders and fed articles to dozens of Anglo-Jewish weekly newspapers. The Yiddish-language press also remained a lively presence in the American Jewish community (although its readership declined substantially by the 1940s, as the immigrant generation was supplanted by native-born Jews). Rabbi Wise paid some attention to the Yiddish newspapers, although probably more as a bellwether of opinion among the grassroots than as a news source; their sometimes sensationalist tone did not always inspire confidence in their reliability.

News about the *Einsatzgruppen* massacres in German-occupied western Russia reached the West gradually. The JTA published the earliest substantive report to appear in the press, on October 2, 1941, nearly three and a half months after the German invasion began: the machine-gun massacre of forty-two hundred Jews in Kamenetz-Podolsk that August, as well as other atrocities in the region around the same time. On October 23 a JTA dispatch recounted the slaughter of "tens of thousands of Jews" in the Kamenetz-Podolsk area, many of them "machined-gunned while praying in their synagogues," with "thousands of Jewish corpses floating in the waters of the Dniester River." Much of this information, attributed to "reliable sources," was published in the *New York Times* on October 26, 1941—the first time news of the mass killings broke through to major American news media. Over the next three weeks, the JTA reported even larger slaughters: six thousand in Lomzha, Poland (October 30), twenty-five thousand in Odessa (November 14), and fifty-two thousand in Kiev (November 16), in what came to be known as the Babi Yar Massacre. The latter report was particularly significant, both because of the unusually large number of victims cited and the fact that the correspondent carefully distinguished the nature of the massacre from previous outbursts of anti-Jewish violence: "The details available here establish that the victims did not lose their lives as the result of a mob pogrom, but by systematic, merciless execution carried out in accordance with [the] cold-blooded Nazi policy of Jewish extermination. Similar measures, though on a smaller scale, have been taken in other conquered towns."[1]

Neither the public activities nor the private correspondence of Rabbi Wise or other U.S. Jewish leaders during this period reflected a recognition of the radically different nature of these atrocities, nor any awareness of the broader Nazi plan that was now being implemented. There were several reasons for this. The early reports of large-scale massacres were infrequent and scattered over many weeks, giving the appearance of random atrocities rather than the result of a coordinated German strategy. Only one of those early reports made it into the authoritative *New York Times*, so Jewish leaders may have wondered if the reports were accurate. Also, accounts of the massacres were appearing simultaneously with many other reports of Jews suffering in aerial bombardments, or from disease, food shortages, and the like—circumstances that may have seemed to be war-related rather than specifically the result of targeted persecution. Furthermore, even as many reports recounted Jews being forcibly deported from one part of Europe to another, none of the sources indicated that such expulsions were part of a systematic mass murder plan.

Nevertheless, the accumulation of reports about massacres, starvation, and mass expulsions or deportations of Jews did provoke some expressions of dissatisfaction in the American Jewish community over the Allies' disinterest in the plight of the Jews. These rumblings of dissent were likely galvanized in part by the refusal of Allied government representatives to share with delegates at a January 13 conference in London a statement prepared by British Jewish leaders concerning Nazi atrocities against Jews.[2] Rabbi Wise's close colleague Maurice Perlzweig, political affairs director for the World Jewish Congress (wjc), reported to Wise in mid-January that many Jews "complain now as a sheer matter of habit. . . . Jewish orators and writers have fallen into the habit of denouncing Roosevelt and Churchill on the alleged ground that they never throw a crumb of comfort to the Jews." Perlzweig's assessment was somewhat overstated—the number of Jewish "orators and writers" willing to publicly criticize either Roosevelt or Churchill in January 1942 was small—but not without foundation. An editorial in the *Reconstructionist* that same week charged that the British government's continuing refusal to admit more than a handful of Jewish refugees into Palestine —reflecting its policy of mollifying Arab opinion—"reveals that she has not yet outgrown completely the policy of appeasement." Even more pointed was the January 5 full-page ad in the *New York Times* challenging Roosevelt and Churchill for not agreeing to establish a Jewish army to fight alongside the Allies against the Nazis. The advertisement was sponsored by the Committee for a Jewish Army, widely known as the Bergson Group (after its founder, Peter Bergson [Hillel Kook]), a small but growing political action committee that would soon become a serious thorn in the side of the established Jewish leadership.[3]

The many additional atrocity reports reaching the West in the weeks and months to follow could not be easily dismissed as reflecting the ordinary travails of war. In March 1942, for instance, a European representative of the American Jewish Joint Distribution Committee reported that in the German-occupied Russian city of Borisov, "the Nazis had ordered Jews to dig a communal grave, into which 7,000 men, women and children—some shot to death, others only wounded—were thrown and covered with earth," and because of "the living breath of those interred," the field was "heaving like the sea." In May the JTA described how "in Vitebsky, the Germans rounded up several thousand men, women and children and loaded them into leaking boats which were towed to the middle of the Dwina River. . . . When the boats reached midstream, the Nazi soldiers turned a murderous stream of bullets upon the Jews, killing thousands of the prisoners and leaving hundreds of others to drown when their leaking craft sank."[4]

A far more extensive and detailed report reached London in June 1942. Smuggled from members of the Jewish Socialist

Bund in Poland to their comrades in the Polish government in exile, the report began: "From the day the Russo-German war broke out, the Germans embarked on the physical extermination of the Jewish population on Polish soil." The Bund listed the names of numerous towns in Poland, Lithuania, and Ukraine where the *Einsatzgruppen* carried out mass killings, the dates of the massacres, and estimates of the number of fatalities in each locale. Significantly, the Bund report also contained the first account of the Germans' use of poison gas to kill Jews: "gassing in the hamlet of Chelmno" was carried out by means of "a special automobile (a gas chamber)," into which "ninety persons were loaded each time." The Bund calculated that from November 1941 through March 1942, about forty thousand Jews and "a number of Gypsies" had been murdered in the vans, which were filled with gas from the vehicles' rewired exhaust pipes. Much of the U.S. news media coverage of the Bund Report did not mention the poison gas, although a Chicago Daily News Service dispatch that appeared in some newspapers did note that "the Nazis are using portable gas chambers in some sections." Overall, the Bund asserted, the Germans had already slaughtered an estimated seven hundred thousand Jews. This was the first time a number of such magnitude was cited in reports reaching the Western media—although the actual total was about two million by then.[5]

In retrospect it might seem the Bund report should have brought about widespread recognition in the West of the transformation from scattered atrocities to systematic mass murder. The fact that it did not have this effect owed in part to the way major news media such as the *New York Times* treated the Bund information and related news. On June 16 the *Times* reported that a massacre of sixty thousand Jews recently took place in Vilna, but added an unusual qualifier that the information was "impossible to confirm now." On June 27 the *Times* published just two paragraphs about the Bund report and buried them at the bottom of a stack of war-related items. The newspaper's publisher, Arthur Hays Sulzberger, was Jewish but thoroughly assimilated and feared that giving prominence to Jewish-related news would provoke antisemites to accuse the *Times* of promoting Jewish interests. The content and placement of stories related to Nazi atrocities against Jews reflected Sulzberger's mindset.[6]

The meager coverage the *Times* accorded the Bund report may have contributed to American Jewish leaders' failure to recognize the significance of the new information. About one month later, the AJCongress, together with several other groups, held a rally at Madison Square Garden to decry Nazi atrocities. The protest was not specifically in response to the Bund report; it was intended to coincide with Tisha B'Av, a traditional Jewish day of fasting and mourning to commemorate the destruction of the Temple in ancient Jerusalem. From Jewish leaders' remarks at the event—Wise, for example, spoke of "the Nazi threat to destroy the Jewish people" rather than a Nazi program of mass murder already underway—it is evident that Rabbi Wise and the other speakers did not yet comprehend the magnitude of what was happening to European Jewry.[7]

"War Rumor Inspired by Fear"

The turning point for Wise came near the end of that summer. On August 8, 1942, Gerhart Riegner, the WJCongress representative in Switzerland, arrived at the American consulate in Geneva with a message he sought to cable to Allied leaders and to Rabbi Wise. It read:

> Received alarming report stating that, in the Fuehrer's Headquarters, a plan has been discussed, and is under consideration, according to which all Jews in countries occupied or controlled by Germany numbering 3½ to 4 millions should, after deportation and concentration in the East, be at one blow exterminated, in order to resolve once and for all the Jewish question in Europe. Action is reported to be planned for the autumn. Ways of execution are still being discussed including the use of prussic acid. We transmit this information with all the necessary

reservation, as exactitude cannot be confirmed by us. Our informant is reported to have close connexions [sic] with the highest German authorities, and his reports are generally reliable.

Riegner had received the information from Eduard Schulte,
a German industrialist with close contacts in the Nazi hierar-
chy. American Vice Consul Howard Elting Jr. forwarded Riegner's request to the U.S. legation in Bern, along with a cover
note affirming that Riegner was "a serious and balanced individual" and recommending that Bern forward the cable to the
State Department. On August 11 the Bern diplomats sent the
telegram to Washington, albeit with a disclaimer asserting that
Riegner's information had the "earmarks of war rumor inspired
by fear." The officials in the State Department's Division of
European Affairs who handled the incoming cable immediately
branded it unreliable. This was consistent with their general
tendency to view reports of anti-Jewish atrocities as exaggera-
tions cooked up by Jewish organizations seeking sympathy or
political advantage.[8]

State Department officials debated whether to forward the
message to Rabbi Wise, as Riegner had requested, or suppress it. Paul T. Culbertson, assistant chief of the Division of
European Affairs, worried that "if the Rabbi hears later that we
had the message and didn't let him in on it, he might put up a
kick." Culbertson recommended sending Wise the cable with
a note saying that State could not confirm its accuracy. His colleague Elbridge Durbrow, however, argued against showing it
to Wise at all, in view of "the fantastic nature of the allegation"
and "the impossibility of our being of any assistance if such
action [against European Jews] were taken." Without examining
whether there was any way in which the United States might
be able to assist the potential victims, Durbrow instinctively
recoiled at the idea of U.S. action to aid the Jews; he treated the
very notion as inconceivable. Consequently the State Department withheld Riegner's telegram from Wise.

Unbeknownst to Washington, however, Riegner gave the

same telegram to the British consulate in Geneva, asking that it be sent to the Foreign Office and to Sydney Silverman, a Jewish member of parliament who also served as head of the British division of the World Jewish Congress. The message to Silverman concluded: "Please inform and consult New York." The cable reached the British Foreign Office on August 10. Officials there spent a week discussing how it might have "embarrassing repercussions," presumably meaning that it might stimulate public pressure on the Allies to take action. Finally, the Foreign Office staff, recognizing they could not reasonably withhold such information from a member of Parliament, gave the message to Silverman on August 17. He spent several days discussing its veracity and implications with colleagues, and seeking governmental permission to telephone Rabbi Wise—that request was rejected on the grounds that the Germans might be listening—or to forward Riegner's cable to Wise, which the foreign office permitted. However, because of the time needed to clear the censorship office and the low priority accorded private telegrams during the war, the cable did not reach Wise until early on August 25.[9]

Wise immediately recognized that Riegner's message differed significantly from previous reports about Nazi atrocities. To begin with, it had been sent and vouched for by a trusted senior representative of the World Jewish Congress, whom Wise knew personally and regarded as "unperturbably and really conservative"—in other words, not the sort of person inclined to spread baseless rumors. In addition, it cited far greater numbers of Jewish victims than those of earlier reports—millions, not thousands or even tens of thousands. Moreover, the summary of German mass murder plans indicated that Riegner's unnamed source possessed inside knowledge of a specific annihilation strategy, rather than haphazard massacres.[10]

After several days of anguished conversations with his WJ Congress colleagues, who were "overwhelmed" by the "shattering" telegram, Wise decided to consult with Undersecretary of State Sumner Welles. When Wise telephoned him on September 2 to tell him of the Riegner cable, Welles gave no hint that he had been aware of the telegram for three weeks (that is, since the day it first reached Washington.) Wise asked Welles if the State Department could obtain additional information regarding the veracity of Riegner's message and let him know the next day—Thursday, September 3—before departing for the long Labor Day weekend. Welles said he would look into it.[11]

Later that afternoon, at a meeting of wj congress leaders, "a heated discussion" broke out over a proposal by A. Leon Kubowitzki, the chairman of its rescue commission. Kubowitzki suggested asking President Roosevelt and other Allied leaders "to issue a warning to Hitler informing him that for all crimes committed against the Jewish civilian population there will be a ra[z]ing and destruction of German towns and villages." Rabbi Wise moved quickly to squelch the idea of asking the president for anything. Launching into what one attendee called "a statesman-like address," Wise argued that Kubowitzki "did not think of the American mind." The problem, in Wise's view, was that "Americans have not yet completely thrown themselves into this war, [so] how could we ask the American people to take a special warlike action on behalf of the Jews?"[12]

Understanding "the American mind" was central to Wise's calculation as to how to respond to the news from Europe. How would non-Jewish Americans react to Jews seeking government action in an area of narrow Jewish concern that might impact the war effort? Were Jews sufficiently secure in their status as American citizens that they could engage in such activities without unpleasant repercussions? In Rabbi Wise's view, a Jewish request for "special warlike action" crossed the invisible line between acceptable behavior and what might be perceived by non-Jews as inappropriate.

Attendee Dr. Max Beer noted with disappointment that after Wise knocked down the reprisals proposal, there was "a general feeling" around the room that "nothing really effective could be done to stop the menace to our people." The next day, Beer circulated to the meeting's participants several possible steps he believed could in fact be taken: through the Vatican or other intermediaries, the Allies could warn "the German military chiefs and the German diplomats" of severe postwar consequences for them personally if they did not stop the killings; German Americans could be mobilized to speak out against the Nazis; and the U.S. authorities could beam radio messages to the German public, threatening retribution unless the mass murder ceased. Beer's suggestions were heard; in one form or another, they were incorporated in the rescue plans later put forward by the wjc and other organizations.[13]

Welles called Wise the next afternoon (September 3) and "tried to be re-assuring," as Wise later reported to his colleagues. The undersecretary said that as far as the State Department could tell, "the real purpose of the Nazi government" in rounding up and deporting Jews "is to use Jews in connection with war work both in Nazi Germany and in Nazi Poland and Russia." Welles asked the rabbi to refrain from publicizing the Riegner telegram until its veracity could be determined.[14]

Wise complied. The rabbi was aware that by doing so, he was—as he wrote at the time—"accepting a great responsibility if the threat [of annihilation] should be executed." Still, he believed there was no alternative but to agree to Welles's request. He had no way to independently verify Riegner's assertions and did not want to publicize claims that might later turn out to be inaccurate, thereby discrediting other, more reliable information he might receive about Nazi atrocities. He knew that some reports of German atrocities in Belgium in World War I later turned out to be false, engendering considerable public skepticism about such allegations.[15]

Additionally, Wise was concerned that defying Welles's request would jeopardize his relationship with State Department officials, whose assistance he might need in responding to the mass killings. Wise also expected—mistakenly—that Welles would have more definitive information within a matter of days. As the rabbi prepared to leave for Labor Day, he instructed his secretary to promptly alert Nahum Goldmann, chairman of the wjcongress executive committee, if Welles called over the weekend with the confirmation. Wise could not imagine it would take not days, not even weeks, but months before Welles would get back to him. His expectation that the information would arrive imminently, thereby releasing him from his pledge of silence, no doubt made it easier on Wise's conscience that he was withholding the news from public view.[16]

A Second Telegram

Even as Wise was still reeling from the Riegner cable, another shocking telegram arrived from Europe. On September 3 the Polish consulate in New York received and forwarded a message sent by the Switzerland-based Orthodox rescue activists Recha and Yitzchak Sternbuch and addressed to Rabbi Jacob Rosenheim, president of the U.S.–based Orthodox organization Agudath Israel. Rosenheim relayed the information in a cable to President Roosevelt, Rabbi Wise, and others that same day: "According to numerous authentical informations [sic] from Poland, German authorities have recently evacuat[e]d Warsaw Ghetto and bestially murdered about one hundred thousand Jews. These mass murders are continuing. The corpses of the murdered victims are used for the manufacturing of soap and artificial fertilizers. Similar fate is awaiting the Jews deported to Poland from other occupied territories. Suppose that only energetic steps from America may stop these persecutions."[17]

A shaken Wise poured out his anguish in a letter to Justice Frankfurter the next day. "My heart is so full that I just must write to you," he began. Wise recounted the contents of the Riegner cable and his subsequent conversation with Undersecretary Welles. Now, there was the latest jarring news. "A moment ago, another message came from Berne," Wise wrote, "saying that in the past days one hundred thousand Jews have been killed in Warsaw, and that their corpses are being used to make soap." The new message appeared to "circumstantially confirm" the Riegner telegram, Wise noted. The rabbi then shared with Frankfurter his conflicting emotions as to whether to bring the information to President Roosevelt's attention. On the one hand, "I was tempted to call up [Treasury Secretary] Henry [Morgenthau] Jr. and ask him to put it before the Chief, just that he might know about it even though, alas, he prove to be unable to avert the horror."

For reasons he did not explain, however, Wise did not contact Morgenthau. Instead, he sent copies of the two telegrams to Frankfurter, leaving it to the justice to decide "whether the Chief ought to know about it. . . . One somehow feels that the foremost and finest figure in the political world today should not be without knowledge of this unutterable disaster which threatens and may now be in process of execution." Frankfurter later told Wise that he did mention the matter to the president. First Lady Eleanor Roosevelt also was aware of the situation, having been sent a copy of the Sternbuch telegram by PACPR chairman James G. McDonald.[18]

That same day, Wise shared the Riegner telegram, and Rosenheim revealed the Sternbuch cable, with attendees at a hastily called meeting of Jewish organizational leaders initiated by the Union of Orthodox Rabbis. The participants now privy to these shocking developments proposed an array of steps, including asking President Roosevelt to make a public appeal to the Germans; mobilizing churches, members of Congress, and newspaper editors to speak out; and seeking permission from the Allies to ship food to Jews in the ghettos. But they were unable to reach a consensus on how to respond, and therefore agreed to reconvene two days later, on September 6. The second meeting concluded with the appointment of a small committee of Jewish organizational leaders, headed by Wise, to recommend possible responses to the crisis. Meeting on September 9, members of this smaller committee decided that "no action would be taken" until Wise could obtain further information from Undersecretary Welles. In their discussions, Wise and his colleagues appear to have conflated the two telegrams from Europe; although Wise's pledge of silence pertained to the Riegner cable, he and the others treated the

Sternburch telegram as if it were somehow intertwined with Riegner's. Either because he privately doubted the veracity of Sternbuch's information, or because he felt that any publicity about the cables would displease the administration, Wise appears to have never considered the possibility of revealing the Sternbuch telegram to the public while awaiting word regarding Riegner's.[19]

Even though Wise was withholding the two cables from public view, fragmentary information about the mass deportations to which the telegrams had alluded was beginning to reach the news media through other sources. The JTA's September 9 bulletin, for example, reported from Geneva that three hundred thousand Jews had been deported from Warsaw to "undisclosed destinations." It quoted Jewish organizations in Switzerland expressing fear that the deportations were related to "unconfirmed alarming information" that "the Gestapo is demanding the annihilation of all Jews in Poland." A second article elsewhere in that day's bulletin disclosed that "unverified reports of renewed Nazi massacres in the ghettos of Poland" had reached Palestine in recent days. However, without more authoritative information, and with the qualifiers about the information being unconfirmed, those who were unaware of the Riegner and Sternbuch telegrams may not have connected the dots—and even those who were aware of the two cables may have felt they needed further verification.[20]

Rabbi Wise traveled to Washington twice in early September to discuss the two telegrams with a number of government officials, including Vice President Henry Wallace, Treasury Secretary Henry Morgenthau Jr., Assistant Secretary of State Dean Acheson (instead of Welles, who was out of town), and the U.S. ambassador to the Vatican, Myron Taylor. On a separate visit to the capital several weeks later, Wise showed the telegrams to Interior Secretary Harold Ickes. Little came out of these meetings in the way of immediate practical action. Acheson said he would "dig into the problem," but then added, to Wise's disappointment, that he would consult with Assistant Secretary of State Long, who was notoriously lacking in sympathy for Jewish refugees. As for Ambassador Taylor, Wise had hoped he would seek Papal intervention such as "using the mighty ban of his Church"—that is, excommunicating Nazi leaders who were at least nominally Catholic, including Hitler himself. There is no indication Taylor ever made such a proposal.[21]

In early September, State Department officials told Wise that the hundred thousand Warsaw Jews whom the Sternbuchs reported were slain had actually been "sent to the new Russo-Polish frontier to build fortifications."[22] Wise felt somewhat encouraged. With hindsight, it is not surprising that he regarded State's assertion as credible. The very idea that the Germans would choose to kill hundreds of thousands of Jews rather than exploit them as slave labor to aid their war effort flew in the face of conventional assumptions about a regime's priorities in wartime. Even after nearly a decade of Nazi persecution of Jews, it was difficult for American Jewish leaders to fathom that Hitler would give his war against the Jews a higher priority than his war against the Allies. Moreover, many of the reports Wise was reading in the JTA's *Daily News Bulletin* during those weeks appeared to be consistent with the State Department's theory. The Jews of Holland were reportedly being prepared for deportation to Nazi-occupied Russia "for forced labor" (September 4). More than 150,000 Polish Jews were said to have been deported "to various parts of Germany for forced labor" (September 6). All Polish Jewish adults were being deported "to work in industrial enterprises in Germany" (September 15). Some Dutch Jews were reported to have received letters from deported relatives who "are now working in the coal mines in Silesia [southwestern Poland]" (September 28). Two thousand Jews were dragged from Warsaw synagogues during Rosh Hashana services and transported "directly to labor camps for forced labor" (October 4). Hundreds of Belgian Jews were deported, some "to work in the coal mines in Silesia," others "to the Nazi-occupied Ukraine for hard labor there" (October 30).[23]

Yet, certain aspects of the JTA's news bulletins must have given Rabbi Wise pause. Many of the reports about deportations made no mention of forced labor. A September 2 dispatch ominously described French Jews being arrested en masse and "sent to unknown destinations." The JTA reported on September 9 and again on October 7 that three hundred thousand Jews had been deported from the Warsaw Ghetto "to undisclosed destinations." Czech Jews were being sent "to Nazi-held devastated sections of Russia" (September 21). Dutch and Belgian Jews were being deported "to the East" (October 15). Jews in Germany were being assembled "for deportation to Nazi-held eastern territory" (October 25).[24] Also unexplained was the fact that many of the deportees were obviously unfit for slave labor. Four thousand Jews "between 65 and 85 years of age" were deported from Germany and other countries "to the fortress prison of Therezin in Czechoslovakia," the JTA reported on September 18; it also noted that forty thousand of the fifty thousand German Jews previously sent there "were aged men and women between 65 and 75 years of age." Five hundred Jewish children were taken from French orphanages "for deportation to occupied territory in eastern Europe" (September 24). All of the residents of the Jewish home for the aged in Nuremberg were "shipped to Nazi-held Eastern European territories" (October 19). Rabbi Wise must have wondered how the deportation of young children and elderly people squared with the State Department's theory of deportees being used for slave labor.[25]

Moreover, Wise would have learned from the JTA that slave labor often meant only a very brief reprieve; some reports indicated that those who were sent for labor were soon murdered. For example, after reporting on September 28 that Dutch Jews had received reassuring letters from deported relatives who were working in coal mines, the JTA revealed two weeks later that "many" Dutch Jews who were "originally sent for forced labor" in occupied territory actually "have been executed by the Nazis." Nearly two thousand Jews "brought from Poland, Belgium and Holland for forced labor building roads" were instead murdered en masse in Nazi-occupied Smolensk (October 22). The "majority" of an estimated 240,000 Hungarian Jews sent to the eastern front as slave laborers for the Hungarian and German armies "were killed by the Hungarians and the Germans as soon as they had completed the tasks assigned to them" (November 11). An October 4 JTA dispatch, citing as its source the Belgian government in exile, bluntly described the expectation of slave labor as a Nazi ruse. "Various pretexts were given by the German authorities when the Dutch or Belgian Jews were sent to the East," such as the claim that they were being sent to undertake "difficult and urgent work, as for example, road building." Instead, the deportees "were executed with the other Jews of the Baltic countries."[26]

In addition, during this same period the JTA published numerous reports detailing mass killings. Some of the articles described massacres that had taken place months earlier, when the *Einsatzgruppen* mobile death squads swept through Soviet territory behind the advancing German army. In Velizh, for example, nine hundred Jews had been confined to a pigsty; many were taken out in groups and shot, while the rest perished when the Germans locked the building and set it on fire (September 9). Eight hundred Jews were herded into a Kovno fire station, where they were starved for eight days and then shot en masse (September 20). In Urechi more than seven hundred Jews were shot into a pit, with some young girls buried alive (October 18). The casualty tolls in some cities were staggering: seven thousand in Vitebsk, eleven thousand in Ponievezh, fourteen thousand in Riga (September 27), and six thousand in Shklov (November 9).[27]

Several JTA dispatches reported that the killings were ongoing, and by the second half of September, the Jewish Telegraphic Agency was no longer asserting that the news was unverified. Whereas on September 9 there were "unverified reports of renewed Nazi massacres in the ghettos of Poland," on September 20 JTA reported that "massacres of Jews on an unprecedented scale are now taking place all over Nazi-occupied Poland" as part of a Nazi program "of total extermination of the Jews in Poland." On October 6 the JTA published what it called "an authentic report from the Jewish underground movement in Nazi-held Poland," which described "mass-executions of thousands of Jews of all ages." Significantly, it also noted: "In Lodz, thousands of Jewish families are taken away from the ghetto systematically and nobody ever hears from them again. They are poisoned by gas." An October 28 JTA report chronicled the "systematic extermination of the Jews in the Nazi-occupied portions of Russia." That same day's bulletin summarized an editorial in London's *Manchester Guardian* which affirmed that "almost two million Jews have already been destroyed in Nazi-occupied Europe, excluding those massacred in the parts of occupied Russia" and "the same fate is awaiting 4,500,000 more Jews in Europe" unless the Allies intervened. If he read these articles carefully, Rabbi Wise would have noticed the striking similarities between the information contained in the Riegner and Sternbuch telegrams and the JTA's reports about "systematic extermination," the use of poison gas, and a Jewish death toll in the millions.[28]

Soon after his meetings in Washington in September, Wise received a report from the Geneva office of the Jewish Agency for Palestine reiterating the points in the Sternbuch telegram and adding many new details that dovetailed with the descriptions in the Riegner and Sternbuch cables. The Jewish Agency report was said to be based on "two reliable eyewitnesses (Aryans), one of whom came from Poland on August 14." All Jews in the Warsaw Ghetto, it stated, "are being taken out of the ghetto in groups and shot," with their corpses used for "fats and fertilizer." Like the Sternbuchs, the Jewish Agency cited a death toll of one hundred thousand. The executions were taking place "in camps especially prepared for the purpose," one of which "is said to be in Belzek." To hide the slaughter of the Jews from public view, the Nazis "must first of all deport them to the east, where outsiders have less opportunity of knowing what is happening. A large part of the Jewish population deported to Lithuania and Lublin has already been executed during the last few weeks." The report also provided details about the cattle cars utilized for the deportations, and the use of Theresienstadt as "an interim station" on the way to the death camps. For Wise the fact that the Jewish Agency report came from a source he trusted and was based on eyewitness testimony from non-Jews added to its credibility. Moreover, the report's consistency with both the Riegner and Sternbuch telegrams strongly suggested the worst was true. Each new report appeared to further substantiate its predecessors. Wise forwarded the Jewish Agency's memorandum to Welles. There was no response.[29]

The strain under which Wise labored during those days in September 1942 is apparent from his correspondence. The meetings with other Jewish leaders on September 4 and 6 had cast him in the unenviable role of advocating patience and restraint in the face of calamity. "I don't know whether I am getting to be a *Jofjude*," he wrote to Frankfurter, invoking the term for a court Jew (language which, ironically, he himself once used to deprecate his rivals at the AJcommittee), "but I find that a good part of my work is to explain to my fellow Jews why our Government cannot do all the things asked or expected of it." To another friend that week, he wrote: "I haven't been able to sleep since that [Riegner] cable to me. . . . I can think of nothing else and, therefore, I am afraid, write of nothing else." Likewise, to Rev. Holmes, he wrote that the Sternbuch telegram "left me without sleep." These were "the unhappiest days of my life," he told Holmes. "I am almost demented over my people's grief."[30]

There is no reason to doubt the sincerity of Wise's expressions of anguish. As the foremost Jewish leader in the Free World, he shouldered the enormous burden of forging a communal response to a Jewish catastrophe of unprecedented dimensions. The responsibility he bore to lead American Jewry in responding to the mass killings was made all the more difficult by the agony of finding himself in the position of actively suppressing the news of the mass murder. Given these circumstances, one would indeed expect that his "heart would be full," that he would be "almost demented in my grief," that he would "think of nothing else and write of nothing else," that he would be unable to sleep, that he would be tormented by the situation in Europe and by his personal predicament. Indeed, one would have expected him to set aside the more mundane matters on his usual daily schedule to focus on the pressing life-and-death situations in Hitler-occupied Europe. He knew from the JTA and other sources that whether or not the Riegner telegram was accurate, huge massacres and other wanton atrocities were taking place.

Yet Wise's activities in September indicate that he did not separate himself from his usual business. A significant portion of his correspondence and meetings during this period was unrelated to the crisis of Europe's Jews. On September 3—the day after telephoning Welles about the Riegner cable and presiding over the WJcongress leadership meeting to discuss how to respond to the cable—Wise corresponded with a rabbinical colleague about disputes within the Reform rabbinate and wrote his associate Robert Szold about traveling to England in the near future for Palestine-related meetings, cautioning that his ability to travel might be affected by "medical, family and personal considerations." He did not list the need to focus on Europe's Jews as one of the potential obstacles to a transatlantic journey. On September 4, in between his letters to Frankfurter and Goldmann about the Riegner cable, Wise wrote a long, chatty letter to Mack about Chaim Weizmann's medical ailments, various personal matters, and the weather. That same week he also wrote several letters to colleagues concerning the state of long-running negotiations with non-Zionists over possible joint activities. Even Wise's heart-rending September 16 "Jofjude" letter to Frankfurter was only partly about his Washington meetings regarding European Jewry; one-third of it dealt with New York State Democratic Party politics and his thoughts on the upcoming gubernatorial race. He corresponded with a rabbinical colleague about a prospective convert to Judaism, and wrote letters of recommendation for the children of friends seeking employment and admission to college. He sparred with Jewish Agency chairman David Ben-Gurion, then visiting from Palestine, over Ben-Gurion's dissatisfaction with Chaim Weizmann's leadership of the Zionist movement. And he presided over a September 17 Emergency Committee for Zionist Affairs meeting focusing on efforts by Hebrew University president Judah Magnes to promote the idea of an Arab-Jewish binational Palestine instead of a Jewish state.[31]

Yom Kippur began on the evening of September 20 that year. Wise's annual High Holiday sermons attracted the Free Synagogue's largest attendance of the year, as well as the possibility of coverage by the *New York Times* or other news media. It was a prime opportunity to call attention to the issue that concerned him most: presumably that would have been the escalating and unprecedented persecution of the Jews in Europe. By this time, even if Wise harbored doubts regarding the veracity of the Riegner and Sternbuch telegrams, he had still read the JTA's reports in the first three weeks of September—that is, the three weeks preceding Yom Kippur—that hundreds of thousands of Jews from France, Holland, and Germany had been deported to slave labor sites; that three hundred thousand Warsaw Jews were being shipped to "undisclosed destinations"; and that nine hundred Jews in Velizh and eight hundred in Kovno had been massacred. And while the JTA had asserted on September 9 that the "renewed Nazi massacres in the ghettos of Poland" were as yet "unverified," by September 20 the news service verified that "massacres of Jews on an unprecedented scale are now taking place all over Nazi-occupied Poland" as part of a Nazi program "of total extermination of the Jews in Poland." That news appeared in the JTA bulletin that landed on Wise's desk on the morning preceding Yom Kippur. Even as Wise understandably felt constrained by his pledge to Welles not to mention the Riegner cable, nothing precluded him from speaking out on that Kol Nidre night about the new September 20 JTA report as well as other reports to date chronicling the plight of European Jewry. Nonetheless, his Yom Kippur evening sermon dealt with the compatibility of Judaism and American citizenship, and on Yom Kippur morning, he spoke about the joy of love and the thrill of everyday life. His choice of topics is all the more puzzling in view of the fact that Wise did not face pressure from the synagogue's board or lay leaders to restrict what he said from the pulpit. As the name of the Free Synagogue indicates, Wise had established it on the basis of the principle that the rabbi should be completely free to speak his mind.[32]

Wise's actions in the weeks to follow continued to reflect a failure to grasp the overwhelming catastrophe that was consuming the heart of world Jewry. On October 1 he wrote to White House adviser David Niles to propose mobilizing prominent Americans—including the president—to endorse the reelection of a U.S. senator with whom Wise was particularly enamored: George W. Norris of Nebraska. (Wise acknowledged the gesture was unnecessary. "I know it is not needed; I suppose he will have a 70% to 80% vote, but just as compliment and tribute to him," the rabbi wrote.) Days later, Wise corresponded with Frankfurter on how to get rid of nettlesome letter writers; with Chaim Weizmann's aide, Meyer Weisgal, about contacts with non-Zionists; and with Mack about everything from the sculpting of a new bust of Justice Brandeis to Wise's request for tickets to the annual Yale-Harvard football game. The rabbi also helped select speakers for several Jewish organizational meetings and attended to editorial matters for *Opinion*.[33]

Throughout September and October, Wise also maintained his heavy load of organizational and institutional commitments. He presided over inaugural exercises at the start of the Jewish Institute of Religion's academic year in September, and continued his regular teaching schedule at the school that semester. He delivered speeches at a Menachem Ussishkin memorial meeting, a Jewish National Fund luncheon, and a dinner honoring the scientist Emanuel Libman. He also corresponded with his daughter Justine about juvenile delinquency (her area of professional interest), and became involved in a time-consuming controversy over whether funds raised by the United Jewish

War Effort to assist the Soviet Union should be used to purchase tanks and planes, or only medical supplies.[34]

The documentary record of Wise's activities grows thin in
early November, because he spent most of the first half of the
month on a previously planned visit to Mexico with Nahum
Goldmann. "In addition to the overwhelming beauty of Mexico," Wise reported to the AJcongress Governing Council, he
and Goldmann were deeply impressed to discover Mexico's
"whole-hearted adherence" to the Allied cause, "the affectionate loyalty of all groups and classes of the Mexican people" to
both their president and President Roosevelt, and the Mexican
Jewish community's "unlimited cooperation" with the World
Jewish Congress. During the visit, Wise and Goldmann had
taken part in a rally celebrating the anniversary of the Balfour
Declaration and persuaded Mexico's foreign minister to permit the Inter-American Jewish Council, a wjcongress affiliate,
to hold its next session in Mexico City.[35]

It would take until November 24, 1942, eighty-one days after
Wise pledged to Undersecretary Welles to suppress the Riegner
cable while it was being investigated, for Welles to report back
on the findings and release Wise from his oath of public silence.
During those tumultuous eighty-one days, when additional and
ever more severe reports about Nazi atrocities were published
by the jTA and other media, much of Wise's schedule had been
devoted to the same kinds of concerns that filled his daily life
prior to the arrival of the annihilation news. He did hold a number of private meetings and conversations, and engage in correspondence, regarding the Riegner and Sternbuch telegrams and
related matters. On the whole, however, Wise's calendar during
those eighty-one days did not accord with someone who was
"almost demented with grief" and could "think of nothing else
and write of nothing else" other than Europe's Jews.

Would it have made any difference had Wise acted otherwise? Publicizing the Riegner telegram in defiance of Welles's
request arguably could have backfired. Not only would Wise
have alienated an important U.S. government official, but the

astounding and unverified claims made in the telegram might have engendered skepticism among the news media and the public as to the believability of reports about Nazi atrocities in general. Yet Rabbi Wise had other options. He was under no obligation to Welles to suppress the Sternbuch telegram or to refrain from commenting on the numerous press reports about Nazi massacres published in September, October, and November. He was likewise free to publicize the Bund Report of the previous May, the accuracy of which had not been challenged. Even disregarding the Riegner cable, then, Wise had ample credible evidence that the Germans had already carried out a deliberate slaughter of hundreds of thousands of European Jews, and were in the process of massacring many more. The American Jewish Congress and World Jewish Congress, under Wise's leadership, could have undertaken a nationwide campaign, beginning in September 1942, to inform the American public of the mass murder. Generating public awareness and sympathy was the necessary first step to securing U.S. government action to aid Jewish refugees—which is what the Bergson Group dissidents would eventually do, in early 1943 (see chapters 4 and 5). But the Bergsonites were at a disadvantage; they did not have a staff, budget, political connections, or interfaith relationships comparable to those of the established organizations. A campaign led by Stephen Wise, centered around the shocking news from Europe, would have had much greater impact, and much more quickly. Precisely how the pace or extent of the Holocaust might have been affected by an earlier and more effective publicity campaign cannot be known. What can be said is that because each passing day brought more Jewish victims, any earlier Allied action to help the Jews, no matter how modest, had the potential to save at least some lives.

Business as Usual

Rabbi Wise was far from the only American Jewish leader who failed to break free from his usual routines and less-urgent concerns during the Holocaust years. On the contrary, a number of commentators publicly noted, and bemoaned, the problem of American Jews—both leaders and the community at large—behaving in a business-as-usual fashion.

One of the most memorable of these critics was Hayim Greenberg, editor of the Yiddish-language newspaper *Yiddisher Kemfer* and chairman of the Labor Zionists of America. In a February 1943 article titled "Bankrupt," Greenberg sarcastically proposed "a day of fasting and prayer for American Jews." He explained:

> No—this is not a misprint. I mean specifically that a day of prayer and of fasting should be proclaimed for the five million Jews now living in the United States. . . . They are not even aware what a terrible misfortune has befallen them. . . . This misfortune consists of the vacuity, the hardness and the dullness that has come over them; it consists in a kind of epidemic inability to suffer or to feel compassion that has seized upon the vast majority of American Jews and of their institutions; in pathological fear of pain; in terrifying lack of imagination—a horny shell seems to have formed over the soul of American Jewry. . . . [A]t a time when the eyes of millions of Jews in Europe who are daily threatened with the most terrible and degrading forms of physical extermination are primarily turned to American Jewry, this American Jewish community has fallen lower than perhaps any other in recent times, and displays an unbelievable amount of highly suspect clinical "health" and "evenness of temper." If moral bankruptcy deserves pity, and if this pity is seven-fold for one who is not even aware how shocking his bankruptcy is, then no Jewish community in the world today . . . deserves more compassion from Heaven than does American Jewry.[36]

In a similar vein, in January 1943 the editors of the monthly magazine *Jewish Spectator* declared it "shocking and revolting" that "at a time like this, our organizations, large and small, national and local, continue 'business as usual' and sponsor gala affairs, such as sumptuous banquets, luncheons, fashion teas, and what not." The *Spectator* editors felt "nauseated" by "the abysmal indifference and heartlessness flaunted by Jewish men and women who can bring themselves to sit down at banquet tables, resplendent in evening clothes, while at the very same evening hundreds of Jews expire in the agonies of hunger, gas poisoning, mass electrocution—and what other forms of death fiendish sadists can invent."[37]

The records of American Jewish organizational life provide more than a few snapshots illustrating this business-as-usual phenomenon. In the spring of 1939, for example—at the same time the refugee ship *St. Louis* hovered off Florida's coast and the Wagner-Rogers child refugee bill was being debated in Congress—AJ committee leaders did not hold regular meetings because so many of them were spending long weekends in the country. Similarly, David Ben-Gurion, visiting New York in the summer of 1942, complained to a colleague that it was impossible to arrange a meeting of Zionist leaders on a Friday afternoon because "even with Rommel nearing Alexandria, everybody left for the country for the week-end." In the midst of delicate talks with State Department officials in July 1943 over a plan to rescue Jewish refugees in Rumania and France, Nahum Goldmann of the World Jewish Congress informed his interlocutors that he was "leaving on his vacation at the end of the week," so any further discussion would have to be handled by one of his deputies. A meeting between American Jewish leaders and Secretary of State Edward Stettinius in August 1944 to discuss Palestine and European Jewry was delayed because Rabbi Wise was at Lake Placid in upstate New York. "The Zionist Movement in these critical war times must conform with the lecture schedule and the vacation schedule of Dr. Wise," his fellow Zionist leader, Rabbi Dr. Abba Hillel Silver, protested. Even if Wise's visits to Lake Placid at this juncture were more for recuperation rather than vacation, the incident points to the related problem of Rabbi Wise's declining health and the extent to which it interfered with his communal responsibilities.[38]

Perhaps the most jarring contemporaneous commentary on American Jewish leaders' business-as-usual mindset was expressed in a message brought by the Polish Underground courier Jan Karski from the Warsaw Ghetto to Szmul Zygielbojm, a Jewish member of the Polish government-in-exile in London, on December 2, 1942. Karski told Zygielbojm that when he asked Jewish leaders in the ghetto what message they wanted him to bring to the American and British Jewish leadership, they said: "Jewish leaders abroad won't be interested. At 11 in the morning you will begin telling them about the anguish of the Jews of Poland, but at 1 o'clock they will ask you to halt the narrative so they can have lunch. That is a difference which cannot be bridged. They will go on lunching at the regular hour at their favorite restaurant. So they cannot understand what is happening in Poland."[39]

Some months later, Zygielbojm, despondent over the murder of his wife and son by the Nazis as well as the news Karski brought from Poland, committed suicide as a protest against international indifference. The stinging "favorite restaurant" statement attracted some attention at the time, as the New York City daily newspaper PM included it in its report on Zygielbojm's suicide. An editorial in the U.S. Labor Zionist journal *Jewish Frontier* also quoted the remark in full. The Jewish Telegraphic Agency, however, only alluded to it, noting that the message Zygielbojm received from Warsaw "expressed doubt that Jewish leaders would do anything to help the Jews in Poland." The publications of the major Jewish organizations went even further: the AJcongress's *Congress Weekly* (which allotted one paragraph to Zygielbojm's suicide), the AJcommittee's *Contemporary Jewish Record* (two paragraphs), and B'nai B'rith's *National Jewish Monthly* (four paragraphs) all reported his death, but omitted the accusation about Jewish leaders lunching.[40]

It may be said that Rabbi Wise did not differ from many of his contemporaries when it came to this business-as-usual mindset. Yet he had chosen to take upon himself the task of guiding the Jewish community in determining the appropriate response to the mass murder of their coreligionists. He had resisted the pressure to turn over the reins of leadership to others. Therefore he bore a unique responsibility in the Jewish people's time of crisis.

"Confirming Your Deepest Fears"

On November 24, 1942, a telegraphed message from Welles arrived in Wise's Manhattan office, asking him to come to Washington. Wise, accompanied by his son James and "sensing that I might hear the direst tidings," took a train to the capital that afternoon. According to Wise's account, Welles handed him a sheaf of documents that had recently arrived from the U.S. legation in Bern, and said, "I regret to tell you, Dr. Wise, that these confirm and justify your deepest fears." The red wax seals on the documents made him think of "the blood of my people pouring forth in rivers," the rabbi later wrote. Welles authorized Wise to release the information to the public, but did not authorize him to attribute the confirmation of the news to the State Department. Welles "couldn't vouch for the truth of these statements," Wise privately explained to AJ Congress colleagues a few days later. "All he said was that he believed they were correct."

State Department officials feared that official U.S. government confirmation would erase any lingering doubts in the minds of the public and the media as to the veracity of the news, and "the way will then be open for further pressure from interested groups for action which might affect the war effort," R. Borden Reams, head of Jewish affairs in State's European Division, confided to colleagues. "The plight of the unhappy peoples of Europe including the Jews can be alleviated only by winning the war."[41]

Leaving the meeting with Welles, Wise immediately organized a press conference in Washington that evening. He told the assembled reporters that Hitler had "ordered the annihilation of all Jews in Europe by the end of the year," and that "this news is substantiated in documents furnished to me by the State Department this afternoon." Wise evidently hoped his carefully nuanced language would give the impression of State Department endorsement without actually saying so. But many editors seemed to notice Wise's hedging and refrained from reporting that State confirmed the news. The Associated Press, for example, reported that Wise "claimed" it was confirmed by the State Department and that he "asserted" the administration had authorized him to release the news.[42]

State did its best to sow seeds of doubt. When the editor of the Protestant journal *Christian Century* telephoned Washington the day after the press conference to inquire about the department's position, M. J. McDermot, head of the Division of Current Information, immediately replied: "I today informed correspondents in confidence and am glad to give to you, not for publication, that Rabbi Wise was in the Department . . . in connection with certain material in which he was interested and he now has this material. The State Department had only sought to facilitate the efforts of his Committee in getting at the truth and the correspondents should direct all questions concerning this material to Rabbi Wise."[43]

The State Department's effort to cast doubt on the information was compounded by the fact that much of the news media declined to give prominence to Wise's announcement. The *New York Times*, which did not send a reporter to the press conference, published five paragraphs from the AP dispatch on page ten, tacked onto the end of another story about the mass murder. The following day, the *Times* published additional details from Wise's press conference, in six paragraphs at the end of a related story on page sixteen. Although some other major daily newspapers—such as the *New York Herald Tribune* and the *Miami Herald*—placed the story on page one, most relegated it to inside pages. The *Atlanta Constitution* buried it on page twenty, next to the train schedules. The major radio networks ignored it altogether.[44]

Wise's attempt to conceal the State Department's noncooperation was challenged most bluntly by the editors of *Chris-*

tian Century. An unsigned editorial declared that "although Rabbi Wise went out of his way to place the responsibility for his charges on the State Department, that branch of the government has conspicuously refrained from issuing any confirmation." The editorial also suggested that Wise's numbers were exaggerated, and that the claim regarding the use of Jewish corpses was reminiscent of World War I atrocity stories that turned out to be false. Wise tried to paper over State's position, asserting in a letter that appeared in *Christian Century* several weeks later, "Had you taken the trouble to inquire, you would have learned that the State Department not only authorized the publication of the statement I made, but for months had been seeking with our help to make sure of the accuracy of the statements with respect to Jewish mass slaughter." The editors fired back, pointing out that they had indeed "taken the trouble to inquire," and "the State Department promptly replied through an accredited officer." They continued: "Unfortunately, it specified that its reply was 'not for publication.' We have that reply in our files; it does not support Dr. Wise's contention. Our editorial comment on his charges was written in the light of the State Department's reply to our question."[45]

At a meeting of leaders of major Jewish organizations soon after the press conference, the attendees decided to proclaim December 2, 1942, a day of prayer and fasting, to mourn "the greatest calamity in Jewish history since the destruction of the Temple." Mourning rallies were held in Jewish communities throughout the United States and abroad. In heavily Jewish New York City, several radio stations observed two minutes of silence, and an estimated half a million Jewish workers staged a ten-minute labor stoppage. Many Jewish newspapers placed black borders around their front page in that week's editions.[46]

After first confirming with the State Department that the president was likely to respond in the affirmative, Wise wrote to FDR on December 2, 1942, asking if he would permit a delegation of Jewish leaders to present him with a memorandum concerning "the Hitler mass-massacres." In his note,

Wise cited his acquiescence in the administration's request to suppress the news. "I have had cables and underground advices for some months, telling of these things," he wrote. "I succeeded, together with the heads of other Jewish organizations, in keeping these out of the press." Wise emphasized that the proposed delegation would ask the president only to "speak a word which may bring solace and hope to millions of Jews who mourn, and be an expression of the conscience of the American people."[47]

The meeting with President Roosevelt took place six days later. Wise was accompanied by the presidents of the AJ committee, B'nai B'rith, the Jewish Labor Committee, and the Union of Orthodox Rabbis. Afterward, Wise told reporters that the president was "profoundly shocked" by the Nazis' mass murder of European Jewry; that Roosevelt said "the American people will hold the perpetrators of these crimes to strict accountability"; and that FDR promised the Allies "are prepared to take every possible step" to "save those who may still be saved."[48]

Wise's reassuring description of the president's intention to take rescue action was not consistent with other accounts of the meeting, such as the report Jewish Labor Committee president Adolph Held circulated in a private memo to his colleagues. According to Held, President Roosevelt began the meeting by joking about his choice of Governor Herbert Lehman, a Jew, to head the postwar administration in Germany. Rabbi Wise then spoke briefly about the Nazi atrocities. The president replied that he was "very well acquainted" with the massacres, but it would be "very difficult" to stop them because Hitler was "an insane man." FDR then asked the Jewish representatives if they had any suggestions. Four of the Jewish leaders spoke, but "the entire conversation on the part of the delegation lasted only a minute or two," Held wrote. "The President took notice [of what the leaders proposed] but made no direct replies to the suggestions." Roosevelt "then plunged into a discussion of other matters." Of the twenty-nine minutes the delegation spent with the president, "he addressed the delegation for 23 minutes." As soon as the president finished speaking, he "pushed some secret button, and his adjutant appeared in the room" to usher the Jewish leaders out.[49] Held made no reference to any promise by Roosevelt to—as Wise put it—"take every possible step" to "save those who may still be saved." Another account of the meeting likewise made no mention of the president promising to take action. Speaking to an AJCongress Governing Council meeting two days after the White House meeting, senior staffer Lillie Shultz stated only that "the delegation was cordially received and was assured by the President that the proposals contained in the memoranda [that they presented to him] would be given full consideration." Those memoranda did not propose specific rescue steps, and Shultz said nothing about Roosevelt promising to help save Jews from the Nazis. Similarly, neither Rabbi Wise's subsequent correspondence nor the minutes of subsequent AJCongress leadership meetings mentioned anything about the president having made such a pledge. It seems Wise embellished Roosevelt's remarks, deliberately making the president appear more engaged in helping European Jewry than he actually was. It would not be the last time Wise would do so.[50]

The Allied Declaration

In Great Britain, the accumulation of published reports in November and early December about the Nazi massacres created a groundswell of pressure for government action. Members of the British Parliament, Jewish organizations, and the Archbishop of Canterbury, head of the Anglican Church, urged the Churchill administration to respond. "Unless we can make them some kind of gesture," a senior British Foreign Office official advised his colleagues, "they will cause a lot of trouble." To alleviate the pressure, London suggested to Washington that the Allies issue a joint statement about the killings. At first the State Department resisted the proposal, fearing that, as one official put it, "the various Governments of the [Allied nations] would expose themselves to increased pressure from all sides to do something more specific to aid these people."[51] Eventually, however, the Roosevelt administration went along with the statement, but only after significantly watering down some of the language. For example, the proposed phrase "reports from Europe which leave no doubt" (that mass murder was underway) was reduced to "numerous reports from Europe."

Released on December 17, 1942, the Allied declaration condemned the Nazis' "bestial policy of cold-blooded extermination." It was signed by the United States, Great Britain, the Soviet Union, and the governments-in-exile of eight German-occupied countries. Pope Pius XII declined to sign because, as the papal secretary explained, the Vatican preferred to condemn war crimes in general rather than single out any particular atrocities. The statement did not include any proposed steps to rescue Jews from Hitler. The idea of including an offer of asylum for Jewish refugees was raised at one point in the discussions but left out of the final statement because, as one British official explained, it would mean making an offer "which would dog our footsteps forever"—in other words, some refugees might try to take them up on it.[52]

After the December 2 fast day and the December 8 meeting with the president, "there was a certain lull in the activities" of the mainstream Jewish organizations on the issue, Nahum Goldmann acknowledged to a colleague. The minutes of the January 12, 1943, AJCongress Governing Council meeting illustrate the Jewish leadership's retreat. Most of the meeting was devoted to discussion of a proposal to establish a new Jewish communal body to combat domestic antisemitism, as well as plans for a national conference "with respect to postwar reconstruction" and Palestine. Even as reports about the mass murder continued to appear prominently in the Jewish press in December and January, and some local rallies were held in various parts of the country, the national Jewish leadership seemed to be gripped by a sense of defeatism and general lack of imagination when it came to responding to the plight of Europe's Jews.[53]

A few isolated stirrings of dissent emerged. A columnist for the Yiddish daily *Der Tog* wondered aloud, "We have fasted, that is, some of us did, but is that all we can do for the Jews in Hitlerland as they walk in the valley of shadows?" An editorial in the *Reconstructionist*, titled "Fasting Is Not Enough," questioned "the desirability of fasting and prayer when unaccompanied by any suggestion of an outlet in action for the emotions evoked" and criticized Jewish leaders for failing to prepare a "program of action" along with the mourning rites. In a sharply worded private letter to Rabbi Wise, A. Leon Kubowitzki, chairman of the wjcongress's rescue department, lambasted Wise for not heeding his proposals for high-profile protests: "If this heavy burden is too heavy, why don't you allow us to share it with you? Why aren't you making use of our despair, of our will to help, of our experience, of our connections? Why do you expose our memories to be spat upon by future generations because we acquiesced in the crime of inaction in such a time and did not try everything I say everything in the world?"[54]

In the months to follow, other voices within the wjcongress as well as the ajcongress would join Kubowitzki in pressing for a more activist response to the plight of Europe's Jews. But at that early stage, in December 1942, critics such as Kubowitzki were too few and far between to influence Rabbi Wise's position. As leader of the American Jewish Congress, the World Jewish Congress, and the American Zionist movement, and as the Jewish leader with the most access to the White House, Rabbi Wise enjoyed a position of unparalleled authority in the organized Jewish community. The more cautious defense organizations, the ajcommittee and B'nai B'rith, were entirely satisfied with the ultra-conservative approach that Wise and his organizations had adopted. The various Zionist organizations deferred to Wise's judgment, as did the organizations representing Jewish religious denominations. The Jewish Labor Committee, attuned by its nature to strikes, grassroots mobilization, and other political and social action, was more inclined to favor public protests on behalf of European Jewry—but, not having Wise's experience and relationships in the national political realm, was unable to offer an alternative to his leadership on the European issue. Brooklyn Jewish Democracy, the activist group that had caused a brief stir in the Jewish community in the mid-1930s, had faded almost entirely from the scene. By all measures, the organized American Jewish community in early 1943 was locked into a position of sitting and waiting.

And then, almost overnight, Rabbi Wise and other American Jewish leaders suddenly swung into action and began protesting in the most forceful terms—but not concerning the Jews in Europe.

Equality in North Africa

On November 8, 1942, American and British forces launched "Operation Torch," invading Nazi-occupied Morocco, Algeria, and Tunisia. It took the Allies just eight days to defeat the Germans and their Vichy French partners in the region.

American Jewish leaders closely monitored the situation in the liberated regions, especially Algeria. They were particularly interested in the status of the Cremieux Decree of 1870. Crafted by French Minister of Justice Adolphe Cremieux, the decree had granted full French citizenship to Jewish residents of French-occupied Algeria, thereby reversing centuries of second-class status that local Arab leaders had imposed on Algeria's Jews. As a result, Jews could enter professions and schools in Algeria from which they previously had been excluded.

In 1940, however, the Germans occupied France and set up a pro-Nazi puppet regime, known as Vichy, to govern the southern part of the country. Vichy authorities were also given control of the regimes that administered France's overseas colonies, including those in North Africa. One of Vichy's earliest actions in North Africa was to repeal the Cremieux Decree. The Vichy administration then stripped Jews of their civil rights, severely restricted their admission to schools and some professions, seized Jewish property, and tolerated periodic pogroms by local Muslims.

Wise and other American Jewish leaders were also aware that many thousands of Jews were being held in slave labor camps operated by the Vichy rulers in North Africa. Life in the camps was characterized by long hours of backbreaking work, random beatings by the guards, extreme overcrowding, poor sanitation, near-starvation, and little or no medical care. While U.S. Jewish leaders were not necessarily acquainted with the details of conditions in the camp, scattered JTA reports in 1941–42 provided reason for alarm. The authorities were reportedly building "huge concentration camps" to which thousands of French Jewish refugees were being deported, in order to build a long-planned trans-Saharan railroad. In the summer of 1941, there were said to be nine thousand inmates, "the majority of them Jews" (the others were Spanish Loyalists and other anti-Nazi political prisoners); by the time of Operation Torch, that number had risen to twenty-five thousand, according to press accounts. One report asserted that some 150 Jews scheduled to be shipped to North Africa from France were so fearful of the rumored conditions there that they resisted deportation, even though that meant risking their lives. Indeed, they were executed en masse as a result.[55]

In the wake of the Allied liberation, North Africa's Jews—and their American coreligionists—expected the Cremieux Decree to be reinstated and the prisoners released. The first obstacle to restoring the former policy was Admiral Francois Darlan, a senior leader in the Vichy French administration. The Allies had taken Darlan prisoner on the first day of the fighting. To hasten the Allies' victory in the region, FDR agreed to leave Darlan in charge of the Allied-occupied North African territories in exchange for Darlan ordering his forces in Algiers to cease fire. Many prominent liberals in the United States were appalled by the president's action. "[It] sticks in the craw of majorities of the British and French, and of democrats everywhere, [that] we are employing a French Quisling as our deputy in the government of the first territory to be reoccupied," an editorial in the *New Republic* protested. These liberal voices understood the Allies' war effort as intending not merely to achieve military victory over the Axis but to bring the values of enlightened democracy to areas that had been under the jack-boot of fascism. Keeping Vichyites in power in North Africa seemed to contradict that aspiration.[56]

In his victory announcement, Roosevelt explained the Darlan deal as a "temporary expedient," not an endorsement of Vichy ideology. FDR asserted that in planning the postwar administration in that region, he already had "asked for the abrogation of all laws and decrees inspired by Nazi governments or Nazi ideologists." U.S. general Dwight Eisenhower, the commander of Operation Torch, made the same promise to a delegation of Algerian Jews. Assistant Secretary of State Adolph Berle Jr. likewise assured U.S. Jewish leaders that abolishing Vichy's anti-Jewish legislation in North Africa was "on the agenda."[57] Thus, despite the fact that Darlan was placed in charge of the interim administration, American Jewish leaders expected that President Roosevelt's pledge would guide the governance of Arab North Africa and its Jewish population. The AJCongress optimistically predicted that the repeal of the Vichy-era anti-Jewish laws would follow the Allied occupation of North Africa "as the day follows the night," and Wise publicly thanked the president for "the promptness of your action regarding the abrogation of all laws and decrees inspired by the Nazi Government of Nazi ideologies in Northern Africa, and the liberation of all persons who have been imprisoned because of their opposition to Nazism."[58]

On the ground, however, not only was Darlan in power; he retained nearly all of the original senior officials of the local Vichy regime. He did dismiss one Vichy official of note—Yves Chatel, the governor of Algeria—but replaced him with Maurice Peyrouton, the very Vichy official who had signed the original anti-Jewish laws implemented in 1940 when the Vichyites had assumed administration of France's colonies. Under Peyrouton, no steps were taken to bring back the Cremieux Decree. Moreover, the Vichy regime's notorious "Office of Jewish Affairs" (Service des Questions Juives) continued to operate. Overall there was little change in the status of the region's Jewish communities (except for a small number of instances in which government-confiscated property was returned to North African Jews). In addition, the slave labor camps in which thousands of Jewish men were imprisoned continued to function.[59]

Contrary to President Roosevelt's public pledge to abrogate the Vichy's anti-Jewish laws, behind the scenes his administration took Darlan's side against the Jews. FDR's envoy to North Africa, Robert Murphy, recommended to Washington that the Cremieux Decree not be reinstated, because it might provoke local Arabs to revolt against the Allied occupation authorities. General George S. Patton, another central figure in carrying out Operation Torch and managing its aftermath, warned General Eisenhower that if steps were taken in North Africa to "favor the Jews," then "we will precipitate trouble and possibly civil war"—that is, an armed Arab uprising against Allied forces in the region. Patton sent Eisenhower a report prepared by Darlan that argued against equal rights for North African Jewry. Eisenhower, in turn, forwarded the materials to the War Department and State Department. Both departments then urged FDR to leave the decisions on Jewish affairs in the hands of the local governments in the region.[60]

Rumblings of concern began to surface in the liberal press. A December 17 editorial in the *New York Times* questioned whether Darlan really intended to bring about "the abrogation of anti-Jewish laws [and] release of prisoners and internees of the United Nations." The editors of the *New Republic* asked: "Who controls French Africa, Darlan or the United Nations [as the Allies were known]? And if the latter, isn't it high time we cleaned up the remnants of fascism that obviously still exist there?" An investigative report in the New York City daily newspaper *PM* asserted that the regime of Darlan's successor, General Henri Giroud, was actively discriminating against Jews, and while some "anti-Vichy Frenchmen" had been released from imprisonment, "thousands" of Spanish Loyalists and others remained "in concentration camps." Questioned by reporters at his January 1, 1943, press conference about the North African prisoner camps, President Roosevelt replied, "I think most of the political prisoners are—have been released," but he offered no further details.[61]

Roosevelt met with Major-General Charles Nogues, a leader of the post-Vichy regime, in Casablanca, Morocco on January 17. The status of Jews in North Africa was one of the items on their agenda. According to the notes of Captain John McCrea, FDR's naval aide, who served as stenographer, General Nogues reported: "The Jews, especially those in Algeria, had raised the point that they wish restored to them at once the right of suffrage." President Roosevelt replied: "The answer to that was very simple, namely, that there just weren't going to be any elections, so the Jews need not worry about the privilege of voting."

Ambassador Murphy, who took part in the meeting, pointed out that "the Jews in North Africa were very much disappointed that 'the war for liberation' had not immediately resulted in their being given their complete freedom," at which point, per McCrea's notes: "The President stated that he felt the whole Jewish problem should be studied very carefully and that progress should be definitely planned. In other words, the number of Jews should be definitely limited to the percentage that the Jewish population in North Africa bears to the whole of the North African population. Such a plan would therefore permit the Jews to engage in the professions, at the same time would not permit them to overcrowd the professions, and would present an unanswerable argument that they were being given their full rights."[62]

General Nogues "agreed generally [with FDR's position]," noting that "it would be a sad thing for the French to win the war merely to open the way for the Jews to control the professions and the business world of North Africa." Roosevelt remarked that "his plan would further eliminate the specific and understandable complaints which the Germans bore towards the Jews in Germany, namely, that while they represented a small part of the population, over fifty percent of the lawyers, doctors, school teachers, college professors, etc. in Germany were Jews." (Actually, about 16 percent of the lawyers, 11 percent of the doctors, 3 percent of the college professors, and less than 1 percent of the schoolteachers were Jewish.)[63]

The same topic arose at another meeting between Roosevelt and Giraud later that afternoon. According to McCrea's account: "The President asked General Giraud as to the Jewish situation in Algeria. This was discussed at some length and the President set forth to General Giraud his views as he had done in this connection to General Nogues. General Giraud did not think the Jewish problem an insurmountable one."[64]

American Jewish leaders were not privy to Roosevelt's remarks in Casablanca about Jews. Still, a steady stream of articles in the New York City press and the JTA in the days to follow contributed to a growing perception that the situation after the Allies' liberation was essentially unchanged from before. Near-daily reports by I. F. Stone in PM in late January featured headlines such as "U.S. Policy in North Africa: Why State Dept. Holds Up Repeal of Nuremberg Laws," and "Hull Admits Anti-Fascist Prisoners Still Being Held in North Africa." The JTA reported on January 17 that Polish Jews interned in "camps near Oran" (in Morocco) lacked basic food and clothing, and on January 24 that some sixty-five thousand "anti-Fascist prisoners," including five thousand Jews, were being held in seventeen camps in Algeria and Morocco. A report in the New York Times on January 29 named prison camps in Morocco, one of them holding three thousand to four thousand "Spanish Republicans, Poles, and Jews," just five miles from where "American troops, dedicated to end government by concentration camp, live."[65]

Several factors militated against any public American Jewish protests over the North Africa situation. Ever deeply loyal to FDR, whom he called "the Great Man" and "the All Highest" in his private correspondence, Rabbi Wise had almost never publicly criticized the administration on any issue. Moreover, Jewish leaders recognized that to disagree with a popular president in the midst of a world war—and a war whose outcome, at that point, was still far from clear—meant risking antisemitic accusations that Jews were not putting the war effort first.

Nonetheless, even as they relegated the issue of European Jewry's annihilation to the back burner in late 1942 and early 1943, mainstream Jewish leaders rose in angry and unprecedented protest against the inferior status of North African Jewry. "North Africa" was the number one agenda item of the American Jewish Congress's Governing Council meeting on February 4, 1943. Rabbi Wise and Nahum Goldmann announced to their colleagues that they had already "conferred with Government officials respecting the situation," and because the meetings had achieved nothing, they "were of the opinion that a statement should now be issued." The thirty AJCongress lay leaders present voted unanimously to publicly challenge the administration on the issue.[66]

On February 14 the American Jewish Congress and World Jewish Congress issued a joint public statement charging that "the anti-Jewish legacy of the Nazis remains intact in North Africa." Despite the passage of three months since the Allied liberation, only a few "grudging concessions have been made" to aid the Jews, while no changes "of an important character have been made in the[ir] political and economic situation." Recalling President Roosevelt's promise to eliminate the Vichy laws—and thus calling attention to his failure to fulfill that promise—the two groups declared that he had pledged "action to insure that the four freedoms shall without further delay be declared as valid for all the peoples in North Africa, which means the total abrogation of all anti-Semitic laws and decrees and . . . the release of those of whatever race or nationality who are being detained because of their support of democracy and opposition to Nazi ideology." This statement from the two mainstream Jewish organizations was only slightly milder than the charge by Benzion Netanyahu, executive director of the militant U.S. Revisionist Zionists, that "the spirit of the Swastika hovers over the Stars and Stripes" in the administration of North Africa.[67]

Rabbi Wise then led an AJCongress delegation to Washington to personally make their case before Welles, and Dr. Gold-mann organized a group of prominent French exiles in the United States to present Welles with a petition of their own. Even organizations that were ordinarily much more reserved than the AJ congress spoke out. Leaders of the AJ committee, for example, confronted Undersecretary Welles to demand abrogation. The Union of American Hebrew Congregations (Reform), for its part, issued a resolution urging the administration to intervene against the Vichyites. These protests induced a number of other prominent individuals to speak up, among them Supreme Court Justice Felix Frankfurter, the exiled French Jewish leader Baron Edouard de Rothschild, and leaders of the American Jewish Joint Distribution Committee.[68]

At first, the Roosevelt administration dug in its heels and dismissed the protests. Ambassador Murphy claimed that some prominent Algerian Jews agreed it was impossible to reinstate the Cremiuex Decree. Undersecretary Welles insisted that, technically, the region was no longer under Allied military occupation and therefore the United States could not dictate how the local government acted. These excuses and misrepresentations only stoked American Jewish anger, triggering new statements of condemnation that were supplemented by ongoing negative press coverage about U.S. policy. Even more-reserved publications, such as the *New York Times*, published news articles and analyses about the North Africa controversy that added to the pressure on the Roosevelt administration.[69]

By March 1943, in response to the avalanche of public protests, the administration instructed the local authorities to repeal the anti-Jewish measures. The implementation process, however, was slow, even after De Gaulle's Free French forces took over Giraud's administration in the late spring. In April the forced labor camps in North Africa were officially shut down, although some of them continued operating well into the summer. The Jewish quotas in schools and professions were gradually phased out. On October 20, 1943, nearly a year after the Allied liberation, the Cremieux Decree was at last reinstated.[70]

The willingness of Rabbi Wise and other American Jewish leaders to publicly criticize Roosevelt administration policy on this one issue may seem remarkable, especially when contrasted with their reluctance to speak out regarding the simultaneous massacre of millions of European Jews. The key to understanding their unusual boldness may be found in the fact that this issue not only affected North African Jews, but also American Jews themselves. The full equality that Jews had enjoyed in the United States was predicated on the American government's unwavering fealty to the principles of liberty at the core of its political, cultural, and social constitution. The U.S. government's willingness to acquiesce in the application of a legal system that deprived Jews of equal rights implicitly posed a challenge to the status of Jews in America—implying that their rights, too, might one day be vulnerable to some circumstance of political or military expediency. Such a prospect would not have been something that Rabbi Wise and his colleagues could abide.

4

Suppressing the Dissidents

MORE THAN MOST OF the Jewish public, Rabbi Wise's students at the Jewish Institute of Religion (JIR) had the opportunity to interact with him and understand his perspective in a direct, personal context. One student in particular had some interesting things to say about his former teacher. Saadia Gelb, a young Labor Zionist in New York City, enrolled at JIR primarily as a cover for his underground activity: smuggling weapons from the United States to the Haganah, the Labor-affiliated militia in Palestine. Although he attended classes, he never had any intention of completing the requirements for graduation, which likely made him feel less inhibited about speaking frankly to Rabbi Wise. In his autobiography, Gelb recalled:

> One of the most interesting folks with whom I was in contact was Rabbi Stephen Wise, the founder and head of the Jewish Institute of Religion. He often would relate off-the-record accounts of his high-level activities, including meetings with President Franklin Roosevelt. Wise asked the president to respond publicly to the news of the Nazi extermination centers, but Roosevelt replied half-heartedly, pointing out the difficulties of waging the world war. Wise then quoted the president as saying: "Stephen, you can always call on me. When the front door

is closed you can always enter through the back door." Hearing the story, I was infuriated and said to Wise: "That's precisely the point. Don't you see? He's conning you with soapy words. The problem is not whether you have access to him, but what he'll do about it." Wise was unconvinced. To this day, I believe Roosevelt took advantage of Wise.[1]

On several occasions, Gelb suggested to Rabbi Wise that Jewish leaders should adopt a more activist policy in response to the persecution of European Jewry. According to Gelb, Wise dismissed his criticism on the grounds that a young person, lacking experience as a Jewish leader, "simply did not understand" the many factors that rendered Gelb's proposals impractical.[2]

Almost without exception, Wise's students at JIR revered him. His political and religious views shaped their view of the world. They consulted him on personal as well as professional matters, and many of them followed his lead by making civil rights and other social justice causes a significant component of their rabbinical careers. One student described how he and the other young men felt "a sense of awe and intimidation" in the presence of a man who kept company with presidents and prime ministers. JIR students seldom expressed disagreement with Wise, both because of their admiration for him and because, as another student later put it, "we were, in a sense, scared to death of him, because our future as rabbis was in his hands."[3]

Each Thursday morning, the entire JIR student body—which during the 1940s totaled about twenty young men—was required to attend a "Practical Rabbinics" class with Wise.[4] He frequently spent much of the time recounting his recent private meetings with political leaders and other dignitaries. For the students, these were indeed exercises in practical rabbinics. While none of them imagined they would reach Wise's level of renown, all of them regarded him as a model of how a modern rabbi could interact with the surrounding world. They were "thrilled" to be privy to these inside descriptions of Wise's activities. "We were these little guys hearing these amazing stories," one recalled.[5]

The students were shaken by Wise's harrowing descriptions of the Nazis' mass murder of European Jewry, including the Riegner telegram, which Wise read aloud in class shortly after receiving it. He also shared his frustration after meetings with President Roosevelt and senior State Department officials who told him the United States could do nothing to aid Europe's Jews except to win the war. The rabbi conveyed to his young charges a sense that, while the administration's unwillingness to extend itself on behalf of Jewish refugees was deeply troubling, American Jews could do little to change U.S. policy.[6] Wise's description of one such meeting left student Howard Singer unsettled: "One day Rabbi Wise called some of his students into his office having returned from Washington. He told of a conference he had with President Roosevelt, and he dramatized it, as was his way. At one point he said, 'And then I said, Franklin, I think . . .' At that point I had the terrifying feeling that for the privilege of calling Roosevelt 'Franklin,' the Jewish people would pay heavily. He had obviously taken so much pride in that accomplishment."[7]

Murmurs of dissent were sometimes heard in the Thursday sessions. One student, Morris Goldfarb, remembered "one or two occasions" when several of the students asked Wise "why we couldn't be more public in protesting what was happening to the Jews in Europe." Wise replied that "the problem was both political and social—non-Jews don't understand these things, and with antisemitic groups such as America First on the rise, it is necessary to be discreet about publicizing such Jewish issues." Another student, Sanford Saperstein, recalled suggesting that American Jews should wear a Star of David on their clothing as a symbol of solidarity with European Jewry; Wise "mused on the idea for a moment, but it went no further."[8]

By and large, Wise's students followed his lead on such issues. In December 1943, for example, the JIR student organization declined to sign a petition to President Roosevelt urging the rescue of European Jewry, because it was sponsored by a dissident group with which Wise had clashed, Peter Bergson's Emergency Committee to Save the Jewish People of Europe. JIR Student Organization secretary Sidney Jacobs informed the Emergency Committee's leaders that the students had rejected the petition because the committee was "not . . . a legitimate, representative group within Jewish life."[9]

Meanwhile, dissent was beginning to brew in the dormitories of another Manhattan college campus: the Jewish Theological Seminary of America (JTS), Conservative Judaism's flagship institution. Three students in particular had become deeply concerned about the plight of European Jewry. Freshman rabbinical student Noah Golinkin, himself a recent refugee from Poland, closely followed news about the fate of the Jews in his native country. Moshe "Buddy" Sachs, a sophomore, happened to share a dormitory room with Max Gruenwald, a German refugee rabbi who was a visiting scholar at JTS and also worked in the WJCongress offices, and who returned to the dorm each evening with news about anti-Jewish atrocities that left Sachs "stunned." Galvanized by the small *New York Times* report of Rabbi Wise's November 1942 press conference, Golinkin, Sachs, and a third friend, sophomore Jerome Lipnick, decided to establish their own committee to promote an activist Jewish response to the mass murder. Lipnick, an articulate and popular figure on campus, became their public spokesman.

Few students or faculty at JTS took an interest in the committee's activities, but in any event, the trio envisioned a movement that would reach far beyond their home campus. Disappointed by the tepid response of the wider community to the news from Europe, and the apparently meager results of the December 8 meeting with President Roosevelt, the JTS activists recruited rabbinical students from their Orthodox and Reform counterparts, Yeshiva University and the Jewish Institute of Religion, to join them as a delegation to meet with Rabbi Wise.[10]

The December 17 meeting began with a brief discussion

about the plight of Jews in Nazi-occupied territories. Rabbi Wise then repeated the main points he had presented at the November 24 press conference. When the students pressed Wise to name ways in which the organized Jewish community might respond to the European situation, he responded by pointing to the December 2 day of fasting and the White House meeting on December 8. He also alluded to unspecified steps that, he said, he and other Jewish leaders were undertaking behind the scenes but could not yet reveal.[11]

Lipnick spoke of the need to "evacuate" the Jews from Poland. Wise bristled. "We don't evacuate human beings; we evacuate cattle," the rabbi shot back. "This is Jabotinsky talk!" He was referring to Vladimir Ze'ev Jabotinsky (1880–1940), founder of the militant Revisionist Zionist movement, who had stirred controversy in the Jewish world in the 1930s by calling for the emergency "evacuation" of the European Jewish masses to Palestine. While Jabotinsky urged rapid emigration from Poland to escape rising antisemitism, Wise, in common with most mainstream Zionist leaders, favored a more gradual approach to the settlement of Palestine, with priority given to young immigrants trained in agriculture. Wise's strong attachment to the principle of equal rights for Jews in the Diaspora clashed with the concept of rapid mass Jewish emigration from Europe, even after the confirmation of mass murder.[12]

Lipnick next broached the idea of seeking to open the Virgin Islands or Alaska to Jewish refugees. Wise cut him short, insisting the Virgin Islands were "too hot" and Alaska "too cold" for Jewish settlement. More likely, however, Wise's opposition was rooted in other factors. In 1940 Wise had opposed using the Virgin Islands as a haven for refugees, "however imminent be their peril," for fear that it "might be used effectively against [Roosevelt] in the [presidential] campaign." And he had refrained from promoting Alaska as a site for Jews escaping Hitler because it would "make a wrong and hurtful impression . . . that Jews are taking over some part of the country for settlement" (see chapter 2).[13]

The students then turned to the main part of their proposal to Rabbi Wise: the building of a broad college campus–based protest movement. They presented a four-part plan: to mobilize fellow divinity students, fellow students in general, college faculty, and alumni to speak out for U.S. action to rescue Jews. They proposed to begin within the world of religious seminaries, where they would "acquaint non-Jewish seminaries with the facts in order to get a joint proclamation of protest and specific demands." Next, they would "acquaint faculties and student bodies of universities and colleges with the situation in order to get public action." After that, they would seek to "activate alumni of our institutions to organize Jewish and interfaith meetings for protest and petition to higher churchmen, public officials, Congressmen, etc." Finally, they would "form an emergency general Jewish youth council to consider youth action." Rabbi Wise was not impressed. "Wise told us that as a veteran Jewish leader, he knew best what methods of protest should be organized," Golinkin later recalled. "He told us to trust his judgment and be patient."[14]

Disappointed but not discouraged, the students decided to take action on their own. In early 1943, they organized an unprecedented "Metropolitian Interseminary Conference to Discuss the Plight of European Jewry Today" to raise public awareness of the mass murder. Several hundred students and faculty attended the February 22 event, held with alternating sessions at the Jewish Theological Seminary and its Protestant counterpart, the nearby Union Theological Seminary. Among the speakers and panel participants were prominent Jewish figures (JTS president Dr. Louis Finkelstein, Jewish Welfare Board director Rabbi Philip Bernstein); Christian leaders (Federal Council of Churches president Rt. Rev. Henry St. George Tucker, Dr. Willard Johnson of the National Conference of Christians and Jews); as well as a number of refugee and relief experts. One such expert was Varian Fry, an editor at the *New Republic*, who during the early months of the war had personally organized the escape of more than two thousand Jewish refugees from Vichy France—until the Roosevelt administration forced him to end his mission because he was, as Secretary of State Hull put, "evad[ing] the laws of governments with which this country maintains friendly relations," that is, the relations between the United States and Nazi Germany.[15]

The conference aimed to begin cracking open the curtain of silence surrounding the Nazi genocide, to alert opinion makers and rising young leaders in the faith communities about the mass murder, and to generate public discussion of the crisis. It achieved at least some small steps in that direction. Although major news media did not report on the symposium, the Religious News Service circulated an account of the event authored by Jerome Lipnick, and the Union Theological Seminary's student journal published a stinging rebuke of American churches' response to the Holocaust, authored by a UTS student who had spoken at the conference. The impact was especially noticeable at Yeshiva College, where students who had attended the conference organized two campus protest rallies and authored articles about the plight of Europe's Jews for the student newspaper. Golinkin, Sachs, and Lipnick also sent copies of the conference resolutions to Jewish leaders and coauthored a stunning essay in the *Reconstructionist*, asking: "What have the rabbis and leaders . . . done to arouse themselves and their communities to the demands of the hour? . . . What have they undertaken to awaken the conscience of the American people?" All of this contributed to the slow but necessary process of educating both the Jewish community and the general public, as a prelude to generating U.S. government action.[16]

The students' most notable achievement was prodding the lethargic Synagogue Council of America—the umbrella group for Orthodox, Conservative, and Reform synagogues—to establish a Committee for Emergency Intercession to publicize the European catastrophe. At the students' suggestion, the new Committee announced a seven-week publicity campaign, linked to the traditional period of semi-mourning between Passover and Shavuot. Many synagogues of different denominations throughout the country adopted the Committee's proposals to recite special prayers for European Jewry; limit their "occasions of amusement"; observe moments of silence and partial fast days; and write letters to political officials and Christian religious leaders. In addition, individual synagogues held memorial rallies nationwide (in some cases with congregants wearing black armbands designed by Noah Golinkin)—culminating in a prayer rally by three hundred rabbis of varying denominations in Manhattan. Ironically, Rabbi Wise was one of the speakers at that rally, which had grown out of the activities proposed by the students and rejected by Wise just months earlier.[17]

All along, Wise's adamant assertion that "he knew best" had struck the JTS students as simplistic and puzzling. In the face of mass murder, it seemed implausible that refuge in a particular region should be rejected because the climate might be uncomfortable, or that a discussion of resettlement prospects should be halted because Lipnick had inadvertently used a phrase that reminded Wise of something he disliked years ago, when Jews still had the luxury of imagining a future in Poland. Now, the fact that Wise himself took part in a rally that had originated in the very proposals he had rejected when the students had presented them to him, reinforced their perception of Wise as capricious, and as someone who dismissed policy suggestions not on their merits but according to whether they originated within his small circle of like-minded friends and colleagues.

"Awaken Their Vacationing Hearts"

The accumulation of news media reports about the mass murder began to stir a grassroots response on both sides of the Atlantic in early 1943. In England there was a rising tide of calls from church leaders, members of Parliament, and the local Jewish community for some kind of Allied assistance to Jewish refugees. To head off this growing pressure, the British Foreign Office initiated discussions with the State Department about convening an Anglo-American conference on the refugee problem. While those discussions were proceeding behind the scenes, Jewish activists in the United States had begun organizing to fill the vacuum left by the inactivity of the established leadership. Much of the new agitation was the work of the aforementioned Bergson Group, which would soon make its presence felt in the political arena and also find itself in a bitter struggle with Rabbi Wise.

"Bergson" was the pseudonym of Hillel Kook, a dynamic twenty-nine-year-old activist from Palestine. (He adopted the name Bergson to shield his family—including his uncle, the chief rabbi of Palestine—from publicity and controversy.) An activist in the Irgun Zvai Leumi, the Palestine Jewish underground, Bergson was involved in smuggling European Jews to Palestine in the 1930s. In 1940 Revisionist Zionist leader Vladimir Ze'ev Jabotinsky sent him and a handful of his comrades to the United States to mobilize political and financial support for the cause of Jewish statehood. The American Friends of a Jewish Palestine, as they called their small group, operated on a shoestring budget and made little headway in its early months.

Bergson tried and failed to solicit Rabbi Wise's endorsement of the American Friends group in 1940. Wise responded that he would not support "the activities of a body like the 'Irgun' which refuses to recognize the authority of the duly constituted national bodies and is responsible to no one but itself." The group experienced much greater success when, in 1941, it became the Committee for a Jewish Army of Stateless and Palestinian Jews. The idea of a Jewish army fighting against the Nazis appealed not only to a segment of the American Jewish community but to many non-Jews as well. Numerous prominent intellectuals, entertainers, labor leaders, and political figures publicly endorsed the Jewish army committee. Ben Hecht, the Academy Award–winning screenwriter and newspaper columnist, authored the group's broadsides and recruited Hollywood celebrities for the cause. The group's full-page advertisements in the *New York Times* and other major newspapers helped put its cause on the map. In late 1941 Wise's Emergency Committee for Zionist Affairs initiated negotiations aimed at bringing the Bergsonites under its wing. The talks, which lasted more than a year, ultimately foundered over the Emergency Committee's unwillingness to permit the activists more than a minimal role in policymaking.[18]

When news of the mass murder of Europe's Jews was confirmed in late 1942, Bergson and his comrades shifted their attention to the plight of European Jewry and looked for ways to publicize the slaughter. This was important, because if the public was uninformed and indifferent, the administration was unlikely to act. In January 1943 a Gallup poll asked Americans: "It is said that two million Jews have been killed in Europe since the war began. Do you think this is true or just a rumor?" Although the Allied leadership had publicly confirmed that two million Jews had been murdered, the poll found that only 47 percent of the public believed it to be true; 29 percent dismissed it as a rumor and the remaining 24 percent had no opinion. The news media's failure to treat the Nazi genocide as a serious issue contributed to the public's skepticism. To some extent, editors were following the lead of the Roosevelt administration, which, in the months following the December 17 Allied proclamation, had made no effort to publicize the tragedy or aid Jewish refugees.[19]

In an attempt to fill this vacuum, Hecht created a full-scale dramatic pageant that he called "We Will Never Die." On a stage featuring forty-foot-high tablets of the Ten Commandments, the production surveyed Jewish contributions to civilization throughout history, described the Nazi slaughter of the Jews, and culminated in an emotional recitation of "Kaddish," the traditional Jewish prayer for the dead, by a group of elderly rabbis. "Will it save the four million [Jews still alive in Europe]?" Hecht wrote on the eve of the opening. "I don't know. Maybe we can awaken some of the vacationing hearts in our government."[20]

Hecht had convinced numerous stars of stage and screen, including Edward G. Robinson, Stella Adler, Sylvia Sydney, and Paul Muni, to headline the cast. Kurt Weill ("The Three-penny Opera") composed an original score; Moss Hart ("You Can't Take It With You") agreed to serve as director, and famed impresario Billy Rose signed on as producer. The Bergsonites rented Madison Square Garden to host the opening perfor- mance on the evening of March 9, 1943.

Since December, Rabbi Wise's colleagues in the AJ congress and WJ congress had been suggesting to him that they hold a protest rally of their own at the Garden. They pointed with alarm to the fact that "the Jewish Army committee is planning a similar meeting," according to the minutes of an AJ congress- WJ congress Planning Committee session. The proposal was made all the more urgent by the arrival on February 9 of a tele- gram to Wise from Gerhart Riegner and Jewish Agency official Richard Lichtheim, reporting the intensification of the mass killings, including the fact that six thousand Jews were being murdered daily at a single death camp in Poland. The AJ con- gress avoided being upstaged by the Bergsonites by booking the site for March 1. Hecht proposed merging the two events, but Wise refused. According to Hecht's later account, Wise urged him to cancel the pageant; the activists turned him down.[21]

The March 1 AJ congress rally drew a standing-room-only audience of more than twenty thousand to Madison Square Garden. That tens of thousands of others had to be turned away illustrated the strong sentiment in the Jewish community for a more forceful response to the European Jewish crisis. After speeches by Rabbi Wise and an array of political, church, and labor leaders, the assembly adopted an eleven-point plan that (among other recommendations) urged the Allies to negoti- ate with neutral countries for the emigration of Jewish refu- gees; create "sanctuaries" in the West for escapees; liberalize immigration procedures to fill U.S. immigration quotas; and open British Mandatory Palestine to Jews fleeing the Nazis.[22]

The rally represented a significant departure from the more than two months of inertia that had characterized the Jewish leadership in the aftermath of the December 17 Allied declara- tion. Wise forwarded the resolutions adopted at the rally to President Roosevelt, with a cover note expressing disappointment that three months had passed "since the United Nations' Declaration without action to stay the executioner's hand." Nearly three weeks later, FDR replied with a boilerplate assurance that the administration would "help the victims of the Nazi doctrines of racial, religious and political oppression"—he pointedly did not say Jews—"so far as the burden of war permits." The later phrase, positing a conflict between rescue and the war effort, was becoming a hallmark of the administration's policy regarding Jewish refugees.[23]

Another twenty thousand people filled Madison Square Garden on the evening of March 9 for the opening of "We Will Never Die." So many people had gathered on the sidewalks outside and were unable to enter the packed hall that the cast decided, on the spot, to do a second performance immediately after the first. The second show, too, filled the Garden. "If there was a dry eye at Madison Square Garden Tuesday night, it wasn't mine," wrote reviewer Nick Kenny in the New York City daily PM. "It was the most poignant pageant we have ever witnessed. It is a story that should be made into a moving picture, just as it was presented at the Garden and shown in every city, town and hamlet in the country."[24]

The Bergson Group did, in fact, take the show on the road. In the months to follow, "We Will Never Die" was performed before sell-out crowds in Chicago Stadium, the Boston Garden, Philadelphia's Convention Hall, the Hollywood Bowl in Los Angeles, and Washington DC's Constitution Hall. Altogether, more than one hundred thousand Americans watched the performances. The audience for the Washington show included over two hundred members of Congress, numerous members of the international diplomatic corps ("ambassadors from everywhere," Hecht called them), six Supreme Court justices, and Eleanor Roosevelt. It was not the first time that the famously independent First Lady failed to toe the president's line.

Mrs. Roosevelt was so moved by the performance that she devoted part of her next syndicated column, "My Day," to the pageant and the plight of Europe's Jews. For millions of American newspaper readers, it was the first time they learned of the Nazi mass murders. Shattering the wall of silence surrounding the Holocaust was the initial crucial step in the process of mobilizing the American public against the slaughter.[25]

Nonetheless, some regional branches of the AJ Congress and like-minded mainstream Jewish organizations attempted to obstruct the pageant's supporters from raising funds for the project. This spectacle of established Jewish groups interfering with efforts by dissidents on behalf of Europe's Jews was just the beginning of what would become a sustained effort by Rabbi Wise—sometimes at the behest of President Roosevelt himself—to silence the dissidents.[26] Wise and other Jewish leaders did not object to the content of "We Will Never Die," which focused on Jewish contributions to civilization and Jewish suffering in Europe, and refrained from explicit criticism of Allied policy. What rankled Wise and his colleagues was the Bergson Group's ability to enlist the endorsement of prominent individuals whose involvement led to significantly greater public and media attention to their cause—and, thereby positioned the group itself as a voice of the Jewish community to the wider world.

The White House, too, looked askance at the pageant. Through White House adviser David Niles, producer Billy Rose had asked the president for a "brief message" that could be read aloud at the opening performance, which would "say only that the Jews of Europe will be remembered when the time comes to make the peace." Rose assured the White House that "There is no political color to our Memorial Service." The problem was that in the Roosevelt White House, the very mention of the Jews was deemed political. White House aides warned the president that sending the requested message would be "a mistake." Despite Rose's assurance, "it is a fact that such a message would raise a political question," Henry Pringle of the Office of War Information advised. In other words, publicizing the slaughter could raise the "political question" of how America was going to respond to the Nazi genocide. Because the president did not want to take any specific steps to aid the Jews, raising that question would be embarrassing. Hence presidential secretary Stephen Early informed Rose that the "stress and pressure" of the president's schedule made it impossible for FDR to provide the requested message.[27]

The White House policy of refraining from drawing attention to the specific plight of the Jews was also evident in statements the president issued in 1942–43 concerning Axis atrocities. At his August 21, 1942, press conference, for example, FDR referred generally to "barbaric crimes against civilian populations." As examples of these crimes, the president cited "the shooting of hostages, not only in France but very recently five or six very important citizens in The Netherlands, and a good many people in Norway," as well as "executions of scores of innocent hostages in reprisal for isolated attacks on Germans." He acknowledged that there "probably" were still atrocities going on "in those other countries like Poland and Czechoslovakia that we don't get much news out of." In an October 7, 1942, statement, the president affirmed that the United States would cooperate with its allies in establishing a war crimes commission, but offered no explanation as to what war crimes were being perpetrated, or against whom. Similarly, in a July 30, 1943, statement, Roosevelt reiterated that the Allies would "make use of information and evidence in respect to barbaric crimes in Europe and Asia and the instigators of those crimes would have to stand in courts of law to answer for their acts." The mention of Asia made it clear that the president did not regard the plight of the Jews as deserving of special mention, much less special action. Ironically, when Rabbi Wise asked the president, in August 1943, to issue a public statement about the massacres of the Jews, FDR replied by citing these three statements as evidence that he had already done so.[28]

Fiasco in Bermuda

Meanwhile, in late 1942 and early 1943, criticism of FDR's refugee policies was beginning to be heard even from staunch Roosevelt supporters in the liberal press. Varian Fry, writing in the *New Republic*, charged: "It is not true that nothing can be done for the Jews until after Hitler has been defeated. By [that] time quite possibly they may all be dead." Unimpressed by the Allies' threat of postwar retribution for Nazi war crimes—one editorial asserted that such "moral condemnations and vague threats [are] not enough"—the editors of the *New Republic* pressed for concrete steps, including the creation of an Allied commission for the specific purpose of rescuing Jews. A February 1943 editorial declared that if the Allies remained indifferent to the slaughter of the Jews, "they will make themselves, morally, partners in Hitler's unspeakable crimes."[29] In the *Nation*, editor Freda Kirchwey declared:

> In this country, you and I, the President and the Congress and the State Department, are accessories to the crime and share Hitler's guilt. If we had behaved like humane and generous people instead of complacent cowardly ones, the two million lying today in the earth of Poland . . . would be alive and safe. We had it in our power to rescue this doomed people and yet we did not lift a hand to do it—or perhaps it would be better to say that we lifted just one cautious hand, encased in a tight-fitting glove of quotas and visas and affidavits and a thick layer of prejudice.[30]

Even the *New York Times*, which seldom took issue with the Roosevelt administration on Jewish-related issues, published an unsigned editorial on March 3 saying it would be a "crime against humanity" to deny haven to Jews fleeing Hitler, and specifically calling on the U.S. government to "set a good example, [by] revising in the interests of humanity the chilly formalism of its immigration regulations." A resolution adopted unanimously by the U.S. Senate the following week, although merely condemning the mass murder without calling for rescue steps, added to the perception that the plight of the Jews was a matter of concern to many Americans.[31]

In the face of this groundswell of public interest, the administration was receptive to the British Foreign Office's proposal for a British-American conference on the refugee problem. The two governments selected the remote island of Bermuda for the assembly, so that lobbyists and protesters would find it difficult to gain access. Recalling the fiasco of the Evian conference in 1938, Jewish leaders feared Bermuda likewise was intended merely as a way of deflecting critics of Allied refugee policy. Arthur Lourie of the Emergency Committee for Zionist Affairs pointed out to colleagues: "The whole procedure adopted by the British and American governments with regard to the refugee question is directed towards quieting public opinion without undertaking anything effective."[32]

In early March, anguished over the continual atrocity reports in the press and pressured by the rise of the Bergson Group dissidents, eight American Jewish organizations established a Joint Emergency Committee on European Jewish Affairs (JEC), with Rabbi Wise and AJcommittee president Joseph Proskauer as its co-chairs. Earlier attempts at intra-organizational unity— such as the aforementioned Joint Consultative Committee and General Jewish Council—had been repeatedly handicapped by turf wars and other rivalries, but the JEC organizers hoped that cognizance of the unparalleled Jewish tragedy in Europe would encourage its member groups to temporarily set aside some of their disagreements.

The JEC quickly initiated efforts in both the public and private realms. To drum up public sympathy for European Jewry, it decided to duplicate the March 1 AJcongress rally, on a much smaller scale, around the country. Ultimately about two dozen such rallies were held in fourteen states during March and April. At the same time, Wise and other JEC representatives repeatedly asked State Department officials to permit a Jewish delegation to attend the Bermuda conference. They also sought an audience with President Roosevelt, intending to urge that the March 1 rescue resolutions be incorporated into the U.S. position at Bermuda. Both requests were denied. The JEC then sought to have a delegation of seven Jewish congressmen meet with the president for the same purpose. That request, too, was initially rejected, but after strong pressure from Rep. Emanuel Celler, FDR relented.[33]

The meeting took place at the White House on April 1. "It was a very unsatisfactory interview," Congressman Daniel Ellison (R-MD) reported afterward. "[We] asked the President about refugees, the White Paper, etc . . . what he proposed to do about these things. [We] made a number of suggestions to him as to what [we] thought he ought to do and the answer to all of these suggestions was 'No.'" Roosevelt hinted that "perhaps visitor's visas would again be issued" for refugees as he did after the 1938 *Kristallnacht* pogrom (in fact, he never did approve any additional visitor's visas). According to Celler, the president claimed Prime Minister Churchill had agreed to "surreptitiously allow Jews to enter Palestine without hindrance as to number." Actually, however, "there wasn't a bit of truth to that ploy," Celler later recalled. The president was simply trying to stop the Jewish congressmen "from, as he put it, 'making waves.' . . . Roosevelt, although he may have desired to help the Jews, didn't raise a finger to help the Jews."[34]

The president showed only minimal interest in the Bermuda conference. He received just one State Department briefing during the preparations, and his role was a limited to a half-hearted attempt to persuade Supreme Court justice Owen Roberts to chair the U.S. delegation. When Roberts declined, Roosevelt said he regretted that the justice "cannot go to Bermuda—especially at the time of the Easter lillies!" Princeton University president Harold W. Dodds agreed to accept the assignment. Joining him on the delegation were Congressman Sol Bloom, a Jewish Democrat from New York who strongly supported the Roosevelt administration's position on Zionism and refugees, and Senator Scott Lucas (D-IL), another staunch supporter of the administration's refugee policy. R. Borden Reams, one of the State Department's fiercest opponents of rescue, was named secretary of the delegation.[35]

Jewish organizational leaders regarded the selection of Bloom, the only Jewish member of the delegation, as a bad omen.

Nahum Goldmann warned his colleagues that Bloom had been chosen to serve as "an alibi" for the conferees in their likely refusal to take real action. Indeed, Breckinridge Long privately considered Bloom "easy to handle" and "terribly ambitious for publicity," two qualities that would ensure he would do as State asked. Rabbi Wise had privately derided Bloom as "the State Department's Jew" prior to the congressman's participation in the U.S. delegation to the 1938 Evian conference. Wise expected a repeat performance from Bloom in Bermuda.[36]

On April 14 the JEC sent Undersecretary Welles its formal proposal regarding Bermuda. The memorandum was signed by Wise and Proskauer, along with the presidents of B'nai B'rith, the Jewish Labor Committee, and the Synagogue Council of America, speaking collectively on behalf of "a large majority of the Jewish population of this country." The unusually blunt communication expressed "anguish" over "the failure of the United Nations [the Allies] to act until now to rescue the Jews of Europe," even as "thousands of Jews continue to be murdered daily." The signatories pronounced themselves "seriously disturbed" by the Allied leadership's ongoing refusal to consult with Jewish groups regarding Bermuda, the rejection of requests to permit Jewish representatives to attend the conference, and the selection of a conference site that was "completely inaccessible to the influences of public opinions or public personalities." Breckinridge Long replied on behalf of Welles to Rabbi Wise six days later. Ignoring the JEC's requests, Long assured Wise that the delegates to Bermuda "are men of wide knowledge and experience in world affairs," who "are well acquainted with the problem." Long's letter was "written of course in a decently friendly strain," Wise commented in forwarding a copy to Proskauer, "[but] it says nothing."[37]

The minutes of Joint Emergency Committee meetings in April testify to its members' mounting frustration over the administration's antagonism. AJCongress representative Carl Sherman proposed launching "a forceful public campaign" to convince President Roosevelt to endorse the Joint Emergency

Committee's rescue program. The State Department's attitude toward rescue "is still very cold," warned Lillie Shultz, the
AJCongress's de-facto executive director. "The President must
be shown that the country is aroused." Even Nahum Goldmann, Wise's usually reliable ally on matters of political strategy, seemed to be losing patience. At the April 18 JEC meeting,
Goldmann suggested organizing an emergency protest meeting of "1,000 to 2,000 people" in New York to publicly chastise the administration for failing to place the JEC's proposals
on the Bermuda conference agenda.[38]

Rabbi Wise labored to prevent the "wild people" in the JEC
from "calling President Roosevelt and the State Department
names," as Wise put it in an April 22 note to Goldmann. Such
public criticism of the president would be "morally and perhaps
even physically suicidal," Wise asserted, seemingly implying
that it might unleash a harsh, perhaps violent, backlash against
American Jews. "It is very easy to hold press conferences and
to call meetings, but we must in advance consider what it will
lead to—that it will shut every door and leave us utterly without
hope of relief as far as FDR is concerned," Wise wrote. "He is
still our friend, even though he does not move as expeditiously
as we would wish. But he moves as fast as he can, in view of
the Congress on his hands, a bitterly hostile and in a very real
sense partially anti-Semitic Congress." Wise understood that the
administration, not Congress, was suppressing the admission
of refugees below the limits allowed by law; he himself had publicly referred to the fact that the administration had not filled the
German quota (see chapter 1). Blaming Congress, however, was
easier than confronting the disappointing record of a president
to whom he felt a strong personal and political attachment.[39]

Wise's vigorous opposition to the calls within the JEC for
greater activism pleased his co-chair. Joseph Proskauer and
the AJcommittee had always advocated backstairs diplomacy
and opposed Jewish public protests; they were unfazed when
critics derided the AJcommittee for using "hush-hush muf-
flers." Proskauer perceived Wise as his ally in the struggle

to suppress the activists within the committee. "The spirit I encountered at the first meetings [of the JEC in March 1943] was to rely entirely on the mass meeting technique," Proskauer confided to a colleague. "I am glad to say that in conference I have changed all this . . . despite the fact that Dr. Stephen Wise and I have disagreed sharply on many issues, we have agreed a hundred percent" that backstairs diplomacy was preferable to public protests.[40]

"Cruel Mockery" in Bermuda

The Bermuda conference began on April 19, 1943. In his opening remarks, U.S. delegation chairman Harold Dodds made it clear there would be no deviation from the administration's view that winning the war was the only way to really help the Jews. "The true and final solution of the refugee problem," he declared, "[is] complete and final victory." Over the course of the twelve days of discussions, it became clear that neither government was interested in taking any significant steps to aid European Jewry. There was to be no special emphasis on the plight of the Jews, nor adoption of any policies that would benefit Jews in particular. The United States would not agree to the use of any transatlantic ships to transport refugees, not even Liberty ships that brought supplies (and later troops) to Europe and then returned empty. There would be no increase in the number of refugees admitted to the United States, despite the many unfilled quota places. For their part, the British delegates refused to discuss Palestine as a possible refuge. The British also blocked any consideration of negotiating with the Nazis for the release of Jews, on the grounds that "many of the potential refugees are empty mouths for which Hitler has no use." The release of any significant number of Jews "would be relieving Hitler of an obligation to take care of these useless people." The Bermuda delegates also rejected the idea of food shipments to starving Jews as a violation of the Allied blockade of Axis Europe, even though the Allies had previously made an exception for German-occupied Greece. With all these options off the table, the Bermuda delegates spent the bulk of their time on smaller-scale steps. When the meetings drew to a close on April 30, the conferees had agreed on only a meager set of recommendations, principally the establishment of a camp in Morocco for several thousand Jewish refugees and another in Libya for a few thousand non-Jewish refugees. Anxious to avoid shining a spotlight on how little had been achieved, the two governments kept the proceedings secret. Two days later, Assistant Secretary of State Adolph Berle sent a statement to a Jewish rally in Boston reiterating that "nothing can be done to save these helpless unfortunates" except to win the war. The Roosevelt administration's policy toward the Jews was unchanged.[41]

The failure of the Bermuda conference provoked the first serious Jewish criticism of the administration's refugee policy. "Since Adolph Berle has now expressed the official view that nothing can be done to save the Jews except by invasion, it seems to be clear that we ought to do everything here and in London to arouse public opinion," World Jewish Congress political director Maurice Perlzweig advised Rabbi Wise. Although Wise remained reluctant to directly challenge the president—he characterized the Bermuda parley as "a woeful failure," but blamed the British—many of his close colleagues now were less reticent. Rabbi Dr. Israel Goldstein, president of the Synagogue Council of America, blasted the conference as "not only a failure, but a mockery," bluntly adding: "The victims are not being rescued because the democracies do not want them, and the job of the Bermuda conference apparently was not to rescue victims of Nazi terror but to rescue our State Department and the British Foreign Office from possible embarrassment." Other Jewish groups were equally outspoken. The Bergson Group placed a full-page advertisement in the *New York Times* and other newspapers, headlined "To 5,000,000 Jews in the Nazi Death-Trap, Bermuda was a 'Cruel Mockery.'" The Labor Zionist journal *Furrows* commented that the conference's "sole contribution to the rescue of European Jews was the great news that the Democracies had established a preliminary committee to call a preliminary conference which is to consider ways of helping Hitler's victims after the war." These Jewish critics may have been emboldened by the strong criticism of Bermuda that appeared in the liberal press. The editors of the *New Republic*, for example, declared after Bermuda: "If the Anglo-Saxon nations continue on their present course, we shall have connived with Hitler in one of the most terrible episodes of history. . . . If we do not do what we can, our children's children will blush for us a hundred years hence."[42]

Jewish congressmen, too, were outraged. Rep. Samuel Dickstein asserted: "Not even the pessimists among us expected such sterility." Congressman Celler accused the Bermuda delegates of engaging in "more diplomatic tight-rope walking," at a time when "thousands of Jews are being killed daily." He also dubbed Bermuda "a bloomin' fiasco," a thinly disguised slap at his congressional colleague's role in the conference. Bloom's unapologetic retort—"as a Jew, I am perfectly satisfied with the results of Bermuda"—quickly turned him into a lightning rod for Jewish anger. Bergson Group activist M. J. Nurenberger, responding to a boast by Bloom that he brought matzohs to Bermuda (Passover had taken place that week), told the congressman he thought "it would have been more important for [you] to eat bread there and save some Jews."[43]

Rabbi Wise, for his part, characterized the Bermuda parley as "a woeful failure," but publicly blamed only the British. Wise's reluctance to directly challenge President Roosevelt explains why he blocked a proposal by Congressman Celler, prior to the Bermuda conference, to hold a "conclave" in Washington of members of Congress who were "sympathetic to active and genuine rescue of refugees." Immediately after Bermuda, Celler renewed his proposal to Wise, arguing that to properly address the refugee crisis, the U.S. needed officials "other than the Charlie McCarthys who represented us at Bermuda" (a reference to a popular ventriloquist's dummy). "We will be ditched again unless extreme pressure is brought to bear upon the authorities," Celler implored Wise. Celler seemed genuinely puzzled that Wise "frowned on" the proposal. But Wise was unwilling to put "extreme pressure"—or, really, any pressure—on FDR.[44]

The Joint Emergency Committee on European Jewish Affairs was slow to respond to Bermuda, partly because its response underwent several drafts as the member organizations quarreled over language and tone. Finally, on June 1, the JEC leaders sent a long letter to Undersecretary of State Welles to explain how "sadly disappointed" they were by the paltry results of the conference. The JEC letter actually went further than any of its individual member organizations had previously gone in criticizing U.S. policy. In a direct challenge to the administration's argument that the only way to rescue Jews was to defeat the Axis powers on the battlefield, JEC leaders stated: "To relegate the rescue of the Jews of Europe, the only people marked for total extermination, to the day of victory is . . . virtually to doom them to the fate which Hitler has marked out for them." Welles replied that there was no way to transport refugees to Palestine; that efforts were being made to bring a small number of Jews out of Bulgaria; and that the State Department was "very closely" following up on the issue of postwar punishment for Nazi war criminals. Welles gave no indication of any substantive change in the Roosevelt administration's Jewish refugee policy.[45]

A Cry from Palestine

A revealing glimpse of the tensions within the Jewish leadership in 1943 and the struggle over American Jewry's response to the Holocaust is afforded by the experiences of two notable Jewish figures from Palestine who visited the United States. Because of their stature in the Zionist movement, Rabbi Meyer Berlin, leader of Mizrachi, the international organization of religious Zionists, and Leib Jaffe, a prominent journalist and poet, were permitted to take part in meetings of the Joint Emergency Committee. Both would leave behind compelling accounts of what they encountered there.

In February 1943 Rabbi Berlin flew to Washington for three days of meetings with Vice President Henry Wallace, leading congressmen, and foreign ambassadors, to make the case for rescuing Jewish refugees and establishing a Jewish state in Palestine. The results, described in a report that Berlin compiled, were not encouraging. Senate majority leader Alben Barkley (D-KY) conceded to the rabbi that he was "quite unfamiliar" with the plight of European Jewry and the British closure of Palestine. Sen. Robert Wagner (D-NY), for his part, claimed he had "no influence" regarding Palestine and tried to change the subject to the status of Jews in the Soviet Union, whom he alleged were "well situated." Rabbi Berlin expressed to Senator Wagner his "astonishment" that "nothing practical has so far been done to help the Jews in their great despair." The rabbi added: "If horses were being slaughtered as are the Jews of Poland, there would by now be a loud demand for organized action against such cruelty to animals. Somehow, when it concerns Jews, everybody remains silent, including the intellectuals and humanitarians of free and enlightened America."[46]

Rabbi Berlin's "most disappointing" meeting was with Vice President Wallace. When the rabbi said Europe's Jews were "threatened with total extinction," the vice president responded by "inject[ing] the curt remark, 'I cannot agree with you on that,'" a curious statement considering that just two months earlier, the Allies had publicly denounced the Germans' "bestial policy of cold-blood extermination." Wallace also refused to endorse Zionism. "Many groups in American Jewry [are] totally against Zionism," he said, "and [I have] no right to consider the opinion of one group in preference to another." Wallace's own diary entry about the meeting was not particularly pleasant. "Rabbi Berlin asked me pointblank for a message which he could take to the Jews in Palestine concerning what I would do for them after the war," the vice president wrote. "I told him with equal frankness that I would not give them any such message. . . . He was very much disappointed. I must confess that there are certain types of religious leaders who have a very poor sense of time and place."[47]

Rabbi Berlin received a different response from the one

Republican congressman with whom he met, House Minority Leader Joseph Martin of Massachusetts. "With tears in my eyes and uncontrolled emotions," the rabbi described the plight of Jews in Hitler Europe. "The congressman was apparently touched by my words. . . . 'That is surely wrong,' [Martin] exclaimed" when Berlin described the British policy of keeping Jewish refugees from reaching Palestine. The congressman promised to "do whatever possible" to facilitate a congressional resolution about European Jewry and to "try to do his very best" to press the British on Palestine. The problem, Rabbi Berlin later wrote, was that "Congressman Martin has, until now, not been approached at all about Zionist or general Jewish matters, and it is truly a pity that we are neglecting people of this calibre. . . . These men must be furnished with proper material which will bring home to them some knowledge of our situation." Rabbi Wise and other American Jewish leaders who strongly identified with President Roosevelt, the New Deal, and the Democratic Party had refrained from forging relationships with Republicans, confining their Capitol Hill contacts instead to those with whom they felt the strongest ideological affinity (see chapter 1).[48]

As a participant in meetings of the JEC and the Emergency Committee for Zionist Affairs (ECZA) during the spring and summer of 1943, Rabbi Berlin repeatedly pressed for greater activism. At one JEC meeting, he "complained bitterly about the indifference, inadequate action and lack of feeling [about European Jewry] on the part of American Jews compared with the Palestine Jews." The Jews of British Mandatory Palestine "engage in street demonstrations, sign huge petitions, [and] close shops," Rabbi Berlin reported. "They are discouraged by the silence of the American Jews." The rabbi proposed a general shutdown of Jewish-owned stores in the United States "for a day or half a day, or an hour or half an hour, including such shops as Macy's, Saks and others, to show to the Jews as well as to non-Jews their sympathy for the Jewish victims of Nazi barbarism." At an ECZA meeting, he called for a concerted public campaign against the White Paper, arguing that "many people in political life here [are] ignorant of the significance of the White Paper and . . . plans should be made to provide the necessary information." He also recommended that the issue "be brought to the attention of the President." The minutes of those meetings record no response by Rabbi Wise to Rabbi Berlin's comments; perhaps out of deference to his distinguished guest, Wise chose not to challenge Berlin's remarks.[49]

Wise and Berlin did clash, however, when Mizrachi decided to open its own lobbying office in Washington DC in May 1943. Berlin explained to Wise that prior to his recent arrival in the United States, "I was under the impression that there is in this country an effective and constant political bureau in Washington which is devoting itself to political Zionist influence exclusively and uninterruptedly. . . . I was amazed to find, however, that there is no such bureau or institute in existence." Thus a Mizrachi office in the capital would pose no competition to the existing Jewish groups but would simply help fill a void, he contended. In fact, World Zionist Organization president Chaim Weizmann had made a similar point in a meeting with U.S. Zionist leaders the previous December. "The work in Washington cannot be done by hit and run methods," he argued. "Unless an office is created in Washington . . . it is not to be expected that anything effective can really be accomplished from New York." But Wise was not prepared to see the opening of an office by a faction he did not control. The day after the Bermuda conference concluded, the ECZA leaders spent much of their time wrangling over a resolution condemning Mizrachi for planning to open an office "without any authorization" from the World Zionist Organization. After considerable debate, the participants accepted Rabbi Berlin's proposed compromise: Mizrachi would "suspend its activities in Washington for the next few weeks to give the Emergency Committee an opportunity to open a Washington office" of its own. In the end, however, it took the Zionist Emergency Committee six months, rather than "a few weeks," to open its office. At a time when more, not less, Jewish political action was needed in Washington, Rabbi Wise and his colleagues succeeded in silencing Mizrachi's work in the capital without producing anything to replace it.[50]

Meanwhile, the other visitor from Palestine was also tugging at Wise's elbow. The journalist and poet Leib Jaffe had arrived in New York City at the end of 1942 to fund-raise for the Jerusalem-based Keren HaYesod (Palestine Foundation Fund). Having grown up in Lithuania and studied in Germany, Jaffe felt a particularly close connection to the events in Europe. In a June 2, 1943, letter to Rabbi Wise, Jaffe urged the Joint Emergency Committee to "proclaim a day of mourning and protest for all American Jews" and bring "hundreds of thousands of Jews into the streets to express their grief and indignation." There were those who "say that street demonstrations are not customary now," Jaffe wrote; "all the more [reason] why we should do it. It would even be more impressive." Jaffe took care to avoid pointing an accusing finger directly at Wise. "I know that our leaders are working beyond their strength, but the masses are not given an opportunity to express their feelings, and if they were, it would strengthen and add force to the efforts of the leaders." Instead, he charged, the American Jewish community "is silent. . . . Life goes on normally and quietly as if nothing were happening." Like Rabbi Berlin, Jaffe contrasted the American Jewish response with that of Palestine Jewry: "In Palestine, an organization has been set up under the name *Al Domi* (Be not silent), whose purpose is to cry out unceasingly day and night. We Palestinians here are constantly receiving reminders from Palestine that we keep on demanding that something be done. . . . We cannot be silent. Jewish history will never forgive it. The blood of our brethren cries out to us."

Six days after Jaffe sent his letter, participants in an AJ congress executive committee meeting proposed "holding a mass street demonstration with respect to the atrocities." Lillie Shultz urged that the demonstration "express Jewish woe not only over the fate that has overtaken the Jews of Europe but woe over the indifference of the civilized world." Wise vetoed the proposal, citing "the undignified character of such demonstrations."[51]

Jaffe requested and was granted permission to speak at the JEC's July 15, 1943, meeting. Alternating between scolding, pleas, and practical proposals, Jaffe spoke with conviction and a sense of desperation. "We, who have come from the Land of Israel, know no peace," he said. "Our spirit is dejected at the reaction of American Jewry to the tragedy of the Jews in Poland and elsewhere in Europe. We cannot understand how American Jewry can keep quiet upon their hearing the last dying groans of European Jewry." If the American public hesitates to believe the reports of the massacres, Jaffe pleaded, then "Make them believe!":

> We have to do something that goes beyond the norm, an event as great as the tragedy that has befallen us, an event that will waken the spirit of the quiet Jews and will shock the cold and cruel world. Many say that we must refrain from hysteria, but it is better if we are hysterical, if this is the way that we can save even just one child: we will be hysterical so long as there is still a spark of feeling left in Jewry and humanity. . . . God shall never forgive us if we do not raise our voices at this time.[52]

Jaffe paraphrased part of the Warsaw Ghetto message that had reached Szmul Zygielbojm (see chapter 3): "We hate you! Why have you not saved us? . . . If you feel our pain, leaders of [Jewry], rise and go to the American representatives, and to the Foreign Ministry offices, and stay there until they put you in jail, and if they arrest you, go on a hunger strike until you die!" Jaffe called for "mass demonstrations" by Jews as well as Christians:

> We have to get hundreds of rabbis out of their houses so that they march in the demonstration with Torah scrolls in their hands. From every synagogue in the [Jewish world], there should be a voice crying out in protest. . . .
>
> We have neglected much in these last months. Now, in this last hour, we can correct these shortcomings and do everything that still may be done. . . . These may be harsh and bitter words, but they are poor and weak in expressing the strangled feelings of our hearts.

The minutes of the meeting do not record Rabbi Wise's response, but according to Jaffe, Wise "reacted emotionally to the extent of being frightened," and "viewed the speeches [by Jaffe and Rabbi Berlin] as a rebuke directed towards him." Jaffe wrote that Wise told him he could not sleep for two nights afterward. Evidently Wise was already on edge going into the meeting; shortly beforehand, he had reported to JEC co-chair Proskauer that "the Yiddish press is severely criticizing the Joint Emergency [Committee]" for its ineffectiveness.[53]

Jaffe elaborated on his thoughts in a letter to Goldmann a week after the meeting. The WJCongress co-chair had opposed Jaffe's July 15 call for demonstrations (even though Goldmann himself had proposed the idea of holding a mass protest meeting in New York City three months earlier, at the April 18 JEC meeting). On July 22, Jaffe wrote him:

> If you don't agree with my proposal for a street demonstration, then something else should be done. I said something exceptional, something compatible with our tragedy should be done. This silence of the Jewish masses cannot continue. You remarked that such demonstrations would not help. I do not know whether this is so. This mass demonstration at Madison Square Garden [the March 1943 rally organized by the AJcongress] had its results. The United States are [sic] a democratic country and they count on the pressure of the masses. Our reaction would perhaps provoke the reaction of many Gentiles who are uncomfortable, who feel that they should not remain inactive and indifferent. You also said that in Washington they would not like such a demonstration, that they are already tired of us, and that some Senators have expressed their displeasure. I think that other Gentiles will think differently. I repeat my words: The Gentiles will respect our outcry more than they are respecting our silence and our indifference.[54]

Jaffe's final extant letter on the subject of American Jewry and the Holocaust was dated August 19, 1943, and addressed to one of his Keren HaYesod colleagues in Jerusalem. "There is not enough air [here in the United States] for me to breathe," he wrote. "What tortures me especially is my complete helplessness." While the established Jewish organizations were calling their coalition for European Jewry an "emergency committee," Jaffe continued, "this *Emergency Committee* [emphasis in original], which supposedly should be working day and night, had not met in over two and a half months." He described how at the July 15 meeting, Nahum Goldmann had "made a long speech" arguing that "demonstrations such as I suggested would not help, and further, that Washington would not like it. Some Senators had complained about the Jews making too much noise." While the subsequent comment was not recorded in the meeting minutes, Jaffe told his colleague that he had then reminded Goldmann: "A demonstration much larger than that held at Madison Square Garden was arranged for the Jewish delegates from Russia. An estimated 50,000 people attended the meeting held for them"—so why assume that a rally to rescue European Jewry would fare any worse?[55]

Only one of the Jewish leaders at the July 15 JEC session openly took Jaffe's side. Benjamin Tabachinsky, national director of the Jewish Labor Committee, "supported me and criticized very harshly the Joint Emergency Committee for its complacency and its indifference," Jaffee wrote. Tabachinsky urged "that an office be created for this Committee (they do not even have an office) and said that the Labour Committee would give $5,000 for this purpose." In the days following the July 15 JEC session, Jaffe reported having "had talks with many people" in Jewish leadership circles, but "all was in vain." Even U.S. Labor Zionist leader Hayim Greenberg—himself a critic of the Jewish leaders—told Jaffe "his hands had fallen," a reference to the biblical episode, chronicled in Exodus 16:11, in which the ancient Jews triumphed in battle when the hands of Moses were raised but were defeated when his hands fell. "I also spoke with Dr. Israel Goldstein and with many others, but it was all to no avail," he concluded. "Our leaders cannot be moved."[56]

Signs of Hope

Amid all the disappointments Jaffe encountered on the American Jewish scene, he did find one hopeful sign: the emergence of the Bergson Group.

Throughout the spring and summer of 1943, the Bergson Group's newspaper ads had helped generate significant public discussion about the rescue issue. The advertisement blasting the Bermuda conference as a "Cruel Mockery" was particularly important in galvanizing criticism of the Allies' refugee policy. Altogether, the Bergson Group placed more than two hundred advertisements in newspapers nationwide featuring headlines such as "How Well Are You Sleeping? Is There Something You Could Have Done to Save Millions of Innocent People from Torture and Death?" and "Time Races Death: What Are We Waiting For?" Congressman Will Rogers Jr., son of the famous entertainer and a leading backer of the Bergson Group, later characterized the ads as "the most effective technique of all of the methods we used. . . . They carried tremendous impact. . . . I can remember when they appeared in the paper, even around the halls of Congress, there was conversation. . . . I would go down to the floor of Congress and they would be talking about it. 'Look at this.' Or, 'Isn't this outrageous?' Or 'Shouldn't something be done?' Very effective. Very effective." On one occasion, Eleanor Roosevelt told Bergson that President Roosevelt complained to her that one of the ads was "hitting below the belt." Bergson replied that he was "very happy to hear that he is reading it and that it affects him." That advertisement described a ghost of a Holocaust victim sitting on the windowsill of the Oval Office, waiting for the president to take action to aid the Jews. According to Bergson Group officials, presidential adviser Bernard Baruch telephoned Ben Hecht "on behalf of President Roosevelt" and asked him "to call off all further criticism of President Roosevelt and his administration."[57]

Rabbi Wise publicly condemned the Bergson Group's newspaper ads as "glaring, garish, [and] sometimes misleading."

One in particular became the focus of the Jewish leadership's ire. In early 1943, Bergson received a telephone call from Herman Shulman, Wise's close colleague and vice chairman of the American Zionist Emergency Council (the new name of the Emergency Committee for Zionist Affairs). Shulman was worried about one of Bergson's upcoming ads. Headlined "Ballad of the Doomed Jews of Europe," it featured a poem by Ben Hecht that blasted international indifference toward the mass murder, and included the line, "By Christmas you can make / Your Peace on Earth without the Jews." That was a reference to a news report, in late 1942, that Nazi propaganda minister Joseph Goebbels had predicted the slaughter of European Jewry would be complete by Christmas. The ad was originally slated for publication in the *New York Times* prior to Christmas, but delayed because of wartime paper shortages. In the interim, someone at the *Times* had alerted Shulman. He asked Bergson to meet him and AJ committee president Joseph Proskauer at Proskauer's apartment. Curious that Jewish leaders who had previously ignored him suddenly wanted to speak with him, Bergson accepted the invitation. Shulman and Proskauer implored Bergson to cancel the ad, on the grounds that its "anti-Christian" tone "could well bring on Jewish pogroms in the USA." Bergson agreed to withhold the ad in exchange for assurances by Shulman and Proskauer that the mainstream Jewish organizations would pay greater attention to the rescue issue. Nine months later, rescue was still not the top priority of the established organizations, so Bergson went ahead and placed the ad in the *Times*. No pogroms ensued.[58]

In a dramatic rejoinder to the Bermuda conference, the Bergsonites sponsored a five-day Emergency Conference to Save the Jewish People of Europe in New York City in July 1943. "They brought to this conference great American statesmen and writers—many of the most important men in America," Leib Jaffe reported to his colleagues in Palestine. The speakers included members of Congress, New York City mayor Fiorello La Guardia, and prominent Christians such as the Right Rev.

Henry St. George Tucker, president of the Federal Council of Churches. Former president Herbert Hoover spoke by telephone to the closing session, and sympathetic messages were sent by Treasury Secretary Morgenthau, 1940 Republican presidential candidate Wendell Willkie, and other notables.[59]

Jaffe also noted the "excellent reception" Bergson's conference was accorded in the press: "The *New York Times* reported on it for five days. I do not know of any other Zionist demonstration that had such wide publicity." The Bergsonites had succeeded in "bringing the Jewish question to the conscience of the American people. They were not afraid of becoming a nuisance to some senators." Jaffe cited a columnist in the Yiddish press who had observed: "This action is a revolt of young energetic men against the inactivity of the old men who cannot get out of their routine. . . . [Moreover], the same idea was expressed by other writers in other Jewish papers which are far from the [Jabotinsky camp]."[60]

Unlike other Jewish conferences, which typically were one-time events, Bergson's conference concluded by transforming itself into the Emergency Committee to Save the Jewish People of Europe. "This group of young men is continuing its work," Jaffe reported. "They have sent [Congressman Will] Rogers to London. They intend to send a representative to Palestine and South Africa. A few days ago they sent a delegation to Secretary of State Hull. Mrs. Roosevelt mentioned in an article of hers a talk she had with a representative of this group. Among the sponsors of the Emergency Committee are some of the greatest writers in the United States, leaders of American public opinion, and American political leaders of both parties." The escalating clamor for rescue that Jaffe observed was given an additional boost in August, when the *New Republic* published a twenty-page supplement titled "The Jews of Europe: How to Help Them." "It is not yet too late," the editors wrote, "to retrieve ourselves and to prevent our being recorded in history as the tacit accomplices of this most terrible of all crimes." A columnist for the Yiddish-language *Morgen Zhurnal* said the supplement "should be in the hands of every Jew and should also be spread through the Christian world." Jewish organizations and others purchased more than forty thousand copies within the first week of its publication.[61]

Another source of pressure on Rabbi Wise came from one of his own closest colleagues. Henry Montor first worked alongside Wise in the 1920s as assistant editor of the ZOA's journal *New Palestine*. Subsequently he served as executive director of the United Palestine Appeal (UPA), then as executive chairman of the United Jewish Appeal, two groups in which Wise was a leading figure. In the late 1930s, Wise and his colleagues became concerned that the Jewish Telegraphic Agency, which was subsidized by the American Jewish Committee, was leaning toward the AJC's line on Zionist issues. (Rabbi Wise privately derided the agency's editor in chief as "the little swine.") As a counterweight, they established the Independent Jewish Press Service (IJPS), with Montor as its editorial writer.

At first Montor's writings reflected his sponsors' perspectives. But in the face of the news from Europe and the slow response of the established organizations, Montor's editorials took on a more forceful tone. A March 12, 1943, column, for example, charged that for the previous ten years, "our dear leaders . . . have been trooping up to the State Department with bated breath and hat in hand—and getting the run-around." He continued:

> Why didn't you report back to us, the Jewish people of America, so that we could try to do something about it before it was too late? What could we have done? We could have done what other Americans do when their kinsmen are threatened with danger and death. We could have brought pressure to bear on Congress, on the President, on the State Department—mass pressure, not just the backstairs "diplomacy" of your hush policy. It is too easy for a government official to say No when he knows it isn't going any further. . . . We could have organized a mass movement to back you up. Instead of doing that, you hushed-up your failure.

Montor also occasionally represented the UPA at meetings of the Joint Emergency Committee, where he spoke up in favor of a more activist approach. At the April 10 meeting, he argued that Jewish organizations should not be satisfied with having only "private and unofficial talks" with government representatives. At the April 18 session, he proposed mobilizing Jews from around the country to gather on Capitol Hill for an all-day lobbying blitz for rescue action. That summer, Montor's IJPS editorials praised Bergson's Emergency Conference for "directing attention with force and conviction to the plight of millions of Jews," and scoffed that the dissidents lacked "a certificate of kashrut from some self-anointed Jewish Sanhedrin." The spectacle of his own longtime associate aiming such barbs at the Jewish leadership was more than a little discomfiting for Rabbi Wise.[62]

Putting Rescue on the Agenda

Another reason Rabbi Wise was not fully devoted to the plight of European Jewry in December 1942 and January 1943 was that he was engaged in a behind-the-scenes scheme to expand his power base in the Jewish community. These developments had their roots in a May 1942 meeting of Zionist groups in New York's Biltmore Hotel, at which for the first time they explicitly and unanimously endorsed the goal of "Palestine as a Jewish Commonwealth," by which they meant a sovereign Jewish state. Palestine Labor Zionist leader David Ben-Gurion, who was visiting the United States, then initiated talks with AJcommittee president Maurice Wertheim in hopes of winning the AJcommittee's affirmation of the Biltmore declaration. The talks, held at Wertheim's home in Cos Cob, Connecticut, concluded in early June with tentative agreement on a statement embracing the 1917 Balfour Declaration—which would have been a first for the AJcommittee—in exchange for dissolving the World Jewish Congress. The WJcongress had always been a sore spot for AJcommittee leaders, because its raison d'être was the notion that Jews in the Diaspora constituted a separate national grouping with loyalties to world Jewry—a concept the AJ committee feared contributed to antisemitism. The essential flaw in the Cos Cob agreement was that neither of the negotiators had his compatriots fully on board. Rabbi Wise adamantly rejected the idea of shutting down the WJ congress, which, after all, had been his brainchild. On the other side, some of Wertheim's colleagues accused him of making too many concessions to the Zionists. As the two sides jockeyed back-and-forth, an exhausted Wertheim resigned as president of the AJ committee and was succeeded by the anti-Zionist Joseph Proskauer.

At about the same time, a faction of dissident anti-Zionist Reform rabbis, alarmed over the spread of Zionist sentiment within the Reform rabbinate, established a new organization, the American Council for Judaism, to lobby against Zionism both within the Jewish community and in contacts with the Roosevelt administration. The council was small in numbers but, much to Wise's chagrin, it received substantial attention in the *New York Times* because the *Times*'s owner and publisher, Arthur Hays Sulzberger, shared the new group's hostility to Zionism.

Proskauer's rise and the creation of the American Council unnerved Rabbi Wise. In the immediate aftermath of the Biltmore conference, in May, Wise had basked in the glow of the newly created impression that Zionism—under his leadership, as head of the U.S. Zionist movement—enjoyed the support of an overwhelming majority in the Jewish community. But by the autumn—at the very time Wise was awaiting confirmation of the Riegner telegram—the Jewish community once again appeared to be deeply divided over Zionism. The gains of the spring seemed to be slipping away. Hence Wise turned a significant portion of his attention to a new plan for demonstrating the primacy of Zionism among American Jews, and thereby shoring up his own position as the community's preeminent leader.

On December 2, 1942—just one week after his press conference confirming the ongoing annihilation of Europe's Jews—Rabbi Wise, together with his ZOA colleague Louis Lipsky and

Nahum Goldmann, met in New York City with Henry Monsky, president of B'nai B'rith. Monsky was personally pro-Zionist and had been trying to steer the officially non-Zionist B'nai B'rith in that direction. In letters to his close colleague Eliezer Kaplan at the Jewish Agency in Jerusalem, Goldmann explained what happened next. Wise asked Monsky to take the lead in convening an "American Jewish Assembly," ostensibly "to work out [postwar] peace demands both for Palestine and the Diaspora" together with B'nai B'rith, the AJ congress, and the Wise-controlled Zionist organizations. Wise could have initiated and headed up the assembly project himself; the very fact that he enlisted Monsky as his stalking horse further indicates he was hiding his role, because otherwise the proposal would have been perceived as blatantly self-serving. "Our main purpose was to have Monsky, a so-called neutral [on Zionism] to call the Conference and to have it without the American Jewish Committee and the [Jewish] Labor Committee" (the JLC was also anti-Zionist), Goldmann wrote. "It was for that reason that we fixed the date [January 24] one week before the annual meeting of the American Jewish Committee, January 31." Monsky was "ready to go along with us," Wise and his cohorts found, because he "always resented" the fact that he had not been included in the Cos Cob discussions. Fragile egos sometimes played an outsized role in intra-Jewish machinations.[63]

As Wise hoped and anticipated, the date made it impossible for AJ committee officials to participate. Monsky's gathering, in Pittsburgh, was attended by representatives of thirty-two organizations, but the AJ committee was not among them. "It was the mistake of [the AJ committee leaders'] life not to have participated," Goldmann gloated afterward, "because with them absent, we took over the real leadership. Had they been there, they would have organized a non-Zionist bloc and even the B'nai B'rith would not have gone along with us 100%, as they did." Some elements within the AJ congress and the Emergency Council for Zionist Affairs, not being privy to Wise's strategy of using Monsky as a stalking horse, complained to

Wise about "the idea of drawing Monsky into the picture and letting him play a leading role," but when the Pittsburgh session concluded, "even the most violent critics admitted they were wrong," Goldmann reported. AJCommittee leaders were not naive about Wise's strategy. Monsky was a "stooge" of Wise and deserved to be known as "Henry Monkey," Morris Waldman groused to Proskauer. "Like a squeezed orange," he will be "thrown into the garbage pail" after Wise was finished exploiting him, Waldman predicted.[64]

The participants resolved to hold, later in the year, "an American Jewish Assembly, organized on democratic lines," focusing on "post-war problems" and "the implementation of the rights of the Jewish people with respect to Palestine." Wise and Goldmann considered the adopted wording a victory, because "it mean[t] that the question of Jewish rights to Palestine, as such, cannot be discussed, but only their implementation is a matter for discussion and action." The Pittsburgh participants also chose the members of the Assembly's Executive Committee, and "the majority of its members are Zionist and American Jewish Congress people," Goldmann informed Kaplan. "If all goes well," Goldmann concluded, "in May or June we will have an Assembly of 500 delegates which, I think, will adopt our Zionist demands and which will really represent the overwhelming majority of American Jewry."[65]

Despite the torrent of news from Europe in the weeks preceding the Pittsburgh meeting—the confirmation of the first Riegner telegram, the numerous press reports of deportations and massacres, the Riegner-Lichtheim telegram—the topic of the mass murder was absent from the assembly's agenda. One delegate, Dr. Isaac Lewin of the Orthodox group Agudath Israel, did urge inclusion of rescue in the agenda, but Monsky rebuffed him, saying the gathering "was called for a different purpose." As preparations proceeded in the months to follow, rescue remained off the agenda, despite such developments as the controversy over the Bermuda conference. When in June the AJCongress announced its ten-point program for the gathering, the list included compensation for Jewish victims of the Nazis, postwar punishment of war criminals, and the right of European Jews to return to their homes, but not rescue. Rabbi Wise's own pre-conference "Forecast," published in his journal *Opinion*, likewise made no mention of rescue.[66]

On June 7 the executive committee chose Monsky, Wise, and Proskauer as the three co-chairs of the forthcoming assembly. That arrangement suited Wise just fine; the AJ committee president was clearly outnumbered. Wise also had earlier acceded to Proskauer's one demand: to change the name from American Jewish Assembly to American Jewish Conference. Proskauer feared that the term "assembly" would enable antisemites to accuse Jews of creating a state-within-a-state.[67]

Wise's expectation of Zionist domination was confirmed when elections took place at the end of June. In thirty-eight communities around the country, local Jewish organizations held meetings at which anyone who was Jewish and twenty-one or older could cast a ballot for "electors" (some of whom ran unopposed). The electors, in turn, chose the delegates to the AJ conference. Zionist groups (including the AJ congress) won 337 of the 501 delegates to the conference. The AJ committee declined to participate on the grounds that it was not a mass membership organization and thus could not meaningfully compete in local elections. By rule, it was awarded three delegates.[68]

The absence of the rescue issue from the pre-conference agenda sparked criticism from some of the participating organizations in the months preceding the gathering. Two Orthodox groups, Agudath Israel and the Union of Orthodox Rabbis, as well as the Jewish Labor Committee and the Synagogue Council of America, repeatedly pressed for inclusion of rescue on the agenda, to no avail.[69]

The criticism soon spilled over into the Jewish press. "Is the Conference to take no measures to save from extermination now what is left of European Jewry?" a columnist for the *National Jewish Ledger* wondered. "If so, of what value will your consideration of postwar Jewish problems in Continental Europe be if there will be hardly any Jews left on the Continent?" An essay in the AJCongress's own *Congress Weekly* acknowledged that "Jews, ordinary Jews with sound national instincts," had responded with "distrust and even fear" when they heard of the conference plans, asking, "Is this the solution for a people that stands on the brink of annihilation? An August 6 message from Undersecretary Welles to Rabbi Wise reporting that "the number of [Jewish] victims [of the Nazis] has reached about 4,000,000" undoubtedly added to the pressure on Wise not to exclude rescue from the conference.[70]

Finally, shortly before the August 29 opening, the conference organizers gave in and added a Committee on Rescue to their roster of committees. The organizers did not offer any explanation of this policy change. American Jewish Joint Distribution Committee chairman Paul Baerwald, who was involved in the planning discussions, later described the decision to add rescue as the result of "a very insistent demand on the part of the delegates." The Independent Jewish Press Service speculated that the Bergson Group's Emergency Conference the previous month had "embarrassed" the AJConference organizers into embracing rescue.[71]

A Third World War

Unbeknownst to the Jewish public, a different controversy threatened to upend the American Jewish Conference. This one related to Allied policy on Palestine.

In late 1942 President Roosevelt dispatched a personal envoy, Lt. Col. Harold Hoskins, to the Middle East to assess Arab public opinion. Hoskins returned with some unabashedly anti-Zionist advice for the president: "If the issues of a Jewish political state and of a Jewish army continue to be pressed at this time," the Arabs will instigate "a very bloody conflict" and drag the Allies into it, he warned. This would plant "the seeds of a possible third World War." Based on Hoskins's report, the State Department proposed issuing an Anglo-American declaration that until the war ended, no decision on Palestine would be made "without full consultation with both Arabs and Jews." In practical terms, that meant Palestine's doors would continue to be almost entirely shut to Jewish refugees fleeing Hitler. The declaration would also assert that all "public discussions and activities of a political nature relating to Palestine" should "cease." The administration had no legal means of enforcing such a speech ban, but the practical impact of such an announcement would be to tar all public expressions of Zionism as undermining the war effort. President Roosevelt jotted "OK—FDR" on the first draft of the proposal on May 7, 1943, and returned it to the State Department.[72]

Even before the statement was issued, its thrust colored Roosevelt's thinking on Palestine. While Jewish leaders were hoping the president would press the British to open the Holy Land to Jews fleeing the Nazis, FDR was in effect assuring King Ibn Saud of Saudi Arabia that he would do no such thing. In a letter to the president at the end of April, the Saudi leader accused the Jews of trying to "exterminate" the Arabs of Palestine and pleaded with the Allies to stop all Jewish immigration and land purchases. In his response, President Roosevelt assured Ibn Saud that "it is the view of the Government of the United States that . . . no decision altering the basic situation of Palestine should be reached without full consultation with both Arabs and Jews."[73]

The declaration itself took some time to wind its way through the requisite stages of approval. Finally, on July 14, the British cabinet assented, and on July 19 FDR approved the final draft. The two governments initially intended to simultaneously release the statement on the afternoon of July 27, but as word of the plan began to leak and Jewish opposition emerged, the release stalled. Rabbi Wise, hearing a rumor "that our State Department or the Foreign Office was to issue a statement enjoining silence with respect to Jewish claims in Palestine," hurried to Washington on July 22 to seek reassurance from the president himself. It was "a most satisfactory talk with the Chief," Wise reported afterward to Chaim Weizmann. The president "seemed completely in the dark with respect to such statement"—a curious posture for Roosevelt to adopt, considering that he had already approved the statement and it was scheduled to be published imminently. Within days Wise was privately expressing suspicion that there might be more to the story than the president was letting on. Wise confided to Goldmann on July 27 that in a telegram, Sumner Welles had reported he "had taken up the matter at once with Secretary Hull by telephone, and . . . Hull promised him to speak to the President." While "I cannot imagine the Chief will do this," Wise wrote, "I must tell you, to my great regret, that nothing in the telegram of Welles indicated surprise on his part."[74]

Nahum Goldmann, meanwhile, rushed to the British embassy to ask information officer Isaiah Berlin "if anything could be done to stop the declaration." Berlin's Jewish background seems to have led Goldmann to overestimate his sympathy for Zionism. Berlin, hoping to stifle any Jewish opposition, warned Goldmann that "the President had made up his mind" and therefore "agitation would not help" but rather would "only serve to irritate the President." Berlin well knew that invoking the specter of annoying the president was a tried and true way of intimidating American Jewish leaders. While Goldmann said nothing publicly, his agitated private conversations with Jewish officials in the administration, including Secretary Morgenthau, Justice Frankfurter, Ben Cohen, and David Niles, stirred up enough chatter in Washington corridors to alarm Secretary Hull, who decided an endorsement from the War Department would help overcome the critics. Hull therefore postponed the release date from July 27 to August 3, so that Secretary of War Henry Stimson could weigh in upon returning from vacation. Berlin suspected the State Department "got cold feet" because of the intense criticism it had recently faced over the administration's deal with the Vichyite Darlan in North Africa. "The Darlan flurry has had its effect here in the sense that the State Department are [sic] determined not to go through such a nightmare again," Berlin informed London.[75]

While Hull awaited Stimson's response, opposition began brewing from a surprising source. Several of the president's top Jewish aides, who seldom broached Jewish issues with FDR, now decided to raise objections. Treasury Secretary Morgenthau regarded the proposed statement as an attempt "to deprive U.S. citizens of their constitutional liberties." Several others, including senior adviser and speechwriter Samuel Rosenman, feared Zionists would ignore the declaration and continue their activities, thereby stirring up antisemitism by making Jews appear unpatriotic. Isaiah Berlin reported to London that anti-Zionists such as Rosenman feared "the Zionists would inevitably issue a shriek, a public controversy involving Senators, etc., would follow, which would ultimately give the Jews, whether Zionists or not, dangerous publicity as playing politics in a time of crisis." Thus this strange sequence of events found anti-Zionist Jews trying to block adoption of an anti-Zionist policy, for fear it would backfire and provoke antisemitism.[76]

Evidently recognizing that the statement was running into trouble, the president decided to leverage Jewish concerns about the declaration as a way to pressure Zionist critics of the administration to quiet down. Discussing Palestine with Rosenman on July 31, FDR complained bitterly about recent newspaper ads sponsored by the Bergson Group and the U.S. Revisionist Zionists criticizing Allied policy on rescue and Palestine. According to Berlin's account of what Rosenman told him, the president instructed Rosenman to stifle "Zionist clamours" by going "to New York to persuade Wise to stop Jewish Army advertisements, etc. in return for suppression of the [Anglo-American] statement." During a lengthy late-night meeting on August 3, Rosenman told Wise that (contrary to what the president told Wise) an Allied declaration on Palestine was indeed forthcoming. However, Rosenman insisted, it was the Jews' own fault, instigated by two recent Jewish provocations. One was a statement in the *New York Times* by the Jewish Agency's Moshe Shertok that Jews in Palestine might undertake "deeds of despair if driven to extremes of exasperation by a [British] decision to persevere in what is to them a cruelly unjust policy." The second was the "hideous advertisement" in the *Times* about which the president had complained. In fact, the Anglo-American statement had been in the works prior to both Shertok's remark and the offensive newspaper ad, but Wise had no way of knowing that.[77]

Rosenman proposed convening a meeting in Washington, under the auspices of State and War Department officials, to which Wise and other Jewish leaders would be invited, together with Bergson Group representatives. The goal would be to pressure the Bergsonites to stop criticizing the Allies on rescue and Palestine. Wise immediately objected. "It would be very bad to have any such honor done to the Jewish Army people," he told Rosenman. Wise promised to seek other ways to "deal with" Bergson. Rosenman intimated it might be possible to head off the Anglo-American statement if Wise and his colleagues postponed the August 29 American Jewish Conference—or, at the very least, restrained the conference from issuing a strong declaration on Palestine.[78]

On August 5, unbeknownst to Wise, Secretary Stimson told Hull that reports of a potential Arab uprising were "alarmist" and there was no need for the Anglo-American statement. Hull cabled British foreign minister Anthony Eden that in view of the War Department's position, "no basis exists, so far as the United States is concerned, for issuing the statement." The British, however, were not yet ready to concede.[79]

In the meantime, news of the proposed statement leaked to the news media, which significantly escalated the controversy. Syndicated columnist Drew Pearson revealed the gist of the State Department's plan "to stifle discussion of the Palestine issue" in his August 8 "Washington-Merry-Go-Round" column. That provoked strong public criticism of the administration from Congressman Emanuel Celler, who charged that the ban "will, with its 'Silence please,' drown the clamor of the tortured Nazi victims pleading for a haven of refuge." Celler also publicly asserted that he had heard from "thoroughly reliable sources" that "the joint statement will be issued with the knowledge and consent of the President." On August 21 British Foreign Minister Eden wrote to Hull in hopes of persuading the administration that "some sedative joint statement is as urgent as ever," given alleged large-scale thefts of weapons by Jews in Palestine and the likelihood of Zionist agitation at the forthcoming American Jewish Conference. From President Roosevelt's perspective, however, the disadvantages of proceeding with the declaration by now outweighed its advantages. At a meeting with Churchill in Quebec the next day, the Allied leaders decided to hold the plan "in abeyance." It was never revived.[80]

Nobody bothered to tell Rabbi Wise, however. He proceeded to prepare for the American Jewish Conference under the false presumption that the joint statement was still hanging over his head like a Sword of Damocles. Rosenman likely calculated that by keeping Wise in the dark about the demise of the declaration, the rabbi might continue his efforts to stifle the Zionist tone of the conference (or, as the State Department's Wallace Murray instructed Goldmann, to ensure that the attendees "behaved with tact"). Just days before the conference, Wise sent Rosenman a heartfelt plea to understand that the delegates would "be thrown into a nasty uproar" if the declaration were to be issued before or during the gathering. It would harm Palestine Jewry "by seeming to approve the White Paper," Wise warned. Moreover, it would provoke "an angry response from genuine liberals all over the country," and it would cause "moral hurt" to Jews in Allied countries because of "its terrible implication that we have put second things first, our own Palestine interests above the triumph of the [Allies]." Wise must have felt he had good reason to fear the statement was imminent, because he then resorted to an argument that he would have done almost anything to avoid invoking: a threat that American Jews would turn against Roosevelt. The president "has come to have a very, very special place in the heart of Jews," he wrote. "They rightly look up to him, revere him and love him." But "this feeling of Jewish homage . . . might change" if the statement were issued.

Although Wise himself promised to "say what I believe is just with respect to the President" in his keynote address, "regrettably, unwise things may be said in the course of the Conference by those who do not understand the immensity of the difficulties and the pressures under which the President rests." Still, Rosenman refused to tell Wise where matters stood regarding the declaration. That set the stage for an epic clash within the American Zionist leadership.[81]

The roots of the conflict reached back to late 1942, when World Zionist Organization president Chaim Weizmann, alarmed by the lethargic state of American Zionism, proposed to Wise that he share his leadership of the Emergency Committee for Zionist Affairs with Rabbi Dr. Abba Hillel Silver, a dynamic forty-nine-year-old orator and activist from Cleveland, who possessed, as Wise had put it a few years earlier, a "very great power of public utterance." At first Wise welcomed the proposal, writing to Weizmann in February 1943 that he would be "glad" if Silver "were to take over the too onerous duties of the chairmanship of the Emergency Committee. . . . The work should come into the hands of a younger and stronger man— and he is the man." But almost as soon as the two men began working together, they found themselves at odds. Wise was not, in fact, ready to hand over the reins of power to another man. Furthermore, the conflict between the two would be greatly exacerbated by the fact that Silver felt no personal or political loyalty to President Roosevelt and advocated challenging the administration on Jewish policy matters when necessary.[82]

At the American Jewish Conference, in August 1943, Wise and Goldmann both delivered major addresses, yet neither even mentioned Jewish statehood, in deference to the president. Infuriated, a number of activist-minded delegates, including some from Wise's own AJCongress, decided to give their time slot to Rabbi Silver. He delivered an electrifying appeal for Jewish statehood that "swept the conference like a hurricane," as one delegate put it. "There was repeated and stormy applause, the delegates rising to their feet in a remarkable ovation." The assembly burst into a rousing version of the Zionist song *Hatikva* (which would later become Israel's national anthem). As much as Wise had wanted to accede to the administration's pressure, now there was no way to prevent a Palestine homeland resolution from being introduced at the conference. "[W]e would be torn limb from limb if we were now to defer action on the Palestine resolution," Goldmann told the AJ committee delegation. The resolution calling for the establishment of a Jewish commonwealth in Palestine passed by 498 to 4. In effect, Silver had pulled the rug out from under Wise. The AJ committee delegates left the hall and, shortly afterward, formally withdrew from the American Jewish Conference.[83]

The plan Rabbi Wise had so carefully hatched at the December 1942 meeting with B'nai B'rith's Henry Monsky had come completely undone. Wise had conceived the American Jewish Conference as a means to demonstrate American Jewry's support for Jewish statehood, under his leadership. Instead, intimidated by the demands from President Roosevelt and the State Department to keep quiet on the issue, Wise himself retreated from calling for statehood at the conference. Wise's silence created a vacuum that Silver filled with the dramatic address that arguably established the Cleveland rabbi as American Jewry's most dynamic leader.[84]

Still, elevating Silver was not exactly the same as demoting Wise. While some AJ congress delegates had been sufficiently dissatisfied by Wise's address that they arranged for Silver to speak, that did not constitute a repudiation of Wise. In fact, on the final day of the conference, the delegates voted to transform the conference into a full-fledged organization and named Wise as its president. The AJ conference actually had no specific role to play in organized Jewish life; it would disband in less than four years. In the meantime, however, Wise was able to use the AJ conference's Commission on Rescue to address the ongoing problem he was having with dissidents inside the Joint Emergency Committee.

The increasingly militant mood within the JEC had reached a crescendo on August 10, 1943, at the JEC's final meeting prior to the AJ Conference. The delegates "devoted considerable time to a discussion of more forceful action which might be taken," the minutes reported. Meyer Weisgal, the Jewish Agency representative and right-hand man to Chaim Weizmann, proposed "a demonstration in the streets of New York." David Wertheim of the Labor Zionists called for a "march on Washington by leaders of various Jewish communities" to dramatize the demand for rescue. The boldest proposal came from an unexpected source. Lillie Shultz, representing the AJ Congress, suggested using Jewish voters as a weapon of political pressure against the Roosevelt administration. "The time has come . . . to be critical of [the president's] lack of action [on rescue]," she said, "and in view of the fact that this is the eve of a presidential election year, ways can be found to indicate to the administration, and possibly through the political parties that the large and influential Jewish communit[y] will find a way of registering its dissatisfaction over the failure of the administration to take any effective steps to save the Jews of Europe."[85]

This would have represented a dramatic departure from Jewish voting trends, because an estimated 85–90 percent of Jewish voters had supported President Roosevelt's reelection in 1936 and 1940. According to the minutes, Rabbi Wise did not respond to Shultz's suggestion, but as a passionate supporter of the president, Wise could not have been pleased by her recommendation. On numerous occasions, Wise had issued appeals to the Jewish community to "vote as Americans, not as Jews"— that is, to not permit ethnic considerations to determine which candidate they would support. To make matters worse—from Wise's perspective—another Jewish figure of prominence at the meeting, Judge Morris Rothenberg of the United Palestine Appeal, seconded Shultz's proposal. The so-called wild people in the JEC seemed to be gaining in number.[86]

This threat from the JEC dissidents prompted Wise to maneuver to tip the balance of power within the committee. In September 1943 Wise proposed that his close ally, Hadassah, the Women's Zionist Organization, be permitted to join the JEC. The other members could not reasonably object, because Hadassah, with more than ninety-five thousand members, was the largest Jewish organization in the United States. Officially, Hadassah was the women's division of the ZOA and Wise enjoyed close relations with its leaders. Bringing Hadassah on board gave Wise a majority of like-minded colleagues within the JEC. And once the numbers were in his favor, Wise began arguing that the establishment of the American Jewish Conference's Commission on Rescue had rendered the JEC obsolete. In early November, at Wise's initiative, the JEC voted, five to four, to dissolve itself and turn over its functions to the AJ conference.[87]

"Who Appointed You?"

Rabbi Wise had first made his name in the Jewish community as a principled dissenter: championing social justice issues when most pulpit rabbis shied away from controversy, advocating for Zionism in a Reform rabbinate dominated by anti-Zionists, creating the AJ congress as a democratic, grassroots alternative to the entrenched oligarchs of the World War I–era Jewish leadership. Yet once he reached the pinnacle of power and influence, Wise was often less than tolerant toward those who dissented from his positions. Peter Bergson recalled a particularly telling example of Wise's efforts, in 1943, to stifle his criticism of Allied policy toward European Jewry. In a conversation with Bergson, Wise not only accused the Bergson Group of "endangering American Jewry," he contested Bergson's very right to act as a public spokesman for Jewish causes. "*Mi samcha?*" ("Who appointed you?" Exodus 2:14), Wise challenged him, referring to the biblical account of two quarreling Jewish slaves in Egypt who challenged Moses's right to intervene in their dispute. Wise's remark sheds light on his stern responses to other dissenters, such as his rabbinical student Saadia Gelb, the Palestine emissaries Leib Jaffe and Rabbi Meyer Berlin, the Jewish Theological Seminary students, and the activist voices within the Joint Emergency Committee. Though his personal loyalty to Roosevelt and his fear of provoking antisemitism in America shaped

Wise's resentment of the dissidents, the *"Mi samcha?"* outburst indicates that his resentment was also provoked by their refusal to submit to his authority as the preeminent American Jewish leader of the era. It seems as if he could not conceive the possibility that outsiders, lacking the experience and knowledge he had acquired through decades of Jewish leadership, might be able to offer better ideas than his on the major issues of the day.[88]

In Wise's view, the very fact that the Bergson Group acted independently, outside the bounds of the organized Jewish community, signaled its illegitimacy. One broadside from Wise's American Zionist Emergency Council claimed that "no member of [Bergson's leadership] has acquired any standing either in the Jewish or the general community. They came to this country unknown and have remained unaccepted and unacceptable." Another AZEC statement emphasized that "none of [Bergson's] committees have had any official relationship, direct or indirect, with any responsible body in American Jewish life." From the AZEC's perspective, the Bergson Group could not possibly play a legitimate role in the Jewish world, because the Jewish Agency alone was "the recognized spokesman of the Jewish people in all matters concerning the future of Palestine, and is so regarded by Jews, non-Jews, and the governments with which it deals." Moreover, the Bergsonites' very independence suggested they might harbor "usurpatory aspirations," as one AZEC denunciation of Bergson asserted.[89]

Wise's difficulty in dealing with dissidents in the community was exacerbated by his marked tendency to overreact to any indication that those with whom he disagreed did not appreciate his importance, the power of his name, or the extent of his efforts on behalf of the community. "Although Silver could hardly bring himself to believe it, there are still people in and outside of the Zionist movement who, curiously enough, imagine that my name means something in American life," he wrote Goldmann in 1943, as his quarrel with Silver gathered steam. To a correspondent in 1945 who inquired about Wise's opposition to the Bergson Group, the rabbi replied: "After fifty years, that is to say, a long life of service to my people in every sense, I do not feel called upon to defend my reasons for having nothing whatever to do with a little group of irresponsible and unrepresentative people who set themselves up as saviours of Jewish life." Treasury Secretary Morgenthau once described to his staff what happened when he had innocently asked, "Doctor Wise, whom do you represent?": "Whew! The roof went off. 'Whom do I represent,' pounding his chest . . . Boom! 'You should ask me that question! I have told the President; the President has told me'—and, Oh, boy!"[90]

In general those dissidents who were the most independent of Wise typically accomplished the most. The criticisms that were voiced within the confines of the Jewish Institute of Religion's classrooms or in private Jewish leadership meetings do not appear to have influenced Wise or his colleagues. But when Rabbi Meyer Berlin went on his own to meet government officials in Washington, when Henry Montor wrote editorials for the Independent Jewish Press Service, and when the rabbinical students confronted the Synagogue Council of America leaders, they circumvented Wise's domain of authority and reached audiences beyond his control. The contrast between Wise's dismissive response to the students, and the Synagogue Council's quick adoption of the students' proposals, is striking. The results—the nationwide educational activities to raise awareness of the Holocaust and the interfaith protest rallies urging U.S. intervention—speak for themselves.

The Bergson activists gained some political advantage by remaining outside the established American Jewish organizational world. When challenged, "*Mi samcha?*"—"Who appointed you?"—Bergson could reply that, indeed, no one had appointed him, and therefore he was beholden to no one. Because he was not elected, he was not accountable to a voting constituency. And because he was not tied to any particular political leader or party, he felt comfortable seeking allies among congress members with whom he may have disagreed on other issues, and succeeded in building relationships on both sides of the aisle. Furthermore, because he was not an American citizen and had no intention of remaining in the United States in the long term, Bergson pursued his single-minded campaign for rescue unburdened by fears that some non-Jews might look askance at loud Jewish protests. Bergson's concern was for European Jewry, not American Jewry. In short, Bergson's decision to forge ahead without "authority" may have infuriated Rabbi Wise, but it was precisely such independence of thought and action that ultimately enabled Bergson to have a direct impact on the American government's response to the Holocaust (see chapter 5). Wise, by contrast, was set in his ways, encumbered by political loyalties, and hamstrung by the dilemma of how to craft American Jewish responses to the Holocaust that would not negatively impact non-Jews' perceptions of Jews—or at least what Wise believed those perceptions to be.

5

The Politics of Rescue

"CLEAR THE WAY FOR those rabbis!"

Surely it was the first time the stationmaster at Washington DC's Union Station ever shouted those words. The crowd before him was unlike any previously seen in the central train station of the nation's capital. The date was October 6, 1943, three days before Yom Kippur, and more than four hundred rabbis had arrived to plead for the establishment of a U.S. government agency to rescue Jews from the Nazis.[1]

This was a novel tactic for American Jews. There never had been a Jewish march on Washington. Other interest groups had staged marches or protest rallies in front of the White House or elsewhere in the capital, but U.S. Jewish organizations had never felt sufficiently secure of their place in American society, or sufficiently convinced that it was politically necessary, to do so. For Stephen Wise and other mainstream Jewish leaders, the spectacle of Jews marching through the streets of the nation's capital, during wartime, to promote specifically Jewish requests such as rescue, was anathema.

Not so for these rabbis. Their distinct garb, use of Yiddish, and strict adherence to traditional Judaism's calendar and religious rituals set them apart from most of their fellow Americans. Precisely because they were not interested in becoming fully acculturated Americans, they were not as worried as other American Jews about how non-Jews might react to their march through the streets of Washington.[2]

By taking to the streets and seeking to directly confront the president, the rabbis were in effect repudiating Rabbi Wise's approach. After years of urging American Jews to trust President Roosevelt and his administration to do whatever was possible to aid Europe's Jews, Wise had little to show for it: U.S. officials continued to insist that nothing could be done to save the Jews except to win the war. The Bergson Group leaders, who conceived of the rabbinical march, rejected that claim. They believed that if there was sufficient will to rescue Jews, ways could be found—and if rescue was left in State Department hands, no meaningful action would ever be taken.[3]

The Bergson Group's pessimistic assessment of the administration's intentions and attitudes was later borne out by the revelation of internal State Department memoranda spelling out, in chilling detail, U.S. officials' hostility toward rescue. Cavendish Cannon of State's Division of European Affairs, for example, argued in November 1941 against rescuing Jews from Rumania because it was "likely to bring about new pressure for an asylum in the western hemisphere . . . a migration of the Rumanian Jews would therefore open the question of similar treatment for Jews in Hungary and, by extension, all countries where there has been intense persecution." Similarly, in October 1943, R. Borden Reams of State's Division of European Affairs wrote to his colleagues: "There was always the danger that the German government might agree to turn over to the United States and to Great Britain a large number of Jewish refugees. In the event of our admission of inability to take care of these people, the onus for their continued persecution would have been largely transferred from the German government to the Allied nations." In a 1943 meeting, British foreign minister Anthony Eden told President Roosevelt and Secretary of State Cordell Hull why he opposed Allied action to help the Jews of Bulgaria: "If we do that, then the Jews of the world will be wanting us to make similar offers in Poland and Germany." Neither Roosevelt nor Hull expressed any disagreement with Eden. Neither government wanted to deal with the burden of where to put large numbers of refugees. The Roosevelt administration had been working over the previous decade to keep Jewish refugee admission far below what the law allowed (see chapter 2). For its part, the Churchill administration was engaged in keeping Jewish refugee immigration to Palestine to a minimum by continuing to enforce the 1939 White Paper.[4]

Bergson no doubt would have been horrified to learn that senior State Department officials seized upon one of his own group's slogans in 1943 to craft a conspiracy theory according to which Hitler was plotting to release refugees to harm the Allied war effort. Soon after a Bergson Group newspaper ad calling for "Action—Not Pity" by the Allies to aid the Jews, Assistant Secretary of State Breckinridge Long drafted a fifteen-page essay arguing that the "action" phrase was actually part of a secret two-part Nazi strategy: Hitler would offer to release Jews in exchange for ransom payments ("which would furnish him with much needed foreign exchange"); and the Nazi leader would also demand "the feeding [by the Allies] of minority groups," which would breach the Allied blockade against sending food or other supplies into enemy territory.[5]

Long's colleagues Howard Bucknell (of State's Division of Current Information) and Robert Alexander (assistant chief of the Visa Division) strongly praised the draft. Bucknell wrote that "it would form the basis for a very useful article" in a major magazine such as *Collier's.* Alexander went a step further, claiming that after Hitler (allegedly) employed the phrase "action—not moralizing" in 1937, "Ben-Gurion, a Zionist leader in Palestine, took up the cry, transplanted it to England, where certain emotionalists and impractical dreamers adopted it and shipped it on to Rabbis Wise and Goldmann in New York. There it was made the keynote of a mass meeting in Madison Square Garden." (This was one of numerous instances in which State Department officials mixed up rival Jewish organizations. The "Action—Not Pity" slogan actually appeared in advertisements related to the Bergson Group's *We Will Never Die* pageant, not the earlier Madison Square Garden rally, with which Wise and Goldmann were associated.) According to Alexander, the reason Hitler promoted the "Action—Not Pity" concept was that in practice it meant "negotiate with Hitler—break the blockade—exchange refugees for internees—relax the immigration procedure of the United States—open the doors to Palestine regardless of the Arabs—and take the burden and the curse off Hitler!"[6]

Even without being privy to these behind-the-scenes machinations at State, Bergson recognized that the administration's record on rescue spoke for itself. Every appeal to U.S. government officials to intervene on behalf of Europe's Jews was met with stock statements about victory as the only means of rescue; every conference that was supposed to devise ways to aid the Jews concluded with little or no aid offered. Thus, Bergson and his colleagues conceived the rabbis' march as a way of advancing the rescue cause from several new angles. First, the dramatic appearance of hundreds of rabbis from around the country would show the president that the plight of Europe's Jews was a matter of urgency to the American Jewish community—which was, after all, an important part of his New Deal coalition and a significant voting bloc in the key electoral state of New York. Second, the Bergsonites hoped that the publicity surrounding the march would arouse the sympathy of the American public, thereby helping to put pressure on the administration to act. More immediately, by having the march begin with a gathering at the Capitol involving leading members of Congress, Bergson hoped to galvanize support for a congressional resolution that would encapsulate the rabbis' demand: the creation of a new government agency, independent of the State Department, to handle refugee matters.

The task of recruiting the rabbinical demonstrators was handled primarily by the Va'ad ha-Hatzala, a U.S. Orthodox group that provided financial aid to beleaguered Torah scholars in Europe and lobbied for visas to bring small numbers of them to America. The Va'ad's efforts were ordinarily undertaken behind the scenes; the march represented the first time the Va'ad was venturing into the realm of public protests.

The majority of the rabbis came from the New York City area, but others hailed from Philadelphia and Baltimore, and some traveled from as far away as Chicago, Cleveland, and Worcester, Massachusetts. Among the participants were leaders and rising leaders of the U.S. Orthodox community, such as Eliezer Silver and Israel Rosenberg, co-presidents of the Union of Orthodox Rabbis; Moshe Feinstein, who would later come to be regarded as the leading authority in America on matters of Jewish religious law; and Joseph Soloveitchik, soon to emerge as the spiritual leader of modern Orthodox Judaism in America. Some Jewish members of Congress, led by Rep. Sol Bloom, "had done all they could to dissuade the Rabbis from making their bearded appearances in Washington," an internal Bergson Group account reported. "At a certain moment they almost succeeded [in dissuading the rabbis], but Mr. Bloom spoiled the soup by telling one of the Rabbis, as an additional inducement for not going, that it would be very undignified for a group of such un-American looking people to appear in Washington. This created a lot of resentment and in the end instead of 250 Rabbis on whom we counted, we had to cope with 400."[7]

Accompanied by marshals supplied by the Jewish War Veterans of America, the rabbis marched solemnly from Union Station to the Capitol. There they were met by Vice President Wallace, who, *Time* reported, "squirmed through a diplomatically minimum answer" to the marchers' plea for rescue. Wallace expressed "grief" at the plight of Europe's Jews but made no mention of the possibility of rescuing any of them. In view of Bergson's strategy of using the march as a prelude to a congressional resolution, it was significant that prominent members of Congress came out to greet the marchers: Senate Majority Leader (and later vice president) Alben Barkley of

Kentucky, Senate Minority Leader (and unsuccessful Republican vice presidential candidate of 1940) Charles McNary of Oregon, and House Speaker Sam Rayburn (D-TX).[8]

Two of the rabbis read aloud the group's petition to the president, in Hebrew and English. "Children, infants, and elderly men and women are crying to us, 'Help!'," they proclaimed. "Millions have already fallen dead, sentenced to fire and sword, and tens of thousands have died of starvation. . . . And we, how can we stand up to pray on the holy day of Yom Kippur, knowing that we haven't fulfilled our responsibility? So we have come, brokenhearted, on the eve of our holiest day, to ask you, our honorable President Franklin Roosevelt . . . to form a special agency to rescue the remainder of the Jewish nation in Europe." Arthur Hertzberg, later a prominent Jewish scholar and World Jewish Congress leader, recalled: "I was a youngster of 22 who was allowed to be present because the leaders, men who were older than me by a generation or two, were friends and contemporaries of my father, Rabbi Zvi Elimelech Hertzberg. I saw their tears and heard their sobs. They were standing before God and praying for the life and safety of people who were their brothers—and who could have been themselves. I cried among them and I could not stop—not that day and nor for many days to come."[9]

From the Capitol, the protesters proceeded to the Lincoln Memorial, where they offered prayers for the welfare of the president, America's soldiers abroad, and the Jews in Hitler Europe, and then sang the national anthem. Then they marched to Lafayette Park, across the street from the White House, and waited there while a small delegation of their representatives approached the gates to present their petition. Although a White House aide had previously turned down their request for a meeting with the president, the rabbis still hoped they might yet be granted a few minutes with him.[10]

"These rabbis were not clean-shaven or well-dressed," Hertzberg would later write. "They were avowedly East European. They represented not 'American types' from the posh synagogues. On the contrary, they might just as well have been the rabbis whom Hitler was then putting in death-camps along with their congregants. They were standing at the gate of the White House begging the president to see them and to do something for the Jews who were being slaughtered by the tens of thousands. I could not get up to the fence of the White House so I had to look on from the park across the road. Eventually someone came out of the White House. He took a letter from the rabbis to the president, but the president himself never greeted them."[11]

White House secretary Marvin McIntyre informed the delegation that the president was unavailable to see them "because of the pressure of other business." Actually, the president's schedule was remarkably light that afternoon. His daily calendar listed nothing between a 1:00 pm lunch with Secretary of State Cordell Hull and his 4:00 pm departure to a ceremony at an airfield outside Washington. All signs point to FDR having made a political decision to refrain from doing so. Meeting the rabbis would have conferred legitimacy on their demands and focused fresh attention on the administration's resistance to pleas for rescue. Indeed, a full-page Bergson Group ad in that morning's *Washington Post* (and in the previous day's *New York Times*) charged that "nothing has been done by the Allied governments to stop the slaughter or to alleviate the torments of five million people. . . . 500 leaders of the Rabbinate . . . have come to Washington to impress upon our Government the tragic plight of the Jews of Europe."[12]

That morning at breakfast, the president was "disturbed" by the ad and "used language . . . which would have pleased Hitler himself," senior adviser and speechwriter Samuel Rosenman told Nahum Goldmann later that day. Apparently Goldmann also shared the anecdote with Meyer Weisgal, staff member of the American Zionist Emergency Council, who reported to a closed session of the council some weeks later that "in very high places utterances were made as a result of this advertisement, which the informant tells us, if he did not know who the person was that spoke, because of his irritation with regard to this particular ad, he would have thought that Hitler was speaking." The exact language used by FDR in that outburst is not known.[13]

Rosenman made it clear to the president that he, too, resented and opposed the rabbis. Presidential aide William D. Hassett noted in his diary that Rosenman "said the group behind this petition [is] not representative of the most thoughtful elements in Jewry. Judge Rosenman said he had tried—admittedly without success—to keep the horde from storming Washington. Said the leading Jews of his acquaintance opposed this march on the Capitol." It is not clear whether Rabbi Wise was one of those "leading Jews" with whom Rosenman discussed the matter prior to the march. Afterward, however, Wise publicly condemned "the orthodox rabbinical parade" as a "painful and even lamentable exhibition." He derided the organizers as "stuntists" and accused them of offending "the dignity of [the Jewish] people." That month's edition of the Jewish Labor Committee organ the *Call* bitterly reported that officials of the Allied governments had "advised us not to make too much fuss about the murder . . . not cry out; not to appeal for help, lest the impression be created that we are fighting the war to save Jews, and this might harm the war effort."[14]

While the rabbis stood across the street, waiting to see if their representatives would be admitted to the White House, President Roosevelt left through a rear exit, thereby eluding the protesters. If he thought he could avoid the controversy by avoiding the rabbis, the president was mistaken. A jarring headline in the next day's *Washington Times-Herald* announced: "Rabbis Report 'Cold Welcome' at the White House." A columnist for a leading Jewish newspaper angrily asked: "Would a similar delegation of 500 Catholic priests have been thus treated?" The editors of the Yiddish-language daily *Forverts* reported that the episode was affecting the president's level of support in the Jewish community: "In open comment it is voiced that Roosevelt has betrayed the Jews."[15]

This criticism in the Jewish community coincided with an intensifying outcry in the liberal press. A major exposé in the daily newspaper PM on October 3, by investigative reporter I. F. Stone, revealed that in 1940 the then-ambassador to the Soviet Union, Laurence Steinhardt, had objected to the granting of emergency visas to a small number of intellectuals and rabbis, on the grounds that the intellectuals were "political agitators" and the rabbis "have never had congregations outside of their own families." Although Stone's article pertained to events from three years earlier, it reinforced the public perception that some Roosevelt administration officials were deeply hostile to any refugees. A second major article by Stone in PM, on October 17, accused the State Department of "giving the run-around" to U.S. congressman Andrew Somers (D-NY), who had been trying for weeks to secure government-authorized transportation to lead a delegation to Turkey, in order to galvanize rescue efforts there. Six days later, another important liberal periodical, the New Leader, published a J'Accuse titled "The Shame of a World" by its literary editor, Melvin Lasky. He condemned the Allies' response to the Nazi genocide as "sympathetic mumbo-jumbo and do-nothingism." Millions of Jews were being murdered, and the most they could expect was "obituary notices" from "eloquent and self-righteous" Allied political leaders, who were motivated "partly out of fear and ignorance, out of weary everyday conservatism, and out of a disgraceful moral emptiness." Lasky concluded: "The continent has become a vast cemetery for a whole people. Relatives and friends will cry and mourn and remember, [but] for the rest, the terrible shame of a world will be forgotten."[16]

The Rescue Resolution

In the days preceding the march, Bergson Group supporter Fowler Harper, a law professor and solicitor general for the Interior Department, began drafting a congressional resolution calling for the creation of a U.S. government agency to rescue refugees. On October 1 Senator Elbert Thomas (D-UT), who intended to co-sponsor the resolution, sent an early draft of it to Assistant Secretary Long for his comment. It took Long four weeks to reply. On October 27 Long wrote back that the administration was already doing its best to help refugees, so the agency proposed in the resolution would be "unwarranted and liable to duplicate functions which are being carried out by the Department."[17]

In the meantime, Bergson had brought his case directly to Long. Their meeting took place at the State Department on October 15. Bergson was accompanied by Henry Pringle, who until recently had been chief of the publications division of the Office of War Information. It was a measure of the growing public interest in the plight of the Jews, along with the Bergson Group's diplomatic skills, that a handful of Roosevelt administration officials, such as Pringle and Harper, would join his cause. (Nor were they the only ones; later that autumn, Interior Secretary Ickes himself would become honorary co-chairman of the Washington DC chapter of the Emergency Committee to Save the Jewish People of Europe.) Bergson explained to Long the need for "some organization of the Government to attend to the affairs of the Jews," as Long put it in his memo of their talk. Long replied that such an organization already existed, in the Visa Division of the State Department, where there was "a section which devoted its entire attention to the refugee problem." Long then pressed Bergson, without success, to stop publishing advertisements calling for Allied rescue action.[18]

In early November Harper presented his final draft of the resolution to the lead sponsor, Senator Guy Gillette (D-IA). It called for "the creation by the President of a commission of diplomatic, economic, and military experts to formulate and effectuate a plan of immediate action designed to save the surviving Jewish people of Europe from extinction at the hands of Nazi Germany." At Bergson's direction, Harper omitted any mention of Palestine as a destination for refugees, so as not to alienate those members of Congress who would be reluctant to challenge British policy in the middle of the war. On November 9 Gillette introduced it in the Senate, and Will Rogers Jr. (D-CA) and Joseph Baldwin (R-NY) presented it in the House of Representatives.[19]

Because it was merely a non-binding recommendation rather than legislation, such a resolution ordinarily would not have necessitated a hearing. But Rep. Sol Bloom, as chairman of the House Foreign Affairs Committee, insisted on the unusual step of holding full hearings. Whether Bloom was acting directly at the request of the administration or simply concurred with its stance against the resolution, the apparent goal was the same: to delay and undermine the resolution. At Bloom's direction, hearings on what became known as the Gillette-Rogers resolution opened on November 19.[20]

Much to the administration's chagrin, the resolution attracted bipartisan support. Prominent Democrats and New Dealers such as 1928 presidential candidate Al Smith and American Labor Party leader Dean Alfange endorsed the rescue measure. So did prominent Republicans, including 1940 presidential nominee Wendell Willkie, newspaper publisher William Randolph Hearst, and New York City mayor Fiorello La Guardia. Hearst repeatedly published sympathetic editorials and news articles about the resolution in his chain of thirty newspapers nationwide. Among those testifying at the House committee hearings in support of the resolution were Alfange and La Guardia, publisher William Ziff Sr., author Frances Gunther, representatives of the American Federation of Labor and the Congress of Industrial Organizations, and Bergson himself.[21]

To Senator Gillette's surprise, the opposition to the resolution emanated from mainstream Jewish groups. He recalled:

> Within twenty-four hours after the introduction of that resolution, I began to have a series of callers, not only phone calls, but personal calls; first calling my attention to the fact that those who had asked me to sponsor the resolution did not represent the Jewish people; that they were upstarts; they were just a little group who desired to aggrandize themselves and were not in a

position to represent the American people of Jewish extraction. I told them that I didn't care whom they represented. It did not make a particle of difference to me whom they represented. They said to me, "Why, Senator, we know that if you had realized who were the sponsors of this proposal, you would not have lent yourself to the introduction of the resolution." And from that time on, these people used every effort, every means at their disposal, to block the resolution. . . . On the day that I was to call it up in the Foreign Relations Committee and we had the vote to report it out unanimously (I had already contacted every member), one of the cosponsors came in and said: "I wish these damned Jews would make up their minds what they want. I could not get inside the committee room without being buttonholed out here in the corridor by representatives who said that the Jewish people of America did not want the passage of this resolution."[22]

Sen. Gillette later wrote that soon after he introduced the resolution, "Dr. Wise called at my office accompanied by two or three other gentlemen and discussed the pending Resolution with me. . . . [T]he tenor of the conversation seemed to suggest their belief that the action as proposed by the Resolution was not a wise step to take, although they professed very strong interest in everything that would look to the saving of the remnant of the Jewish people in Europe from destruction."

In another indication of Wise's position, former congressman William S. Bennet, a Bergson supporter, later told Treasury Secretary Morgenthau that Sen. Albert Hawkes of New Jersey "told me he would sponsor [a similar] resolution, but later the influence of Rabbi Stephen S. Wise and others changed his mind." When a letter-writer privately questioned Wise about the Hawkes incident, the rabbi replied: "I have never opposed any resolution which promised to be of service to the Jewish people. I have strenuously opposed any proposal which surrendered the Jewish position or which threatened to do hurt to the Jewish people."[23]

The only mainstream Jewish leader who testified at the hearings was Rabbi Wise. He told the congressional committee that "of course we favor" the resolution, but then proceeded to criticize it as "inadequate" and urged that it be amended to mention Palestine as a destination for Jewish refugees.

Bergson Group leaders believed Wise was stubbornly refusing to set aside his Zionist ideology—the focus on Palestine as a future refuge—at a time when havens, anywhere in the world, were the need of the hour.[24] In fact Wise was more flexible on this point than the Bergsonites realized. Wise's private correspondence reveals he was willing to have Jewish refugees temporarily settled in countries other than Palestine in order to get them out of dangerous areas. In 1938, for example, he wrote to a friend that while Palestine was "the Mother Country," he "would be perfectly willing," in view of the urgent situation then prevailing, "to negotiate with Soviet Russia with regard to [the Siberian region of] Birobijan" or "to deal with the British government concerning Uganda or Kenya" as sites for Jewish refugees. In the aftermath of that year's *Kristallnacht* pogrom, Wise suggested to James McDonald, chairman of the President's Advisory Committee on Political Refugees, that the committee explore settling German Jews in the Soviet Union.[25]

If the issue was not Zionist ideology, then why did Wise criticize the rescue resolution in his testimony? In Congressman Rogers's view, Wise was trying to defeat the resolution without appearing to be against rescue. Inclusion of Palestine was likely to antagonize congress members who would not support implicit criticism of Great Britain. "I knew as well as Rabbi Wise knew that putting Palestine in was just going to kill it," Rogers later noted. Wise's insistence on adding Palestine "was a method, a means which he used to try and kill this resolution. He did not openly oppose it. He really couldn't. There was no way, nobody can openly oppose trying to be a humanitarian. But they just wanted to wiggle around and sabotage and change the wording or do something else."[26]

Wise told reporters afterward that "the allegation that I

wanted to kill the Gillette-Rogers resolution is a lie, and its authors know that it is a lie." The minutes of a November 6 AJConference executive committee meeting suggest otherwise, however. There Wise was quoted as telling his colleagues that he "did not favor this bill" and that he had initially succeeded in having its introduction "postponed." There was no mention of Palestine in the discussion and Wise did not offer any specific explanation as to what was wrong with the resolution, other than a general complaint that Bergson's efforts were causing "confusion" on Capitol Hill. Likewise, a press release issued by the AJConference to explain Wise's position quoted him as calling the resolution "inadequate," but did not say why; nor did it mention the omission of Palestine as the problem. In all likelihood, then, the real reason Wise sought to undermine the resolution was not Palestine but rather a combination of Wise's deference to the Roosevelt administration and his strong resentment of Bergson for usurping his own role as the most prominent Jewish spokesman on the rescue issue.[27]

Aside from Wise, the other witness to testify against the resolution was Assistant Secretary of State Long. Appearing on November 26, Long set aside the standard Roosevelt administration claim that rescue was impossible, and instead testified that the United States was already rescuing Jews. "We have taken into this country since the beginning of the Hitler regime and the persecution of the Jews, until today, approximately 580,000 refugees," he asserted; therefore, a resolution demanding the creation of a rescue agency would be a "repudiation" of the life-saving work that was already (supposedly) underway. In fact, the background memo on this subject from his aide Robert Alexander had referred to "visas of all kinds [that] were issued" all over the world—not just to those fleeing the Nazis and also not confined to those who actually entered the United States. The real number was under 250,000, and not all of the immigrants were Jews.[28]

The congressmen, however, were unaware they were being misled, and since the testimony was given behind closed doors,

Long's assertions initially escaped public notice. As a result, Long's testimony, combined with Wise's, persuaded a majority of the House Foreign Affairs Committee members to oppose the resolution. However, because the congressmen now feared that the public might perceive their casting votes against the resolution as voting against the rescue of innocent victims of Nazism, they chose to quietly shelve the resolution without a formal vote. They also requested Long's permission to publicize his testimony, which they believed would help justify their action. Long, carelessly confident that the transcript would put the final nail in the resolution's coffin, readily agreed. His testimony was made public on December 10. The *New York Times* ran a major front-page article headlined "580,000 Refugees Admitted to United States in Decade." It was the most prominent coverage the *Times* ever accorded, or would accord, Holocaust-related news. But it was based on a lie.[29]

The backlash came quickly. Two leading political affairs journals, the *Nation* and the *New Republic*, denounced and refuted Long's statistics. House Immigration Committee chair Samuel Dickstein accused Long of making "no effort of any kind to save from death many of the refugees who could have been saved." Congressman Emanuel Celler blasted Long's professions of sympathy for Jewish victims of Hitler as "crocodile tears," demanded that he explain "how many Jews were admitted during the last three years in comparison with the number seeking entrance," and urged him to resign. Mainstream Jewish organizations also challenged Long. Even the ultracautious AJ Committee, which normally refrained from public protests, issued a statement citing Immigration and Naturalization Service figures that contradicted Long.[30]

Long had hoped to bury the rescue issue, but the release of his testimony instead ignited a fresh, and even louder, debate over the administration's harsh policy toward Jewish refugees. The escalating controversy not only embarrassed the administration, but also energized the rescue resolution's supporters, including those on the Senate Foreign Relations Committee.

The senate committee's chairman, Tom Connally of Texas, took ill in December and initially blocked any consideration of the resolution in his absence. Just before Christmas, though, Senator Thomas of Utah temporarily replaced him as chairman and immediately placed the resolution before the committee. "It is not a Jewish problem alone," the sponsoring senators wrote in their preamble. "It is a Christian problem and a problem for enlightened civilization. We have talked; we have sympathized; we have expressed our horror; the time to act is long past due." The resolution passed unanimously and headed for the full Senate.[31]

Some veteran Washington lobbyists believed Gillette-Rogers had a good chance to pass in the Senate. Dorothy Detzer, the Washington DC representative of the Women's International League for Peace and Freedom, wrote:

I found that on many questions I disagreed profoundly with Peter Bergson, though there was always logic in his point of view provided one accepted his premises. But in spite of disagreement on many matters, I was convinced that on the crucial question of rescuing Jews from the occupied countries, Bergson's plans were sound. The policies of those other Jewish groups, with which I felt in more general sympathy, did not, it seemed to me, approach this problem with nearly as much clarity and directness. For Peter Bergson had sharpened the focus of his Emergency Committee to one objective. On that it concentrated; on that Peter Bergson hammered. "The problem is not how to save the Jews," he would reiterate with tireless persistence. "The problem is only where to send them when they've been rescued." (. . .)

[After the Gillette-Rogers resolution was introduced], an active and vigorous campaign of lobbying was initiated at once: hearings, interviews, publicity, persuading, explaining. . . . For months, the Capitol was the seat of unremitting pressure. I had other Congressional irons in the fire, but I helped the Emergency Committee as much as I could. Finally, toward the middle of January, a poll of both houses promised a sufficient margin of votes to insure passage. The measure was then slated for the calendar, and on Monday, January 24th, it was scheduled to come up for vote [before the Senate].

The political wind does not blow where it listeth; it runs along the ground. Now its murmur carried to the Administration the angry rumblings of the grass roots. The country, no longer indifferent to the plight of the Jews, was roused to a fever of indignation over the government's failure to act to save them. If that bill went through the Congress, Republicans might be able to take equal credit with the Democrats for forcing through this humanitarian move. For [Republican Senator] Bob Taft's name was on the measure [as a cosponsor], and his skill and energy behind it. Hence, its successful passage would be due in part to the minority party.

The Assault on Bergson

Bergson's success in moving the rescue resolution forward triggered the Jewish leadership's first all-out public attack on his group. Earlier attempts to undermine Bergson had been kept behind closed doors, as for example when Wise helped pressure Undersecretary of State Sumner Welles and Ambassador Myron Taylor to reject invitations to speak at the Bergson Group's July 1943 rescue conference.[32] But in the wake of Bergson's efforts on Capitol Hill, Wise concluded the time had come to go public. On December 29, while Gillette-Rogers remained undecided, the AJConference issued an eight-page memorandum denouncing the Bergson Group. The memo skirted substantive policy issues, focusing instead on the legitimacy of the group itself. The Bergson activists have "assumed to speak for the Jewish people in this country without having . . . a mandate from any constituency"; "they have sought to undermine . . . the recognized national Jewish agencies"; they engaged in "competitive activities"; their "separatist activities" served only to "bring confusion in the minds of well-meaning people"; and the rescue resolution was introduced "in complete disregard" of the established groups' own rescue advocacy.[33]

More than anything else, the tone and content of the AJ conference attack gave the appearance of a petty turf war. Resentment at Bergson's success, rather than substantive disagreement with his positions, appeared to be fueling the Jewish leadership's opposition to the upstarts, to judge by internal memos from Wise-led organizations in 1942–43. Bergson's rescue campaign "is stealing the thunder of the Joint Emergency Committee and perhaps of the American Jewish Conference," one such internal WJ congress staff memo candidly warned. Longtime AJ congress leader Louis Lipsky acknowledged that the Bergsonites "write very good advertisements, and we ought to compete with them." Rabbi Wise, for his part, was particularly anguished over Bergson's ability to attract support from individuals of prominence. "They are a disaster to the Zionist cause and the Jewish people," he wrote to a friend in 1944. "Yet see how many names they capture of persons who are well-meaning and friendly to Jews! It is too sad for words."[34]

Throughout 1944 Rabbi Wise and his colleagues undertook a number of steps to undermine the Bergson Group. Learning that Interior Secretary Ickes had agreed to co-chair Bergson's Washington DC division, Wise urged him to "withdraw from this irresponsible group, which exists and obtains funds through being permitted to use the names of non-Jews like yourself." (Ickes rejected Wise's request.) Representatives of the American Zionist Emergency Council visited Jewish members of Congress, former Republican presidential nominee Wendell Willkie, and other public figures to urge them to stay away from Bergson. Lillie Shultz, of the AJ congress, persuaded the editors of the *Nation* to stop accepting paid advertisements from the Bergsonites.[35]

Rabbi Wise himself "mentioned Bergson in the most violent terms," John Pehle of the Treasury Department would later report to his colleagues. When Pehle met Wise in New York City, the rabbi "even said that he had told his family that if he were found dead in the alley some night that they would know who did it and that he seriously felt that Bergson might kill him." Wise might genuinely have harbored such fears; he knew Bergson and some of his comrades were previously allied with the militant Irgun Zvai Leumi group in Palestine. Still, the most intense rhetoric employed in these quarrels—"Hitler," "gangster," "liquidate," and the like—came from the established leaders against Bergson, not the other way around.[36]

Nahum Goldmann, for example, wrote to Secretary Morgenthau's assistant, Henrietta Klotz, in May 1944 that the Bergson Group "is now becoming a public menace and everything must be done to liquidate them." Goldmann visited the State Department to explain how "distressed" he was "to see Bergson received in high places." The wjcongress leader said he and his colleagues "could not see why this Government did not either deport Bergson or draft him." Goldmann also told State Department officials that Rabbi Wise "regarded Bergson as equally as great an enemy of the Jews as Hitler, for the reason that his activities could only lead to increased anti-Semitism." Goldmann's personal files bulge with carbon copies of letters he sent to foreign diplomats in Washington, urging them to refuse to see Bergson. (The letters were sent to "all the Embassies in Washington," Goldmann assured Wallace Murray of the State Department.) AZEC staffers compiled a list of several hundred individuals who had signed Bergson Group newspaper ads and contacted each one of them to urge them to withdraw. Next to each name was a note, such as "Finds principles of [Bergson Group] laudable; following up"; "States he is ready to work with all groups for Palestine; no withdrawal"; and "Will be governed by our statements in the future." Those who failed to respond, or did not respond as desired, received three follow-up letters over the next three months.[37]

Goldmann was not the only one urging U.S. government officials to have Bergson deported or drafted. Congressman Bloom urged similar actions, fearing that "if Kook [Bergson] were not deported from the United States, he would eventually provoke sufficient antagonism among the citizens of the United States to cause anti-Semitic pogroms." The British government, which dubbed Bergson "a Semitic Himmler," likewise wanted Bergson deported to Palestine, where British authorities would be able to arrest him for belonging to the Irgun, an illegal organization. But London thought the chances of that happening were unlikely "in view of the influential friends who seem to be able to protect him." Counter-pressure from Bergson's allies in Congress, combined with the State Department's fear that such action would "make a martyr out of Bergson," did indeed stymie consideration of drafting or deporting him.[38]

Still, there were other ways to make Bergson's life difficult, and the Roosevelt administration did not need much prodding from Jewish leaders or British officials to pursue them. Breckinridge Long was also complaining that the group's newspaper ads "made it very difficult for the [State] department." Consequently the Roosevelt administration sent the FBI and the Internal Revenue Service after Bergson. Although they were ostensibly pursuing evidence of criminal wrongdoing, political motives were clearly the impetus. "This man has been in the hair of [Secretary of State] Cordell Hull," an internal FBI memo bluntly noted in 1944, in its explanation of the reasons for U.S. government action against Bergson.[39]

The FBI's investigation of Bergson proceeded along two tracks simultaneously—to find evidence that the Bergson Group was assisting the Irgun, and to determine if the Bergsonites were Communists. The FBI eavesdropped on Bergson activists' phone conversations, opened their mail, sifted through their trash, and used informants (whom FBI reports characterized as "persons in New York City who are familiar with Israelite matters") to gather information and take documents from Bergson's office. Ultimately, however, despite an exhaustive, years-long investigation, the FBI was unable to document any Irgun or Communist activity by the group.[40]

Meanwhile, the IRS sought out evidence of financial irregularities that would enable the administration to revoke Bergson's tax-exempt status. IRS agents repeatedly visited the Bergson Group's Manhattan headquarters—once from morning until night for more than two weeks—but, like the FBI, ultimately uncovered nothing untoward. As they were departing Bergson's headquarters on the final day of their inquiry, each of the IRS agents reportedly made a small cash contribution to the group.[41]

"The Acquiescence of This Government"

While this Jewish effort against Bergson was proceeding, a conflict of considerably greater consequence was unfolding behind the scenes, at the Treasury and State Departments. Under ordinary circumstances, matters involving Jewish refugees would not have come to the attention of Treasury officials. But in the spring of 1943, Gerhart Riegner, the Geneva representative of the World Jewish Congress, asked Rabbi Wise and his colleagues in New York to provide funds to facilitate the rescue of Jews from France and Rumania. Because sending funds into enemy territory was against the law, the WJCongress needed to obtain a special license from the Treasury Department to carry out the transaction. Its request landed on the desk of Josiah E. DuBois Jr., a young attorney in the Foreign Funds department, who quickly gave it his approval.[42]

When the application reached the State Department, however, it ran into unexplained roadblocks. Investigating the reasons for the delay, DuBois enlisted a friend inside State to surreptitiously provide him with the Department's file on the WJCongress request. The purloined documents revealed that State Department officials were not only deliberately dragging their feet on the funds transfer request; they had also ordered U.S. diplomats in Switzerland to stop sending Washington information about the mass murder of the Jews, fearing that circulation of such reports would increase pressure on the Roosevelt administration to assist the refugees.[43]

Meanwhile, the long delays in granting the WJCongress's application to send funds to Europe prompted Rabbi Wise to seek an audience with President Roosevelt. It took almost two months of requests and reminders for Wise to finally secure the July 22 appointment. According to Wise's account, when he explained the funds problem, FDR immediately responded, "Stephen, why don't you go ahead and do it?" The president telephoned Treasury Secretary Morgenthau on the spot and told him, "This is a very fair proposal which Stephen makes about ransoming Jews out of Poland into Hungary." Wise told reporters afterward that the president exhibited "a profound and penetrating interest in these victims of Hitler." In a private note to the president the following day, the rabbi exclaimed, "I am happier than I can say" at the president's evident sympathy.[44]

Wise rejoiced too soon. Three weeks later, the rabbi received a "Dear Stephen" letter from the president informing him that Morgenthau had already approved the transfer request, and "the matter is now awaiting a further exchange of cables between the State Department and our mission in Bern regarding some of the details." This meant that FDR's dramatic phone call to Morgenthau, ostensibly to break the bureaucratic logjam holding up the license, had been nothing of the sort. In fact FDR's intercession had been of no help at all, because Treasury had approved the license a week before Wise even met with FDR. The true obstacle was not Morgenthau at Treasury, but Hull at State. It would take yet another six months, and only after additional developments (discussed below), before State would finally approve the license.[45]

As the months wore on, Secretary Morgenthau and his aides grew increasingly frustrated by the delays. "I don't know how we can blame the Germans for killing them when we are doing this," staff member Randolph Paul remarked at one meeting. "The law calls them *para-delicto*, of equal guilt." Morgenthau agreed, asserting during one staff discussion that the State Department's obstruction of rescue meant that "we find ourselves aiding and abetting Hitler."

By the autumn of 1943, several Treasury staffers were insistently making the case to Morgenthau in staff meetings that disinterest in the Jewish refugees was rife in the State Department, and rescue action would be impeded unless the refugee issue was taken completely out of State's hands and assigned to a new government agency focusing exclusively on rescue. "The bull has to be taken by the horns in dealing with this Jewish issue, and get this thing out of the State Department into some agency's hands that is willing to deal with it frontally," DuBois argued. "You get a committee set up with their heart in it, I feel sure they can do something." His colleague John Pehle agreed: "It seems to me the only way to get anything done is for the President to appoint a commission or committee consisting of sympathetic people of some importance." White House adviser Oscar Cox, who had been invited to take part in the Treasury discussions on rescue, pointed out that "on the Hill there has been pending before the House Foreign Affairs Committee the so-called Rogers-Gillette resolution to create a special commission to handle this problem. There has been a fight within the House Foreign Affairs Committee on the thing." Cox feared the controversy could turn into "a domestic political problem" for the president. The opposition of Rabbi Wise and Assistant Secretary Long notwithstanding, the momentum in favor of the rescue initiative on Capitol Hill was now converging with the sentiment of Morgenthau's advisers and paving the way for dramatic developments.[46]

Going to the President

The Treasury-State conflict reached its climax when DuBois asked State to provide a copy of a telegram related to reports of atrocity news that U.S. diplomats in Switzerland had sent to Washington. Long doctored the telegram to hide State's role in suppressing the transmissions; he did not know that DuBois already had a copy of the original telegram, furnished to him by his source inside State.[47]

DuBois revealed to Morgenthau what Long had done. The furious treasury secretary instructed his staff to undertake a full investigation of State's actions with regard to European Jewry. Their eighteen-page "Report to the Secretary on the Acquiescence of This Government in the Murder of the Jews," authored primarily by DuBois, was delivered to Morgenthau at the end of December. The document exposed how State Department officials "were so fearful that this Government might act to save the Jews of Europe if the gruesome facts relating to Hitler's plans to exterminate them became known" that they suppressed the information, obstructed rescue opportunities, and undermined attempts by private organizations to facilitate rescue. The officials "not only failed to use the Governmental machinery at their disposal to rescue Jews from Hitler, but have even gone so far as to use this Government machinery to prevent the rescue of these Jews," for example through "the administrative restrictions which have been placed upon the granting of visas to the United States," as a result of which "the admission of refugees to this country does not come anywhere near the quota." Dismissing the administration's claim that such restrictions were necessary for national security, the report argued that "even if we took these refugees and treated them as prisoners of war, it would be better than letting them die."[48]

The Treasury staff urged Morgenthau to deliver the report to President Roosevelt. Furthermore, they prepared a draft of an executive order creating an independent rescue agency that they asked Morgenthau to present to FDR. Concerned that more explicit political pressure might be needed to move the president, Morgenthau's aides emphasized that the ongoing battle over the Gillette-Rogers rescue resolution could be used as leverage in approaching the president. Ansel Luxford explained:

> There have been hearings before both the House and the Senate on the ridiculous operations of State on the refugee problem. The Senate Foreign Relations Committee reported out unanimously a resolution calling for the establishment of a commission by the President to take this thing out of State and to handle the Jewish refugee problem. Now, the House Foreign Relations Committee, Bloom's committee, had been holding hearings on the same problem, and Bloom is having to

do everything he can possibly do to keep that resolution from being reported out of the House Foreign Relations Committee. . . . [H]e probably feels that it will be a blow to the Administration to have this thing thrown out onto the Floor of the House and debated on the basis that it will be debated. It will not be any pleasant thing.[49]

Randolph Paul interjected: "Therefore, [our] remedy is an Executive Order—let's do it without a statute." White House aide Ben Cohen then counseled: "[T]here is also a factor which you don't want to put in the memorandum which will influence the President and influence Hull. We all know that during this political year minorities are being exploited." Likely alluding to the Jewish vote in the 1944 presidential election, Cohen continued: "It is not that the minorities are trying to exploit politics. There may be some of that, but all the politicians are trying to exploit the value of minority groups, and the situation has gotten to the point where something has to be done." Morgenthau agreed that the congressional activity would give him crucial ammunition. "I personally hate to say this thing, but our strongest out [with the President] is the imminence of Congress doing something," the secretary remarked. "Really, when you get down to the point, this is a boiling pot on the Hill. You can't hold it; it is going to pop, and you have either got to move very fast, or the Congress of the United States will do it for you."[50]

Before going to the president, Morgenthau had one more hurdle to clear: presidential adviser Samuel Rosenman. On January 13, 1944, he called Rosenman and invited him to take part in a Treasury staff meeting to prepare for their approach to the president about a rescue agency. Rosenman replied that it would not be "wise . . . to get the president in on any refugee problem, right now." Seeing that Morgenthau would not back off, Rosenman urged him to make it clear to the president that he was not "only talking about Jewish refugees," but "Poles and Greeks as well, and all who are willing to get out." Told that two Jewish non-Treasury figures, Ben Cohen and Oscar Cox, would participate, Rosenman complained that if word of the meeting were to leak out, it would look "terrible" that three Jews took part. Morgenthau assured him there would be no leaks to the press. "Don't worry about the publicity," the treasury secretary said. "What I want is intelligence and courage—courage first and intelligence second."[51]

On January 16, 1944, Morgenthau, accompanied by Pehle and Paul, met with President Roosevelt in the Oval Office. The treasury secretary handed the president an abbreviated version of the "Acquiescence" report (with the toned-down title, "Report to the President"), together with a draft of an executive order establishing a "War Refugee Board." DuBois had suggested that Morgenthau tell the president that if Roosevelt did not act, he (DuBois) would "resign and release the report to the press," but Morgenthau did not need to go that far. He told the president he was "deeply disturbed" to discover that State Department officials were "actually taking action to prevent the rescue of the Jews." Citing his father's efforts on behalf of victims of the Armenian genocide, Morgenthau said he was "convinced that effective action could be taken"—contradicting everything the president and his spokesmen had been claiming for years. Morgenthau then asked Pehle "to explain to the President the facts which the Treasury had uncovered" regarding State's actions.

When Pehle began describing Breckinridge Long's role, Roosevelt came to the defense of his old friend. "The President seemed disinclined to believe that Long wanted to stop effective action from being taken," according to Pehle's account of the meeting, which he dictated later that day. FDR explained Long's actions by blaming the Jews. He "said that Long had been somewhat soured on the problem when Rabbi Wise got Long to approve a long list of people being brought into this country many of whom turned out to be bad people." Secretary Morgenthau interjected to "remind the President that at a Cabinet meeting [Attorney General Francis] Biddle had indicated that only three Jews of those entering the United States during the war had turned out to be undesirable." FDR did not budge, according to Pehle: "The President said that he had been advised that the figure was considerably larger." He did not say who had advised him in that regard, or what he believed the number to be.

In any event, President Roosevelt undoubtedly recognized how embarrassing it would be for him—in an election year—to have the full Senate approve the Gillette-Rogers rescue resolution, thus calling attention to his administration's stark humanitarian failure. The political cost of taking no action now outweighed his longstanding principle of not taking special steps to aid Europe's Jews. Preempting congressional action by unilaterally establishing a rescue agency was the politically advantageous route. At the end of the twenty-minute discussion, the president said, "We will do it." Six days later—just two days before the scheduled Senate debate on the rescue resolution— FDR issued Executive Order 9417, establishing the War Refugee Board and empowering it to "take all measures within its power to rescue the victims of enemy oppression who are in imminent danger of death." It also required the State, Treasury, and War Departments "to execute at the request of the Board, the plans and programs [developed by the board]."[52]

When the battle to establish the board ended, the fight to claim credit began.

Some Jewish organizations sought to downplay the Bergson Group's role in the creation of the new rescue agency. Rabbi Wise and the AJcongress claimed Bergson's "chief accomplishment is the creation of confusion and bewilderment." Some leading newspapers, however, saw things differently. An editorial in the *Christian Science Monitor* called the board's establishment "the outcome of pressure brought to bear by the Emergency Committee to Save the Jewish People of Europe [the Bergson Group], a group made up of both Jews and non-Jews that has been active in the capital in recent months." Likewise, a *Washington Post* editorial argued that in view of the Bergson Group's "industrious spadework," the group was "entitled to credit for the President's forehanded move [in creating the board]." In their internal discussions in the weeks to follow, Secretary Morgenthau and his staff cited the Bergson Group and the congressional rescue resolution as the impetus for the board's creation. "The thing that made it possible to get the President really to act on this thing," Morgenthau said, "[was that] the resolution at least had passed the Senate to form this kind of a War Refugee Committee." Pehle agreed that the Bergson Group was "the crowd that got the thing that far."[53] In another discussion, Morgenthau referred to "the Resolution in the House and in the Senate by which we forced the President to appoint a Committee [the War Refugee Board]" and that FDR would not have wanted "to have him forced by Congress to do this." On a different occasion, Pehle remarked that the Bergson Group "brought considerable pressure on Congress to pass a resolution which called for the setting up of an agency such as the War Refugee Board." Likewise, DuBois later said of Bergson: "I think a lot of his activities, in terms of advertisements, put a lot of pressure on the government, particularly before the formation of the War Refugee Board. It all helped create an atmosphere."[54]

"Rescue as Many as We Can"

The War Refugee Board (WRB) was handicapped from the outset because the Roosevelt administration had never wanted it to come into existence in the first place. President Roosevelt gave the new agency a token initial $1 million. That covered only about 10 percent of the board's expenses; the remaining 90 percent had to be raised. Private Jewish organizations, primarily the American Jewish Joint Distribution Committee and the World Jewish Congress, contributed more than 90 percent of its budget.

Officially, the board consisted of Secretary of State Hull, Secretary of State Stimson, and Secretary of the Treasury Morgenthau, but only Morgenthau made a serious effort on behalf of rescue. The State Department and War Department often refused to cooperate with the board's initiatives, and the White House generally showed little interest in its work.

Morgenthau and his senior aides hoped to secure a well-known public figure to serve as the WRB's executive director, in the belief that a person of stature would carry more weight when interacting both with other U.S. government agencies and foreign representatives. The White House, however, vetoed Morgenthau's suggestion of 1940 Republican presidential nominee Wendell Willkie, concerned that choosing him would give FDR's once and perhaps future rival too much favorable publicity in the run-up to the 1944 presidential campaign. Rather than waste precious time wrangling over the question of executive director, Morgenthau then suggested giving the post to his aide John Pehle, with Josiah DuBois as general counsel. The White House had no objection.[55]

The core WRB staff consisted of about a dozen individuals working out of offices within the Treasury building. The total staff never exceeded thirty. They were young—Pehle was thirty-five, DuBois thirty-two—but their energy, dedication, and creativity helped compensate for their lack of experience in such work. They carried out operations in Europe and the Middle East through a combination of representatives sent from the United States, American refugee relief workers who were already on the scene, and, occasionally, helpful U.S. diplomats abroad. The board's agent in Istanbul, Ira Hirschmann, noted that the agency was created "at five minutes to twelve [midnight]." Fourteen months had elapsed since the Roosevelt administration had verified the news of the Nazi genocide, and more than four million Jews had already been slaughtered.

Often at great risk to themselves, War Refugee Board representatives in Turkey, Switzerland, North Africa, Portugal, and Italy employed unorthodox means of rescue, including bribery of border officials and the production of forged identification papers and other documents to protect refugees from the Nazis. As a result of negotiations undertaken by the board's agents, approximately forty-eight thousand Jews were moved out of Transnistria, where they would have been in the path of the retreating German army, to safe areas in Rumania. About fifteen thousand

Jewish refugees, as well as twenty thousand non-Jewish refugees, were evacuated from Axis-occupied territory, and at least ten thousand more were protected through such board initiatives as providing funds to underground groups to hide them.[56]

In Hungary the board orchestrated a series of condemnations and threats from the United States, the Vatican, and other governments against its rulers to end the deportation of Hungarian Jews to Auschwitz in July 1944. That effort came too late for the 440,000 Jews who had already been deported from around the country, but approximately one hundred thousand Jews were then still in Nazi-occupied Budapest. The WRB's agent in Stockholm, Iver Olsen, persuaded Swedish businessman Raoul Wallenberg to undertake rescue work in Budapest. With WRB funds and logistical assistance, Wallenberg traveled to the Hungarian capital, where he was appointed first secretary of Sweden's diplomatic mission (to shield him from arrest). The courageous and resourceful Wallenberg designed a Swedish protective passport and distributed thousands of them to Jews in Budapest to prevent the Germans from deporting them. He also used bribery, threats, and blackmail to interfere with the deportation process. In one instance, Wallenberg actually leaped atop a train of deportees as it was leaving the station and frantically handed protective documents to the Jews inside as German bullets whizzed around him.

The War Refugee Board also urged President Roosevelt to grant temporary haven to hundreds of thousands of Jewish refugees. The idea was to circumvent any possible controversy over the immigration quotas by admitting refugees only for the duration of the war. In his proposal for this action, DuBois also argued that if the United States demonstrated its willingness to take in a significant number of refugees, other countries would likely follow suit.

To stimulate public interest, DuBois shared the idea with syndicated columnist Samuel Grafton, who then wrote about what he called "free ports for refugees," comparing it to the government's policy of allowing goods in transit to stay temporarily in American ports without payment of custom duties. "We do it for cases of beans," Grafton wrote. "It should not be impossible to do it for people." Grafton's article appeared in forty newspapers nationwide, with a combined circulation of more than four million.

As a result of the WRB's behind-the-scenes efforts, the "free ports" idea was publicly endorsed in April and May by numerous leading newspapers, prominent Christian groups such as the Federal Council of Churches, and leading labor unions such as the AFL and the CIO, as well as major Jewish organizations. The Bergson Group sponsored full-page newspaper advertisements backing the plan. At the other end of the spectrum, Secretary of War Stimson tried to pour cold water on the proposal, arguing that Jewish refugees were "unassimilable" and would negatively affect America's "racial stock." To gauge public sentiment, the White House arranged for a Gallup poll, which found 70 percent of Americans in favor of such temporary havens. This represented a startling change from the 1930s, when polls had consistently shown strong public opposition to admitting more refugees, even at times when the plight of the Jews was receiving the most sympathetic publicity. For example, Opinion Research polls around the time of the Anschluss (March 1938) and Kristallnacht (November 1938) found 75 percent and 71 percent of Americans respectively opposed to "allowing a larger number of Jewish exiles from Germany to come to the United States to live." A Gallup poll in 1939 found 66 percent of Americans opposed to "admitting 10,000 refugee children from Germany to be brought into this country." But once the tide of the war had turned in mid-1943 (with the defeat of the Germans at Stalingrad and the liberation of Italy) and Americans learned more about the mass killings, a significant shift in public opinion took place, as the April 1944 poll revealed. The level of support no doubt increased because the poll specified the refugees would stay in America only for the duration of the war.[57]

In the midst of these developments, word reached the WRB in mid-May that large numbers of refugees from Yugoslavia were flooding into Allied-liberated Italy. In a message to the White House, Pehle cited this new situation as an instance where the immediate granting of temporary haven could help alleviate a crisis. The president initially resisted, telling reporters at his May 30 press conference that "it is not, in my judgment, necessary to decide that we have to have a free port right here in the United States," because "there are lots of other places in the world where refugees conceivably could go to." With public pressure mounting, however, the president decided to make a one-time gesture. At his June 9 press conference, turning his attention to the refugees who had reached Italy, Roosevelt announced that "we are going to bring over a thousand, that's all, to this country." (The final number was 982.) By contrast, some much smaller countries had taken in far larger numbers; Sweden, for example, had given refuge to more than seven thousand Danish Jews fleeing the Nazis in October 1943, and Switzerland had admitted an estimated twenty-seven thousand Jewish refugees during the war. In the end, President Roosevelt's view as to who should be permitted to enter the United States was more in line with Stimson's than the WRB's. (Roosevelt's perspective is explored in detail in chapter 8.)[58]

Rabbi Wise's organizations were effusive in their praise of the president's gesture. The American Jewish Conference declared that the admission of the 982 refugees "may yet help stave off the death sentence which the puppet government of Hungary has decreed for the last surviving Jews of Europe," because it might encourage Hungarians to shield Jews. An editorial in the AJCongress's *Congress Weekly* acknowledged that while some "skeptics" might say that "the rescue of a thousand souls is somewhat puny compared with the magnitude of the catastrophe and the vastness of this country," such criticism would be unwarranted because "there are circumstances which prevent the full expression of the traditional humanity of this Republic." A few voices in the community responded differently. U.S. Labor Zionist official Marie Syrkin wrote in *Jewish Frontier* that the admission of 982 refugees was "impressive neither as a practical measure of alleviation nor even as a gesture." A *National Jewish Ledger* editorial called the admission of such a small number "an insult and an affront to a greatly afflicted and martyred people." *Morgen Zhurnal* columnist Jacob Glad-stone called it "no more than a token, a symbolic gesture, a Christian Science rescue, and the conscience of the world may continue to doze."[59]

Altogether, the War Refugee Board's efforts played a major role in saving about two hundred thousand Jews and twenty thousand non-Jews during the period from its inception in January 1944 to the end of the war in Europe in May 1945. Its work provided a forceful answer to longstanding claims by the Roosevelt administration and its supporters that there was no way to rescue Jews except by winning the war.[60]

6

FDR, Wise, and Palestine

"YOU KNOW THERE IS not room in Palestine for many more people," President Roosevelt told a surprised and dismayed Rabbi Wise in early 1938. "Perhaps another hundred or hundred and fifty thousand."

Throughout FDR's twelve years in office, Wise and his colleagues labored to convince the president that there was in fact room in Palestine for many hundreds of thousands, and ultimately millions, of Jewish immigrants. Justice Felix Frankfurter, among others, periodically sent the president newspaper clippings and Zionist memoranda to demonstrate Palestine's promising future, especially its ability to absorb large numbers of new immigrants.

Mass immigration was the key to the Zionist vision of creating a modern, functioning Jewish state. In Rabbi Wise's view, the building of a Jewish homeland in Palestine was the answer to the increasingly pressing need for a refuge for persecuted Jews. The United States had endorsed Great Britain's promise, in its 1917 Balfour Declaration, to facilitate the creation of a Jewish national home there. Rabbi Wise and his colleagues hoped that with sufficient American encouragement, the British would follow through on that pledge.[1]

In the 1930s President Roosevelt displayed little interest

in Zionism, aside from boiler-plate expressions of sympathy with Jewish development initiatives in Palestine. A presidential message to a Zionist convention in 1935 praised the goal of "creating in Palestine a home of happiness" for the Jews; the watered-down term "home," rather than "homeland," had been chosen after input from the State Department, where opposition to Zionism was vehement and unyielding.[2] Rabbi Wise drafted FDR's greeting to another Zionist gathering, in 1936; the president and his aides subsequently removed the sentences urging Britain to "open wide the doors of Palestine" to Jewish refugees.[3] The lone but important exception to Roosevelt's hesitant Palestine policy was his aforementioned pre-election pressure on London, in the autumn of 1936, to postpone British plans to severely restrict Jewish immigration.

By early 1937 rumors were circulating that a British investigative body, the Peel Commission, was preparing to issue recommendations regarding Palestine that would be unfavorable to the Jews, such as restrictions on immigration or land purchases. When Rabbi Wise visited the White House in April 1937 to discuss the matter with President Roosevelt, he was alarmed to hear the president insist that Palestine had "reached the point of Jewish saturation." Wise protested to the contrary, but to no avail; when he saw FDR nine months later, in January 1938, the president was still maintaining that "there is not room in Palestine for many more people"—100,000 to 150,000 at most, according to Wise's account of the conversation. Dismissing Wise's arguments, Roosevelt further asserted that because "Palestine possibilities are going to be exhausted" soon, "your people" had better "find some large areas [elsewhere in the world] as a second choice for the Jews." By the spring of 1938, David Ben-Gurion had heard enough private reports of these and other remarks by the president to conclude that for all practical purposes, FDR was "an anti-Zionist."[4]

Jewish leaders had hoped to leverage U.S. support for Zionism to counter England's vacillation on Palestine. In the face of Britain's steady retreat from the pledges of the Balfour Declaration, Roosevelt's weakening stance on Zionism was all the more alarming. In July 1937 the Peel Commission recommended partitioning western Palestine into Jewish and Arab states, with the Jews allotted less than 20 percent of the territory. The following year, another British government inquiry, undertaken by the Woodhead Commission, proposed creating an even tinier Jewish homeland consisting of a thin coastal strip divided in two portions. Wise and most other American Zionist leaders opposed both partition plans and scrambled for ways to stave off the shift in British policy. Increasingly it appeared that the White House would not be of much help.

Alarmed that President Roosevelt was so "mis-educated" regarding Palestine's absorptive capacity, a deeply worried Frankfurter visited the White House in October 1938 to discuss the matter face to face with the president. The Supreme Court justice asked Roosevelt to press the British on immigration to Palestine, if for no other reason than because of the country's "symbolic value" to world Jewry. FDR asked Frankfurter to draft a letter to that effect, which he would then send to Prime Minister Neville Chamberlain. Frankfurter drafted the letter, but FDR never sent it. Two months later, Roosevelt recommended to Morgenthau that one million German, Polish, and Rumanian Jews be spread around the globe. For five years, he suggested, twenty thousand could enter the United States annually (although that was 25 percent less than what the existing quota laws permitted); assorted African and South American countries and colonial territories would each take some; and just fifteen thousand would be admitted to Palestine—which, as it happens, was exactly the benchmark the British were then contemplating for the Holy Land.[5]

Proposals for dispersing most Jewish refugees around the world were the handiwork of Roosevelt's adviser on population settlement issues, Isaiah Bowman, an internationally renowned geographer and president of Johns Hopkins University. Their relationship began after the president read Bowman's 1937 study, *Limits of Land Settlement*, "with great interest." Bowman contended that there were virtually no places left in the world to which large numbers of people could migrate. Concerning Palestine, Bowman maintained that it was incapable of absorbing any significant number of immigrants, and that an influx of Jewish refugees would provoke significant conflicts with the local Arab populace. British officials put forward similar arguments to justify the restrictions on Jewish immigration and land purchases, which they began imposing in the 1930s. Soon Bowman was firmly ensconced as a senior presidential adviser. Roosevelt enlisted him to undertake a two-year examination of settlement possibilities for Jewish refugees in South America, the Caribbean, and Africa. Bowman and his team found virtually every country they studied to be unsuitable for "a large foreign immigrant group." He advised FDR that it would be best to "keep the European elements within the framework of the Old World"—that is, to discourage Europeans from leaving Europe.[6]

When First Lady Eleanor Roosevelt seemed receptive to a report by the Agriculture Department's Walter Clay Lowdermilk that found room in Palestine for several million immigrants, the president asked Bowman to have a talk with her. Annoyed that the "mischievous" Mrs. Roosevelt was meddling in "questions beyond her understanding," Bowman lectured her on Palestine's very limited ability to absorb Jewish refugees, the danger of angering the Arab world, and the risks of America being drawn into a Mideast conflict.[7]

By the late 1930s, the question of Palestine's future increasingly became intertwined with international diplomatic and military developments. Nazi Germany's military buildup in the 1930s and its leaders' assertions of a German right to expand its territory convinced British leaders that war between England and Germany was likely. Looking ahead to the probability of such a conflict, British officials worried that Arab unrest in Palestine could tie down British forces that would be needed elsewhere. They also feared that anger over the Palestine issue throughout the Arab world could lead to Arab support for the

Germans in such a war, potentially endangering British control over strategic and oil-rich regions of the Middle East. By early 1939 British prime minister Neville Chamberlain and his administration decided the only way they could keep the Arab world on their side in a conflict with Germany would be to retreat from their Balfour Declaration pledge supporting a "national home for the Jewish people" in Palestine.

The Chamberlain government invited Jewish and Arab representatives to take part in a conference at the St. James Palace, to begin on February 7, 1939, ostensibly to negotiate a Palestine solution, but in reality to lay the groundwork for British abandonment of the Zionist cause. Rabbi Wise was slated to lead an American Jewish delegation to the talks. Fearing London planned to "bamboozle" the Jewish representatives, Wise requested an appointment with President Roosevelt, hoping a few words from the White House would strengthen the Zionists' position at the conference. FDR declined to see him. In the face of widespread isolationist sentiment at home—a Gallup poll that February found only 18 percent of Americans supported sending U.S. military forces to aid England or France in the event of war with Germany—Roosevelt did not want to be perceived as taking sides in the Arab-Jewish conflict. Nor was he willing to "put pressure on a friendly state in such time of trial," Ben-Gurion privately lamented.[8]

The Arab delegates' refusal to consider the establishment of a Jewish state of any size in Palestine guaranteed the failure of the St. James conference. London's behind-the-scenes support for the Arab position was exposed when a private British diplomatic note to that effect, intended for the Arab representatives, was accidentally delivered by a clerk to the Zionist delegates instead. The conference lurched to its inevitable end shortly afterward.

The evening before Rabbi Wise's return to the United States from St. James, he and the other Zionist delegates gathered to discuss post-conference strategy. Ben-Gurion and the other Palestine Jewish leaders urged Wise to lead a public campaign in the United States against England's Palestine policy. His response was "disappointing and disheartening to all present," according to the diary of Moshe Sharett (Shertok), the Jewish Agency's political director (and a future prime minister of Israel). Wise told them that "for years, he and his American colleagues have been fighting to convince American public opinion of the need to march shoulder to shoulder with England in the war against fascism; he could not deviate from this position, even if the Zionist cause suffered." As Wise later recalled it, he said that U.S. Zionist leaders "would be put in a most precarious position if we set out to move the American people against England, when at any time we might be compelled to give our unmeasured and unequivocal support to Britain" if it went to war against Germany. Ben-Gurion did not share Wise's concern about American Zionists being put in a "precarious position." As he saw it, the prospect of Wise and his colleagues feeling uncomfortable was a small price to pay for advancing the Jewish cause. Another participant in the meeting reported that "He [Ben-Gurion] told [Wise], 'You are Jews who look out only for your own skins' . . . Wise was insulted."[9]

Wise was genuinely torn in his feelings regarding Great Britain. Warm memories of the summer he had spent at Oxford working on his doctoral dissertation had helped nurture his deep-seated admiration for England's culture and political tradition. The Balfour Declaration, and the generally pro-Zionist policy pursued by the British government in the 1920s, had strengthened his affection for England as the most civilized and progressive nation in Europe. Wise would describe himself as "an Anglophile almost to the point of Anglo-mania." The shifts in British policy in the 1930s left him disappointed and bewildered. "I have grown to be very distrustful of England," he had confided to a friend in May 1938. "They will use us while they can, and they will kick us when they want." By later that year, he had reached the conclusion that "the British government's mind is made up—yield as much as necessary to the Arabs, deny as much as necessary to the Jews." Moreover,

Prime Minister Chamberlain's "ignominious surrender" of western Czechoslovakia to Hitler in that September's Munich agreement struck Wise as a bad omen for the Jewish people. If "England, France, and my own country . . . can thus betray the Czecho-Slovakian Republic," he wondered in his private correspondence, "how much may we Jews hope for in the matter of amelioration or saving from them?"[10]

In March 1939, in the aftermath of the failed St. James conference, the British government began preparing to enact a new policy, known as the White Paper, to severely limit Jewish immigration to Palestine for five years and then make further immigration conditional on Arab approval. Catching wind of the plan, Rabbi Wise and other leading American Zionists repeatedly sought President Roosevelt's intervention. Justice Frankfurter once again encountered the familiar pattern: FDR suggested Frankfurter draft a letter from the president urging the prime minister to keep Palestine open, Frankfurter wrote the letter, and FDR never sent it. For his part, Justice Brandeis made four separate appeals to the president to intervene. In his final plea, Brandeis asked if the president could at least spare "a few minutes" to see wjcongress co-chair Nahum Goldmann. Roosevelt's reply: "Can't see him—Sec. State is all that is possible." Privately, FDR expressed dissatisfaction with the British decision. On the eve of the White Paper's publication, he instructed State Department officials to inform London that the United States hoped "no drastic changes" were intended in its Palestine policy. But he was unwilling to put any substantive pressure on the British over the issue.[11]

In retrospect Rabbi Wise would regret that he and his colleagues had not made a greater effort to secure U.S. intervention to avert the new British policy. "I cannot help feeling," he wrote to the zoa's Solomon Goldman soon after the White Paper was implemented, "that if we had [protested] sooner, say a month ago, and gotten both Houses of the Congress to work in our behalf and to 'pressure' the State Department, we might conceivably have had a different result."[12]

Dilemmas of an Anglophile

The approach of war was the key factor shaping Wise's view of how American Jews should respond to British policy. In his view, the broader cause of international opposition to fascism, and the likelihood of a German war with England, had to take precedence over Zionist needs. Just as he would refuse to fight for the admission of Jewish refugees to Alaska or the Virgin Islands because he felt it might harm the more important cause of reelecting President Roosevelt, so too Wise believed it was necessary to sacrifice the smaller cause of Zionism for the sake of what was best for civilization as a whole. "[Even if] for a time Palestine is the sufferer, the fortunes of the Jewish people are bound up with the triumph of England," Wise wrote to a colleague in 1940. "Loyalty to Palestine will help us little if Jews practically cease to be. . . . If Hitler wins the war, the appeasing fascists of America will make their peace with Hitlerism. . . . What then will be the Jewish position? . . . England is in direst extremity. To add the weight of a feather to the crushing burdens now borne by England is to sin against the Holy Spirit."[13]

Not only did Rabbi Wise refrain from organizing any public protests against England's Palestine policy during those years, he sometimes pressured others to keep quiet as well. When the U.S. Labor Zionists told him of their plan, in July 1939, to hold "a great parade and demonstration in Madison Square Garden" to protest British restrictions, "I found it necessary to kill this thing," Wise told a friend. "After all, anything done in that direction would just now further complicate the neutrality legislation; and attacks upon England, however justified, will give still another handle to the attacks of the Isolationist folk against FDR."[14]

Similarly, although Rabbi Wise was disturbed to learn in September 1939 that the British government intended to treat German Jewish refugees seeking haven in England the same as all other German nationals, he chose to keep quiet about it. "I cannot find it in my heart, because of my deep pro-British sympathy, to feel very strongly about it," he wrote Frankfurter. "I am fearful chiefly that it would alienate public opinion in America if this purpose became known." When the matter was discussed at a President's Advisory Committee meeting, Wise's chief concern was protecting England's reputation; he wanted the committee to quietly advise British officials that American public opinion would be "alienated" if the new policy "became known."[15]

In early 1940 the British severely restricted the right of Jews to purchase land in Palestine. Wise advised ZOA president Solomon Goldman to refrain from criticizing the new policy. "[E]ven though it will be difficult to undo this damage, we must look to the peace terms [at the end of the war] to annul this lamentable decision," he told Goldman. "[A]ny and every right in Palestine would mean little in the event of the defeat of the democracies, [so] our business is now to support the democracies even when they gravely blunder, as England does."[16] Rabbi Wise did lead a delegation to the British embassy in Washington that November to express concern over the sinking of the Jewish refugee ship *Patria* in the Haifa harbor (Haganah saboteurs attempting to prevent the refugees from being deported accidentally used an excessive quantity of explosives)—but he still refused to publicly blame British policy for leading to such tragedies. "[W]e have only one objective—the immediate and ultimate destruction of Hitlerism," he explained to Frankfurter. "Anything that stands in the way must be ignored. . . . [M]y decision was not to give any further publicity to the matter [of the *Patria*] although, of course, we must for the record have a considered editorial in the [ECZA journal] *New Palestine*."[17]

Just days after the *Patria* disaster, the British sent a large army and police contingent into the Atlit detention center near Haifa, where unauthorized Jewish immigrants were being held. During the course of a six-hour-long operation on December 9, more than one thousand refugees were forcibly taken from the camp and loaded onto ships that would deport them to the African island of Mauritius. British censors subsequently prevented local newspapers from reporting on what had occurred. In early 1941, however, details of the brutal episode began reaching Zionist organizations in the United States, likely from their colleagues in Palestine. An editorial in the March edition of *Hashomer Hatzair*, the journal of the left-wing Zionist youth movement of the same name, declared that "the way Jews were removed from the Athlit prison camp [was] like the gruesome stories of Nazi concentration camps." Refugees who resisted deportation "were beaten and bludgeoned, and their emaciated bodies, bare and naked, were thrown into the lorries at the point of a bayonet." The editors asked: "Shall this be part of the Zionist bargain with Great Britain—to witness such action and be silent?" For Rabbi Wise and his colleagues at the Emergency Council for Zionist Affairs, the answer to that question was, in effect, "yes." During a meeting between an eight-man ECZA delegation and the British ambassador in Washington on March 17, the council's executive director, Emanuel Neumann, reported that the group had received "some details of the shocking treatment meted out at Athlit to the refugees of the *Atlantique*, [but] in the interests of the British war effort, these facts had been kept from the general public." After the meeting, Wise confided to Frankfurter, "I saw to it that things were not pressed too hard. I stressed and stressed, as you may well imagine, my own identification with the British cause."[18]

Appeasing the Rattlesnake

President Roosevelt's statements regarding Palestine after the United States entered World War II indicate he was heavily influenced by a fear that American backing for Zionism would provoke anti-American violence in the Arab world and Arab support for the Axis. He rebuffed a proposal from president Chaim Weizmann in 1942 that the Allies mobilize a Jewish army in defense of Palestine against a German invasion; such a move would antagonize the Egyptians, FDR insisted. (A frustrated Weizmann compared Roosevelt's strategy to "trying to appease a rattlesnake.") FDR rejected a request to allow the Palestine (Jewish) Symphony Orchestra to name one of its theaters the "Roosevelt Amphitheatre," heeding Secretary Hull's warning that it was inadvisable for the administration to be linked too closely with the Zionist endeavor "in view of the strong feeling against Zionism among the Arab peoples." Likewise, President Roosevelt's support for the aforementioned joint Anglo-American statement on Palestine in 1943 (see chapter 4)—the aim of which was to silence Jewish discussion of Palestine—was based on advice from Lt. Col. Harold Hoskins that Allied support for Zionism would provoke "a very bloody conflict" with Arabs that would drag in the Allies and plant "the seeds of a possible third World War." The same concerns also influenced the Bermuda conference: when the delegates raised the idea of settling a few thousand refugees in Allied-occupied portions of North Africa, the War Department objected on the grounds that allowing any Jews "into the Moslem countr[ies] of North Africa" would "stimulate the religious situation there [and] might result in the death and destruction of several hundred thousand American soldiers." President Roosevelt agreed that no more than a handful of Jewish refugees should be given haven in that region. "I know, in fact, that there is plenty of room for them in North Africa but I raise the question of sending large numbers of Jews there," FDR instructed the State Department. "That would be extremely unwise."[19]

In 1942 the State Department created the Office of Post-War Planning, together with an advisory council. FDR named Isaiah Bowman to head both. Housed in the Library of Congress, the operation had a staff of eight to ten as well as twenty to thirty researchers and consultants. From this new perch, Bowman undertook, at the president's behest, a series of studies known as the "M [for Migration] Project," producing for various branches of the administration hundreds of reports and memoranda on possible population resettlement sites. He also figured prominently in wartime administrative discussions regarding Jewish refugee settlement issues and Zionism. FDR remarked to Bowman on more than one occasion that "U.S.

policy on Palestine followed your lead," although it is not clear whether the president meant that literally or was merely flattering Bowman.[20]

Saudi Visitors

During Rabbi Wise's aforementioned July 22, 1943, meeting with President Roosevelt, FDR mentioned—according to the rabbi's account—that "after having arranged to help Saudi Arabia in certain respects, he had invited the Heir Apparent of the Old Man to come to this country and that he would be here soon." The president was alluding to his recent decision to declare Saudi Arabia eligible for U.S. military assistance and his approval of the construction of a new pipeline in Saudi Arabia by the Aramco oil company, to ensure U.S. access to Saudi oil in the years ahead. The "Old Man" to whom Wise referred was Saudi king Ibn Saud; the "Heir Apparent" was his son and foreign minister, Faisal. Recalling Ibn Saud's recent statement to *Life* magazine that Jews had no right to live in Palestine and should stay "in Europe or America," Wise told Roosevelt "how very, very bad it would be if the Heir Apparent were to make any statement in this country with regard to Jews in Palestine, for such statement would be certain to evoke most acrimonious and unwholesome discussion." Nahum Goldmann, apparently repeating what Wise told him, said at the time that the president indicated to Rabbi Wise "that he expected no attacks would be made by the Zionists" on the royal Saudi visitor.[21] In effect the president was warning American Jewry to keep quiet about the Arab visitors.

Meanwhile, concerned that some Jewish members of Congress might publicly challenge Foreign Minister Faisal, the State Department enlisted Sol Bloom to help keep potential critics quiet. At State's request, Bloom informed the Jewish congress members that Faisal, accompanied by his brother, Crown Prince Khalid, would arrive on October 3 and "the State Department had expressed the confident hope that Ibn Saud's son[s] would not be publicly attacked by any Jewish or Zionist

group." All of the congressmen acquiesced to the administration's request, except for Emanuel Celler. According to Bloom's
account, Rep. Celler told the group "he planned to attack Ibn
Saud and his son in a radio broadcast"; all of Bloom's efforts
"to dissuade [sic] Mr. Celler not to do this were in vain." Bloom
asked Nahum Goldmann to intervene with Celler and also
with the Jewish news media. Bloom feared that some Jewish
journalists "might attack Ibn Saud's son[s], which would also
make a bad impression."[22]

Goldmann told Bloom he agreed that "it would certainly be
bad taste and bad politics to attack a man who comes here as
a guest of the President." He assured Bloom that Rabbi Wise
would "discuss the matter with Mr. Celler and warn him not
to make any public attack." Goldmann also promised to "discuss the matter with the editors of the Yiddish and Anglo-
Jewish press and request them to refrain from making any
attacks." At the same time, Goldmann cautioned Bloom that
if the Saudis made any "anti-Zionist statements" during their
visit, "the Zionists would have to issue a counter-statement."
Likewise, Rabbi Wise told presidential aide Samuel Rosenman that if the Saudi visitors spoke out against Jewish statehood, "it would evoke very unpleasant Zionist repercussions
and that, of course, would be undesirable from every point of
view." Bloom assured Goldmann he would "make it clear to the
State Department that no such statements should be made" by
the Saudis. It appeared that the Jewish leaders and the administration had a deal: the Jews would keep quiet, and the Saudis
would say nothing about Palestine.[23]

Although exactly what Wise said to Celler or what Goldmann
said to various Jewish newspaper editors remains unknown, it
seems the Jews kept their side of the bargain. The major Jewish
and Zionist organizations did not issue any statements about
the Saudis' visit. Congressman Celler's radio address mentioned the visiting princes but did not directly criticize them;
instead, Celler merely expressed hope that President Roosevelt
would explain to the Saudis why Jewish development of Pales-

tine was beneficial to the Middle East. For its part, the Jewish Telegraphic Agency optimistically reported: "It is understood that the Arabian delegation is not expected to make any anti-Zionist statements during its stay in the United States."

Ibn Saud's sons, however, did not live up to that prediction. Prince Faisal told the Washington press corps that British Mandatory Palestine should become an Arab state and join a "United States of Arabia" that would include Egypt, Iraq, and Syria. Despite Faisal's remark, Ibn Saud's sons left Washington with an agreement for a badly needed U.S. loan, to be followed soon afterward by U.S. military equipment (via the Lend-Lease program). American Jewish leaders, fearful of crossing the president, did not publicly respond to Faisal's statement about Palestine. They watched in silent frustration as the administration failed to fulfill its promise to keep the prince from raising the Palestine issue.[24]

"Going to Town for Palestine"

By the autumn of 1943, there were signs that the expected contenders for the 1944 Republican nomination, New York governor Thomas Dewey and previous nominee Wendell Willkie, intended to target Jewish voters in the next presidential election. After Dewey and Willkie sent strongly worded pro-Zionist messages to a New York City rally commemorating the Balfour Declaration, Vice President Wallace noted in his diary "how vigorously Willkie is going to town for Palestine," while Rabbi Wise wrote to David Niles, Roosevelt's liaison to the Jewish community, that he was "very much disturbed by the things that Dewey is saying about Palestine."

Could the administration's unsympathetic policies regarding Palestine and refugees drive some Jewish voters away from Roosevelt? Lillie Shultz of the AJcongress thought so—and recommended using that prospect as leverage on the White House. As noted in chapter 4, Shultz had recently argued at a Joint Emergency Committee meeting that "ways can be found to indicate to the administration, and possibly through the political parties that the large and influential Jewish communit[y] will find a way of registering its dissatisfaction over the failure of the administration to take any effective steps to save the Jews of Europe." Similarly, Eri Jabotinsky of the Bergson Group reported to his colleagues that the fight in Congress over the Gillette-Rogers rescue resolution could have electoral consequences:

> It is felt in Democratic as well as Republican circles that the issue involved, if not handled carefully, may lose for the Administration a good million of Jewish voters, especially in New York City. . . . The debate around the Resolution has certainly succeeded in awakening widespread Jewish interest, and the failure of this Resolution to be adopted by Congress would certainly create a deep rift between the Jews on the one side and the State Department, even the President, on the other side. It is typical today to hear public orators at Jewish gatherings saying that Jesus was not the Messiah, nor apparently is Mr. Roosevelt.[25]

Jabotinsky's assessment of attitudes among grassroots Jews is noteworthy because he and his comrades were well positioned to take the pulse of Jewish public opinion. Bergson Group officials lived in working-class Jewish neighborhoods, attended less-Americanized synagogues, and read the Yiddish-language press. They were keenly attuned to the criticism of President Roosevelt's positions on European Jewry and Zionism, which appeared in Jewish newspapers with increasing frequency in late 1943 and early 1944.

With the White Paper scheduled to expire in May 1944, Rabbis Wise and Abba Hillel Silver visited the White House on March 9, seeking an expression of presidential opposition to renewal of the British policy. They also hoped to secure FDR's endorsement of a recently introduced congressional resolution—sponsored by Senator Robert Taft (R-OH) and Representatives Ranulf Compton (R-CT) and James Wright (D-PA)—calling on the administration to "use its good offices and take appropriate measures" to persuade the British to open Palestine to the "free entry" of Jewish immigrants. They did not know that during a February 18 cabinet meeting, President Roosevelt, Acting Secretary of State Edward Stettinius Jr., and Secretary of War Stimson were all "in complete accord that the Moslem world was all ready to be set on fire all the way from Morocco to Arabia and the military situation would be imperiled by any action taken [by Congress] at the present time," Vice President Wallace wrote in his diary. Wallace also noted that Stimson, apparently annoyed by Jewish protests regarding Palestine, dismissively called the State Department "the wailing wall for the Jews."[26]

Wise and Silver told the press after the March 9 meeting that President Roosevelt assured them "the American Government has never given its approval to the White Paper of 1939" and that "When future decisions are reached, full justice will be done to those who seek a Jewish National Home for which our Government and the American people have always had the deepest sympathy and today more than ever in view of the tragic plight of hundreds of thousands of homeless Jewish refugees." Wise told Niles after the meeting that "the Chief never was kinder nor more friendly nor more helpful." That evening, Wise quoted the president's statement in his address to a Zionist dinner in Washington. He did not mention that the president had declined to endorse the congressional resolution.[27]

Rabbi Silver concurred with Wise's upbeat assessment. He told Vice President Henry Wallace later that day that he, too, was "very much pleased" with the outcome of the meeting with Roosevelt. However, other accounts of the next day's cabinet meeting indicate there was more to the story. According to Wallace and Treasury Secretary Morgenthau, FDR boasted to the cabinet that he had told Wise and Silver "where to get off." He berated the Jewish leaders, "Do you want to start a Holy Jihad? . . . If you people continue pushing this recommendation [for the pro-Zionist congressional resolution] on the Hill, you are going to be responsible for the killing of a hundred thousand people"— because "enraged Arabs" would attack Americans in the Mideast as revenge for U.S. support of Zionism. The vice president noted in his diary that after this dressing-down, Roosevelt proceeded "to cause Wise and Silver to believe that he was in complete accord with them and the only question was timing." Wallace observed: "The President certainly is a waterman. He looks one direction and rows the other with the utmost skill."[28]

Roosevelt also led Silver and Wise to believe he would be willing to issue a pro-Zionist statement based on their conversation. Four days after their meeting, on March 13, the Zionist leaders sent the president a draft of the proposed statement. Yet in the meantime, FDR hurried to assure Arab leaders he did not really mean what Wise and Silver were claiming he meant. On March 15 Secretary Hull sent a telegram—the draft of which bore the words "Approved by the President" in the margin—to American ambassadors in the Arab world, instructing them to inform Arab leaders that FDR had spoken to Silver and Wise only of a "national home" rather than a state; that the United States promised nothing would be done regarding Palestine "without full consultation with both Arabs and Jews"; and that the United States "has never taken a position in regard to the White Paper." Hull was correct; at the time of the White Paper's proclamation in 1939, Roosevelt had refrained from saying he approved of it, but he also carefully refrained from disapproving of it, as the president himself reminded Hull five years later.[29]

Roosevelt's unfulfilled March 9 promise to Wise and Silver soon became tangled in the swirl of developments abroad. Ten days later, on March 19, 1944, the Germans occupied Hungary. The last major Jewish community in Europe not yet engulfed by the Holocaust, eight hundred thousand in number, was now in Hitler's grasp. For several weeks, the War Refugee Board had been pressing the White House to issue a statement warning civilians in Axis-occupied countries to refrain from assisting any Nazi persecution of Jews. FDR objected that the draft was "too much for the Jews." The occupation of Hungary made such a warning all the more urgent. After several weeks of wrangling, the president agreed to issue the statement, but only after making a significant change in the text: the word "Jews" was to be removed from the first four paragraphs and downplayed elsewhere and refrences to Japanese war crimes and the mistreatment of American POWs were added.

The president issued the warning on March 24. Although the statement never mentioned Palestine, Roosevelt and Hull decided its publication relieved the administration of any obligation with regard to the proposed Wise-Silver statement on Palestine. Hull told FDR that the Zionist leaders' request for a Palestine statement "is really fully answered in the Statement of March 24, 1944," so there was no need to act on the other statement; the president readily concurred. Two entirely different issues—Palestine and rescue—were under discussion, but it was as if throwing one bone to "the Jews" would suffice.

Despite these developments, Rabbi Wise's political faith remained essentially unshaken. He still believed Roosevelt and the Democratic Party on the whole represented decency, fairness, and the liberal humanitarian values he cherished as a Jew and as an American. The Republicans, on the other hand, represented the forces of reaction, bigotry, and exploitation of the working man. They were nothing more than canny politicians trying to lure Jewish voters on the basis of promises they would never fulfill. As a result, whenever Wise was disappointed by a Roosevelt policy concerning Jews or Zionism, he characterized it as an aberration caused by specific circumstances or advisers, and not as a genuine reflection of the president's views. "I am still greatly worried about the Chief's attitude" toward Palestine, Wise confided to a friend in November 1943. "He seems to be completely and hopelessly under the domination of the English Foreign Office and . . . the Colonial Office in London." Wise convinced himself that FDR was a good man surrounded by bad influences. And even in the worst-case scenario—if Roosevelt absolutely refused to alter his policies on Jewish refugees and Palestine—Wise still believed the president's political and social agenda was best for society, and therefore Jews needed to support him when they cast their ballots.[30]

The electoral math in the forthcoming presidential election gave Wise and other prominent Jewish Democrats reason for concern about Thomas Dewey. He was the popular governor of the state with the most electoral votes. New York's forty-seven votes (the next largest was Pennsylvania, with thirty-five votes) could be the key to the election, and the state's large Jewish voting bloc—comprising about 14 percent of New York's electorate—could swing the state. Congressman Celler was particularly vocal about this danger. In a memo to presidential secretary Marvin McIntyre, Celler warned that "the Jews in New York and other areas like Philadelphia, Chicago, Boston, Sanfrancisco [sic], [and] Cleveland are greatly exercised over the failure of our Administration to condemn the MacDonald White Paper. . . . It would not surprise me in the least to have Governor Dewey make a pronouncement in the not too distant future to the effect that Palestine cannot be liquidated as a homeland for the Jews and that the MacDonald White Paper must be abrogated . . . as far as the race of Abraham, Isaac and Jacob is concerned, [Dewey] would steal the show right from under our noses."[31]

Ironically, the Republicans' interest in Palestine was connected in part to the lobbying efforts of Wise's own co-chair at the (recently renamed) American Zionist Emergency Council, Abba Hillel Silver. The fact that one of the GOP's most powerful figures, Senator Robert Taft, hailed from Silver's home state of Ohio gave Silver frequent opportunities to interact with the senator. Although Silver himself was not a Republican, he recognized the value in having connections on both sides of the aisle, and over the years had carefully cultivated a close relationship with Taft. Wise could not object to Silver's friendly relations with an important United States senator, but the fact that Silver was close to the nation's most prominent conservative Republican politician, while Wise embraced the liberal Democrat president, made it almost inevitable that the Wise-Silver relationship would quickly deteriorate. Their personality differences only exacerbated the tensions. Wise was known for his short temper; Goldmann recalled the rabbi's tendency to "flare up terribly and become quite rude." By November 1943 one of Wise's close colleagues, Meyer Weisgal, was reporting that Silver's independent spirit and the perceived threat Silver posed to Wise's leadership was driving Wise into "a state of uncontrollable fury." Weisgal described a recent example of Wise's "intermittent convulsions" over Silver: "Lipsky and I were beneficiaries, last Friday, of the first thunderous outburst that rocked the offices of the American Jewish Congress to its foundation. 'Either Silver will learn to consult, collaborate, cooperate, or I will resign from the Emergency Committee.' The *keles uvrokin* [the deafening thunder and lightning] on Mt. Sinai [at the time of the giving of the Torah, Exodus 19:16] could not have been much louder. We tried to pacify him but it was useless."[32]

The private correspondence of Wise and Silver soon overflowed with harsh insults behind each other's backs. As far as Silver was concerned, Wise suffered from a "hysterical prestige-complex." To Wise, Silver was "arrogant" and "vulgar." It may have been only a rhetorical flourish, but soon Wise was writing to a colleague: "Pray for me. I need the intervention of divine protection, unless I want to perish at the hand of the co-Chairman of the Emergency Council." The Republican and Democratic party conventions in the summer of 1944 would bring the Wise-Silver conflict to a climax.[33]

Showdown at the Conventions

Senator Taft was slated to chair the resolutions committee at the 1944 GOP convention. Rabbi Silver's ties to Taft led to an invitation to Silver to deliver the benediction at the convention. It also gave him an opportunity to speak with Taft and other Republican leaders about adding a plank about Palestine to the party's campaign platform. Neither major political party had ever before taken that step.[34]

Additional spadework in promoting the Palestine issue to the Republicans was undertaken by Benzion Netanyahu, an energetic scholar and emissary of Revisionist Zionism who had come to the United States in 1940 to organize rallies and full-page newspaper ads challenging the Allies for abandoning European Jewry and the Zionist cause. In the months leading up to the convention, Netanyahu met with a number of influential Republicans, including Senator Taft, former president Herbert Hoover, and Connecticut congresswoman Clare Booth Luce, who had been chosen to deliver the keynote address at the convention and would also serve on the resolutions committee. Netanyahu pressed his Republican contacts to adopt a plank supporting Jewish statehood in Palestine.[35]

The GOP had good reason to embrace the Palestine cause, whether out of genuine sympathy for the Jews or simply to take advantage of political circumstances. The result was a plank that actually went further than either Silver or Netanyahu had requested:

> In order to give refuge to millions of distressed Jewish men, women and children driven from their homes by tyranny we call for the opening of Palestine to their unrestricted immigration and land ownership, so that in accordance with the full intent and purpose of the Balfour Declaration of 1917 and the resolution of a Republican Congress in 1922, Palestine may be reconstituted as a free and democratic commonwealth. We condemn the failure of the President to insist that the Palestine Mandatory carry out the provisions of the Balfour Declaration and the Mandate while he pretends to support them.[36]

Rabbi Wise was enraged by the inclusion of the anti-Roosevelt sentence, for which he blamed Silver, although in fact the language was added over Silver's objections. Neither Silver nor Netanyahu's Revisionists had ever explicitly criticized FDR in public; both men understood the political pitfalls of attacking a popular president in the midst of a world war. Nonetheless, a furious and embarrassed Wise immediately informed the president that he was "deeply ashamed" of the plank's wording, and he issued a public statement criticizing the GOP for casting "an unjust aspersion" on Roosevelt.[37]

Originally, Wise had not planned to attend that summer's Democratic convention in Chicago, but the Republicans' embrace of Palestine forced his hand. "I now think I shall go there," he wrote Frankfurter, "in order to be certain that the Resolution on Palestine which must now be adopted shall more than neutralize the damage done by the Silver-inspired attack upon the Chief." For his part, Silver was delighted to see that even as the Republican plank infuriated Wise, it galvanized him. "For the first time, our [Zionist] Movement finds itself in the fortunate position where both major political parties are competing for its approval," a delighted Rabbi Silver wrote to a colleague. He counseled Wise to use the GOP plank "as a lever to put through a similar and, if possible, a better plank in the Democratic platform." At the same time, however, Silver cautioned his rival that anti-Zionists in the State Department "will bring pressure to bear . . . to have a watered-down, meaningless plank on Palestine" in the Democrats' platform. Thus, Silver wrote to Wise, "You might have to go to the very top [meaning President Roosevelt] to force through a strong resolution."[38]

As much as he resented Silver, Wise evidently realized that in this instance his arch-enemy had a point. Hence, in the days preceding the Democratic convention, Wise repeatedly asked White House aides for a meeting with FDR to secure his "personal and administration support of [the] Zionist program" and "affirmation of his desire to bring about maximum rescue [of] Jewish civilians." Wise's request was denied.[39]

Soon after arriving at the convention, Wise found himself shut out of the deliberation over the Palestine resolution. "It's all so confusing and distressing," he complained to a colleague. "I can't break through a cordon of bell boys." In a letter to President Roosevelt that went unanswered, Wise reported: "My information is that either no plank concerning Palestine is to be adopted or that the Platform will include a plank which is utterly inadequate." Wise caught wind of rumors that presidential speechwriter Samuel Rosenman was pushing for a Palestine resolution that would be so weak it would constitute, as

the rabbi put it, "a great gift to [Republican presidential nom-
inee] Tom D[ewey]." Wise did secure permission to address
the Committee on Resolutions—only to find that Rabbi Morris Lazaron, a leader of the anti-Zionist American Council for
Judaism, was being granted equal time to testify to the committee against a Palestine plank. In his remarks to the committee,
and in the draft he circulated, Wise proposed that the Palestine plank call for "its establishment as a free and democratic
Jewish commonwealth." In the version that was adopted, that
phrase was watered down to "the establishment there of a free
and democratic Jewish commonwealth." AZEC officials inter-
preted the softer wording as "implying partition." Moreover,
the Democrats' plank made no mention the plight of European
Jewry. Still, the language on Palestine was arguably as strong as
the GOP's with regard to Palestine, and its reference to a "Jewish" commonwealth was arguably more explicit than that of the
Republicans. Rabbi Wise concluded that on balance, "we did
rather well" in securing the Democrats' pro-Zionist position.[40]

Wise attributed this achievement to his "personal friendships
with many leaders of the Party," which he said "gave us the resolution that we finally got despite those who would have denied
us." Synagogue Council of America president Israel Goldstein,
who accompanied Wise at the convention, believed their success was the result of old-fashioned one-on-one lobbying. He,
Wise, and their colleague Herman Shulman had positioned
themselves near a revolving door directly downstairs from the
room where the platform was being discussed, "so that every
politician that came in would be bound to bump into Wise. . . .
He knew most of them by their first names. . . . And he col-
lared every one of these politicians and I was standing there at
his side as a kind of junior assistant and the two of us together
would indoctrinate that person in the two or three minutes that
were available, and that person was on his way to the meeting of the Platform Committee which was upstairs. So by the
time he got to his meeting, he had already had some indoctri-
nation at the hands of Wise plus Goldstein—mostly Wise."[41]

An additional ingredient contributed to Rabbi Wise's success. Some of the arguments he made at the Democratic convention were anchored, explicitly or implicitly, in the electoral ramifications of the party's stance on Palestine. Assistant Attorney General Norman Littell, a convention delegate, later recalled how Wise buttonholed him to warn of the electoral dangers: "'They are refusing to give us a plank on the establishment of an independent state in Palestine,' [Wise] said, seizing both my hands. 'Judge Proskauer, through Sam Rosenman at the White House, has influenced the President against such a plan. It will hurt the president. It will lose the President 400,000 or 500,000 votes.'" The Republicans had adopted "a satisfactory plank" on Palestine, Wise reminded Littell; therefore the Democrats needed to match it.[42]

Wise's threats at the convention concerning the Jewish vote did not necessarily contradict his own many public statements emphatically denying that a Jewish vote existed and decrying the very concept of such a voting bloc. There was a significant difference between talking about a Jewish vote in public and talking about it in private. A public affirmation of a "Jewish vote" would have gone beyond what Wise felt American Jews could legitimately and comfortably say out loud concerning their political behavior. In his eyes, it would have indicated to the general American public that unlike them, Jews were not fully loyal Americans—that Jews' voting preferences were based on narrow ethnic concerns rather than patriotic considerations of what was best for America as a whole. To be welcomed by non-Jews as equal citizens, Jews had to give lesser priority to ethnic interests, and make sure that non-Jews knew they were doing so. What Wise said in a private setting that was unlikely to reach a wider audience, however, was another matter. In specific situations where it was necessary, he was prepared to invoke the Jewish vote.

As a result, owing to the interrelated pressures of the GOP plank and Rabbi Wise's use of the Jewish vote as a rhetorical weapon, the Democrats adopted a pro-Zionist plank. It was, if nothing else, a concession to political reality. "With the plank in both platforms the thing is lifted above partisanship," Wise exulted after the resolutions committee vote. The adoption of the two party planks ensured that support for Zionism, and later for Israel, would have an enduring place in American political culture.[43]

Countering Dewey

Keenly sensitive to Arab opinion, the State Department was alarmed by Rabbi Wise's achievement in Chicago. In the wake of the Democratic convention, Secretary of State Hull advised President Roosevelt that Arab leaders were justifiably worried American Zionists had "take[n] advantage of the political situation in this country to commit both major parties to a course which would not be in accord with the war aims of the United Nations [the Allies]." Hull urged FDR to "refrain from making statements on Palestine during the campaign that might tend to arouse the Arabs or upset the precarious balance of forces in Palestine itself." Several weeks later, the secretary of state again lamented to the president that "the susceptibilities [sic] of the Arabs have been aroused" by the two parties' platforms.[44]

Meanwhile, Wise and his colleagues at the American Zionist Emergency Council learned of rumors that Governor Dewey intended to issue a pro-Zionist statement in the weeks prior to Election Day. To counter Dewey's move, they decided to seek a public affirmation by President Roosevelt supporting the Democrats' Palestine plank. Wise wrote to the president to request a meeting. "I would not press this if I did not know how important it was from certain points of view to see you now," he explained. "There are things afoot which I do not like, designed to hurt you. These must not be permitted. Nearly everything can be done to avoid them if we can talk to you and have from you a word which shall be your personal affirmation of the Palestine plank in the Chicago platform of the Party. Easy enough for the Republican candidate to make the broadest and most reckless of promises, as indeed he is doing in many directions."[45]

Samuel Rosenman shared Wise's concerns. In a September 16 memo to the president, Rosenman warned of indications that Dewey "is going to make quite a play" on Palestine. FDR offered to "say something" in an upcoming speech "about preparations being necessary [in Palestine] because I do not want to see an immediate mass influx before the country is ready for it." A remark along those lines would have accurately reflected Roosevelt's longstanding convictions, but the president's public assertion that Palestine was not yet ready for a large number of immigrants might have increased Jewish support for the Republican nominee.[46]

Wise, meanwhile, did not receive a reply from the president, so he turned to Rosenman. In a note on September 26, the rabbi wrote:

> I may say to you in confidence that it would be definitely helpful to THE cause if we could see the Chief with the least possible delay, and get from him a statement that would be little more than one of assent to the plank in the Democratic platform, together with some word that would indicate that either in this or his next term of office he will do what he can to translate that platform declaration into action together with the British Government. Believe me, dear Judge [Rosenman's pre-White House position], that I would not press this as I do if I did not have reason to fear that fullest advantage might be taken of the Chief's failure to speak on this at an early date. It would be a mistake to let that word come just before the elections; the sooner the better, as you well understand."[47]

Meanwhile, in Jerusalem on September 28, Nahum Goldmann was briefing the Jewish Agency. He described Wise's strategy: "Wise will tell [Roosevelt] that this declaration could secure for him 200,000 additional votes in New York, and there is a chance that at the end of October the president will perhaps issue the declaration."[48]

While waiting for Rosenman's reply, Wise and Silver enlisted Senator Robert Wagner to help them reach the president. Perhaps pressure from a senator could move the president where the Zionist leaders could not. The senator had recently let them know he was looking for a way to impress his state's Jewish voters prior to Election Day. Wise and Silver decided to have Wagner ask Roosevelt to meet with them to prepare a presidential statement on Zionism, which Wagner could read aloud at the Zionist Organization of America's annual convention in mid-October.[49]

At last, after repeated inquiries from Wagner, Wise, and Silver (and probably also with Rosenman's recommendation), the president agreed to see Wise—but not Silver—on October 11. At about the same time, Wise gave Rosenman a draft of the message he hoped the president would send to Wagner to be read at the Zionist convention. No transcript of the Roosevelt-Wise conversation exists, but some indication as to what transpired was provided by Wise's colleague Herman Shulman, speaking on Wise's behalf at a subsequent AZEC board meeting (as Wise was too ill to attend). Shulman reported that FDR affirmed to Wise "that the Palestine plank in the Democratic Party platform had [the president's] full support." The two men then discussed Wise's proposal for Roosevelt to "send a message to Senator Wagner." According to Shulman's account, Wise believed electoral considerations—both Wagner's as well as FDR's—constituted the decisive factor in convincing Roosevelt to send a statement to Wagner. It seems likely Wise said something to the president along the lines of what Nahum Goldmann had told the Jewish Agency leadership Wise was planning to say. "There was a reference to the [election] campaign," Shulman reported to his AZEC colleagues. "There was no doubt that the question of the campaign for Senator Wagner's re-election in New York in particular and the problems of the political campaign in general had been an important factor in the whole matter."[50] The only public statement Wise made afterwards was a joke to reporters that afternoon that he was not sure whether he would vote "for the President or for the Democratic candidate."[51]

The day following the FDR—Wise meeting, Governor Dewey announced his endorsement of the GOP's Palestine plank. "I am for the reconstitution of Palestine as a free and democratic Jewish commonwealth in accordance with the Balfour Declaration of 1917," the Republican nominee declared. "I have also stated to Dr. Silver that in order to give refuge to millions of distressed Jews driven from their homes by tyranny, I favor the opening of Palestine to their unlimited immigration and land ownership. . . . The Republican Party has at all times been the traditional friend of this movement. As President I would use my best offices to have our Government, working together with Great Britain, achieve this great objective for a people that have suffered so much and deserve so much at the hands of mankind."[52]

President Roosevelt needed to quickly counter the attention Dewey attracted with his pro-Zionist announcement. The proposed presidential message to Wagner provided the vehicle. Rosenman gave the president Wise's draft, cautioning that the draft "takes you out very far in favor of a Jewish Commonwealth—too far." FDR agreed. Over the course of the next twenty-four hours, the president made four changes that weakened the text. The original draft's explicit pledge to support a Jewish commonwealth was changed to a vague promise that unspecified "efforts" would be undertaken to determine the "appropriate ways and means" to bring about a commonwealth. The promise that a Jewish homeland would be established "as soon as practicable" was deleted. Wise's version referred to "an undivided Palestine"; in Roosevelt's edited version, "undivided" was removed. Also, the pledge "I shall do all in my power" (to facilitate a Jewish homeland) was reduced to just "I shall help to bring about." FDR did not want to explicitly commit to facilitating the creation of a Jewish state. He also did not want to rule out the possibility that the Jews would be given only a small portion of Palestine.[53]

If the delegates to the Zionist convention where the message was read had been aware of the differences between Wise's draft and FDR's final version, they might have been disturbed by the evidence of the president's lukewarm commitment to Jewish statehood. Not knowing how the draft had been watered down, however, they heard what sounded like boilerplate presidential praise of the Zionist cause, and cheered accordingly.

The pro-Zionist congressional resolution that Wise and Silver had discussed with President Roosevelt back in March 1944 had been temporarily set aside. As noted earlier, President Roosevelt, Stettinius, and Stimson had all agreed, during a cabinet discussion, that the resolution should be prevented from being considered by Congress, for fear that its passage would spark a violent reaction throughout the Arab World. By September, however, buoyed by the inclusion of Jewish statehood in the Democratic and Republican party platforms, AZEC sought to have the resolution introduced anew. Silver mobilized hundreds of local Zionist groups throughout the country to press their congress members to back the resolution. Silver's activist approach created a new point of friction with Rabbi Wise, who preferred a quiet campaign limited to private contacts in the administration. Silver's supporters characterized these differing strategies as a clash between "vigorous public action as against timidity and a reversion to *Shtadlanut* [backstairs diplomacy]."[54]

The resolution's lead sponsors—Taft in the Senate, Wright and Compton in the House—were ready to reintroduce their measure. The administration, however, was still opposed. Acting Secretary of State Edward Stettinius informed Wise on November 15 that the president continued to regard the resolution as "unwise." Wise hurriedly convened an AZEC meeting without Silver's knowledge, and persuaded his colleagues not to take action on the resolution so long as the president opposed it. Rabbi Silver was engaged in "the needless and ruthless exacerbation of FDR, who is our friend despite Silver," Wise contended. When Silver, together with Senator Robert Wagner, arrived at the office of Secretary Stettinius on December 4, they were shocked to see the telegram Wise had sent Stettinius earlier in the day, assuring him that American Jewish leaders "do not wish to have action taken [on the resolution] contrary to your and the president's recommendation." Two days later, Stettinius persuaded the Senate Foreign Relations Committee to set the resolution aside.

In the wake of these developments, Rabbi Wise sensed an opportunity to strike at his archenemy. On December 12 Wise dramatically announced he could not remain co-chairman of AZEC if Silver was part of the leadership, because his continued support of the Taft-Wright-Compton resolution contravened the council's position.[55]

Wise then enlisted the secretary of state to help silence the rabbi's Jewish critics. Wise drafted a message for Stettintius to send to him, in which he assured Wise that although the administration wanted the resolution "deferred for the time being," it still adhered to the president's October 15 statement on Palestine. In the past, the president and his aides had used Wise to keep Jewish dissidents quiet; now Wise was utilizing the secretary of state for the same purpose—a strategy with which Stettinius was glad to cooperate.

The gambit strengthened Rabbi Wise's hand as he jockeyed with Silver for control of the Zionist movement. To Zionist activists, it appeared that the administration was sincerely, and of its own accord, expressing continued support for Zionism; they had no way to know that Wise himself had choreographed the entire maneuver. Eight days later, AZEC convened an all-day session at which Silver was essentially placed in the docket. Taking umbrage at the accusations and intemperate tone of his critics, Silver stormed out of the meeting and resigned his co-chairmanship of AZEC. Wise was pleased to bid good riddance to Silver and resume his sole leadership of the council.[56]

Five Minutes with Ibn Saud

There was to be one more troubling episode in the history of President Roosevelt's Palestine policy. Returning from the Yalta Conference in February 1945, FDR stopped in the Middle East for meetings aboard the USS *Quincy* with, among others, King Ibn Saud of Saudi Arabia. The king came aboard "with his whole court, slaves (black), taster, astrologer, & 8 live sheep," Roosevelt wrote with amusement to his confidante, Margaret Suckley. "Whole party was a scream!" One of the topics he and the king discussed was whether or not the Arabs could accept the creation of a Jewish homeland in Palestine. According to the official notes of the conversation—recorded by the U.S. ambassador to Riyadh, William Eddy, and signed afterward by both the president and the king—Roosevelt asked Ibn Saud for his view of "the problem of Jewish refugees driven from their homes in Europe." The king responded that the Jews should be "given living space in the Axis countries which oppressed them," not in Palestine. Roosevelt replied that "Poland might be considered a case in point. The Germans appear to have killed three million Polish Jews, by which count there should be space in Poland for the resettlement of many homeless Jews." Ibn Saud protested against "continued Jewish immigration and the purchase of land [in Palestine] by the Jews," insisting that "the Arabs and the Jews could never cooperate, neither in Palestine, nor in any other country." President Roosevelt "replied that he wished to assure his Majesty that he would do nothing to assist the Jews against the Arabs and would make no move hostile to the Arab people."[57]

FDR reiterated that assurance in a subsequent exchange of correspondence with the king. On March 10 Ibn Saud wrote to Roosevelt, asking him to oppose the continued development of a Jewish homeland in Palestine. In his April 4 reply, recalling "the memorable conversation which we had not so long ago," FDR reaffirmed that "no decision [will] be taken with respect to the basic situation in that country without full consultation with both Arabs and Jews," and reiterated his assurance "that I would take no action, in my capacity as Chief of the Executive Branch of this Government, which might prove hostile to the Arab people."[58]

Rabbi Wise never knew the full details of Roosevelt's conversation or correspondence with Ibn Saud; the transcripts were not revealed until many years later. But FDR's allusion, in public, to one part of his discussion with the Saudi king was more than enough to shock and alarm Wise. Speaking to a joint session of Congress on March 1, 1945, FDR departed from his prepared text to offer an ad-libbed comment about Palestine: "I learned more about the whole problem, the Moslem problem, the Jewish problem, by talking with Ibn Saud for five minutes than I could have learned in the exchange of two or three dozen letters."[59]

Roosevelt's assertion ignited a firestorm of criticism from members of Congress and the American Jewish community. "The choice of the desert king as expert on the Jewish question is nothing short of amazing," Colorado Senator Edwin Johnson declared. "I imagine that even Fala [the president's dog] would be more of an expert." Rabbi Wise visited the White House on March 16, hoping for some reassurance that FDR had been misunderstood. The president began the meeting by berating Wise for failing to realize that seeking Jewish statehood would lead to an Arab massacre of Palestine's Jews: "You are a minister of religion. Do you want me to encourage five or six hundred thousand Jews to die?" At the same time, the president also assured Wise that he still stood by the pro-Zionist (if watered down) message he had sent to Senator Wagner the previous October at Wise's request. Emerging from the meeting, Wise announced that the president's position on Zionism was unchanged, despite the Ibn Saud episode. In a letter to James McDonald shortly afterward, Rabbi Wise said he was "encouraged" by FDR's "reaffirmation," adding that the problem was that "the President's will is not carried out by the State Department. He plans and recommends one course; they execute another." Wise did not explain how the State Department could have been responsible for Roosevelt's evidently spontaneous remarks regarding Ibn Saud, nor how State would have been able to conduct its own foreign policy in defiance of the president.[60]

Four days after FDR's meeting with Rabbi Wise, the president met with anti-Zionists Joseph Proskauer and Jacob Blaustein of the AJcommittee. According to Proskauer, FDR told them that "the project of a Jewish state in Palestine was, under present conditions, impossible of accomplishment." The president then recounted how he had told Wise that he, "as a rabbi," had no right to provoke an Arab pogrom in Palestine, or a third world war, by continuing his agitation for a Jewish state. Proskauer suggested to the president that there seemed to be a contradiction between what he was saying now and his remark to Wise just a few days earlier that his position on Zionism had not changed since the October 1944 statement. FDR replied: "Don't I know that, Joe? That's why I'm telling it to you. I went out on a limb for those goddamn Zionists and I have been to Yalta and I have talked to Ibn Saud. . . . You can't get a Jewish state in a country that's two-thirds Arab." Proskauer's account is consistent with what Lt. Col. Hoskins privately recorded after he and the president met that same week: "Roosevelt said there were 15,000,000 or 20,000,000 Arabs in and around Palestine and that, in the long run, he thought these numbers would win out."[61]

Several months after President Roosevelt's sudden passing, on April 12, 1945, from a cerebral hemorrhage, Proskauer told a number of other Jewish leaders about his and Blaustein's conversation with FDR regarding Palestine. This triggered what would be the first of several controversies in which Rabbi Wise vigorously defended the late president's record on Jewish issues. Upon learning of Proskauer's remarks, Wise wrote a private letter to an old friend, Rabbi William Rosenblatt, accusing Proskauer of deliberately misrepresenting the president's position on Zionism and describing Proskauer as "a congenital and incurable liar . . . one of the vilest human beings I have ever known . . . without a shred of honor." Proskauer, catching wind of the letter, telephoned Wise, who "categorically denied" having written it. Rabbi Rosenblatt, however, would neither confirm nor deny the authenticity of the letter, prompting Proskauer to demand that Wise disavow it in writing. Rabbi Wise stalled for a week, then wrote to

Proskauer, admitting that he had authored the letter; explaining that he had denied writing it because he had simply "forgotten" about it; and justifing his outburst on the grounds that Proskauer had put him "in an explicable mood of bitter wrath [because Proskauer] dared . . . to misquote the President when he could no longer speak for himself." In a private letter to Felix Frankfurter a few days later, Wise said he had admitted authorship of the "intemperate" letter to Proskauer because "he could probably sue me for several million dollars for libel," although Wise continued to believe that what he wrote about Proskauer was true.[62]

As for the substance of the issue, Wise wrote Frankfurter in November 1945 that he was especially chagrined by Proskauer's purported claim that Roosevelt also said to him, "Go to San Francisco and see if you can hold Stephen and the Zionists in check." This was a reference to the then-forthcoming founding conference of the United Nations in San Francisco in April 1945. Zionist delegates to the gathering, led by Wise, promoted the cause of Jewish statehood among the delegates; the AJ committee delegation, led by Proskauer, lobbied in favor of general human rights principles for the postwar international community. "It is unthinkable," Wise wrote Frankfurter, "that FDR was so treacherous as to urge Joe to neutralize us Zionists as far as he could at San Francisco." Yet the president or his representatives had indeed sought to "hold Stephen and the Zionists in check" on multiple occasions. As previously noted, Roosevelt had personally thanked Ambassador Dodd for "checking the Chicago agitation" after Dodd acted to cause the cancellation of the planned second staging of Wise's mock trial of Hitler in 1934. Two years later, Felix Frankfurter, conveying the president's sentiments, had warned Wise "not to make any outcry" against the British Royal Commission investigating Palestine. Also in 1936 FDR had spoken directly to Wise about "the necessity for a time of Jews lying low." In 1938 Roosevelt pressed Wise to neuter the planned American Jewish plebiscite. In 1943 the president asked Rabbi Wise to ensure that American Jews refrained from publicly criticizing the two Saudi princes during their visit to the

United States. That same year, FDR approved the proposed Anglo-American statement to suppress public discussions of Palestine during the war, then he used the imminent publication of that statement as leverage to try to get Wise to "stifle Zionist clamours" (such as the Bergson Group's newspaper ads) and to drop all references to Jewish statehood from the rabbi's forthcoming address to the American Jewish Conference. The following year, President Roosevelt tried to pressure Wise and Silver to stop promoting a pro-Zionist congressional resolution by claiming that their activities would provoke "a Holy Jihad" that would lead to "the killing of a hundred thousand people."[63]

The Proskauer episode was not the only instance in which Wise responded so vigorously to those who questioned FDR's commitment to the Jewish people. When, in 1946, he heard that former vice president Henry Wallace had referred to Roosevelt as having been "never very keen on Zionism," Wise enlisted former undersecretary of state Sumner Welles to write a letter to the AZEC official who had reported Wallace's statement to Wise, to "dispel the illusion" that, Wise alleged, had been fostered by "the campaign to blacken the name and record of the President." Several factors were likely at work in compelling Wise to engage in such posthumous efforts in defense of Roosevelt. In general Wise found it extremely difficult to admit that he was wrong. In this instance acknowledging that FDR was not the friend of Zionism that Wise had portrayed him to be would constitute an admission that Wise's entire political strategy over the past decade—anchored in faith in Roosevelt—had been fundamentally flawed. That, in turn, would have severely undermined Wise in his ongoing struggle with Silver for primacy in the American Zionist leadership. In short, Wise had strong psychological and political reasons to leap to the defense of the late president. In a sense, Wise's own position as a Jewish leader depended on it.[64]

The Return of Abba Hillel Silver

Rabbi Wise's maneuver to induce Abba Hillel Silver's resignation from the AZEC leadership was by no means the final battle in their war. Almost immediately upon Silver's resignation at the end of 1944, his backers began pressuring the Zionist council's leadership to take Silver back. They pointed to the obstruction of the Taft-Wright-Compton resolution on Palestine and the Ibn Saud incident as evidence that Wise's strategy of trusting FDR had failed. Moreover, with Roosevelt gone, Wise was no longer enjoying far greater access to the White House than any other Jewish leader. Now it was anybody's guess as to which Jewish leaders would have the strongest ties to the Harry S. Truman administration. Furthermore, later that spring, as newsreel footage of the liberated death camps began reaching America's movie theaters, the nature and extent of the Holocaust, which until then some in the Jewish community had not fully realized, strengthened the argument that Wise's politics of caution were no longer appropriate. The call for leaders who would more vigorously promote the Zionist cause gained increasing support. The AZEC and ZOA offices were deluged with mail urging Silver's return. Articles in the Jewish press called on Wise to reconcile with Silver. When Christian Zionist author Pierre van Paassen spoke in support of Silver at Zionist rallies in New York City and Washington DC in early 1945, "the house literally rose to its feet and cheered" at the mention of Silver's name, he reported. Local Zionist activists with whom van Paassen met in Brooklyn were "boiling with indignation," he informed Silver: "They want to sweep the administration into the ash can. I think they will. The Jews are sick and tired of appeasement and whispers and dark hints. Their kinsmen are dying in Europe. The White Paper is in force. Tomorrow the British will tell us: there are no Jews clamoring to enter Palestine. The Jews are dead. Hitler killed them. Before this argument is advanced they want action. And they feel that you ought to lead them. They are waiting for word from you. They are deeply stirred."[65]

Nahum Goldmann shared with State Department officials his concern over the increasingly militant mood in the Jewish world. For the past five years, he explained, Rabbi Wise and Chaim Weizmann had heeded the Roosevelt administration's request that they "urge their people to follow a policy of moderation and not expect a solution of the Palestine question along Zionist lines before the end of the war in Europe." They "had succeeded to a notable degree in imposing a policy of restraint upon the Jews of the world" and had "persuaded [our] people to accept in a disciplined manner the terrible misfortunes which had been visited upon world Jewry in the last few years." But now American Jewry's patience had reached the breaking point. "At least 70% of American Zionists" were now "backing Rabbi Silver strongly and it was not at all certain that the extremists would not prevail." There was a growing likelihood, Goldmann said, that those who favored a moderate political line "might be ousted in favor of Rabbi Silver and other advocates of a stronger policy."[66]

Meanwhile, Silver was for the first time publicly condemning Wise's leadership. "All too often Dr. Wise treated the Zionist movement of the United States as a piece of personal property and has bitterly resented any new leadership which threatened his monopoly," Silver asserted in a January 1945 statement to the press. "His 'shtadlanuth' in Washington has been an egregious failure for many years, and not only as far as Zionism is concerned. This weak-kneed 'shtadlanuth' policy has accomplished next to nothing for our people during these tragic years of slaughter and annihilation." Wise bristled at Silver's charges. "I have never been a 'Stadtlan [sic],' which means a cringing and appeasing beggar at Royal doors," Wise wrote indignantly to one correspondent in the heat of the struggle. "[I] have always been not a non-militant Zionist, as he claims, but militant." Yet in the wake of the recent controversy over the Taft Palestine resolution, Silver's accusations resonated with a growing segment of the Jewish community. The grassroots pressure became so formidable that by July 1945, an AZEC "peace committee" prevailed upon an exhausted and disheartened Rabbi Wise to accede to Rabbi Silver's return to co-chairmanship of the movement.[67]

Would It Have Mattered?

What if Rabbi Wise had not heeded the administration's demand that he urge American Jews "to follow a policy of moderation," as Goldmann charitably put it? Would it have made any practical difference? Would it have mattered if Wise and other Jewish leaders had publicized and protested the Atlit beatings, or if Wise had openly called for a Jewish state in his address to the American Jewish Conference, or if he had lobbied for the Taft resolution in defiance of the president?

These questions are important because the British closure of Palestine to all but a trickle of Jewish refugees, a policy that the Roosevelt administration supported, was one of the Allies' most consequential steps in obstructing the rescue of Jews from the Holocaust. And the converse was true: opening Palestine to refugees likely would have saved a greater number of lives than many of the other rescue steps debated at the time. Because of its proximity to the European front, Palestine was much more realistic as a haven than the far-flung Caribbean islands or African nether-regions that were occasionally mentioned as possible sites for refugee settlement.

While there is of course no definitive way of knowing how things might have turned out had Rabbi Wise adopted a different strategy, several observations are in order.

First, part of what made Wise's stance problematic was that it was anchored in the assumption that England's fate in the war would be substantially affected by whether or not American Zionists criticized London's Palestine policy. That assumption was questionable at best.

Second, in his zeal to protect the British from Jewish criticism, Rabbi Wise repeatedly took steps beyond what was necessary to maintain his position. For example, not only did Wise refrain from organizing any public protests against England's Palestine policy during those years, but he sometimes pressured others to keep quiet as well. When the U.S. Labor Zionists told him of their plan, in July 1939, to hold a demonstration at Madison Square Garden to protest British restrictions, Wise intervened "to kill this thing," as he put it.

Third, while the administration's claim that a pro-Zionist position by the Allies would have driven the Arabs into the arms of the Nazis may seem weighty at first glance, mainstream Zionist leaders at the time offered substantive reasons for disputing it. At the aforementioned meeting between American Zionist leaders and the British ambassador in Washington in 1941, for example, Dr. Israel Goldstein argued that while the British had defended the White Paper policy on the grounds that there was a danger of "strong Axis influence among the Arabs," in the ensuing two years "this factor had been shown to be grossly exaggerated, [so] the continued enforcement of the White Paper policy on the basis thereof seemed unjustifiable." Similarly, Rabbi Wise wrote to First Lady Eleanor Roosevelt in 1942 that "the [pro-Nazi] rebellion in Iraq, the presence of the Mufti [the Palestinian Arab leader Haj Amin el-Husseini] in Berlin and Rome, [and] the failure of Egypt to live up to her treaty of alliance [with England]" proved that some Arabs would side with the Axis no matter what the Allies did, so there was no reason to keep the Jews out of Palestine. Likewise, Nahum Goldmann declared at a Boston rally in 1943 that it was "foolish and immoral" to continue shutting off Palestine in order to "appease Arab Nazis," because those Arabs did not respond by gratefully joining the Allies but rather "express their gratitude for this [White Paper] policy by sitting today in Berlin and Rome, calling on the Arab world to revolt against the British."[68]

The passage of congressional resolutions or the staging of vigorous public protests in New York or Washington might not have resulted in any changes to the White Paper policy. On the other hand, both before and during the war, the British desperately needed American military, financial, and diplomatic support. Substantial American Jewish pressure on the Roosevelt administration, conducted through quiet lobbying, loud protests, and behind-the-scenes warnings involving the "Jewish vote," conceivably could have led to increased U.S. pressure on London, thereby creating the possibility of a British policy change. It is worth noting that in late 1943, observers would have scoffed at the notion that in the middle of a world war, President Roosevelt could have been pressured into creating a government agency to rescue refugees, a task he and his administration had always claimed was impossible. Yet in January 1944, because of a confluence of circumstances, the War Refugee Board came into being. Whether a similar effort regarding the White Paper could have likewise succeeded will never be known, in large measure because the American Jewish community's foremost leader, compromised by his deference to President Roosevelt, his acquiescence in the demand that Jewish needs be set aside because of the war, and his minimalist perception of what Jewish political action might attain, refrained from leading such a protest campaign.

7

The Failure to Bomb Auschwitz

JEWS WERE NOT THE only ethnic group whom Breckinridge Long disdained. He did not think much of Poles, either. In a 1944 diary entry complaining about Polish American pressure on the Roosevelt administration, he wrote, "by temperament they are not a reasonable race."

When it came to U.S. military strategy, however, the Jews and the Poles were treated very differently. Roosevelt administration officials adamantly rejected the idea of using U.S. planes to stop the mass murder of European Jews. Yet they sent U.S. planes to aid the Polish underground.[1]

Flexing Political Muscle

In Polish tradition the day after Easter Sunday is "Dyngus Day," a holiday dating back to medieval times. Polish American communities celebrate it with parties, polka contests, and an ancient custom in which young men and women flirtatiously swat each other with willows and sprinkle water on one another.

In a city such as Buffalo, New York, home to a large Polish American community, politicians who attended Dyngus Day gatherings on April 10, 1944, knew that the swatters and sprinklers of April would also be voters come November. The holiday was at once a cultural celebration and a de facto reminder of Polish American political power.

That same day, four thousand miles away, two young Jews staged one of the very few successful escapes from Auschwitz (Oswiecim, in Polish). While hiding in a woodpile on the outskirts of the death camp, Rudolf Vrba and Alfred Wetzler heard Allied planes flying overhead. Soon those planes would figure prominently in the fate of both Jews and Poles.[2]

Over the course of the next eleven days, Vrba and Wetzler walked eighty miles across southwestern Poland. They crossed into Slovakia, where they met with local Jewish leaders and dictated a thirty-page report that came to be known as the "Auschwitz Protocols." They provided details of the mass-murder process and drew maps pinpointing the location of the gas chambers and crematoria. In response to the Auschwitz Protocols, rescue activists in Slovakia, led by Rabbi Michael Dov Weissmandl, sent a series of letters to Allied officials and Jewish leaders in the Free World, urging the bombing of "the death halls" of Auschwitz and the railway lines and bridges leading to the camp.[3]

The bombing requests reached the West at a time when the Allies were in fact well positioned to carry out such raids. By early 1944 the Allies had established control over the skies of Europe, and throughout the spring, U.S. planes flew repeated reconnaissance missions in the area around Auschwitz. Allied military planners were very interested in that region because the Nazis were using its rich coal deposits to manufacture synthetic oil to power their war machinery, including the German air force.[4]

Polish Americans, too, were extremely interested in what was happening in Poland, but not for the same reason. As Soviet troops advanced into eastern Poland in early 1944, Polish Americans grew increasingly concerned that the Russians would seek to permanently occupy part of the country. The Dyngus Day celebrations in Buffalo and other Polish American communities that spring were tinged with apprehension, especially after a February 22 statement by British Prime Minister

Winston Churchill acquiescing to Soviet demands for changes along the Soviet-Polish border. "We Poles are wild as a result of Mr. Churchill's statement," declared Victor Alski, editor of *Pittsburczanin*, a Pittsburgh Catholic weekly. "It seems to us that Mr. Churchill is ready to sell the Poles down the river."[5]

Galvanized by fears that President Roosevelt might follow in Churchill's steps on Poland, grassroots activists in the Polish American community pressured the moderate-leaning Polish American Council to convene the founding conference of the Polish American Congress, in Buffalo, in May 1944. The Office of Strategic Services (oss) warned the White House that the Buffalo gathering "is expected to draw 5,000 delegates . . . to demonstrate 'in defense of Poland.' . . . This is counted upon in a year of presidential election to impel the Administration toward action of some kind favorable to Poland." In the end some ten thousand people took part in the Buffalo event—more than 2,600 delegates from twenty-six states, as well as nearly seven thousand other attendees. Senior presidential adviser Jonathan Daniels reported to FDR that strongly nationalist elements dominated the proceedings, and that some leaders of the new group were "anti-Administration Republicans who hope to swing some votes to the Republican camp by agitating the Polish boundary issue."[6]

Assistant Secretary of State Long observed these developments with alarm. "This Polish question is a great problem for us here," he wrote in his diary on June 13. "Detroit, Chicago, Buffalo, etc contain great settlements which are especially articulate in an election year. . . . Their Buffalo convention popped off in a nationalistic direction. . . . The appeal to former allegiance apparently had a deciding effect on the delegates. . . . [A] solution (or a position) satisfactory to the Poles here seems difficult—and they may hold the balance of power in votes" in key electoral states.[7]

President Roosevelt, too, was keenly aware of the important role Polish American votes might play in the 1944 presidential election. At the Teheran conference the previous autumn,

FDR privately told Josef Stalin that while he agreed with Soviet demands for border adjustments that would give Polish territory to the USSR, he was unwilling, because of "internal American politics," to do anything soon on the subject. According to the transcript of the meeting, Roosevelt explained that "there were in the United States from six to seven millions Americans of Polish extraction, and as a practical man, he did not wish to lose their vote[s]." What he was willing to do to secure their votes, as compared to his considerations regarding Jewish votes, would soon become apparent.[8]

Bombing Auschwitz

Rabbi Wise turned seventy in March 1944, at a time when the average life expectancy of an American male was under sixty-four years. He suffered from—among other maladies—an enlarged spleen; polycythemia, a blood disease; and a double hernia that was inoperable because of the risk of uncontrolled bleeding. As early as 1939, he had begun to experience periodic bouts of Meniere's disease, which caused severe spells of prolonged dizziness, sometimes at public events. These ailments, the frequent x-ray treatments he was required to undergo, and the general stress inevitably experienced by a man shouldering so many responsibilities at a time of such extreme crisis for world Jewry, took their toll. Photographs of Wise taken in 1943 and 1944 show him as haggard, stooped, and seemingly exhausted. Yet this was precisely the time when a robust and energetic leader was most urgently needed at the helm of the Jewish community.[9]

On March 15, 1944, two days before Wise's seventieth birthday, the Germans marched into Hungary, imperiling the lives of the country's approximately 800,000 Jews. Unlike previous phases of the Holocaust, which the Germans partially succeeded in hiding from the international community, the destruction of Hungarian Jewry was reported in considerable depth, and often in timely fashion, by the American news media (although not necessarily with the prominence it merited). On May 10, one week before mass deportations to Auschwitz began, the *New York Times* quoted a European diplomat's warning that the Germans were preparing "huge gas chambers in which the one million Hungarian Jews are to be exterminated in the same fashion as were the Jews of Poland." On May 19, two days after the deportations started, a telegram to Rabbi Wise from Jewish Agency headquarters in Jerusalem reported: "Refugees who reached Palestine yesterday relate terrible facts regarding Jews in Hungary. There is clear evidence that mass extermination is prepared there according to methods in Poland. Over 300,000 [Hungarian] Jews from Sziget and Carpatho-Russia are already interned in camps and ghettoes." Rabbi Wise did not doubt the veracity of the information; in the May issue of *Opinion*, he wrote: "Tragic news comes to this country through indisputable channels that three vast extermination camps are being prepared for 600,000 and more [Hungarian] Jews and, alas, it is true that, while Hitler never keeps a promise, he seems never to fail to execute the most terrible of his threats." Wise concluded by expressing his faith that "our Government will do what it can."[10]

As the deportations of Hungarian Jews proceeded, American Jewish organizations proposed various ways the Allies might intervene. *Congress Weekly* revived the idea of staging retaliatory bombings. Recalling that an earlier request from the Jews of Warsaw for retaliatory air strikes was "treated as a fantastic encroachment upon the plans and designs of the Allied High Command," the AJ congress journal nonetheless argued:

> Is immediate retaliation still impossible and fantastic? Is there no way of telling Budapest not with words but with deeds that humanity will not stand for the murder of the last million? . . . Can not this Hungarian government be made to learn through fire and devastation that murder begets murder?
>
> Thousands of Allied planes swarm through the European skies every day. . . . A fleet of Allied planes, raining down the warnings against this inhuman crime together with the more

eloquent bombs, may save those lives. Is this, too, a fantastic encroachment upon the plans of the Allied High Command? If it is we must be forgiven for being fools.[11]

Likewise, the editors of the Orthodox magazine *Jewish Forum* contended: "For the sake of saving many thousands of Jews among other vassals of Hitler, Hungary must be taught a lesson similar to that of Berlin. Air squadrons must be sent to Budapest until it is wiped off the face of the earth." Several similar editorials appeared in the Independent Jewish Press Service; one called for "vengeance now—to be wreaked in terms of explosive tonnage upon the cities from which the Jews are deported to their death. . . . Only this may stop the carnage." In later editorials, the Press Service urged the Allies to use both "diplomacy and bombings" to pressure the Hungarians. "Bomb ruthlessly the cities from which Jews are deported, so it becomes a matter of personal security for the enemy to have the Jews remain. Follow this up with a warning that the bombings will continue until the Jews are permitted to depart for neutral lands."[12]

A lone contrary perspective was offered by G. George Fox, an anti-Zionist Reform rabbi, in the *Sentinel*, Chicago's Jewish weekly. Chiding "our more emotional Jewish editors who are demanding that the government of our country strafe the Hungarians for their brutal treatment of our people," Fox declared he "would not agree with any action in this war . . . which would select any special group to be avenged. . . . Let us face this situation as a part of the American Allies, and do all that we can, rather than as a particular group, whether religious, national, or ethnic."[13]

Overall, however, the idea of petitioning for retaliatory bombings was not widely discussed by Jewish advocates in 1944. Perhaps that was in part because the idea had been raised in Jewish leadership meetings two years earlier (see chapter 3) and failed to gain traction. More significant was that, by the spring of 1944, a different method of military intervention—one that could more directly impact the pace of the slaughter—became viable: to directly interrupt the mass murder process either by bombing the railroad lines and bridges leading to Auschwitz, over which the Hungarian Jews were being deported, or by bombing the gas chambers and crematoria in Auschwitz itself. Once the Allies gained control of the skies of Europe in early 1944, Auschwitz was for the first time within striking range of their bombers. Indeed, beginning in April, American, British, and South African planes carried out surveillance flights within a few miles of the Auschwitz gas chambers, in preparation for air strikes on German synthetic oil factories in the vicinity.[14]

On June 18, 1944, Jacob Rosenheim, president of a New York–based Orthodox Jewish organization, Agudath Israel, wrote to the War Refugee Board, urging bombing of the railways based on the information the two Auschwitz escapees had provided. WRB director John Pehle relayed Rosenheim's request to Assistant Secretary of War John McCloy. Two days later, before Rosenheim heard back from McCloy, he sent his associate Meir Schenkelowski to Washington to present the proposal in person to Secretary of State Hull and Secretary of War Stimson, the two cabinet members whose areas of responsibility were the most relevant to implementation of the proposal. Hull responded by pushing the subject off as something concerning the military authorities and not the State Department. An equally uncooperative Stimson disingenuously claimed to Schenkelowski that "the whole matter is within the competence of the Russian Military Command." He said nothing to the Jewish lobbyist about the fact that American planes were already in the Auschwitz area.[15]

On July 4 Stimson's deputy, Assistant Secretary of War John McCloy, formally replied to Agudath Israel's bombing requests. He wrote that a war department study had found bombing the railways was "impracticable" because it would require "the diversion of considerable air support essential to the success of our forces now engaged in decisive operations." In reality, no such study was ever undertaken, and no significant diversion of airplanes would have been necessary, because they were already in action near the death camp. Nonetheless, McCloy continued to make that claim in response to subsequent appeals to bomb Auschwitz or the railways lines and bridges.[16]

What made the Roosevelt administration's claims about the unfeasibility of sending planes to Auschwitz all the more remarkable was that it did send American airplanes into battle in the skies over Auschwitz—but not to strike the mass-murder apparatus. Throughout the summer and autumn of 1944, U.S. bombers repeatedly attacked German oil factories close to the death camp. A detour to strike the death camp or the railway lines and bridges leading to it would have taken them mere minutes. On July 7, for example, American bombers began attacks on the Blechhammer oil factories, forty-seven miles from Auschwitz. Nine more such raids took place between July and November. On August 7 U.S. bombers attacked the Trzebinia oil refineries, just thirteen miles from Auschwitz. Between August 7 and August 29, the United States conducted additional bombing raids on oil refineries within forty-five miles of Auschwitz. On August 20 a squadron of 127 U.S. bombers, accompanied by one hundred Mustang fighters piloted by the all–African American unit known as the Tuskegee Airmen, struck oil factories less than five miles from the gas chambers. Sixteen-year-old Elie Wiesel, who was part of a slave labor battalion stationed just outside the main camp of Auschwitz, witnessed that raid. Years later, in his best-selling book *Night*, Wiesel recalled: "[I]f a bomb had fallen on the blocks [the prisoners' barracks], it alone would have claimed hundreds of victims on the spot. But we were no longer afraid of death; at any rate, not of that death. Every bomb that exploded filled us with joy and gave us new confidence in life. The raid lasted over an hour. If it could only have lasted ten times ten hours!"[17]

Moreover, it was no secret that the Allies were bombing oil factories close to Auschwitz. Ernest Frischer of the Czech government in exile, writing to World Jewish Congress leaders on September 15, noted that "fuel factories" in the vicinity of Auschwitz had recently been "repeatedly bombed." In August and

September, the *New York Times*'s coverage of the Allies' "oil war" against the Germans mentioned "Oscwiecim" (the Polish name for Auschwitz) as one of the targets.[18] Nahum Goldmann told General John Dill of the Allied High Command in October that "the few dozen bombs needed to strike the death camp would not influence the outcome of the war," pointing out that "the Royal Air Force was regularly bombing the I.G. Farben factories, a few miles distant from Auschwitz." Dill rebuffed the proposal, insisting that the Allies "had to save bombs for military targets." During World War II, the U.S. and British air forces dropped an estimated 5.4 billion bombs in Europe.[19]

More Requests, More Rejections

Jewish officials in the United States, Palestine, and Europe made many additional requests to bomb Auschwitz in the weeks and months to follow. At first the Jewish Agency leadership in Jerusalem mistakenly believed that Auschwitz was only a slave labor camp, and on that basis decided to refrain from asking the Allies to bomb it. But several weeks later, at the end of June, the Agency leadership learned the truth about the camp (from the same escapees' report that had reached Agudath Israel and others) and reversed its position. As a result, throughout the summer and fall of 1944, Agency representatives met with American, British, or Soviet diplomats in Jerusalem, Cairo, London, Geneva, Budapest, and Istanbul to press for bombing. None of these requests made any headway, however.[20]

In Washington, Nahum Goldmann, co-leader of the wjcongress alongside Rabbi Wise, handled most of the lobbying for bombing. Wise was almost entirely absent from Jewish discussions regarding the bombing proposal; he was focused on that summer's Democratic Party convention (see chapter 6) and other issues, to the extent his declining health permitted. That summer and fall, Goldmann repeatedly asked U.S., British, and Soviet diplomats to "look for a way to destroy these camps by bombing or any other means." He also broached the request to representatives of the Polish and Czech governments in exile, London-based government officials who had fled their native countries when the Germans invaded, and took an interest, to varying degrees, in the fate of their respective Jewish citizens.[21] Wise must have supported Goldman's advocacy of bombing, considering Goldmann could not have undertaken his lobbying without Wise's assent. Moreover, Wise was the co-recipient, along with Goldmann, of multiple telegrams from Jewish Agency officials in Jerusalem urging them to press the Roosevelt administration to bomb Auschwitz or the railways, and there is no indication that Wise ever objected to the proposal. In addition Rabbi Wise's journal *Opinion* published an article in September 1944 by a regular columnist, Rabbi Theodore Lewis, that mentioned some Britons were urging their governments to bomb the death camps. According to Lewis's much later recollection, he had actually referred to both Britons and Americans in the column he submitted, but Wise edited it by deleting the reference to Americans. If Lewis's memory was accurate, Wise's action would have been consistent with his overall effort to shield the Roosevelt administration from Jewish criticism; he supported the private efforts by Goldmann and others to advance the bombing proposal, but did not want to draw attention in public to the fact that Americans were urging the Roosevelt administration to take action that the administration was refusing to take.[22]

During 1944 at least thirty other Jewish officials or organizations in various countries were involved, at one time or another, in advocating bombing the camps or the railways. Usually these requests were made in private meetings with Allied officials. On July 24, for example, the Emergency Committee to Save the Jewish People of Europe (the Bergson Group) wrote to President Roosevelt urging bombing of the railway lines "and the extermination camps themselves"; the president did not reply. The U.S. wing of the Labor Zionists became involved in the issue at the instigation of Golda Meir (then Goldie Myerson), who was serving as a senior official of the Histadrut, the powerful Jewish labor federation in Palestine. In July she sent her American colleagues a report from Europe about the mass murder, together with a request that they ask U.S. officials to undertake "the bombing of Oswienzim [sic] and railway transporting Jews" to the death camp. The Histadrut's American representative, Israel Mereminski, then made that proposal to the War Refugee Board. It was probably not a coincidence that an editorial in the August 1944 issue of the Labor Zionists' *Jewish Frontier* called for "Allied bombings of the death camps and the roads leading to them"—the first instance of an American Jewish organization publicly demanding the bombing of the death camps.[23]

The idea of bombing Auschwitz was also the focus of some discussion in the American Jewish press at the time. Jacob Fishman, columnist for the Yiddish-language daily *Morgen Zhurnal*, offered three suggestions: the Allies should warn that Bucharest and Budapest "will be bombed and reduced to ashes" if the transports to Auschwitz continued; the Allies should bomb Hitler's Berchtesgaden residence, "saying that this is punishment for the mass murders"; and they should "bomb the death camp at Oswiecim [Auschwitz], with its gas chambers, and also the other death camps in Poland." An Independent Jewish Press Service editorial urged the Allies to rain "explosive tonnage . . . upon the camps where death is meted out to the Jews." In addition, the Jewish Telegraphic Agency reported from London that "liberal circles are demanding that Britain and the United States act to save the Jews of Hungary by first bombing the extermination camps of Oswiecim and Birkenau in Poland."[24]

One wjcongress official dissented from the position advocated by Goldmann and other mainstream Jewish representatives. Fearing that aerial bombing might harm the inmates, A. Leon Kubowitzki, chairman of the group's Rescue Department, favored an attack on Auschwitz by Soviet paratroopers and Polish underground forces. Kubowitzki was the only representative of a Jewish organization known to have taken this position in contacts with Allied officials. Other Jewish officials had weighed the risk of casualties and come to the conclusion that bombing was justified, because the camp inmates were doomed to be murdered imminently.[25]

Jewish leaders had no way of knowing which method of military action was militarily feasible or would be the most effective. Hence in many of their meetings with Allied officials, they urged both bombing the railways and bombing Auschwitz itself. On several occasions, Kubowitzki himself sent the War Refugee Board appeals he had received from Europe to bomb the camp, while attaching a cover note saying he felt using ground troops would be preferable. Jewish leaders also had no way of knowing which of the Allies would be most capable, or most willing, to act. Therefore they raised the issue with American, British, and Soviet diplomats alike. This also explains why the American Jewish Conference chose to use broad language regarding Allied intervention on behalf of Hungarian Jewry. The leaders of an AJ conference rally at Madison Square Garden on July 31, 1944, adopted an eight-point plan for the rescue of Hungary's Jews; one point read: "All measures should be taken by the military authorities, with the help of the underground forces, to destroy the implements, facilities, and places where the Nazis have carried out their mass executions." Similarly, the WJ congress's eleven-point plan, issued on August 14, stated, "Immediate measures [should] be adopted to destroy the murder installations and facilities of the extermination camps"; such wording covered all bases by not specifying precisely what sort of "measures" should be taken.[26]

Each of the three proposed methods of military intervention had advantages and disadvantages. Bombing the railway tracks would have involved relatively little risk to Allied servicemen. On the other hand, the effectiveness of bombing the tracks depended upon the bombers' ability to hit their targets— something impossible to determine in advance—and the speed with which the Germans could repair damaged railway lines. Bombing bridges along the rail routes would have been more effective, because the bridges took longer to repair. Another advantage of striking the railways or the bridges was that such actions would have been directly consistent with the war effort, since the Germans also used those routes for transporting troops and military supplies.

As for bombing the gas chambers and crematoria, it was impossible to predict how successful Allied bombers would be in carrying out such precision attacks. In addition some inmates could be harmed in such bombings, although that possibility was not why the Allies rejected the proposal. Yet those considering the feasibility of such an attack had before them an example of a highly successful precision raid. In August 1944 U.S. planes struck a v-2 rocket factory located in the Buchenwald concentration camp, destroying the munitions area of the camp while sparing the nearby prisoners' barracks. The commander of the attack said in a postwar interview that he and his crew were specifically instructed to avoid hitting the area where inmates were situated.[27]

The other proposed method of action against Auschwitz, sending ground troops, almost certainly would have resulted in Allied casualties. It therefore had the least chance of being accepted by the Allied leadership. In fact War Refugee Board executive director John Pehle refused to forward such requests to the War Department. He felt it was "not proper" to ask the War Department even to consider "a measure which involved the sacrifice of American troops." Calling for a ground attack would have also meant risking the accusation that Jews were willing to endanger the lives of Allied soldiers for their own narrow interests, a concern Rabbi Wise and other Jewish leaders had articulated on various occasions.[28]

Each of the military options raised—bombing the railways and bridges, bombing the gas chambers and crematoria, retaliatory bombings of German cities, and using ground forces—faced the same obstacle: as a matter of principle, the Roosevelt administration opposed taking any substantive special action to aid Jewish refugees. Consistent with that mindset, senior officials of the War Department had decided—long before receiving the first Jewish request for military intervention—that they would have nothing to do with aiding refugees. In response to the creation of the War Refugee Board, the War Department assured the British government: "It is not contemplated that units of the armed forces will be employed for the purpose of rescuing victims of enemy oppression unless such rescues are the direct result of military operations conducted with the objective of defeating the armed forces of the enemy." Internal War Department memoranda the following month stated unequivocally that "the most effective relief which can be given victims of enemy persecution is to insure the speedy defeat of the Axis." This attitude governed the War Department's responses to the requests to bomb Auschwitz.[29]

A Reason to Divert Planes

While Roosevelt administration officials were insisting they could not "divert" planes to Auschwitz, they found plenty of reasons to divert them to Warsaw.

In August 1944 the Polish Home Army rose up against the Germans in Warsaw. Beginning on August 8, Britain's Royal Air Force air-dropped supplies to the Polish rebels. The flight route between the Allied air base in Italy and Warsaw took the planes within a few miles of Auschwitz. They flew that route twenty-two times during the two weeks to follow. The British also pressed the United States to do its share of air-drops. An internal Roosevelt administration assessment of the British effort warned that "the [Polish] Partisan fight was a losing one" and "large numbers of planes would be tied up for long periods of time and lost to the main strategic effort against Germany." In fact England's own air force commanders had concluded that the air-drops "achieved practically nothing" because the Germans were intercepting most of the supplies. Nonetheless, President Roosevelt ordered U.S. planes to take part in the mission. The largest air-drop took place on September 18, when a fleet of 107 U.S. bombers dropped more than 1,200 containers of weapons and supplies into Warsaw. Fewer than three hundred of the containers reached the Polish fighters; the Germans confiscated the rest. Thus the administration chose to divert planes from the war effort to aid a revolt it knew was doomed to defeat—all the while falsely claiming it could not spare a few bombs to hit the Auschwitz gas chambers or railway lines and bridges because that would divert resources from the war effort.[30]

Developments on the political front help explain some of the decisions made on the battlefront. The presidential election was ninety days away, and the Democrats were worried. The Republicans had scored well in the 1942 midterm congressional elections. If the GOP could hold on to the states it won in the 1940 presidential race, and if the states that went Republican in the 1942 senatorial and gubernatorial races remained Republican in 1944, the GOP's candidate would win 323 electoral votes—twenty more than the number needed to capture the White House. FDR himself estimated in one private conversation that of the anticipated fifty million voters, twenty million each were solid for the Democrats and the Republicans, and the other ten million were up for grabs.[31]

Because Republican candidate Thomas Dewey was the governor of New York, Democratic Party officials were seriously concerned that Dewey might win his home state, which had the most electoral votes of any state and could be the key to the election. "New York State's electoral votes are by no means certain for the Dem. Party," one party official noted in an internal memo. Another warned that Dewey could carry upstate New York "by 625,000 to 650,000 votes. . . . I deem it imperative that everything be done to cut this down in order to [e]nsure carrying the state for Roosevelt." Campaign officials felt the situation was sufficiently dire to warrant FDR making a special campaign trip to New York. As late as October 2, just weeks before Election Day, one Democratic Party activist warned FDR aide David Niles that "if nothing happens between now and the election date, Dewey will carry NY state." During the same weeks in which the president and his aides were discussing the merits of taking part in the Warsaw air-drops, Dewey was pub-

licly criticizing the administration for not standing up unequivocally for an independent Poland. "The rights of small nations
and minorities must not be lost in a cynical peace," the Republican candidate warned.[32]

Polish Americans did not hesitate to flex political muscle.
Archbishop Edward Mooney of Detroit, an important leader
of Catholic Polish Americans, let it be known that he was prepared to endorse Governor Dewey if Roosevelt failed to air-
drop supplies to the Polish fighters in Warsaw. Monsignor
Zygmunt Kaczynski, the Polish government-in-exile's liaison
to the American Catholic Episcopate, relayed Mooney's threat
to Joseph Dasher, head of the Polish Section of the oss, telling Dasher that "even token aid to Warsaw would create [a]
favorable impression. . . . Poles would be appeased and possible far-reaching Catholic political actions avoided." Dasher
gave the information to the U.S. ambassador to Great Britain,
John Winant, who in turn passed the message to FDR aide
Harry Hopkins—with a note saying he himself (Ambassador
Winant) had just had a similar conversation with Archbishop
Francis Spellman of New York. The White House got the message. The president could not risk being seen by Polish American voters as abandoning Poland.[33]

Abandoning the Jews, however, did not seem to carry much
political risk. The president likely calculated that his two
election-year gestures, the creation of the War Refugee Board
and the admission of 982 refugees, would suffice to quell any
serious danger of Jewish defections in the November election.
Furthermore, unlike their Polish American counterparts, Rabbi
Wise and other American Jewish leaders were not willing to
raise the specter of Jewish voters turning against Roosevelt—
even in private contacts with administration officials—as a
means of seeking U.S. military intervention against the Hungarian deportations.

In an ironic twist, the deportations were, in fact, halted (albeit
belatedly) as a result of Allied bombings. During May and June,
the War Refugee Board secured public statements by members

of Congress and other American public figures, as well as the International Red Cross, the king of Sweden, and the Vatican, urging the Hungarian government to halt the deportations. These reinforced President Roosevelt's March 24 statement threatening postwar Allied retribution against collaborators (see chapter 6). Although the references to Jews had been removed or downplayed in the American statement, it still held value, because a warning from the president of the United States could not be easily disregarded, especially by Hungarian officials who were hoping to escape Allied punishment. In Hungary the local authorities' cooperation had been crucial in enabling the heavily burdened German occupation forces to carry out large-scale deportations. The Allies conveyed the warnings against collaborators through diplomatic channels, the European press, radio broadcasts, and leaflets dropped by Allied planes. It was easier for the Roosevelt administration to assent to the War Refugee Board's persistent appeals to issue such warnings than to get tangled up in a potentially embarrassing clash with the board over the matter. The threat initiative involved relatively minimal effort and no political risk—and thus was preferable to enduring constant pestering by board representatives.[34]

The tipping point came in early July, when the Hungarian authorities intercepted appeals from Hungarian Jews to the Allied leadership asking for bombing of the railways to Auschwitz. As a result, when Allied airplanes struck railway marshaling yards in and around Budapest (hitting them because they were military targets), Hungary's leaders mistakenly believed the raids were undertaken in response to the Jewish requests. On July 6 the Hungarian regent, Admiral Miklos Horthy, ordered the Hungarian military and police forces to cease assisting in the deportations. By then more than 430,000 Hungarian Jews were dead; but 120,000 remained alive, mostly in Budapest.[35]

8

Antisemitism in the White House

AT FIRST GLANCE IT might seem that President Roosevelt's policies with regard to European Jewry during the Nazi years were guided entirely by political, diplomatic, and strategic calculations. Facing strong public opposition to increased immigration, FDR did not want to risk losing votes if he was perceived as opening America's doors to more foreigners. Policy initiatives that required congressional approval might have been jeopardized if he alienated southern Democrats by clashing with them over immigration, which they vehemently opposed. Pressuring the British to open Palestine to refugees might have strained Anglo-American relations and provoked Arab anger.

These factors do not, however, resolve the central mystery of Franklin Roosevelt's response to the Holocaust. During FDR's years in office, 1933–45, immigration to the United States was governed by a quota system that severely limited the admission of refugees in general, and impacted European Jewish refugees in particular. Yet despite these legal limitations, nearly 200,000 more Jews could have entered under the existing law than actually did. For the entire period of the Nazi regime, 1933 to 1945, more than 190,000 quota spaces from Germany and Axis-occupied countries sat unused. In large part this was because the officials responsible for implementing the existing immigration law quietly went beyond the law, with the president's knowledge and approval. The State Department, which administered the president's immigration policy, severely reduced the number of refugees who were granted visas by imposing additional requirements on would-be immigrants and looking for any possible reason, no matter how trivial, to disqualify applicants.

Assistant Secretary of State Wilbur Carr, who was in charge of immigration visas during FDR's first term, assured congressional restrictionists in 1934 that thanks to the manner in which immigration policy was being administered, "there is no chance of any material increase in immigration." Two years later Carr proudly pointed out to a colleague that the department had "achieved administratively" what congressional advocates sought in their unsuccessful attempts to further restrict immigration. The problem was not just that Carr was unabashedly hostile to Jews and bitterly opposed to immigration (especially by what he called "Russian or Polish Jews of the usual ghetto type"), but that the president stood by him when Secretary of Labor Frances Perkins or refugee advocates sought to compel Carr to administer the immigration laws less harshly. Perkins sought to challenge Carr's actions during an April 1933 cabinet meeting presided over by the president, but was forced to "back off completely" in the absence of support for her position, Secretary Hull reported to Carr afterward. As for Breckinridge Long, whom FDR later appointed to fill Carr's position, he was likewise antisemitic and anti-foreigner, and initiated additional restrictions on the granting of immigration visas. Long regularly briefed the president on his practices, and found FDR to be "100% in accord with my ideas" (see chapter 2).[1]

Why did Roosevelt adopt an approach that would produce such a harsh result? Why not quietly instruct the State Department—without any public controversy or fight with Congress—to permit the existing quotas to be filled?

Even when special circumstances might have moved the president to permit greater immigration—within the existing laws—he still preferred to take the most rigid approach. In 1934, for example, Labor Secretary Perkins devised a way, within the current law, to facilitate increased Jewish refugee immigration through the posting of bonds by friends or relatives. The State Department, which administered the immigration system, opposed the plan; FDR sided with State.[2] In the spring of 1939, the 907 refugees aboard the ship *St. Louis* could have been saved by allowing them to stay temporarily, as tourists, in the U.S. Virgin Islands, an American territory. Instead, the administration found a technicality to disqualify them from receiving tourist visas. The Wagner-Rogers bill would have admitted twenty thousand refugee children who, because of their age, would have posed no competition to America's labor force and would have been supported entirely by private sources. The president nonetheless declined to support the measure; the following year, however, FDR supported bringing British children to the United States to escape the German bombing of London. Why the double standard? In 1944 the War Refugee Board urged Roosevelt to permit the creation of temporary havens in the United States, where Jewish refugees would be housed until the end of the war. A Gallup poll commissioned by the White House found that 70 percent of Americans supported the proposal. Yet FDR agreed to create only one token haven, for just 982 refugees, in Oswego, New York. Why not admit greater numbers, when there was plenty of room and ample public backing?

Roosevelt and Race

A closer look at Roosevelt's private views on race and immigration offers a possible answer. Given the prevalence of anti-Jewish prejudice in the upper strata of New York society in the late 1800s and early 1900s, it is hardly surprising that FDR's mother, Sara Delano Roosevelt, subscribed to common stereotypes about Jews and other minorities.[3] As one Roosevelt biographer put it: "[T]here lingered in [FDR] a residue of the social anti-Semitism he had inherited from his mother and other relatives such as his half-brother Rosy and his uncle Fred Delano, all three of them anti-Semites." On one occasion in 1928, Sara Roosevelt objected to inviting FDR adviser Belle Moskowitz to join the family for lunch because she did not want "that fat Jewess," as she called her, in the Roosevelt home. Sara once wrote of Elinor Morgenthau, the wife of future Treasury Secretary Henry Morgenthau Jr.: "The wife is very Jewish but appeared very well." FDR's half-brother Rosy was not fond of Jews, either; he wrote from his European and Caribbean travels in the 1920s about the "awful lot of Jews, mostly of the detestable American variety," whom he encountered on the Continent. Similar sentiments are occasionally to be found in Franklin's adolescent correspondence, such as a letter to his mother, at age fifteen, in which he contemptuously referred to a renowned European concert pianist as "a long-haired Polish Jew."[4]

Mother and son shared a keen interest in their family's bloodlines. Sara "could recite pedigrees from a repertoire that seemed to include half the aristocracy of Europe and all that of the Hudson River Valley," FDR biographer Frank Freidel wrote. "At least a dozen lines of Mayflower descent converged in Franklin, and Sara could name every one of them. There were times when she thoroughly irritated her daughter-in-law [Eleanor] with her genealogical talk." As for Franklin, he "had effortlessly acquired the knowledge from his mother, [and] could as a matter of course plunge into similar recitations," according to Freidel. "One of the main bodies of knowledge he mastered at Harvard—if one were to judge only by his letters to his mother—was genealogy. He unearthed several Puritan Pomeroys to add to the family records, and [authored] a history thesis on the 'Roosevelts in New Amsterdam.'" Even decades later, Freidel noted, FDR made much of his ancestors, "whose exploits he recounted frequently in his presidential small talk." Eleanor Roosevelt's biographer, Blanche Wiesen Cook, likewise noted: "The Delanos were very proud of their lineage, which Sara could—and did, repeatedly, recite, back to William the Conqueror. The first American de la Noye [Delano], a Huguenot, settled in Plymouth in 1621. . . . She hated, with considerable verve and in no particular order, ostentation, vulgarity, shabby politicians, the new resorts of the new rich, and virtually all races, nationalities, and families other than her own."[5]

For FDR pride in his family's racial pedigree melded easily with the common early twentieth-century perception in America that the Caucasian, or Aryan, race was locked in an ages-old struggle with inferior races. A speech Roosevelt gave in 1912, when he was a New York State senator, illustrated his perspective: "If we go back through history," he asserted, "we are struck by the fact that as a general proposition the Aryan races have been struggling to maintain individual freedom . . . in almost every European and American country this has been the great and fundamental question in the economic life of the people."[6]

FDR's position on immigration flowed naturally from this view. As he saw it, only certain types of foreigners should be admitted to the United States, in limited numbers and under conditions that would quickly lead to the elimination of their ethnic distinctiveness. In a July 18, 1920, interview with the *Brooklyn Eagle* when he was the Democratic vice presidential candidate, Roosevelt said he could accept the principle of some immigration, provided that the newcomers were dispersed and quickly assimilated:

> Our main trouble in the past has been that we have permitted the foreign elements to segregate in colonies. They have crowded into one district and they have brought congestion and racial prejudices to our large cities. The result is that they do not easily conform to the manners and the customs and the requirements of their new home. Now, the remedy for this should be the distribution of aliens in various parts of the country. If we had the greater part of the foreign population of the City of New York distributed to different localities upstate we should have a far better condition. Of course, this could not be done by legislative enactment. It could only be done by inducement—if better financial conditions and better living conditions could be offered to the alien dwellers in the cities.[7]

FDR expressed similar views in *Asia* magazine in 1923, and in columns he wrote for the *Macon Daily Telegraph*, when he was living part-time in Warm Springs, Georgia in the mid-1920s, shortly before he ran for governor of New York. In *Asia* he expressed sympathy for what he said was the widespread view "that the mingling of white with oriental blood on an extensive scale is harmful to our future citizenship." He added: "As a corollary of this conviction, Americans object to the holding of large amounts of real property, of land, by aliens or those descended from mixed marriages. Frankly, they do not want non-assimilable immigrants as citizens, nor do they desire any extensive proprietorship of land without citizenship." In a demonstration of presumed even-handedness, he expressed confidence that Americans would not insist on "the privilege of entry into an oriental country to such an extent as to threaten racial purity."

In his April 23, 1925, column for the *Daily Telegraph*, Roosevelt explained that he did not oppose all immigration; he favored the admission of some Europeans, so long as they had "blood of the right sort." He endorsed the need to restrict immigration for "a good many years to come" so the United States would have time to "digest" those who had already been admitted. He also proposed limiting future immigration to those who could be quickly and easily assimilated, including through dispersal around the country. He argued: "If, twenty-five years ago, the United States had adopted a policy of this kind, we would not have the huge foreign sections which exist in so many of our cities."[8]

Expanding on this perspective in his April 30, 1925, column, Roosevelt took aim at what he saw as the dangers posed by Asian immigrants. "Californians," he asserted, "have properly objected [to Japanese immigration] on the sound basic ground that Japanese immigrants are not capable of assimilation into the American population." FDR continued: "Anyone who has traveled in the Far East knows that the mingling of Asiatic blood with European or American blood produces, in nine cases out of ten, the most unfortunate results."[9]

Roosevelt's long-held views regarding the characteristics of Asians later would influence his policies as president. Soon after the 1941 Japanese attack on Pearl Harbor, some of his military advisers began pushing for mass detention of Japanese Americans on the grounds that, as Secretary of War Stimson put it, "their racial characteristics are such that we cannot understand or trust even the citizen Japanese"—even though no actual cases of treason had been uncovered. FDR's conviction that "Japanese immigrants are not capable of assimilation" contributed to his willingness to take such a radical step. It also helps explain why he chose to imprison Japanese Americans, while never contemplating similar action against German Americans or Italian Americans, despite the fact that they, too, had family ties to countries America was fighting in the war.[10]

FDR and "Jewish Blood"

"Orientals" were not the only ethnic group whose blood FDR viewed as undesirable.

A conversation in 1939 between President Roosevelt and Senator Burton Wheeler (D-MT), a close political ally, sheds light on Roosevelt's view of what he called "Jewish blood." At the time of the conversation, FDR had not yet declared his intention to seek reelection, and the two men were discussing possible Democratic candidates for president and vice president in 1940. Roosevelt expressed doubt that a ticket composed of Secretary of State Cordell Hull for president and Democratic National Committee chairman James Farley for vice president could be elected. Wheeler's response was preserved in a memorandum he composed following the meeting: "I said to the President someone told me that Mrs. Hull was a Jewess, and I said that the Jewish-Catholic issue would be raised [if Hull was nominated for president, and Farley, a Catholic, was his running mate]. He said, 'Mrs. Hull is about one quarter Jewish.' He said, 'You and I Burt are old English and Dutch stock. We know who our ancestors are. We know there is no Jewish blood in our veins, but a lot of these people do not know whether there is Jewish blood in their veins or not.'"[11]

Roosevelt's sentiments concerning "Jewish blood" did not preclude him from having individual Jews as friends, advisers, or occupants of certain other government positions. Still, only one Jew, Henry Morgenthau Jr., served in Roosevelt's cabinet, and only one, Abe Fortas, reached the level of undersecretary or assistant secretary. Roosevelt also appointed very few Jews to policymaking positions in the major government departments and regulatory agencies. He had Jewish advisers, but there was a limit to how far they could advance. New York attorney Ben Cohen, for example, was useful to FDR as one of the architects of his New Deal legislation. Yet Roosevelt rejected a suggestion by Interior Secretary Ickes to name Cohen assistant secretary of the treasury; according to FDR confidante and biographer Joseph Lasher, Roosevelt told Ickes that "he questioned the wisdom of appointing a Jew under Morgenthau." Likewise, Fortas, as undersecretary of state, worked under the non-Jewish Interior secretary.[12]

Even as FDR had Jewish associates, he also had his share of antisemitic ones.[13] Stephen Early, a senior aide since Roosevelt's 1920 vice presidential campaign who stayed with him through the White House years, often groused about "the goddamned Jews."[14] Edward Flynn, a close friend of Roosevelt's who chaired the 1940 election campaign and the powerful Bronx chapter of the Democratic Party, was "very much prejudiced against the Jews," Vice President Wallace noted in his diary. "He bemoan[s] the fact that Jews had control of all phases of the amusement business, movies, radio, song writers, theater, etc" and were thereby able to "impose on all the people in the United States their own ideals of what culture really is."[15] Isaiah Bowman, FDR's longtime adviser on population settlement issues, strongly opposed Jewish refugees immigrating to the United States or Palestine, and as president of Johns Hopkins University, instituted a quota on the admission of Jewish students on the grounds that they wanted to attend Hopkins "for two things: to make money and to marry non-Jewish women."[16]

Just Joking?

Among friends and relatives who shared his prejudices, FDR felt comfortable indulging in unkind jokes about Jews and their alleged character traits. A number of such instances are known, and probably many others are not. In a letter he wrote to Eleanor in 1908, Roosevelt poked fun at her for donating funds to organizations involved in settlement-house work in New York City's mostly Jewish neighborhoods: "You can pat your little back about fifty times and with eyes raised Heavenward exclaim in accents of deep content 'Yea! I have saved the lives of a score of blessed little ones of the Chosen Race!'" After the Roosevelts' fifth child was born, FDR joked that family members opposed his idea of naming the child Isaac (after one of his great-great-grandfathers) because, as he put it, "the baby's nose is slightly Hebraic & the family have visions of Ikey Rosenvelt, though I insist it is very good New Amsterdam Dutch."[17] During a 1923 fishing trip with Roosevelt off the coast of Florida, biographer Geoffrey Ward reported, FDR's friend Lewis Ledyard Jr. "hooked and landed a 42-pound Jewfish [then a real name for a fish that has since officially been changed]. 'I thought we left New York to get *away* from the Jews,' his wife said, and Franklin thought the remark so good he included it in his log." Elsewhere in that log, FDR added a little Jewish joke of his own: "The tip end of Florida is where Jonah had his trying experience—he was a Hebrew and hence cast up." Roosevelt's friend and closest political adviser, Louis Howe, later presented FDR with an album of anecdotes, photos, and illustrations from the trip, including one of "a Jewfish with a prominent nose and a sort of crest from which hung the triple balls of a pawnbroker's sign."[18]

Curtis Roosevelt, one of the president's grandchildren, said that he "recalled hearing the President tell mildly antisemitic stories in the White House" in which the protagonists were always Lower East Side Jews with heavy accents."[19] Even at the February 1945 Yalta conference, in the waning months of his life, Roosevelt was still telling jokes about Jews. When FDR mentioned to Stalin that he would soon be seeing Saudi Arabian leader Ibn Saud, Stalin asked if he intended to make any concessions to the king. "The President replied," according to the transcript, that "there was only one concession he thought he might offer and that was to give him the six million Jews in the United States."[20] Charles Bohlen, the State Department translator who recorded Roosevelt's remark to Stalin, added a postscript to that episode in the unpublished first draft of his memoir. After Roosevelt's meeting with the king of Saudi Arabia, Bohlen said to the president: "If you put any more kikes in Palestine, he is going to kill them." According to Bohlen, "Roosevelt laughed" at that statement.[21]

Some of Roosevelt's private remarks about Jews seemed to allude to a distinction in his mind between "good" and "bad" Jews, as for example in a May 29, 1942, conversation at the White House between the president, his adviser Harry Hopkins, and Soviet Foreign Minister Vyacheslav Molotov. At one point, Hopkins remarked that the American public's view of Soviet Communists had been damaged by the presence in the American Communist Party of "largely disgruntled, frustrated, ineffectual, and vociferous people—including a comparatively high proportion of distinctly unsympathetic Jews." According to the translator at the meeting, Harvard University professor Samuel H. Cross, "On this the President commented that he was far from antisemitic, as everyone knew, but there was a good deal in this point of view." Molotov, Roosevelt, and Hopkins then apparently agreed that "there were Communists and Communists," which they compared to what they called "the distinction between 'Jews' and 'Kikes,'" all of which was "something that created inevitable difficulties."[22]

Roosevelt's unflattering statements about Jews consistently reflected one of several interrelated notions: that it was undesirable to have too many Jews in any single profession, institution, or geographic locale; that America was by nature, and should remain, an overwhelmingly white, Protestant country;

and that Jews on the whole possessed certain innate and distasteful characteristics. In 1937, for example, he privately told
U.S. Senator Pat Harrison of Mississippi that the Sulzberger
family—publishers of the New York Times—had used "a dirty
Jewish trick" to find a legal loophole to resolve a tax problem
that threatened their control of the newspaper. In Roosevelt's
mind, the ability to find a "dirty" way to maneuver out of a difficult legal or financial dilemma was a Jewish characteristic.[23]

In the years to follow, FDR voiced many additional remarks
about excessive Jewish prominence and influence. As noted in
chapter 2, he asserted in a 1938 conversation with Rabbi Wise
that Jews in Poland were responsible for provoking antisemitism because they dominated the Polish economy.[24] During
a November 1941 cabinet meeting, FDR remarked that there
were too many Jews among federal employees in Oregon. Morgenthau subsequently asked FDR, in private, if that statement
"wasn't giving the cabinet officers the impression that he did
not want too many Jews in government." The president replied
by citing an incident in 1923, when he was a member of Harvard University's Board of Overseers: "Some years ago a third of
the entering class at Harvard were Jews and the question came
up as to how it should be handled . . . I asked [a fellow-board
member] whether we should discuss it with the Board of Overseers and it was decided that we should. . . . It was decided that
over a period of years the number of Jews should be reduced
one or two per cent a year until it was down to 15%. . . . I treat
the Catholic situation just the same. . . . I appointed three men
in Nebraska—all Catholics—and they wanted me to appoint
another Catholic, and I said that I wouldn't do it. . . . You can't
get a disproportionate amount of any one religion."[25] In January
1942, according to Morgenthau's diary, White House adviser
Leo Crowley reported to him that during a recent lunch with
the president, FDR commented, "Leo, you know this is a Protestant country, and the Catholics and Jews are here on sufferance. . . . It is up to both of you [Crowley and Morgenthau] to
go along with anything that I want at this time."[26]

"Spread the Jews Thin"

Roosevelt did not merely complain about what he saw as the problem of Jewish influence; he had specific ideas on how to address it. At the 1943 Casablanca conference—where FDR and local officials discussed the governance of Allied-liberated North Africa—Roosevelt argued that strict quotas should be imposed so that Jews in the region would not "overcrowd" various professions. This approach, he asserted, "would further eliminate the specific and understandable complaints which the Germans bore towards the Jews in Germany, namely, that while they represented a small part of the population, over fifty percent of the lawyers, doctors, school teachers, college professors, etc, in Germany, were Jews." In effect Roosevelt's statement rationalized German antisemitism as an "understandable" response to Jewish behavior.[27] A related conversation took place several months later, during a White House luncheon on May 22, 1943, at which Prime Minister Winston Churchill and President Roosevelt were discussing postwar plans. According to the diary of Vice President Henry Wallace, who was present, at one point the conversation turned to the status of the Jews after the war. FDR told Churchill he had commissioned his adviser on refugee matters, Isaiah Bowman, to study "the problem of working out the best way to settle the Jewish question." According to Wallace, FDR approvingly described Bowman's plan, which "essentially [was] to spread the Jews thin all over the world. The president said he had tried this out in [Meriwether] County, Georgia [which Roosevelt often visited in the 1920s] and at Hyde Park on the basis of adding four or five Jewish families at each place. He claimed that the local population would have no objection if there were no more than that."[28]

FDR's plan for the Jews was remarkably similar to what he envisioned for Japanese Americans. At a November 21, 1944, press conference, the president was asked how soon he intended to permit Japanese Americans to return to their homes from the internment camps in which some 120,000 of them had been detained since early 1942. He replied:

> A good deal of progress has been made in scattering them through the country, and that is going on almost every day. . . . There are about roughly a hundred thousand Japanese-origin citizens in this country. And it is felt by a great many lawyers that under the Constitution they can't be kept locked up in concentration camps. And a good many of them, as I remember it somewhere around 20 or 25 per cent of all those citizens have re-placed themselves, and in a great many parts of the country.
>
> And the example that I always cite, to take a unit, is the size of the county, whether it's in the Hudson River Valley or in western Georgia which we all know, in one of those counties, probably half a dozen or a dozen families could be scattered around on the farms and worked into the community. . . . And they wouldn't—what's my favorite word?—discombobulate the existing population of those particular counties very much. After all—what?—75 thousand families scattered all around the United States is not going to upset anybody.[29]

A common theme underlay Roosevelt's perceptions of both Jews and Japanese Americans. Their "blood"—that is, their innate racial characteristics—made them suspect. If admitted to the country in large numbers, they would soon come to overcrowd certain professions, dominate aspects of society, or harm America's character or culture in other ways. They needed to be "spread out thin" so as to keep them in check. America as FDR envisioned it should be overwhelmingly white and Protestant, with only a modest number of Catholics and Jews included "on sufferance." The entry of significant numbers of "non-assimilable" Jewish or Asian immigrants did not fit comfortably in that vision. Even though the immigration quotas for European Jewish refugees were unfilled by nearly two hundred thousand; even though twenty thousand German Jewish refugee children would not threaten any American's job; even though the 930 Jews on the *St. Louis* could be placed in the Virgin Islands; and even though 70 percent of Americans supported granting temporary haven to large numbers of refugees—doing so did not comport with Franklin Roosevelt's conception of the ideal America.

Roosevelt was not the only president of the United States to have harbored negative stereotypes concerning Jews. Harry Truman and Richard Nixon privately disparaged Jews, too.[30] Their policies regarding Jewish affairs, however, do not seem to have been negatively influenced by their private prejudices. Roosevelt, by contrast, allowed his prejudices to influence his policies regarding America's response to the persecution of European Jewry. Still, like Truman and Nixon, FDR could bend to political considerations. He would have preferred not to antagonize the British by raising the Palestine immigration issue in 1936—but the prospect of increased Jewish support in that year's reelection campaign proved more pressing and made him amenable to Rabbi Wise's appeal for intervention. Roosevelt was in no hurry to insist that the rulers of Allied-liberated North Africa abolish their anti-Jewish policies—but Jewish protests, from Rabbi Wise and others, led him to do so. Furthermore, the president strongly opposed the congressional resolution calling for creation of a U.S. government refugee rescue agency in 1943. Yet when threatened with an embarrassing election-year scandal over his administration's non-response to the Holocaust, Roosevelt reversed course and established the War Refugee Board.

Conclusion

A President's Strategy and a Rabbi's Anguish

FRANKLIN D. ROOSEVELT WAS "fundamentally a political animal, self-centered and always alert to what might constitute a political advantage," according to FDR biographer Robert Dallek. That description arguably could apply to almost every American president. Yet it is noteworthy because it contrasts so sharply with the self-image Roosevelt sought to project. As a presidential candidate in 1932, Roosevelt presented himself to the public as a warm-hearted champion of the "forgotten man," a term he memorably coined during his first campaign for the White House. Yet some of those who were closest to Roosevelt perceived him very differently. Harry Truman, for example, called FDR "the coldest man I ever met."[1]

President Roosevelt understood the political advantage of creating the impression that in his heart, he was genuinely concerned about the plight of Europe's persecuted Jews. Shortly after an October 1943 conference of American, British, and Soviet foreign ministers in Moscow, a reporter asked him whether the meeting included any discussions about helping "Jewish victims of atrocities or persecution." The president, seemingly caught off-guard by the question, replied: "That I don't know. I won't be able to tell you that until I see Mr. Hull because that is, as you know, that whole problem is—the heart's all right—it's a question of ways and means."[2]

The disingenuous explanations that the president and his various spokesmen offered as to why no "ways and means" could be found to aid the Jews left some in the Jewish community wondering as to FDR's actual sentiments. Assistant Secretary Long claimed in his November 1943 congressional testimony that "most neutral shipping disappeared from the seas" at the beginning of the war and therefore "there just is not any transportation" to carry refugees. Congressman Emanuel Celler likewise recalled that Roosevelt administration officials told him that to rescue Jews, the United States would have to "divert shipping for the transportation of war materials and troops for the refugees." In fact, Portuguese liners traveled between Lisbon and the United States every six weeks, and other neutral ships also were available. Liberty ships that brought troops and soldiers to Europe returned to the United States empty and needed ballast to weigh them down so they would not capsize. U.S. officials in Allied-liberated Algiers complained to the War Department in early 1943 of a severe shortage of materials to use as ballast.[3]

The ballast problem was no secret, and some in the American Jewish community made a connection to the refugee issue. An editorial in the *Baltimore Jewish Times* in May 1943 noted that empty Liberty ships were "frequently going out of their way to find ballast," and that the Allies had managed to find ships to bring tens of thousands of Polish refugees to Iran, Uganda, and Mexico—"the very ships [that] all the apologists for failure to aid the Jewish refugees denied were available." The Allies had also found enough boats to take twenty thousand Muslims from Egypt to Mecca, for a religious pilgrimage, in 1944. The Bergson Group's magazine, *The Answer*, noted in 1943 that rubble from England that had served as ballast was being used to construct a new highway on Manhattan's east side (FDR Drive) and remarked: "[I]t is as important to devote shipping space to help secure the foundations of humanity by saving lives as it is to bring rubble for filling foundations for River driveways." Nahum Goldmann, briefing the Jewish Agency leadership during a visit to Palestine in April 1943, said, it was "nonsense that there are no ships to bring out refugees—the ships go from America full, and return empty." Isador Lubin, head of the Bureau of Labor Statistics, informed presidential secretary William Hassett in early 1945 that there were "some five or six hundred Jewish refugees in the Mediterranean area" who had visas for Palestine and could travel there on UNRRA relief ships "if they got the 'go ahead' sign from the President." Lubin received no response.[4]

Celler characterized Roosevelt as "silent, indifferent, and insensitive to the plight of the Jews." Likewise, others in the Jewish community who had contact with the president were not persuaded that his heart was "all right" when it came to the fate of Jews under the Nazis. Jewish activist Cecilia Razovsky, who unsuccessfully negotiated with the White House regarding the refugee ship St. Louis, reported to her colleagues that "our State Department was un-sympathetic and Franklin Delano was apathetic." The chief rabbi of British Mandatory Palestine, Yitzhak Herzog, who met with President Roosevelt at the White House on April 29, 1941, subsequently characterized FDR as "cold and indifferent" to his appeal for U.S. action to aid Europe's Jews.[5]

No doubt, the obstacles to influencing Roosevelt's refugee policy were many and formidable. Regardless of who stood at the helm of the American Jewish community, there was the reality of an unsympathetic White House, an antisemitic State Department, a Congress that was largely anti-immigration, and a public that was strongly isolationist prior to 1941. Nonetheless, political circumstances sometimes created opportunities to change the government's positions, and Jewish leaders who exhibited energy, creativity, persistence, and—especially— the ability to learn from their mistakes were able to influence American policy.

The latter quality assumes particular significance in any discussion of Rabbi Stephen Wise, because in a number of instances in the 1930s and 1940s, fears or expectations that initially shaped Jewish policy decisions were soon proven groundless. A Jewish leader's ability to recognize new information and adjust accordingly became an important attribute for effective Jewish leadership in the Hitler era. The leaders of B'nai B'rith, for example, declined to participate in AJCongress-sponsored protests against the Nazis in 1933 on the grounds that their involvement might result in German government retaliation against B'nai B'rith lodges in Germany. In the wake of attacks on a number of Berlin lodges in 1934, AJCongress officials noted B'nai B'rith's "refusal to join with us in our protest against the Hitler regime did not serve as protection to their lodge abroad, as witness what happened in Berlin." Nevertheless, B'nai B'rith did not change its position on public protests.[6]

The AJCongress was correct about B'nai B'rith, but the same thing could be said regarding Rabbi Wise and the Bergson Group. Wise's fear that strident newspaper ads or the rabbis' march to the White House would foment antisemitism were not borne out by events. Neither the publication of more than two hundred often provocative newspaper ads sponsored by the Bergsonites nor the march by four hundred rabbis through the streets of Washington caused the antisemitic backlash Wise feared. Despite these circumstances, he did not modify his assumptions about Bergson provoking antisemitism. On the contrary, Wise's comparison of Bergson to Hitler ("for the reason that his activities could only lead to increased anti-Semitism") in 1944 indicated that his attitudes had, if anything, hardened even further as time went on.

The shifts in American public opinion in the 1940s concerning immigration point to another example of how a Jewish leader could have taken strategic advantage of changing circumstances. As noted in chapter 5, there was overwhelming public opposition to immigration in the 1930s, owing to fear of foreigners, antisemitism, and Depression-era competition for jobs. However, concerns about immigrants taking jobs lessened significantly following America's entry into World War II, when war production put an end to unemployment. After the tide of the war turned in 1943, with the defeat of the Germans at Stalingrad and the liberation of Italy, public attitudes toward immigration increasingly gave way to humanitarian sympathy for Hitler's Jewish victims. The new sentiment was not exclusive to one political camp. In September 1943 the presidents of both the National Democratic Club and the National Republican Club jointly called for the temporary admission of all refugees until six months after the war. By the spring of 1944, a Gallup poll commissioned by the White House found that 70 percent of Americans favored the creation of emergency refugee shelters in the United States for European Jewish refugees. The trends in public opinion that had once intimidated Jewish leaders were not so inflexible as they first imagined. An undaunted Jewish leader might have used these shifts in public opinion to initiate a public campaign for temporary havens in America. Jewish organizations' lists of rescue recommendations, such as the one submitted for consideration at the Bermuda conference, had included a call for creating "temporary sanctuaries" for refugees in the Allied countries, but the administration had not adopted that proposal, and the idea of publicly pressing the Roosevelt administration for something that the administration clearly did not want was still inconceivable to Rabbi Wise.[7]

Another important mark of a Jewish leader's effectiveness was the ability to keep personal opinions from clouding one's overall political judgment. Rabbi Wise had strong opinions and many years of experience dealing with politicians at all levels. His relationship with President Roosevelt was his most important political asset and elevated his stature among American Jews. Yet it was precisely in this area that he stumbled. Franklin Roosevelt took advantage of Wise's adoration of his policies and leadership to manipulate Wise through flattery and intermittent access to the White House. Calling Wise by his first name made the rabbi feel he was a personal friend of the most powerful man on earth. FDR's inclusion of a sentence by Wise in the president's 1937 inaugural address must have strengthened that perception. All of this made Wise especially susceptible when the president implored him to help silence those in the Jewish community who challenged the administration's policies, from the Bergson Group with its rallies and newspaper advertisements to the American Jewish Conference delegates who insisted on promoting Jewish statehood. Wise's first biographer, Melvin Urofsky, has noted that for all of Wise's private criticism of old-line Jewish leaders for preferring the role of *shtadlan*—quiet intercessor—to that of activist, his own relationship with "the princes of power made him a *shtadlan* and it was his downfall." No doubt Wise genuinely believed that access often equaled influence. But the historical record indicates otherwise.[8]

Some of Wise's closest colleagues faulted the way he related to the president. Eliahu Elath, a Jewish Agency representative at the 1945 UN conference in San Francisco, recorded in his diary a conversation he had there with longtime ZOA leader Morris Rothenberg: "In a long talk we had on the American administration's position on the Palestine question, Morris Rothenberg cautioned against Wise's optimism. He feels that Wise did not realize the late president's true character and that Roosevelt did not always keep the promises he made to Wise or, indeed, to other Jewish and Zionist leaders. Wise was too often satisfied by extracting a declaration from Roosevelt, whose practical value Wise did not scrutinize enough when it came out or examine in the light of other, often conflicting, declarations or acts by the president himself or members of this administration."[9]

Looking back years later, Elath said Wise was "trusting maybe too much Roosevelt's practical desire of helping. . . . Roosevelt charmed him, but didn't promise him anything." He noted that FDR and Secretary of State Hull had not "done anything about [the White Paper]. Influencing Great Britain—the contrary: there is a telegram [to Arab leaders] I have seen in which Cordell Hull says, 'Don't pay attention to what we are saying [to Jewish leaders]; this is all for internal consumption.' Roosevelt knew about that. There's no question about that." With regard to the issue of Jewish statehood, "It's true that before the elections he issued this statement in favor of, in support of, the Jewish commonwealth. But then immediately after he was elected, and probably 80 or 90% of the Jews voted for him, he stopped, as you know it only too well, the deliberations of the Congress." In short, "when it came to crucial situations Roosevelt wasn't helpful," Elath concluded. "Roosevelt probably, with time, disappointed more and more the Jewish and Zionist public. They were very disappointed when he didn't support the demand for improving the possibilities for Jewish immigrants, to permit persecuted Jews from Europe to enter America." Despite it all, Rabbi Wise's support for Roosevelt was unshaken, Elath said, because "he knew him as the man of the New Deal, as the man who revolutionized the social and economic structure of the pre-New Deal Society in America."[10]

Similarly, Nahum Goldmann recalled: "There is something [to the argument] that Rabbi Wise was too close to Roosevelt to be effective, he was too close to really be an opposition leader. . . . Wise exaggerated his appreciation of Roosevelt. The accusations against Roosevelt are partly justified. No question. And [Wise] was so attached to him and they were buddy-buddy."[11] Wise's fawning "Dear Boss" and "Dear Chief" letters were emblematic of the problem, in Goldmann's view. "For instance, in my opinion, which Wise would never accept, Roosevelt would never agree to a Jewish state. . . . In this respect a certain criticism applies that Wise was prejudiced in favor of Roosevelt, there is something in it."[12]

Arthur Lourie, a loyal deputy to Wise as a senior staff member of the American Zionist Emergency Council, was more diplomatic than Goldmann but likewise concluded that Wise erred in his political judgment: "Wise was convinced that the only way to achieve what we wanted in the way of American assistance was through Roosevelt and by the friendship, Roosevelt's friendship on the personal level, as well as through the support of Jews for the Democratic Party. And Wise accordingly was always very careful not to find himself in conflict, in direct confrontation with Roosevelt, which [Abba Hillel] Silver was quite prepared to do, when he felt it necessary. . . . Silver was always skeptical of Roosevelt's bona fides, really, as far as Zionism was concerned. And I think to a large extent he was proved right by history."[13]

Carl Hermann Voss, an American Christian Zionist leader who was a close friend of Wise and would later author a book about Wise and edit a volume of his letters, said he felt "very embarrassed by this because I loved the man so much and he was hoodwinked by Roosevelt. . . . Because over and over again, from 1933 on, Roosevelt had promised to do something, promised to say something, and never once would he move, either utter a word, or take an action. Secondly, I think he [Wise] was taken in by him [Roosevelt] in the early 1940s. Again, Roosevelt did not speak out and did not instruct [officials of his administration] to do anything. . . . I felt that Wise was betrayed by Franklin Roosevelt, a man whom I admired, [b]ut I have to be objective on this score." Wise "got to know Roosevelt very well and was thoroughly charmed by him at that time. . . . There was an adoration [by Wise] of the man [FDR], a trust in him which I think was not justified."[14]

Rabbi Dr. Israel Goldstein, who served as president of the Synagogue Council of America and the Zionist Organization of America, collaborated closely with Rabbi Wise, and felt "a personal love and admiration for him," but was nonetheless critical of Wise's political strategy, in retrospect. "I always felt about Wise that he was a man of generous nature who could be easily taken in," Goldstein recalled. "And I believe that he was taken in, to a large extent, by President Roosevelt, in this respect. Roosevelt was of course himself an outgoing personality and a man of tremendous charm and great cleverness, and I think that more than once he disarmed Wise by his manner. . . . I'm sure that Roosevelt was more clever than Wise, and Wise was no fool. But I think that Roosevelt had a deeper understanding of human nature and how to play up to its weaknesses." Goldstein later elaborated: "When Roosevelt would put his arm around Wise's shoulder and say 'You're wonderful. You don't have to worry. Everything is fine.' . . . well, Wise, I think, had in him enough of that beautiful quality of trusting to be at times deluded and deceived."[15] In a blunt mea culpa he wrote for the *Jerusalem Post* in his final years, Goldstein added:

I have an uneasy feeling that many occupying Jewish leadership positions [in the 1940s] were misled by hollow assurances "from on high" and were lulled into complacency by eminent Jewish colleagues who innocently, but mistakenly, believed that they had found sympathetic ears in Roosevelt's administration.

Everyone—including the writer—who held a position of Jewish leadership, major or minor, during that tragic period of our history should feel, in retrospect, a sense of his own inadequacy and of contrition in the light of what transpired.

Thus in the end, six million Jews perished while the United States dithered and temporized, while the British doggedly sealed off ports of embarkation, and while we Jews in the Free World naively heeded assurances that "everything possible would be done" to save lives.[16]

These friends and colleagues of Rabbi Wise may not have realized that Wise, too, later harbored private doubts about Roosevelt. As he worked on his autobiography in his final years, Wise gave expression to some of those doubts. These are on display in the dramatic discrepancies between the first and final drafts of his book, *Challenging Years* (1949).

The unpublished draft included a lengthy section on the 1942 telegram revealing Hitler's intention to annihilate Europe's Jews, Wise's efforts to publicize the mass murder, and President Roosevelt's statements condemning the atrocities. It concluded with a paragraph that fell noticeably short of defending FDR's response to the Holocaust:

The record of Franklin D. Roosevelt is what it is. History will do him justice, though his detractors cannot. He was the embodiment of his country's ideals as he understood them and strove to put them into practice. Not failure but low aim is crime, said Lowell. Roosevelt rarely aimed low. If he sometimes, rarely enough, did aim low, he acted not for advantage nor out of fear. It is in his rendezvous with destiny that he was equal to its measureless and majestic responsibility. Woe to them who vainly sought and seek to divert this heroic figure from his definitely appointed rendezvous.[17]

Wise seemed to be struggling with his own feelings, torn between what he had hoped Roosevelt would do for the Jews and the reality of what the president did not do. In the unpublished version, Wise could not bring himself to explicitly praise Roosevelt's record concerning the Jews; the most he could say was that the record "is what it is." His sentence "History will do him justice" likewise was steeped in ambiguity. FDR "was the embodiment of his country's ideals as he understood them and strove to put them into practice," Wise wrote, almost implying that FDR might have misunderstood those ideals, or might have failed to practice them. His assertion that the president did, sometimes—albeit rarely—"aim low" seemed to refer to Roosevelt's failure to make a substantial effort to aid the Jews. The phrase "rendezvous with destiny," to which Wise alluded, had been famously invoked by FDR in outlining his vision for America under the New Deal, in his 1936 speech accepting renomination. For Wise to conclude a discussion of Roosevelt's response to the Holocaust by saying that "in his rendezvous with destiny [Roosevelt] was equal to its measureless and majestic responsibility" seemed to imply that although he fell short in helping the Jews, at least FDR succeeded in other ways.

None of this ambivalence made it into the published version of Wise's autobiography, however. He scrapped the draft and replaced it with an adulatory chapter titled "I Remember Roosevelt," in which he emphasized his many happy interactions with the president. He heaped praise on FDR for "grasping what was occurring [concerning Europe's Jews] with more feeling and understanding" than did his State Department. Wise even presented the 1945 meeting with Ibn Saud as a demonstration of Roosevelt's sympathy for Zionism, asserting that the president had meant well in trying "to secure [Ibn Saud's] assent to the development of Palestine," but had been misled by "the poor advice of some counselors in our State Department and in the Colonial Office in England." In his chapter focusing on the Holocaust years, Wise wrote of the "delay and sabotage by State Department bureaucrats" of the wJcongress's 1943 request for a license to send funds to Europe to rescue Jews, without addressing why the president did not press State to follow through on the license. In these passages, his final comments for the record concerning Roosevelt and the Nazi genocide, Rabbi Wise set aside the doubts that had beset him while writing the first draft of the book, and instead spoke only in positive, even glowing, terms of the president's record.[18]

The very fact that Wise repeatedly felt compelled to publicly exaggerate what the president said to him behind closed doors is telling. Wise claimed after the December 17, 1942, meeting at the White House that President Roosevelt promised the Allies "are prepared to take every possible step" to "save those who may still be saved," when there is ample evidence that he never said anything of the sort (see chapter 3). Similarly Wise emerged from his March 9, 1944, meeting with the president portraying him as strongly pro-Zionist, papering over Roosevelt's refusal to support a pro-Zionist congressional resolution then pending (see chapter 6). Had FDR been genuinely sympathetic to Wise's positions, there would have been no need for him to mislead the public regarding the president's sentiments.

Admittedly, it would have been no simple matter to influence Franklin D. Roosevelt. Anyone in Wise's position would have encountered the same disingenuousness and evasiveness from the president that Wise experienced. In a 1944 briefing of David Ben-Gurion and other Jewish Agency leaders, Nahum Goldmann described a typical conversation with FDR: "It is impossible to educate him, because you get to see him only once every six months, for thirty minutes, ten of which are spent by him telling anecdotes, after which he expects to hear you tell him anecdotes, and then there are only ten minutes left for a serious conversation—what can one accomplish like this?"[19] It was precisely because of the inherent difficulty of influencing Roosevelt that the Bergson Group crafted a strategy of circumnavigating the White House and mobilizing congressional pressure to force the president's hand on the rescue issue.

To Rabbi Wise, the notion of going around the president was inconceivable. His interactions with Roosevelt were shaped by his deep personal loyalty to the man, his policies, and his party. In private correspondence, Wise revered FDR as "the Great Man" and "the All Highest." "[I]n the District of Columbia, we have a great, good Friend," he wrote a colleague in 1937. "He is thinking about us and for us. He is planning for us. We are in his mind and on his heart." Wise came to view Roosevelt's political fate in near-apocalyptic terms. "[T]he future of our American democracy" was at stake in the 1936 election, Wise wrote to a friend. "Against Roosevelt, in very large part, are those forces which I consider to be inimical to the highest interests of democratic life . . . [his] election is not only essential to the well-being of America, but to the highest interests of the human race."[20]

Wise's ability to lead effectively was further compromised by his reluctance to develop relationships across the political spectrum. Even the upstart Bergson Group, which had far fewer resources than Wise and whose leaders were not even Americans, understood that building coalitions was the sine qua non of political advocacy. Yet Rabbi Wise was profoundly uncomfortable at the thought of developing relationships with Republicans and conservative Christians. Nor did Wise easily make peace with the activist elements within the Jewish community; he viewed them not as potential partners but as threats to his position. Leib Jaffe was a nuisance who could be dismissed because he was a lone wolf. Rabbi Meyer Berlin, although the leader of a substantial Zionist faction, was an irritant who could be ignored—at least until he threatened to open a lobbying office in Washington DC, which forced Wise to take him seriously, if only to squelch the competition. Similarly, student activists, whether Saadia Gelb at Wise's own Jewish Institute of Religion or the rabbinical students at the Jewish Theological Seminary, could be brushed aside as mere youngsters, even if an offer to organize college students for rescue did not come along every day. The irony is that in his early years, Wise had established the American Jewish Congress to give the immigrant masses a voice. By the 1930s, however, Wise saw the Jewish masses as something of a threat; he contemptuously dubbed them the "pesterers and preachers of a thousand Brooklyn street corners." He engineered the dismantling of the Joint Emergency Committee for European Jewish Affairs—which had been created to organize a unified and effective Jewish response to the plight of European Jewry—out of concern that the "wild people" on the committee were pressing for rallies and marches and the mobilization of Jewish voters. Each of these activist elements was anxious to work with Rabbi Wise on behalf of rescue; in some cases they were practically begging him to utilize them as resources in a campaign to change U.S. refugee policy. But Wise was not prepared to lead a campaign against the policies of a president who had made it clear on more than one occasion that he wanted the Jews to keep quiet.[21]

Yet another untapped resource was the Jewish delegation in the U.S. House of Representatives. With the exception of Rep. Sol Bloom, interactions between Rabbi Wise and the Jewish members of Congress typically consisted of Wise or his deputies trying to restrain the congress members from being too forthright in their efforts for European Jewry. For all of Wise's acerbic comments about Bloom (behind his back), the rabbi's ardent efforts to protect the Roosevelt administration from Jewish criticism indicate he had more in common with Bloom than he cared to admit. On multiple occasions Wise and his colleagues pressed representatives Emanuel Celler and Samuel Dickstein to withdraw, or at least water down, proposals to increase refugee immigration—in one instance for fear that it might provoke an antisemitic congressman "to make another *Protocols of the Elders of Zion* speech," in another because it might discomfit the Roosevelt administration on the eve of the Evian conference.

Rabbi Wise also "frowned on" the proposal by Celler, made twice in 1943, to organize a conference in Washington of congress members to promote the rescue cause. Furthermore, at the administration's request, Wise and Goldmann pressured Celler to refrain from criticizing Saudi Arabia's foreign minister when he visited Washington in 1943, despite a recent assertion by the Saudi king, in *Life* magazine, that Jews had no right to Palestine and should stay "in Europe or America." It was as if Wise had become a kind of unofficial enforcer of FDR's desire to keep the Jews quiet. The only instance in which Wise's AZEC leadership sought to mobilize the Jewish congressmen for concerted action was when it tried to enlist them in a complicated ruse in which they would invite a Bergson Group leader to a meeting and then collectively ambush him with embarrassing questions. (The congress members declined to take part in the scheme.)[22]

Perhaps there was no realistic possibility of Wise cooperating with Bergson; perhaps the Bergsonites were too independent-minded to collaborate effectively with the mainstream Jewish leadership. But treating the Bergson Group as an enemy was not Rabbi Wise's only option. He could have simply left them alone. The amount of time and energy expended on trying to undermine the Bergson Group constituted a significant drain on the Jewish leadership's resources. At a War Refugee Board staff meeting on May 24, 1944—at the height of the well-publicized deportation of Hungarian Jews to Auschwitz—John Pehle reported to his colleagues, "We have been left alone this week by Jewish organizations, except the few who came in to see me and tell me what they thought of Bergson; because they are so busy fighting Bergson, they are neglecting everything else." Every letter sent by AZEC to a foreign ambassador urging him to boycott Bergson could have been a letter sent to a U.S. government official urging the rescue of Jewish refugees. Every request sent to a celebrity urging him or her to stop signing Bergson newspaper ads could have been a request for that individual to become more, not less, involved in speaking out against the mass murder of Europe's Jews.[23]

Rabbi Wise's health problems also significantly affected his leadership ability. His increasingly serious ailments during the 1930s and 1940s were compounded by frequent and painful treatments that themselves were often temporarily incapacitating. In late 1936 and early 1937, he was sidelined for weeks with an acute respiratory infection and severe back pain. In the summer of 1937, as American Zionist leaders were bracing for a momentous British decision on the future of Palestine, Justice Brandeis stopped updating Wise on his diplomatic contacts, "wishing to save [Wise's] strength." Illness caused Rabbi Wise to miss the 1938 Evian conference, after which he had to take a month off to recover. "Ceaseless" bleeding from his gums forced Wise to leave the ZOA's 1939 national convention after the opening sessions. He likewise missed the 1939 World Zionist Congress and a White House conference on refugees later that year because of his declining health. During the crucial period preceding the proclamation of the 1939 British White Paper, Wise confided to Brandeis about his "constantly troublesome spleen, which interferes with the normal behavior of other organs, and gives me great discomfort until from time to time I get x-ray treatment." A bout of "ear trouble which afflicts me with constant dizziness" prevented him from participating in a meeting with Brandeis and other Jewish leaders about the Jewish refugee crisis in the autumn of 1939; Wise later explained that "my otologist forbade me to spend the night in a Pullman car, which was the only way I could have gone to Washington." In late 1939 and early 1940, respiratory infections left Wise in "wretched health" and again prevented him from working. While vacationing in Lake Placid in the summer of 1941, he wanted to "go down to New York

[City] and ask for a special meeting of the Emergency Committee [for Zionist Affairs]," to counteract recent anti-Zionist activity, but could not because, as he told a friend, "I am not equal to the strain of the journey, and I should not get off my back, and the excitement would be too much for me now."[24]

Nonetheless, Wise proved incapable of admitting that he was no longer physically able to undertake the duties expected of him, the logical consequence of which would have been to at least partly relinquish the reins of leadership. Wise's correspondence betrays brief flashes of such recognition, but only in theory. As early as 1935, Wise harbored doubts about his stamina, acknowledging to a friend "the unwisdom of a man getting on in years keeping the leadership of a movement instead of putting in younger and stronger men while he lives." The following year, he had a similar exchange with another colleague. "You are right about my being over-burdened," Wise wrote. "At present I happen to have the major responsibility for half a dozen institutions, including [the Free] Synagogue, [the Jewish] Institute [of Religion], U.P.A., Z.O.A., American and World Jewish Congresses." In a note to a Chicago rabbi in 1939, Wise remarked that "the younger men like [ZOA president Solomon] Goldman and you must now take up the torch, which we elders have carried too long." He told friends in 1940 that after construction of the synagogue's new building was complete, he would serve for a year and then "retire to *otium cum dignitate* [leisure time]." Similarly, Wise first responded positively when Chaim Weizmann proposed in 1943 to bring Abba Hillel Silver into the national Zionist leadership; "younger and stronger" men were needed, Wise acknowledged. Yet such brief flashes of realism never moved Wise from theory to practice. He never loosened his grip on his various longstanding leadership posts.[25]

The larger issue, perhaps, was Rabbi Wise's misplaced faith. From his correspondence and other accounts of the period, it seems clear that Wise desperately wanted to believe that the New Deal policies he so cherished reflected a humanitarian impulse that Roosevelt would extend, in some way, to the plight of European Jewry. He seems to have convinced himself that the president was doing whatever was realistically possible to aid Jewish refugees. If the administration's policies fell glaringly short when it came to Jewish concerns, the State Department, or the British Foreign Office, or anti-Zionist Jews were to blame—never the president, who actually made the final decisions on U.S. policy.

By taking upon himself the task of making excuses for Roosevelt and shielding him from Jewish criticism, Wise was in effect implementing what FDR said to him in 1936 about "the necessity of Jews lying low." He was also helping to facilitate policies that neither he himself, nor most American Jews, supported, from Roosevelt's pursuit of cordial—sometimes even friendly—diplomatic and economic relations with Nazi Germany in the 1930s, to his closing of America's doors to refugees despite unfilled quotas, to his refusal to take even minimal steps to interrupt the mass murder process. In assuming the mantle of communal leadership, Rabbi Wise had a duty to distinguish between hopes and reality, to speak truth to power, to translate privately expressed doubts about Roosevelt's policies into concrete political action, and to step aside if he was no longer able to do so. Those are the criteria by which history will judge him as a Jewish leader.

President Roosevelt's record with regard to the Holocaust has been judged in the past on such criteria as his lack of humanitarian sympathy for the plight of Europe's Jews, his reliance on advice from the State Department, and his tendency to follow public opinion rather than lead it. But other factors were also involved. He expended substantial political capital preparing America for war in the face of strong isolationism. The attention he could have devoted to Hitler's Jewish victims was limited by the tremendous burden he shouldered in addressing the Great Depression. His room to maneuver was also constrained by the failure of his proposal to restructure the Supreme Court and the Democrats' losses in the 1938 congressional elections.

Still, these important accomplishments and considerations

do not mitigate his record with regard to the Holocaust, because they did not conflict with many of the steps he could have taken regarding the Jews. He would not have had to incur substantial political risks had he permitted immigration up to the limits set by U.S. law, admitted refugees temporarily to a U.S. territory, utilized empty Liberty ships to carry refugees, or authorized dropping bombs on Auschwitz or the railways from planes that were already flying over the camp and its environs.

A more comprehensive understanding of FDR's response to the Holocaust must now include recognition of a number of crucial additional facts. While Roosevelt abhorred Nazism and sharply criticized Hitler in private conversations, he was still so committed to maintaining diplomatic and economic relations with Nazi Germany, despite its persecution of the Jews, that his representatives attended Nazi rallies in New York City and Germany and he personally removed anti-Hitler references from a cabinet member's speeches. He made no serious effort against the British White Paper immigration restrictions; in fact, he repeatedly broke his promises to Jewish leaders to issue strongly pro-Zionist statements, and even pressured them to hold back on their own Zionist advocacy. Perhaps most important, the evidence suggests that Roosevelt's harsh immigration policy and his refusal to take military steps that might have left large numbers of European Jews on his hands stemmed in part from the same bigoted notions that underlay his internment of more than 120,000 Japanese Americans. Franklin D. Roosevelt was proud that he had "no Jewish blood," and he bemoaned "the mingling of Asiatic blood with European or American blood." He believed Jews possessed certain innate and distasteful characteristics. He feared having too many Jews in a particular university or profession. Similarly, he advised against having too many Jews or Japanese in one locale, preferring that they be "spread thin" or "scattered all around the United States." He doubted that Japanese were "capable of assimilation." He saw America as "a Protestant country" with "the Jews" and people of other backgrounds present only "on sufferance." Perhaps, then, it is not surprising that he was disposed to policies that would exclude, restrict, disperse, or silence such minorities.[26] To stifle Jewish criticism of these policies, Roosevelt exploited the insecurities of a mostly immigrant and not yet fully accepted community and maneuvered Rabbi Wise to help ensure that the Jews would keep quiet.

NOTES

Abbreviations

AHS	Abba Hillel Silver Papers, The Temple, Cleveland OH
AIA	Agudath Israel Archives, New York
AJCA	American Jewish Committee Archives, YIVO Institute, New York
AJConf	American Jewish Conference Papers, American Jewish Historical Society, New York
AJCong	American Jewish Congress Papers, American Jewish Historical Society, New York
AFLP	American League for a Free Palestine Collection, American Jewish Historical Society, New York
AZEC	American Zionist Emergency Council Papers, Central Zionist Archives, Jerusalem
BAP	Benjamin Akzin Papers, Jabotinsky Archives-Metzudat Ze'ev, Tel Aviv
BGC	Bergson Group Collection, Jabotinsky Archives-Metzudat Ze'ev, Tel Aviv
BLP	Breckinridge Long Papers, Library of Congress, Washington DC
CWP	Chaim Weizmann Papers, Weizmann Institute, Rehovot, Israel
DRP	Daniel C. Roper Papers, Duke University Library, Durham NC
DSW	Archives of The David S. Wyman Institute for Holocaust Studies, Washington DC
ECP	Emanuel Celler Papers, Library of Congress, Washington DC
EMH	Edward M. House Papers, Yale University, New Haven CT
FBI	Federal Bureau of Investigation files, in possession of the author via the Freedom of Information Act

FDRL   Franklin D. Roosevelt Presidential Library and Archives, Hyde Park NY

BGR   Bernard G. Richards Papers, Jewish Theological Seminary, New York

HH   Harry L. Hopkins Papers, Franklin D. Roosevelt Presidential Library and Archives, Hyde Park NY

HHPL   Herbert Hoover Presidential Library, West Branch IA

HMP   Harold Manson Papers, The Temple, Cleveland OH.

IGP   Israel Goldstein Papers, Central Zionist Archives, Jerusalem

JLC   Jewish Labor Committee Records, Tamiment Library and Robert F. Wagner Labor Archives, New York University, New York

JMP   Julian Mack Papers, Central Zionist Archives, Jerusalem

JGM   James G. McDonald Papers, Columbia University, New York

JTA   Jewish Telegraphic Agency

LIN   Louis I. Newman Papers, American Jewish Archives, Cincinnati OH

LJP   Leib Jaffe Papers, Central Zionist Archives, Jerusalem

LSP   Lewis Strauss Papers, Herbert Hoover Presidential Library, West Branch IA

PRO   Public Record Office, London

PSGC   Palestine Statehood Groups Collection, Yale University, New Haven CT

SD   Records of the State Department, National Archives, Washington DC

SGP   Solomon Goldman Papers, American Jewish Archives, Cincinnati OH

SRP   Samuel I. Rosenman Papers, Franklin D. Roosevelt Presidential Library and Archives, Hyde Park NY

SSW-AHA   Stephen S. Wise Papers, American Jewish Archives, Cincinnati OH

SSW-AJHS   Stephen S. Wise Papers, American Jewish Historical Society, New York

SSW-CZA   Stephen S. Wise Papers, Central Zionist Archives, Jerusalem

WJC   World Jewish Congress Papers, American Jewish Archives, Cincinnati OH

WRB   War Refugee Board Papers, Franklin D. Roosevelt Presidential Library and Archives, Hyde Park NY

YGP   Yitzhak Gruenbaum Papers, Central Zionist Archives, Jerusalem

Introduction

1. Stephen Wise to James Waterman Wise, February 16, 1943, SSW, Box 4.

2. "Text of Declaration of the Allied Nations on Nazi Slaughter of Jews," JTA, December 18, 1942.

3. Freidel, *A Rendezvous with Destiny*, 99; Burns, *Roosevelt: The Lion and the Fox*, IX; Breitman and Kraut, *American Refugee Policy and European Jewry*, 222, 227; Morgenthau III, *Mostly Morgenthaus*, 255; Morgan, *FDR*, 772.

4. Breitman and Kraut, *American Refugee Policy and European Jewry*, 227; Adler, "The Roosevelt Administration and Zionism," 133.

5. The victim was Rep. E. Michael Edelstein (D-NY). See "Edelstein Dies After Clash with Rankin in House over Anti-Jewish Speech," JTA, June 5, 1941. For the polls, see Stember et al., *Jews in the Mind of America*, 8, 210, 215.

6. Wyman and Medoff, *A Race Against Death*, 5–6.

7. "Washington Sees Similarity Between Lindbergh's and Berlin's Anti-Jewish Propaganda," JTA, September 14, 1941; Shapiro, "The Approach of War," 59–62; Gartner, "The Two Continuities of Antisemitism," 317–18.

8. Olitzky, "The Sunday-Sabbath Movement in American Reform Judaism"; Ashton, *Hanukkah in America*, 4.

9. Frommer and Frommer, *Growing up Jewish in America*, 112–13.

10. Wyman, *The Abandonment of the Jews*, 71; Max Beer, "A Few Remarks About the Jewish Attitude in This War, Especially in the Field of Propaganda," September 2, 1942, File 268/90, WJC Papers, AJA, Cincinnati. Pressure from labor activists ultimately compelled Wise and his colleagues to accept a ten-minute stoppage, with the time to be made up by each participating worker on the following day.

1. "Nothing but Indifference"

1. "Talk by Rabbi Stephen S. Wise at Free Synagogue-May 15th, 1938," 2, SSW-CZA, A243/69.

2. Urofsky, *A Voice That Spoke for Justice*, 6–7; Rudin, *Pillar of Fire*, 109–11.

3. Urofsky, *A Voice That Spoke for Justice*, 7–8.

4. Voss, *Rabbi and Minister*, 236–38.

5. Smith, *The Shattered Dream*, 178; Urofsky, *A Voice That Spoke for Justice*, 255.

6. Wise to Grossman, March 20, 1933, and Wise to Cunningham, May 1, 1933, SSW-AJHS, Box 106.

7. "Hitler Sworn in As German Chancellor; Names Nazi Aides to Two Key Cabinet Positions," JTA, January 31, 1933; "Tension of German Jews Increases As Sporadic Nazi Attacks Occur; Report Goebbels Will Be Police Head," JTA, February 1, 1933; "Nazi Demonstrations Against Jews in Berlin," JTA, February 1, 1933; "News Brief," JTA, February 2, 1933; "Nazis Break into Cafe Frequented by Jews," JTA, February 3, 1933; "Aged Jew Attacked by Nazis," JTA, February 5, 1933; "Suspension for Abuse of Religious," JTA, February 7, 1933.

8. Wise to Mack, March 8, 1933, Box 115, SSW-AJHS; Strauss to Richey, March 23, 1933, HHPL, File: Correspondence with Lewis Strauss, 1933-June 1934, Post-Presidential Individuals; Strauss to Hoover, June 29, 1933, and Hoover to Strauss, July 5, 1933, LSP, File: Correspondence with Herbert Hoover, January–July 1933.

9. Wise, *Challenging Years*, 234–35; American Jewish Committee Executive Committee minutes, February 12, 1933, AJCA; Shafir, "American Jewish Leaders."

10. Wise to Mack, March 1, 1933, and Wise to Montague, April 18, 1933, SSW-AJHS, Box 115; Wise to Brunswick, April 6, 1933, SSW-AJHS, Box 106; Wise, *Challenging Years*, 250.

11. Wise to Frankfurter, May 6, 1933, SSW-AJHS, Box 109; Wise to Mack, March 8, 1933, and Wise to Mack, March 29, 1933, SSW-AJHS, Box 115; Wise to Gottheil, April 17, 1933, 3, SSW-AJA, Box 947; Wise to Cunningham, November 21, 1933, SSW-AJHS, Box 77.

12. Diary entry for July 9, 1935, in Breitman, Stewart, and Hochberg, *Advocate for the Doomed*, 780.

13. Wise to Gottheil, April 17, 1933, SSW-AJA, Box 947; Wise to Goldman, September 23, 1938, SSW-AJHS, Box 45; Gotttlieb, "The Anti-Nazi Boycott Movement," 198–99.

14. Wise to Gottheil, March 20, 1933, SSW-AJA, Box 947; Shapiro, "A Reform Rabbi in the Progressive Era," 382, 388.

15. Wise, *Challenging Years*, 240–42.

16. Shafir, "The Impact of the Jewish Crisis," 53; Wise to Brandeis, March 23, 1933, SSW-AJHS, Box 106.

17. Adler and Margalith, *With Firmness in the Right*, 3–4, 101–2, 287–88, 304; Cohen, "The Abrogation of the Russo-American Treaty of 1832"; Best, "The Jewish 'Center of Gravity'"; Greenberg, "An 1869 Petition"; Gartner, "Roumania, America, and World Jewry."

18. Fromer, "The American Jewish Congress," 311–12; Wise to Mack, April 15, 1933, cited in Voss, "Let Stephen Wise," 37; "Frown on Parades as Hitler Protest," *New York Times*, April 28, 1933; "Nazi Foes Here Calmed by Police," *New York Times*, March 20, 1933.

19. Adler to Lazaron, April 13, 1939, in Robinson, *Cyrus Adler: Selected Letters*, Vol. 1, 262.

20. Waldman to Proskauer, August 8, 1933, in Waldman, *Nor By Power*, 49; Waldman, "Effects of Hitlerism," 117.

21. Rosen to Hyman, 21 March 1933, File: German: Boycott (Demonstrations and Protest Meetings), 1933–36, 42–43, AJCA, Box 5.

22. Wise to Montague, April 18, 1933, SSW-AJHS, Box 115; Wise to Holmes, April 3, 1933, SSW-AJHS, Box 109.

23. Wise, *Challenging Years*, 245; Wise to Brandeis, September 19, 1933, SSW-AJHS, Box 106.

24. Rosen to Hyman, March 21, 1933, AJCA, Box 5, File: German: Boycott (Demonstrations and Protest Meetings), 1933–36, 42–43; Wise to Mack, March 29, 1933, SSW-AJHS, Box 115; Wise to Brunswick, April 6, 1933, SSW-AJHS, Box 106; "55,000 Here Stage Protest on Hitler Attacks on Jews; Nazis Order a New Boycott," *New York Times*, March 28, 1933; "Vast Crowds Flock to Monster Demonstration at Madison Square Garden to Express Indignation Against Nazis," JTA,

March 29, 1933. For the full text of Hull's cable, see Gottlieb, "The Anti-Nazi Boycott Movement in the American Jewish Community," 51. Regarding Dunn's cancelation, see Wise to Gottheil, April 17, 1933, 2, SSW-AJA, Box 947; Wise to Mack, March 29, 1933, SSW-AJHS, Box 115; Wise to Holmes, April 3, 1933, SSW-AJHS, Box 109; Wise, *Challenging Years*, 251.

25. Wise to Mack, March 29, 1933, SSW-AJHS, Box 115.

26. Voss, *Rabbi and Minister*, 80, 212.

27. Wise's 1925 sermon presenting his view of Jesus provoked strong criticism in the Orthodox Jewish community and some segments of the Yiddish press, and led to an unsuccessful attempt by the Mizrachi religious Zionist movement to oust Wise as chairman of the United Palestine Appeal. See Urofsky, *A Voice That Spoke for Justice*, 193–202.

28. Wise to Lipsky and Shultz, June 7, 1938, AJCong, File: American Jewish Congress; Wise to Frankfurter, March 17, 1941, SSW-AJHS, Box 109.

29. For more on how the Emergency Committee for Zionist Affairs, under Wise's leadership, focused its mobilization of Christian clergy almost exclusively on the liberal denominations, see Merkley, *The Politics of Christian Zionism*, 142–43.

30. Voss, *Rabbi and Minister*, 287–88; Wise to Worrell, October 4, 1934, in Voss, *Servant*, 199; "Mass Meeting Protests Hitler's Anti-Jewish Program" (editorial), *Christian Century*, April 26, 1933, 574.

31. Pickett to MacMaster, March 30, 1933, in Abzug, *America Views the Holocaust*, 27–28.

32. Clinchy to Wise, May 14, 1934, Wise to Clinchy, May 24, 1934, Wise to Newman, June 21, 1934, Newman to Wise, June 22, 1934, and Wise to Newman, June 25, 1934, LIN.

33. Wise, *Challenging Years*, 295.

34. Wise to Mack, March 1, 1933, Wise to Mack, April 5, 1933, and Wise to Montague, April 18, 1933, SSW-AJHS, Box 115; Wise to Brandeis, April 5, 1933, and Wise to Brunswick, April 6, 1933, SSW-AJHS, Box 106; Wise, *Challenging Years*, 250; Wise to Frankfurter, April 3, 1933, SSW-AJHS, Box 109; Wise to Gottheil, April 17, 1933, SSW-AJA, Box 947.

35. Wise, *Challenging Years*, 247–48, 250.

36. Wise to Montague, April 18, 1933, SSW-AJHS, Box 115; Wise to Gottheil, April 17, 1933, SSW-AJA, Box 947.

37. Wise to Mack, April 15, 1933, SSW-AJHS, Box 115.

38. Jonas, *The United States and Germany*, 213–14.

39. Wise to Gottheil, April 17, 1933, 3, SSW-AJA, Box 947.

40. Lipstadt, *Beyond Belief*, 14; "Conversation of Dr. Stephen S. Wise with Bernard S. Deutsch–May 4, 1933," SSW-AJHS, Box 106.

41. Wise to Mack, April 10, 1933, CZA, A243/148; Wise to Frankfurter, April 15, 1933, SSW-AJHS, Box 109.

42. Frommer, "The American Jewish Congress," 327–28.

43. Wise to Frankfurter, May 17, 1933, SSW-AJHS, Box 109; "Anti-Nazi Protest March Through New York Voted by American Jewish Congress," JTA, April 21, 1933.

44. Dodd Jr. and Dodd, *Ambassador Dodd's Diary*, 5.

45. Minutes of the American Jewish Congress Administrative Committee, September 23, 1933, File: Administrative Committee Minutes-1933, AJCong, Box 2; Wise to Mack, July 14, 1933, in Voss, *Servant*, 191.

46. American Jewish Congress Administrative Committee minutes, September 23, 1933, 2, File: 1933, AJCong, Box 2.

47. Gottlieb, "The Anti-Nazi Boycott Movement in the American Jewish Community," 57, 86; "Nazi Foes Here Calmed by Police," *New York Times*, March 20, 1933; "Conference Called for Jewish Congress Decides on Protest Demonstration to Initiate Nationwide Demonstrations on German Situation," JTA, March 21, 1933.

48. "The Anti-German Boycott: A Statement of the Position of the American Jewish Committee," cited in Gottlieb, "The Anti-Nazi Boycott Movement in the American Jewish Community," 37–38, 514–15; "Proskauer Opposes Anti-Reich Agitation," *New York Times*, December 11, 1934; "B'nai B'rith and the Boycott," *National Jewish Monthly*, November 1933, 56.

49. Gottlieb, "The Anti-Nazi Boycott Movement in the American Jewish Community," 85, 90; Richards to Sherman, April 13, 1933, File: Carl Sherman, BGR; Wise to Frankfurter, April 15, 1933, SSW-AJHS, Box 109; Hawkins, "Samuel Untermyer"; Urofsky, *A Voice That Spoke for Justice*, 272; Frommer, 315, 326, 371–372.

50. Wise to Frankfurter, April 15, 1933, and Wise to Frankfurter, April 16, 1933, SSW-AJHS, Box 109; Wise to Mack, April 10, 1933, SSW-AJHS, Box 115; "Protest Meeting at Madison Square Garden Decided On by American Jewish Congress," JTA, March 14, 1933; "Anti-Nazi Protest March Through New York Voted by American Jewish Congress," JTA, April 21, 1933; "Jews Here Decree Boycott on Reich," *New York Times*, May 15, 1933; Wise to Gottheil, April 17, 1933, SSW-AJA, Box 947; Memorandum by Stephen Wise and Bernard Deutsch, April 28, 1933, JMP, A405/83-A; Shafir, "The Impact of the Jewish Crisis," 200; Frommer, 315, 326, 371–72; Wise to Mack, April 10, 1933, SSW-CZA, A243/148; Wise to Mack, May 4, 1933, SSW-CZA, A243/148.

51. Urofsky, *A Voice That Spoke for Justice*, 271.

52. Wise, *Challenging Years*, 253.

53. Wise, *Challenging Years*, 247–48, 250.

54. Wise to Brandeis, September 1, 1933, SSW-AJHS, Box 106; Wise to Frankfurter, July 24, 1933, SSW-AJHS, Box 109; "Rabbi Wise Backs Boycott on Nazis," *New York Times*, August 15, 1933.

55. "Administrative Committee Meeting, Thursday evening, August 17, 1933," File: Administrative Committee Minutes-1933, AJCong, Box 2.

56. Brandeis to Wise, September 18, 1933, SSW-AJHS, Box 106; Wise to Brandeis, September 19, 1933, SSW-AJHS, Box 106.

57. In his autobiography, Rabbi Wise rewrote the history of the boycott movement in such a way as to obscure his six months of hesitation. In one passage, he asserted that "the American Jewish Congress, together with the American Federation of Labor, had launched the boycott." In another section, he wrote: "At the beginning of the Hitler regime, the American Jewish Congress had been the only responsible Jewish body in America to call for and support the economic boycott of Germany." Because Untermyer's organization called itself nonsectarian, and because Rabbi Wise considered Untermyer to be an irresponsible hothead, Wise presumably believed his sentence was technically correct, although it was obviously misleading. Wise proceeded to chastise those Jewish leaders who opposed the boycott, even though he himself had once been among their ranks: "[I]t is a painful to recall that the boycott was unapproved in certain Jewish quarters—and by those same self-appointed Jewish leaders who had urged silence at a time when silence on our part would have resulted in silence on the part of all the forces of civilization." See Wise, *Challenging Years*, 239, 260–61.

58. Sheramy, "When Silence is a Sin"; Hawkins, "Samuel Untermyer"; Kupsky, "Germanness and Jewishness"; Wise to Brandeis, October 17, 1933, SSW-AJHS, Box 106. Boycott advocates believed a serious and sustained boycott could engender "ruin and disaster" for the German economy, at which point "the end of German resources, and the end of all hope of the rehabilitation of Germany," would result in "putting Adolf Hitler out of power." Whether the German economy in 1933 was indeed sufficiently fragile enough to be toppled by a foreign boycott continues to be debated by historians, although ample evidence exists that German officials were profoundly distressed by the boycott. "Hitler had promised to end the depression and unemployment, and his base of popular support would diminish unless he could produce some results," Wise's biographer, Melvin Urofsky, has noted. "A foreign boycott of German goods could have serious effects on the economy, a fact the chancellor's economic advisers well knew." Moshe Gottlieb, a historian of the boycott, concluded that "the boycott hurt Germany . . . in almost every area of German industry, especially exports"; in a few instances, it even resulted in "a temporary halt to the public manifestations of Hitler's virulent anti-Semitic campaign." See Tenenbaum, "The Anti-Nazi Boycott Movement"; Gottlieb, *American Anti-Nazi Resistance*, 438–39, 442; Urofsky, *A Voice That Spoke for Justice*, 266.

59. Wise to Frankfurter, April 15, 1933, and Wise to Frankfurter, April 16, 1933, SSW-AJHS, Box 109; Wise to Mack, April 10, 1933, SSW-AJHS, Box 115; "Protest Meeting at Madison Square Garden Decided On by American Jewish Congress," JTA, March 14, 1933; "Jews Here Decree Boycott on Reich," *New York Times*, May 15, 1933; "Anti-Nazi Protest March Through New York Voted by American Jewish Congress," JTA, April 21, 1933; Wise to Gottheil, April 17, 1933, SSW-AJA, Box 947; Memorandum by Stephen Wise and Bernard Deutsch, April 28, 1933, JMP, A405/83-A; Shafir, "The Impact of the Jewish Crisis," 200; Frommer, "The American Jewish Congress," 315, 326, 371–372; Wise to Mack, April 10, 1933, SSW-CZA, A243/148.

60. Wise to Frankfurter, Mack, and Brandeis, May 23, 1933, SSW-AJHS, Box 109. There were no Jewish members of the U.S. Senate at the time. The Jewish congress members who did not participate in the meeting were Isaac Bacharach (R-NJ), Theodore Peyser (D-NY), Herman Kopplemann (D-CT), and William Citron (D-CT).

61. Wise to Frankfurter, Mack, and Brandeis, May 23, 1933, SSW-AJHS, Box 109.

62. Wise to Frankfurter, Mack, and Brandeis, May 23, 1933, SSW-AJHS, Box 109.

63. Wise to Frankfurter, June 1, 1933, SSW-AJHS, Box 109.

64. Gottlieb, "The American Controversy," 184–85.

65. Gottlieb, "The American Controversy," 199, 203.

66. Gottlieb, "The American Controversy," 202, 208.

67. Gottlieb, "The American Controversy," 211; Wenn, "A Tale of Two Diplomats," 42.

68. For a summary of U.S. press coverage of the 1936 Olympics, see Lipstadt, *Beyond Belief,* 80–85.

69. "Report of a Visit of Dr. Stephen S. Wise to President Franklin D. Roosevelt at Hyde Park, Mon. October 3, 1936," 2–3, SSW-CZA, A243/83; Wise to van Paassen, November 9, 1936, SSW-CZA, A243/92.

70. American Jewish Congress Administrative Committee minutes, September 23, 1933, 2, AJCA, File: 1933, Box 2; Wise to Mack, October 18, 1933, SSW-AJHS, Box 115.

71. Cohen to Wise, February 7, 1940, SSW-AJHS, Box 64. Brandeis, who was not a Roosevelt appointee, was a partial exception; he was more willing than the others to broach Jewish and Zionist concerns with FDR. But his contacts with the president dwindled in his final years, and he passed away in October 1941.

72. Wise to Mack, April 15, 1933, SSW-AJHS, Box 115; Wise to Holmes, June 1, 1933, SSW-AJHS, Box 109; Cook, *Eleanor Roosevelt,* 324; Breitman and Kraut, *American Refugee Policy,* 18; Leff and Medoff, "New Documents Shed More Light on FDR's Holocaust Failure," *American Jewish World,* April 30, 2004.

73. "Swastika to Wave Tonight at German Day Celebration," JTA, December 6, 1933.

74. "'Heil Hitler' Resounds as Steuben Society Denounces Boycott, Acclaims New Germany," JTA, December 8, 1933; "An Address by Daniel C. Roper, Secretary of Commerce, at the Celebration Commemorating the 250th Anniversary of the First German Settlement in North America, Madison Square Garden, New York City, December 6, 1933," DRP.

75. Dodd Jr. and Dodd, *Ambassador Dodd's Diary,* 95.

76. Dodd Jr. and Dodd, *Ambassador Dodd's Diary,* 86–87.

77. Some of the details of the Hitler-Dodd conversation are to be found in Dodd Jr. and Dodd, *Ambassador Dodd's Diary,* 89; others are in "Memorandum by the Ambassador in Germany (Dodd)," United States Department of State, *Foreign Relations of the United States Diplomatic Papers, 1934,* 218–20.

78. Morgenthau Diaries, November 26, 1941, FDRL.

79. "Nazis 'Convicted' of World 'Crime' by 20,000 in Rally," *New York Times*, March 8, 1934.

80. Dodd to House, March 24, 1934, EMH.

81. Dodd to House, March 24, 1934, and House to Dodd, March 31, 1934, EMH; Larson, *In the Garden*, 231–34, 239–241; Dodd Jr. and Dodd, *Ambassador Dodd's Diary*, 95, 103; Anthes, "Publicly Deliberative Drama." Dodd suspected that Jewish members of the U.S. embassy staff had been leaking information to the press. He complained to House that American journalists had been informed that he himself had recently protested to Hitler about Nazi propaganda activities in the United States. "It's another proof of the risky fact of certain people in confidential positions," Dodd wrote to House. "I am almost sure the information was given once more by one of the 'Chosen people.'"

82. "Organization Formed against Discrimination," JTA, February 26, 1934; "B'klyn Jewish Democracy to Fight Hate," JTA, March 6, 1934.

83. Weinstein to Wise, February 19, 1934, plus enclosure, SSW-AJHS, Box 43; Wise to Weinstein, February 20, 1934, SSW-AJHS, Box 43; "Political Club Hit by Head of B'nai B'rith," JTA, March 13, 1934; Memorandum, Abels to Waldman and Schneiderman, April 29, 1938, File: Immigration, 1936–1939," AJCA, Box 6.

84. Wise to Goldberg, March 6, 1934, SSW-AJHS, Box 43.

85. "Preached in City Pulpits," JTA, March 7, 1934.

86. Wise to La Guardia, May 29, 1934, SSW-AJHS; Wise to Leuterstein, JTA, June 14, 1934; Wise to Niles, April 11, 1944, CZA A243/83.

87. Dodd Jr. and Dodd, *Ambassador Dodd's Diary*, 36, 103, 113; Dodd to Roosevelt, August 15, 1934, FDRL, President's Personal File 1043.

88. "Only One Held by Brodsky," *New York Times*, September 15, 1935.

89. "Reich Press is Enraged," *New York Times*, September 8, 1935; "German Government Protests Brodsky Ruling," JTA, September 9, 1935; "Germany Expresses Resentment," September 9, 1935; "Overseas," *New York Times*, September 15, 1935.

90. "Year 5696 Greeted by Jews of the City," *New York Times*, September 28, 1935.

91. "La Guardia Suggests Hitler in World 'Horror Chamber' as an Example," JTA, March 4, 1937; "La Guardia Bitterly Assailed by Nazi Press for Hitler Slur," JTA, March 5, 1937; "U.S. to Protest Nazi Press Attacks; Spurred by Slur on A.J.C. Women," JTA, March 12, 1937.

92. "U.S. Takes Germany to Task for Nazi Press Attacks," JTA, March 14, 1937; "Germany Refuses Regrets for Press Attacks on United States," JTA, March 15, 1937.

93. "Reich Protests to Hull Who Informally Voices Regrets," JTA, March 5, 1937; "U.S. Apologizes to Germany," JTA, March 7, 1937; "Mayor Stands by Statement," JTA, March 7, 1937; "Untermyer Hits Hull for Apology on La Guardia Address," JTA, March 8, 1937; "La Guardia Gets Support in Attack on Hitler," JTA, March 8, 1937; "Reich Embassy Shuns Function to be Addressed by La

Guardia," JTA, March 9, 1937; "Luther to Protest New La Guardia Jibe; Nazis Hit in Congress," JTA, March 18, 1937; "Hull Asks End of La Guardia-Hitler Feud; Mayor Stands Firm," JTA, March 19, 1937.

94. Straus to Early, May 8, 1935, FDRL, Office File 6; Early to Straus, May 9, 1935, FDRL, Office File 6.

95. Diary of Harold L. Ickes, entry for March 30, 1938, 2676–77, and entry for April 2, 1938, 2681–82, Library of Congress.

96. Ickes, *Secret Diary*, 504. Most Roosevelt historians have ignored FDR's censorship of Ickes's speeches about Nazism. An exception was Breitman and Lichtman, *FDR and the Jews*, 103, who cast the April 1938 episode in a positive light, reporting: "FDR authorized Ickes to deliver an address on the CBS radio network blasting countries persecuting Jews. Ickes scheduled the speech for April 3, the fiftieth anniversary of the Chicago-based *Daily Jewish Courier*." They claimed FDR required Ickes to make only "a few minor changes," and those changes did not significantly affect the content of the speech. This assertion was based on two entries in Ickes's diary, but Breitman and Lichtman misrepresented what the entries said, and altered the wording in the diary's key sentence about this episode.

First, it was misleading to state that FDR "authorized" the speech and Ickes then "scheduled" it. That made it sound as if the president came up with the idea for Ickes to give such a speech, as a way of speaking out for the Jews. In fact Ickes wrote in his diary that he was the one who "accepted" an invitation to speak at a celebration of the *Jewish Courier*'s fiftieth anniversary. The diary indicates that it was Ickes's idea, not Roosevelt's, to speak out about the persecution of the Jews.

Second, the disputed phrases in the draft of the speech were not just about "fascism" generally, as Breitman and Lichtman asserted. According to the diary, President Roosevelt told Ickes that Secretary Hull wanted to "cut out the reference that I [Ickes] had made to Naziism [*sic*] as well as references I had to current dictators." FDR then said to Ickes that he wanted him "to make Cordell happy." Later in the entry, Ickes indicated that the "current dictators" to whom he had intended to refer were "Hitler and Mussolini." Thus we see that both Roosevelt and Hull objected to any mention of Hitler, Mussolini, or Nazism. The president permitted Ickes to refer to fascism only in a general way. Hull even insisted that one reference to the term "fascist" be removed, lest it be seen as implicitly referring to Mussolini and thereby harm U.S.-Italian relations.

By deleting the word "Nazism" from Roosevelt's remarks to Ickes, Breitman and Lichtman in effect altered FDR's words and intentions. In reality Roosevelt said (according to Ickes) that Ickes should not mention Nazism; but Breitman and Lichtman removed the word Nazism from the discussion. Then they went one step further, making it appear as if Roosevelt fully backed Ickes's version of the speech, when in fact Roosevelt had backed Hull in demanding the removal of references to Nazism, Hitler, and Mussolini.

97. Press conference #143, September 7, 1934, FDRL, 9–10; John McV. Haight Jr., "Roosevelt and the Aftermath of the Quarantine Speech," *Review of Politics* 24:2 (April 1962): 233–59; Press Conference 534 March 31, 1939, FDRL, 1-2; Kinsella, "The Prescience of a Statesman," 74–84; Jonas, *The United States and Germany*, 218–20, 225.

98. James A. Walsh, "The Helium Controversy of 1938," M.A. thesis, University of Arizona, 1964, 4–5, 33–34, 58–61; Harold L. Ickes, The Secret Diary of Harold L. Ickes, Vol. II. 398, 418. Cordell Hull, who vigorously supported the helium sale and clashed bitterly with Ickes over it, later took a swipe at Ickes in his published memoirs, asserting that the interior secretary "was often quite far to the left and hence frequently out of line with many of us, and he had an unfortunate approach to problems which not infrequently antagonized others." (Hull, *The Memoirs of Cordell Hull*, 209).

99. Norwood, "Entertaining Nazi Warriors," 156, 183.

100. Norwood, "Entertaining Nazi Warriors," 159–60, 180.

101. Wise to Roosevelt, September 9, 1937, FDRL, Office File 198; "U.S. Diplomat to Attend Nazi Congress for First Time," JTA, August 27, 1937; "Boycott Group Protests to Hull," JTA, August 27, 1937; Dodd to Roosevelt, January 22, 1938, President's Secretary's File: Dodd.

102. Larson, *In the Garden*, 345–47.

103. For Secretary of State Hull's defense of the Nuremberg decision, see Memorandum for the President, January 25, 1938, FDRL, President's Secretary's File: Germany-Dodd.

104. Rabbi Wise believed, erroneously, that Dodd resigned "due to the Nazi government's wrath at his urging the State Department not to be represented at the September Nuremberg show." See Wise to Florence, June 28, 1938, SSW-AJHS, Box 94. For the background to Dodd's resignation, see Larson, *In the Garden*, 327, 341–43.

105. Freidel, *A Rendezvous with Destiny*, 113, 329; Stephen S. Wise, Memorandum on White House Conference on Refugees, April 13, 1938, SSW-AJHS, 74–47.

106. For the text of the speech, see https://www.americanrhetoric.com /speeches/fdrarsenalofdemocracy.html.

107. Noack, "William L. Shirer."

108. "Anti-Nazi Protest March Through New York Voted by American Jewish Congress," JTA, April 21, 1933; Feis, *1933*, 159.

109. Urofsky, *A Voice That Spoke for Justice*, 259; Wise to Niles, October 21, 1935, SSW-AJHS, Box 118; Wise to Niles, November 4, 1935, SSW-AJHS, Box 118. Wise's colleague Max Rhoade suspected the need for Jewish votes motivated Roosevelt to seek the reconciliation. See Rhoade to Wise, January 18, 1936, SSW-AJHS, Box 118.

110. Wise to Brandeis, January 12, 1936, SSW-AJHS, Box 106; Wise to Weiss, February 11, 1941, CZA, A243/72.

111. Wise to Brandeis, January 12, 1936, SSW-AJHS, Box 106; James G. McDonald Diary entries dated December 17, 1934, 579 and February 21, 1935, 626, and McDonald to Eleanor Roosevelt, July 31, 1935, 788–89, reprinted in Breitman et al., *Advocate for the Doomed*.

112. "Zionists Map Plan to Raise $3,500,000 in United States, Major Portion to Be Allotted for German Refugees," JTA, February 4, 1936; Penkower, *Palestine in Turmoil*, 242–44.

113. Wise to Weizmann, March 6, 1936, SSW-AJHS, Box 121.

114. Wise to Frankfurter, March 2, 1936, SSW-AJHS, Box 109; Norwood, *The Third Reich*, 63.

115. Early to Commissioner of Education, January 29, 1936, FDRL, President's Personal File 995; "Britain's Palestine Policy Scored at Mizrachi Convention," JTA, February 18, 1936; "Ickes Calls on United Synagogue to Aid in Correcting Social Order," JTA, March 17, 1936.

116. Wise to Brandeis, September 1, 1936, SSW-AJHS, Box 106; Roosevelt to Wise, January 23, 1937, SSW-CZA, A243/83.

117. "Delegates to Jewish Congress Shocked by Simpson Report," JTA, October 22, 1930; Wise to Weizmann, May 29, 1936, SSW-AJHS, Box 121.

118. Wise to Niles, October 7, 1936, SSW-AJHS, Box 118.

119. Brandeis to Szold, May 4, 1938, SSW-AJHS, Box 106; "Jewish Committee to Shun Plebiscite," *New York Times*, June 2, 1938; Wise to Lipsky and Shultz, June 7, 1938, AJCA, American Jewish Congress File; Wise to Frankfurter, January 24, 1938, SSW-AJHS, Box 109.

2. In Search of Havens

1. Wise to Mack, June 7, 1933, SSW-AJHS, Box 115.

2. Wise to Brandeis, September 19, 1933, SSW-AJHS, Box 106.

3. Neuringer, "American Jewry," 211.

4. Mashberg, "The West and the Holocaust," 21.

5. Roosevelt to Lehman, July 2, 1936, FDRL, Box 1, Office File 133.

6. Breitman and Kraut, *American Refugee Policy*, 47.

7. Zucker, *In Search of Refuge*, 239.

8. Meyer, "The Refugee Scholars Project," 364.

9. Laemmle to Hull, April 12, 1938, SD, File 150.069-Laemmle, Carl; Neal Gabler, "Laemmle's List: A Mogul's Heroism," *New York Times*, April 13, 2014.

10. Dodd Jr. and Dodd, *Ambassador Dodd's Diary*, 17.

11. Einstein to Paran, June 25, 1937, DSW.

12. Zucker, *In Search of Refuge*, 81–82, 139.

13. Zucker, *In Search of Refuge*, 93–94; Breitman and Kraut, *American Refugee Policy*, 48–49; Stewart, *United States Government Policy*, 259–61; Mashberg, "The West and the Holocaust," 21.

14. Long to Berle and Dunn, June 26, 1940, BLP, Box 211; Breitman et al., *Refugees and Rescue*, 291.

15. Wyman, *The Abandonment of the Jews*, 125–29; Kraut, Breitman, and Inhoof, "The State Department," 27.

16. Wyman, *The Abandonment of the Jews*, 136.

17. Diary of Breckinridge Long, entries for October 3, 1940, and October 10, 1940, BLP.

18. Roosevelt to Lehman, November 13, 1935, FDRL, Box 1, Office File 133.

19. American Jewish Congress Administrative Committee minutes, September 23, 1933, 25–26, AJCong. Wise's private correspondence also contains allusions to his awareness that the quotas were unfilled. For example his acquaintance Simon Sobeloff, a prominent Baltimore attorney and future U.S. solicitor general, wrote Wise after the 1938 Evian conference: "[T]here has been no abatement in the harsh insistence by our consuls abroad upon difficult conditions in excess of legal requirements with respect to immigration visas." As a result, Sobeloff continued, "We have . . . the anomalous picture of the president calling the nations into conference at Evian to consider the problem of refugees, while our own government refuses admission even to the restricted number permitted by our laws." See Sobeloff to Wise, August 15, 1938, SSW-CZA, A243/138.

20. William R. Conklin, "La Guardia Advises on Refugees' Entry," *New York Times*, November 21, 1938; "Who Will Save the Jews?," *New Republic*, August 2, 1943, 124; Dan Shelton, "War Refugee Board Perpetrates Hoax On Nazi Victims," *Militant*, March 25, 1944, 4; "Declaration and Resolution," *Congress Weekly*, March 5, 1943, 16; "The Bermuda Affair," *Congress Weekly*, May 14, 1943, 13; "Asylum in America," *Congress Weekly*, September 24, 1943; "Free Ports for Refugees," *Congress Weekly*, May 26, 1944;, 10–11 "Revival of Conscience," *Jewish Frontier*, November 1943, 3; "Refugee Groups Disappointed at Decision to Shift Anglo-U.S.A. Parley to Bermuda," JTA, March 29, 1943; "Jewish Comment: The Bermuda Affair," *Congress Weekly*, May 15, 1943; I.F. Stone, "Justice Dept. Immigration Figures Knock Long's Story into Cocked Hat," PM, December 20, 1943; Laura Z. Hobson letter, *New Republic*, June 19, 1944.

21. "State Department Calls for Full Report on German Situation from U.S. Embassy and Consulate Following Visit by Wise, Deutsch," JTA, March 23, 1933; "Nazi Persecution Stressed by Wise," *New York Times*, March 22, 1933; "Admission to U.S. of Relatives of American Citizens, Refugees of German Persecutions, Directed in Resolution by Dickstein," JTA, March 23, 1933.

22. "Carr Fights Easing of Curbs on Aliens," *New York Times*, March 30, 1933; Neuringer, "American Jewry," 134.

23. Zucker, "Frances Perkins."

24. Wise to Neumann, February 8, 1938, SSW-CZA, A243/83; Wise to Szold, October 29, 1937, SSW-AJHS.

25. "Report of Meeting of S.S.W. with F.D.R., Saturday morning, Jan. 22, 1938," SSW-CZA, A243/83.

26. Similarly, although Wise generally accepted the fact that there was no future for Jews in Germany, he was loath to concede the principle that they

had a right to live there. "We will not surrender the right of the Jews or of any other group to live as free men in Germany," he asserted at 1936 luncheon of the AJ Congress Women's Division. See "Wise, Bohn Attack Proposals for Exodus of German Jews," JTA, February 27, 1936.

27. "Report Poland to Base Claim for Colonies on Surplus of Jews," JTA, October 5, 1936; "Poland to Seek Aid for Emigration at London and Geneva Parleys," JTA, October 27, 1936; "Forced Emigration of Jews Demanded in Polish Parliament Debate," January 12, 1937; "A.J.Congress Cables Protest on Poland's Emigration Proposals," JTA, January 14, 1937; "Conference on Poland Demands Restoration of Equal Rights for Jews," JTA, February 1, 1937; "Dealing Responsibly with Poland," Opinion, November 1936, 7; Tomaszewski, "Stephen S. Wise's Meeting," 110. The fear of the Polish situation being duplicated in the United States also induced Wise to propose a sentence that Roosevelt included in his 1937 inaugural address: "We will never regard any faithful, law-abiding groups within our borders to be superfluous." See Wise to Brandeis, Mack, and Frankfurter, February 2, 1937, SSW-AJHS, Box 106.

28. Shirer, Rise and Fall of the Third Reich, 477-78; G.E.R. Gedye, "Austrian Jews Set Adrift on Borders," New York Times, April 20, 1938; "Children of the Storm" (editorial), New York Times, April 21, 1938; "51 Jews Cast Adrift by Nazis in Mid-Danube," JTA, April 21, 1938; "15 Danube Refugees Find Shelter on French Boat," April 22, 1938; "Expulsion of Jews is Laid to Gestapo," New York Times, April 23, 1938; Milka Salmon, "Forced Emigration of the Jews of Burgenland: Test Case," Shoah Resource Center, yadvashem.org.il.

29. Shirer, Rise and Fall of the Third Reich, 477–78; Wyman, Paper Walls, 43–44; Breitman and Kraut, American Refugee Policy, 57.

30. Stewart, United States Government Policy, 286–87. The State Department issued invitations to countries that it perceived as possible sites for refugee settlement. Only Italy declined, evidently out of deference to its ally, Germany. No Asian countries were invited to Evian, although Japanese-occupied Shanghai would soon become a haven for Jews fleeing Hitler; the first refugees reached Shanghai later that summer. See Bartrop, The Evian Conference, 56–57; press conference #472, July 5, 1938, p. 7, FDRL.

31. Memoraudum, Harry Schneiderman to Morris Waldman, "Proposed Immigration Legislation, April 5, 1938," AJCA, Box 6, File: Immigration 1936–39; Elliot, "Conferees Talk of Stimson as Refugee Chief," New York Herald Tribune, July 12, 1938.

32. Wise to Niles, April 14, 1938, SSW-AJHS, Box 118; Wise to Frankfurter, May 19, 1938, SSW-AJHS, Box 109.

33. Long diary entry for October 10, 1940, BLP.

34. President Advisory Committee on Political Refugees minutes, May 16, 1938, 4, 6, 8, SSW-AJHS, File: President Advisory Committee on Political Refugees; Wise to Brandeis, May 17, 1938, SSW-AJHS, Box 106. Breitman, Stewart, and Hochberg, Refugees and Rescue, 130–31.

35. Wise to Bakstansky, June 27, 1938, ssw-ajhs, Box 106.

36. Wise to Bakstansky, June 27, 1938, ssw-ajhs, Box 106.

37. Wise to Bakstansky, June 27, 1938, ssw-ajhs, Box 106; Wise to van Paassen, November 9, 1936, ssw-cza, A243/92.

38. Laffer, "The Jewish Trail of Tears," 350.

39. George Rublee Oral History (1951), Columbia University, 283–84.

40. "No Human Dumping," *Opinion*, August 1938, 4.

41. Feingold, *Bearing Witness*, 107.

42. Feingold, *The Politics of Rescue*, 121; Kaplan, *Dominican Haven*, 81, 103; Wells, *Tropical Zion*, 114.

43. Wyman, *Paper Walls*, 73; Morse, *While Six Million Died*, 239–40.

44. Press Conference #499, November 11, 1938, 4, fdrl.

45. Press Conference #500, November 15, 1938, 2–3, fdrl.

46. Press Conference #500, November 15, 1938, 2–3, fdrl.

47. Stewart, *United States Government Policy*, 407.

48. Press Conference #501. November 18, 1938, 3–4, fdrl. Breitman and Kraut (*American Refugee Policy*, 62) noted that Roosevelt's response to Kristallnacht "paled beside the British response." Breitman did not include that acknowledgment when writing about FDR's response to Kristallnacht in his 2013 book with Allan Lichtman, *FDR and the Jews*. Instead, they asserted that Roosevelt's extremely limited steps after Kristallnacht "reflected reasonable political judgment" (123).

49. Wise to Niles, November 14, 1938, ssw-ajhs, Box 118; Stewart, *United States Government Policy*, 407–8; Kraut et al., "The State Department," 21–22.

50. Feingold, *The Politics of Rescue*, 150.

51. Meacham, *Franklin and Winston*, 32; Dallek, *Franklin D. Roosevelt*, 336; Wyman, *Paper Walls*, 95.

52. Wyman, *Paper Walls*, 75–98; Feingold, *The Politics of Rescue*, 149–53.

53. "Virgin Islands Too Offer Haven for Oppressed Jews," *The Daily News* (St. Thomas, U.S. Virgin Islands), November 21, 1938; Wyman, *Paper Walls*, 111–15; Feingold, *The Politics of Rescue*, 155–57.

54. Morgenthau Diaries, June 5, 1939, 2, fdrl.

55. Medoff, "Revisiting."

56. "Tragedies On the Seas," *Congress Bulletin*, June 9, 1939, 3.

57. Jacob Lestschinsky, "Where Do We Stand?," *Congress Bulletin*, June 16, 1939, 5.

58. Daniela Gleizer, *Unwelcome Exiles*, 182-88; Stephen J. Morewitz and Susan B. Lieberman, "The Saving of the S.S. Quanza in Hampton Roads, Virginia, on September 14, 1940: A Prelude to the Nazi Holocaust," unpublished manuscript.

59. Cook, *Eleanor Roosevelt*, 317, 321.

60. Penkower, *The Holocaust and Israel Reborn*, 117, 272–76; Cook, *Eleanor Roosevelt*, 122–25, 312.

61. Cook, *Eleanor Roosevelt*, Vol. 2, 571.

62. Cook, *Eleanor Roosevelt*, Vol. 2, 315–17.

63. "Polish Army's Only Jewish General Slain in Defense of Kattowice; Gestapo Executes Hundreds," JTA, September 26, 1939; "Chief Rabbi Schorr Reported Among Jewish Leaders Killed by Nazis in Poland," JTA, October 2, 1939; "Nazis Impose Slave Status on Jews in Polish Area; Property Seized, Temples Closed," JTA, October 12, 1939; "German Soldiers Describe Arrests, Executions of Jews in Poland," JTA, October 13, 1939; "Hundreds of Aged Jews Executed by Nazis as 'Snipers,' Polish Refugees Reveal," JTA, October 26, 1939.

64. Wise to Perlzweig, September 21, 1939, SSW-AJHS, Box 90; Wise to Easterman, September 9, 1939, SSW-AJHS, Box 90.

65. Press Conference No. 649-a, June 5, 1940, 45, FDRL.

66. Wise to Nathan, September 17, 1940, SSW-AJHS, Box 115.

67. Entry for April 22, 1941, in Israel, *The War Diary*, 96; "Memorandum for the Secretary of the Interior," December 18, 1940, FDRL, Office File 3186.

68. Berman, "Reaction to the Resettlement."

69. Berman, "Reaction to the Resettlement."

70. Wise to Frankfurter, October 19, 1939, SSW-AJHS, Box 109; "New Frontiers in Alaska," *Jewish Frontier*, May 1940, 3–4; "Another Alaska Bill," *Jewish Frontier*, February 1941, 5–6; Zionist Organization of America Executive Meeting Minutes, October 11, 1939, 11–12, SGP, Box 21, Folder 1; Goldman to Wise, April 5, 1939, CZA, A243/125; "Hearings Scheduled on Alaska Refugee Bill; Ickes Backs Measure," JTA, May 9, 1940; "Alaska Colonization Essential for National Defense, Ickes Tells Senate Group," JTA, May 19, 1940.

71. Berman, "Reaction to the Resettlement," 272; Draft of Ickes address to the Cleveland Zionist Society, December 8, 1938, FDRL, Office File 6; Memorandum from Hasslet, December 9, 1938, and text of Ickes address, December 18, 1938, FDRL, Office File 6.

3. Silence and Its Consequences

1. "Thousands of Jews Executed by Nazi Troops in the Ukraine," JTA, October 2, 1941; "Thousands of Jews Killed in Ukraine by Nazis; Bodies Floating in Dniester," JTA, October 23, 1941; "Slaying of Jews in Galicia Depicted," *New York Times*, October 26, 1941; "6,000 Jews Mowed Down by Nazi Machine-Guns in Poland; Children Executed," JTA, October 30, 1941; "Mass-Execution of 25,000 Jews in Odessa Reported In London," JTA, November 14, 1941; "Nazis Execute 52,000 Jews in Kiev; Smaller Pogroms in Other Cities," JTA, November 16, 1941.

2. "Jewish Statement on Nazi Atrocities Ignored at Inter-allied Conference in London," JTA, January 14, 1942.

3. "600 Jews Massacred by Nazis in Rostov Before Retreating; Other Atrocities Reported," JTA, January 4, 1942; "Jews Freezing to Death in Ghettos; Starvation Mounting in Warsaw, Lodz," JTA, January 6, 1942; "60,000 Jews Killed in Rumania; Jewish Population Deprived of Medical Aid," JTA, January 7, 1942; "Jews to Be Expelled from Belgium; Must Surrender All Property," JTA, January 9,

1942; Perzlweig to Wise, January 19, 1942, Box 92, SSW-AJHS; "Revisionist Agitation for a Jewish Army," *The Reconstructionist*, January 23, 1942, 5; "Jews Fight for the Right to Fight" (advertisement), *New York Times*, January 5, 1942, 7–8.

4. "What Jews Must Remember," *Congress Weekly*, May 1, 1942, 3; "Accounts of Nazi Pogroms in Occupied White Russia Related at Moscow Jewish Rally," JTA, May 25, 1942.

5. Yehuda Bauer, "When Did They Know?" *Midstream*, April 1968, 57–58 (the full text of the Bund Report, translated into English); Chicago Daily News Foreign Service report in David M. Nichol, "700,000 Jews Reported Slain," *Seattle Daily-Times*, June 26, 1942.

6. Leff, *Buried by* The Times, 22–24.

7. Bernard Valery, "Vilna Massacre of Jews Reported," *New York Times*, June 16, 1942; "Big Rewards Paid in Heydrich Case," *New York Times*, June 27, 1942; "Roosevelt Pledges American People Will Hold Nazis Responsible for Atrocities Against Jews," JTA, July 22, 1942; "Churchill, Lehman, Wise Score Nazi Annihilation of Jews in Europe," JTA, July 23, 1942.

8. Wyman, *The Abandonment of the Jews*, 43.

9. Wyman, *The Abandonment of the Jews*, 43–44; Penkower, *The Jews Were Expendable*, 66–67; Laqueur, *The Terrible Secret*, 79–80; Gilbert, *Auschwitz*, 58–59.

10. Wise to Frankfurter, September 4, 1942, SSW-AJHS, Box 109.

11. Wyman, *The Abandonment of the Jews*, 43–44.

12. Dr. Max Beer, "Memorandum on Ways and Means to Stop Nazi Deportation of Jews and Their Plan of General Extermination, as Well as Other Atrocities," September 3, 1942, WJC, File 268/90.

13. Dr. Max Beer, "A Few Remarks About the Jewish Attitude in This War, Especially in the Field of Propaganda," September 2, 1942, WJC, File 264-Rescue; Dr. Max Beer, "Memorandum on Ways and Means to Stop Nazi Deportation of Jews and Their Plan of General Extermination, as Well as Other Atrocities," September 3, 1942, WJC, File 268/90.

14. Wise to Frankfurter, September 4, 1942, SSW-AJHS, Box 109.

15. Wise to Goldmann, September 4, 1942, SSW-AJHS, Box 109.

16. Penkower, *The Jews Were Expendable*, 67–68; "Minutes of Interviews-Washington, DC, October 6, 1943-Dr. Wise and Dr. Goldmann," CZA, Z6/279. Wise's suppression of the telegram was the subject of a remarkable exchange in *Commentary* in 1984 between Richard Breitman and Alan Kraut, on the one hand, and several of their critics. One of the critics, David Kranzler, referred unsympathetically to the fact that Wise withheld the telegram from the public until November 24. Breitman and Kraut countered by presenting what appeared to be a significant revelation: "Our sources provide a much different picture of Rabbi Stephen S. Wise from Mr. Kranzler's account here," they announced. "To give only one example, we have evidence that Wise made the [Riegner telegram] public on September 28, 1942, almost two months before the date [November 24] Mr. Kranzler gives."

Breitman and Kraut's announcement attempted to turn the existing historiography on its head. Every previous book about America's response to the Holocaust had reported Wise's three-month-long suppression, from late August through late November. Now, Breitman and Kraut were declaring that they had uncovered new "evidence" from unnamed "sources" showing that Wise suppressed the telegram only for a few weeks. Instead of revealing the new evidence, however, Breitman proceeded to quietly reverse himself. In the *Journal of Contemporary History* the following year (1985), Breitman described Wise as having revealed the Riegner information in late November. He again gave November as the date in his (co-authored) book, *Breaking the Silence* (1986); said it again with Kraut in *American Refugee Policy and European Jewry* (1987), and once again with Lichtman in *FDR and the Jews* (2013). To this day, neither Breitman nor Kraut has ever revealed the "evidence" to which they dramatically alluded in *Commentary*, which supposedly would have revised the public's view of Rabbi Wise. See Breitman, "The Allied War Effort," 143; Laqueur and Breitman, *Breaking the Silence*, 160; Breitman and Kraut, *American Refugee Policy and European Jewry*, 157; Breitman and Lichtman, *FDR and the Jews*, 205; and Breitman, *Official Secrets*, 143, 287.

17. Rosenheim to Roosevelt, September 3, 1942, NA, SD File 740.00116-European War/570.

18. Wise to Frankfurter, September 4, 1942, SSW-AJHS, Box 109; McDonald to Eleanor Roosevelt, September 4, 1942, JGM, File P-43.

19. Rosenblum to Wertheim, September 9, 1942, AJCA Box II, File: Poland 1942.

20. Penkower, *The Jews Were Expendable*, 68–69; Rosenblum to Wertheim, September 6, 1942, Box 11-Poland 1942, AJCA; Shuster to Waldman, September 8, 1942, AJCA, Box 11, File: Poland 1942; "Deportation of 300,000 Jews from Warsaw Ghetto Reported," JTA, September 9, 1942; "Palestine Hears of Nazi Massacre of Jews in Poland," JTA, September 9, 1942.

21. Wise to Frankfurter, September 16, 1942, SSW-AJHS, Box 109; Wise to Korn, September 9, 1942, in Voss, *Servant*, 249–50; Zuccotti, *Under His Very Windows*, 104–6, 294–96.

22. Wise to Frankfurter, September 16, 1942, SSW-AJHS, Box 109.

23. "Nazis in Holland Plan to Deport Young Jews to Russia, Others to Germany," JTA, September 4, 1942; "150,000 Jews Transported from Poland to Reich for Hard Labor," JTA, September 6, 1942; "All Jews Between 18 and 65 Will Be Deported from Poland," JTA, September 15, 1942; "Deported Dutch Jews Report They Are Working in Coal Mines in Germany," JTA, September 28, 1942; "Gestapo Raids Warsaw Synagogues; Seizes 2,000 Jews for Forced Labor," JTA, October 4, 1942; "Nazis Deport Jewish Women from Belgium; Many Sent to Coal Mines in Silesia," JTA, October 30, 1942.

24. "Drive on Jews Renewed in Unoccupied France; Even Street Cars Raided," JTA, September 2, 1942; "Deportation of 300,000 Jews from Warsaw Ghetto Reported," JTA, September 9, 1942; "Nazis Set Date on Which Czechoslovakia Will Be Completely 'Judenrein,'" JTA, September 21, 1942; "Only 100,000 Jews

Left by the Nazis in Warsaw Ghetto; Mass-Deportations Continue," JTA, October 7, 1942; "Nazis Resume Mass-Deportations of Jews from Holland and Belgium; Suicides Reported," JTA, October 15, 1942; "Nazis Deport German Jews to Poland and Ship Polish Jews to Germany," JTA, October 25, 1942.

25. "New Deportations of Jews from Czech Protectorate to Poland Reported," JTA, September 3, 1942; "4,000 Aged Jews Deported from Reich and Western Europe to Therezin Fortress," JTA, September 18, 1942; "France Deports 500 Jewish Children from Institutions; Refugees Need Clothing," JTA, September 24, 1942; "Nuremberg Home for Aged Jews Closed; Inmates Deported to Eastern Europe," JTA, October 19, 1942.

26. "Nazis Resume Mass-Deportations of Jews from Holland and Belgium; Suicides Reported," JTA, October 15, 1942; "1,850 Jews from Poland and Western Europe Executed by Nazis in Smolensk Area," JTA, October 22, 1942; "240,000 Hungarian Jews Driven to Death at Forced Labor for Nazis on Russian Front," JTA, November 11, 1942; "Esthonian Officer Goes Mad Witnessing Execution of 14,000 Jews in Riga," October 4, 1942.

Historian Elizabeth Bryant speculates it is "likely" that the real reason Wise refrained from publicizing these autumn 1942 reports about the mass murder was "because he realized that by pushing Roosevelt too hard he would be unable to get him to undertake any rescue or relief efforts." She provides no evidence to substantiate that conjecture. See Bryant, "Rabbi Stephen S. Wise's Actions," 190.

27. "Only Seventeen Jews Escape Massacre by Nazis in Russian Town of Velizh," JTA, September 9, 1942; "Nazis Massacre 800 Jews in Kovno After Pillaging Their Homes, Eye-Witness Reports," JTA, September 20, 1942; "715 Jews Murdered By Nazis in Russian Town of Urechi; Girls Buried Alive," JTA, October 18, 1942; Entire Jewish Population in Many Ukrainian Cities Exterminated, Nazi Soldiers Reveal," JTA, November 9, 1942; "Only One Jew Left Alive in Vitebsk; 11,000 Jews Massacred in Ponievezh by Nazis," JTA, September 27, 1942.

28. "Estonian Officer Goes Mad Witnessing Execution of 14,000 Jews in Riga," JTA, October 4, 1942; "Palestine Hears of Nazi Massacres of Jews in Poland," JTA, September 9, 1942; "Unprecedented Pogroms Raging in Poland; Large Scale Deportations of Jews Reported," JTA, September 20, 1942; "Jews in Poland Are in Constant Fear of Death, Says Underground Report," JTA, October 6, 1942; "About Two Million Jews Already Exterminated by Nazis, British Paper Reports," JTA, October 28, 1942.

29. Welles to Taylor, September 23, 1942, SD, File: 740.00116 European War/597A.

30. Wise to Frankfurter, September 16, 1942, SSW-AJHS, Box 109; Wise to Korn, September 9, 1942, SSW-AJHS, Box 113; Wise to Holmes, September 9, 1942, SSW-AJHS, Box 109.

31. Wise to Szold, September 3, 1942, SSW-AJHS, Box 121; Wise to Newman, September 3, 1942, LIN; Wise to Mack, September 4, 1942, SSW-CZA, A243/148; Wise to Wertheim, September 3, 1942, SSW-CZA, A243/100; Wise to Emer-

gency Committee for Zionist Affairs, September 9, 1942, A243/100, CZA; Wise to Eisenstein, August 21, 1942, SSW-AJHS, Box 44; Wise to Eisenstein, September 8, 1942, SSW-AJHS, Box 44; Wise to Committee on Admissions, September 24, 1942, SSW-AJHS, Box 121; Wise to Neumann, September 24, 1942, and Wise to Rosenberg, September 28, 1942, SSW-AJHS, Box 121.

32. See the transcripts of Wise's sermons on September 20, 1942, September 21, 1942, SSW-AJHS, Box 23.

33. Wise to Niles, October 1, 1942, SSW-CZA, A243/83; Wise to Mack, October 9, 1942, SSW-CZA, A243/148; Wise to Frankfurter, October 14, 1942, SSW-AJHS, Box 109; Weisgal to Wise, October 22, 1942, SSW-CZA, A243/100; Wise to Mack, October 27, 1942, A243/148, SSW-CZA; Wise to Mack, November 2, 1942, SSW-AJHS, A243/148; Wise to Marks, October 2, 1942, SSW-AJHS, Box 66; Neumann to Wise, October 6, 1942, SSW-AJHS, Box 66; Wise to Weisgal, October 9, 1942, SSW-AJHS, Box 121; Rosenberg to Wise, November 4, 1942, SSW-AJHS, Box 66; Wise to Rosenberg, November 18, 1942, SSW-AJHS, Box 66; Wise to Rosenberg, November 20, 1942, SSW-AJHS, Box 66.

34. "Jewish Institute of Religion Inaugurates 21st Academic Year," JTA, September 29, 1942; "Pledge to Liberate Nazi-tortured European Jewry Given at Ussishkin Memorial Meeting," JTA, September 24, 1942; Wise to Justine Polier, October 2, 1942, SSW-AJHS, Box 54; "JNF Launches $2,500,000 Loan in America; Hadassah Discusses U.S. Jewish Problems," JTA, October 18, 1942; "Dr. Emanuel Libman to Be Honored on His Seventieth Birthday," JTA, October 25, 1942; "United Jewish War Effort Not Against Aid to Russia, Rabbi Wise Declares," JTA, September 6, 1942; "Jewish Campaign for Tanks to Russia Abandoned; Drive for Watches Launched by Abidjan," JTA, October 28, 1942.

35. American Jewish Congress Governing Council minutes, December 3, 1942, 1–2, SSW-AJHS; "Wise Leaves for Mexico to Confer on Jewish Matters; Will Be Received by the President," JTA, November 3, 1942; "Dr. Wise Leaves Mexico After Conference with Foreign Minister," JTA, November 15, 1942.

36. Greenberg, "Bankrupt."

37. "A People in Mourning," Jewish Spectator, January 1943, 4–5.

38. Lazin, "The Response of the American Jewish Committee to the Crisis of German Jewry, 1933–1939," 304; Ben-Gurion to Shertok, July 8, 1942, reprinted in Klieman and Klieman, American Zionism, Volume 8, 80; "Memo of conversation between Dr. Nahum Goldmann and Bernard Meltzer, Acting Chief of the Division of Foreign Funds Control, State Department," July 14, 1943, SD, 840.48 Refugees/4063; Silver to Neumann, August 22, 1944, CZA, A123/315; Lookstein, We Were Our Brother's Keepers?, 215–16.

39. Frederick Kuh, "Grieving Polish Leader Suicide," PM, May 18, 1943.

40. "The Last Stand," Jewish Frontier, June 1943, 3; "Zygelbojm Inquest Adjourned for Three Weeks," JTA, May 19, 1943; "Chronicle of the Week," Congress Weekly, May 21, 1943, 2; "Poland-in-Exile," Contemporary Jewish Record, August 1943, 410; "Compassion," National Jewish Monthly, July-August 1943, 352.

41. Wise, Challenging Years, 276; Laqueur, Terrible Secret, 226–27.

42. "Hitler Has Ordered Annihilation of All Jews by End of 1942, Washington Hears," JTA, November 25, 1942; Lipstadt, *Beyond Belief*, 181.

43. "Minutes of Meeting of Sub-Committee of Special Conference on European Affairs, Held at the Office of the American Jewish Congress, Monday, November 30, 1942," 3, AJCong; Laqueur, *Terrible Secret*, 227.

44. Wise, *Challenging Years*, 275-76; "Wise Gets Confirmations," *New York Times*, November 25, 1942; "Slain Polish Jews Put at a Million," *New York Times*, November 26, 1942; Lipstadt, *Beyond Belief*, 183.

45. "Horror Stories from Poland," *The Christian Century*, December 9, 1942, 1518-19; "From Rabbi Wise," *The Christian Century*, January 13, 1943, 53.

46. "Minutes of Meeting of Sub-Committee of Special Conference on European Affairs, Held at the Office of the American Jewish Congress, Monday, November 30, 1942," 1-2, AJCong; Wyman, *The Abandonment of the Jews*, 71; "Jews in Twenty-Nine Countries Observe Impressive Day of Mourning for Nazi Victims," JTA, December 3, 1942.

47. Gottschalk to Waldman, November 27, 1942, AJCA, File: Germany-Nazism '42-'43; Wise to The President, December 2, 1942, SSW-AJHS, Box 68.

48. "Roosevelt Receives Jewish Delegation, Promises Aid to End Nazi Massacres of Jews," JTA, December 9, 1942.

49. Adolph Held, "Report on the Visit to the President" (December 8, 1942), JLC. Held's description is consistent with other accounts of how President Roosevelt comported himself in such settings. For example, in October 1940, James McDonald, chairman of the President's Advisory Committee on Political Refugees, and several colleagues met with FDR to plead for more visas. Henry M. Hart Jr., assistant to the solicitor general, who was present, later recalled how "a very cordial Roosevelt spun a succession of stories. Whenever McDonald tried to confront the President with the refugee issue, Roosevelt would be reminded of something else and another anecdote would result. This entertainment continued until the half hour was up and 'Pa' Watson came in to mention that the next appointment was due. Then followed a few rushed minutes of trying to present the problem before the group left." See Wyman, *Paper Walls*, 147.

50. "Roosevelt Receives Jewish Delegation, Promises Aid to End Nazi Massacres of Jews," JTA, December 9, 1942; Held, "Report on the Visit," 1; American Jewish Congress Governing Council minutes, December 10, 1942, AJCong.

51. Wasserstein, *Britain and the Jews of Europe*, 170-72.

52. Wyman, *The Abandonment of the Jews*, 74-75.

53. Goldmann to Greenbaum, April 5, 1943, Z6/302, CZA; "Governing Council-Meeting Held Tuesday, January 12, 1943 at 8:00 P.M.-Congress Offices," AJCong.

54. Samuel Margoshes, "News and Views," *Der Tog*, December 16, 1942; "Fasting is Not Enough," *The Reconstructionist*, December 25, 1942, 4; Kubowitzki to Wise, December 4, 1942, WJC, File: 268/90.

55. "150 Refugees in France Reported Killed Resisting Extradition," JTA, June 18, 1941; "Vichy Plans Internment of Foreign Jews in North Africa; Round-Up

Intensified," JTA, April 21, 1941; "General Weygand Orders Census of Jews in Algeria," JTA, August 27, 1941; "Abolishment of Anti-Jewish Laws and Release of 25,000 Refugees Expected in Algeria," JTA, November 11, 1942.

56. "Darlan," *New Republic*, December 28, 1942, 840.

57. Abitbol, *The Jews of North Africa*, 153.

58. Abitbol, *The Jews of North Africa*, 153; "American Jews Hail Roosevelt's Abrogation of Nazi-Inspired Laws in North Africa," JTA, November 20, 1942; "Wise Thanks Roosevelt for Abrogation of Anti-Jewish Laws in North Africa," JTA, November 23, 1942.

59. Details of the mistreatment of prisoners at the Hadjerat M'Guil camp in Algeria were spelled out in testimony that was given at the 1944 trial of the camp's administrators before an Allied military tribunal. One former inmate reported: "The internees were not treated as human beings. . . . The camp was literally starving; some would eat anything and because of this became seriously ill. Others died from this state of affairs. Despite their physical weakness, the men were assigned particularly strenuous work. . . . The guards, armed with cudgels, beat up the workers . . . without any reason, just to hit. . . . The internees [who were] being disciplined were piled up in the cells and were forced to go to the bathroom in their [food] tins. . . . Sometimes the interned doctors were forbidden to bandage their fellow prisoners, who having been grievously beaten by their guards were nothing but one open wound." A survivor of the Djelfa camp, also in Algeria, recalled: "Often up to three prisoners were piled up in a cell [of less than ten square feet]. No straw mattresses were given and it was forbidden to bring in more than one blanket. . . . Food consisted of six ounces of bread per day and two measures of always meatless camp soup. In winter it was freezing." See Abitbol, *The Jews of North Africa*, 98–100.

60. Breitman and Kraut, *American Refugee Policy*, 169–70.

61. "Darlan's Statement," *New York Times*, December 17, 1942; "Queer Doings in Morocco," *New Republic*, December 28, 1942, 840; Victor H. Bernstein, "Jews Discriminated Against By Darlan After U.S. Lands," PM, January 1, 1943; Press Conference #871, January 1, 1943, 4, FDRL.

62. Aandhal et al., *Foreign Relations of the United States, The Conferences at Washington*, 608.

63. Aandhal et al., *Foreign Relations of the United States, The Conferences at Washington*, 608; Wyman, *The Abandonment of the Jews*, 313; Freidel, *Franklin D. Roosevelt*, 461. Roosevelt's source for these figures is unknown. Winston Churchill seems to have harbored similar sentiments, at least circa 1938. See Wasserstein, *Britain and the Jews of Europe*, 207:78.

64. Aandhal et al., *Foreign Relations of the United States, The Conferences at Washington*, 608.

65. I. F. Stone, "Why State Dept. Holds Up Repeal of Nuremberg Laws," PM, January 18, 1943; I. F. Stone, "Hull Admits Anti-Fascist Prisoners Still Being Held in

North Africa," *PM*, January 21, 1943; Drew Middleton, "African Political Shake-Up Urged; Allies' Friends Hounded or Jailed," *New York Times*, January 29, 1943.

66. "Governing Council-Meeting held Tuesday, February 4, 1943 at 8:30 P.M.-Congress Offices," AJ Cong. Wise was chairman of the World Jewish Congress executive committee; Goldmann chaired its administrative committee; in practice, they functioned as co-chairs of the organization.

67. "Jewish Groups Charge Nazi Laws Stay in North Africa," *Los Angeles Times*, February 15, 1943.

68. "Jewish Delegation Sees State Department on Giraud's Abolition of Cremieux Law," JTA, March 19, 1943; "U.S. Help In Reviving Cremieux Law Asked," *New York Times*, May 21, 1943; Proskauer, *A Segment*, 206; Cohen, *Not Free to Desist*, 268; "Giraud's Stand on Jews Scored," *New York Times*, April 5, 1943; "Welles Answered on Cremieux Law," *New York Times*, April 4, 1943; Murphy, *Diplomat*, 147.

69. Edwin L. James, "Giraud Ruling on Jews Forms Algerian Puzzle," *New York Times*, March 21, 1943; "Jews' Rights Lost as War Measure," *New York Times*, March 22, 1943.

70. Abitbol, *The Jews of North Africa*, 163.

4. Suppressing the Dissidents

1. Gelb, *The Chase is the Game*, 74. Fellow student Martin Zion recalled the incident in which Gelb challenged Wise; other students, while not remembering the specific episode, remarked that it "sounds just like what Saadia would have done" and "if anyone would have spoken up, it would have been Saadia." Martin Zion interview with Rafael Medoff, July 30, 2002; Morrison Bial interview with Rafael Medoff, August 25, 2002; Joel Zion interview with Rafael Medoff, July 30, 2002; Morris Goldfarb interview with Rafael Medoff, July 26, 2002. (The dates of all Medoff interviews appear the first time they are referenced in this chapter's Notes. Unless otherwise indicated, all references to interviews in this chapter relate to interviews with Rafael Medoff.)

2. Saadia Gelb interview with Rafael Medoff, October 4, 2001.

3. Joel Zion interview. Other former students interviewed by the author expressed similar sentiments. Elihu Schagrin interview with Rafael Medoff, July 26, 2002; William Kramer interview with Rafael Medoff, July 26, 2002; Morris Goldfarb interview; Martin Zion interview; Bial interview.

4. Sanford Saperstein interview with Rafael Medoff, July 26, 2002; Schagrin interview; Friedman interview, September 11, 2002.

5. Martin Zion interview.

6. Friedman interview.

7. Howard Singer recollection, quoted in Wells, *Who Speaks for the Vanquished?*, 246–47.

8. Saperstein interview; Goldfarb interview; Joel Zion interview. Other former students interviewed by the author expressed similar sentiments: Schagrin interview; Kramer interview; Goldfarb interview; Martin Zion interview.

9. Jacobs to Smertenko, December 6, 1943, PSGC, File 15.

10. Noah Golinkin interview with Rafael Medoff, February 28, 1996.

11. Golinkin interview.

12. "Dealing Responsibly with Poland," *Opinion*, November 1936, 4; Tomaszewski, "Stephen S. Wise's Meeting."

13. Golinkin interview.

14. Golinkin interview.

15. Marino, *A Quiet American*, 189–90.

16. "Rabbis Plead for Aid to Stricken People," *New York Times*, May 25, 1943.

17. For a summary of the students' efforts, see Medoff, "Retribution is Not Enough."

18. Wise to Bergson, June 4, 1941, PSGC, Box 1; Wyman and Medoff, *A Race Against Death*, 21–28.

19. Wyman, *The Abandonment of the Jews*, 79.

20. Hecht to Eleanor Roosevelt, April 6, 1943, PSGC, Box 1.

21. Welles to Wise, February 9, 1943, WJC, File 267/8; Minutes of World Jewish Congress Planning Committee Meeting, December 29, 1942, WJC, File 185/2; Hecht, *Child of the Century*, 564.

22. "Huge Demonstration in New York Appeals to All Governments to Save Jews in Europe," JTA, March 2, 1943; "75,000 Sought Entrance to New York Meeting Protesting Nazi Massacres of Jews," JTA, March 3, 1943.

23. Wise to Roosevelt, March 4, 1943, FDRL, PPF 5029; Roosevelt to Wise, March 23, 1943, FDRL, PPF 5029.

24. Nick Kenny, "Nick Kenny Speaking," PM, March 10, 1943.

25. Eleanor Roosevelt, "My Day," April 14, 1943, United Feature Syndicate.

26. "Report on attempts to stage 'We Will Never Die' in Kingston, Rochester, Buffalo, Baltimore, Gary and Pittsburgh," undated (early 1944), PSGC, Box 1.

27. Rose to Niles, February 22, 1943, Pringle to Hassett, March 3, 1943, and Early to Rose, March 4, 1943, FDRL, OF 76-C.

28. Roosevelt to Wise, August 30, 1943, SSW-AJHS, Box 68; Press Conference #842, August 21, 1942, FDRL; W. H. Lawrence, "President Warns Atrocities of Axis Will Be Avenged," *New York Times*, August 22, 1942; Leff, *Buried by The Times*, 152.

29. "Help the Jews Now," *New Republic*, January 18, 1943, 69; "The Bermuda Conference," *New Republic*, April 26, 1943, 548.

30. "While the Jews Die," *Nation*, March 13, 1943, 366.

31. "Sanctuary for Europe's Jews," *New York Times*, March 3, 1943; "Congress Adopts Resolution Condemning Nazi Mass-Murder of Jews," JTA, March 9, 1943.

32. Goldmann to Gruenbaum, April 5, 1943, YGP, Z6/302; Lourie to Akzin, March 25, 1943, BAP, 8/15-peh; Joint Emergency Committee for European Jew-

ish Affairs minutes, May 24, 1943, AJCA, Box 8, File: Joint Emergency Committee for European Jewish Affairs.

33. Feuer to Silver, March 24, 1944, AZEC, F39/24; Joint Emergency Committee on European Jewish Affairs minutes, April 10, 1943, I, AJCA, Box 8, File: Joint Emergency Committee for European Jewish Affairs.

34. Celler interview with Laurence Jarvik, October 4, 1978, DSW; Feuer to Silver, March 24, 1944, AZEC, F39/24; Joint Emergency Committee on European Jewish Affairs minutes, April 10, 1943, I, AJCA, Box 8, File: Joint Emergency Committee for European Jewish Affairs.

35. "Memorandum of Telephone Conversation: Conference with the British in Ottawa," March 19, 1943, BLP, Box 202, File: Refugees 1943; Roosevelt to Roberts, April 8, 1943, and Roberts to Roosevelt, April 10, 1943, FDRL, Office File 3186.

36. Urofsky, A Voice That Spoke for Justice, 305; Feingold, Politics of Rescue, 195; Joint Emergency Committee on European Jewish Affairs minutes, April 10, 1943, I, AJCA, Box 8, File: Joint Emergency Committee for European Jewish Affairs.

37. Wise et al. to Welles, April 14, 1943; Long to Wise, April 20, 1943; Trager to Schultz [sic] et al., May 10, 1943, and Wise to Proskauer, April 23, 1943, AJCA, Box 8, File: Joint Emergency Committee for European Jewish Affairs.

38. Joint Emergency Committee for European Jewish Affairs minutes, April 2, 1943, April 10, 1943, and April 18, 1943, AJCA, Box 8, File: Joint Emergency Committee for European Jewish Affairs.

39. Wise to Goldmann, April 22, 1943, and Wise to Goldmann, April 23, 1943, SSW-AJA, Box 1001.

40. Proskauer to Gerstenfeld, March 25, 1943, AJCA, Box 8, File: Joint Emergency Committee for European Jewish Affairs.

41. "Refugee Aid Linked to Victory in War," New York Times, April 20, 1943; Rabinowitz to Jonah Wise, July 2, 1943, BGC, File: Emergency Committee to Save the Jewish People of Europe, First Emergency Conference to Save the Jewish People of Europe-2/1/11-chet; Wyman, The Abandonment of the Jews, 115–18; "20,000 at Garden in Appeal for Jews Under Heel of Nazis," Boston Herald, May 3, 1943; "[World Jewish Congress] Office Committee Meeting," May 7, 1943, CZA, A185/2; Penkower, The Jews Were Expendable, 330:37.

42. Perlzweig to Wise, May 4, 1943, Box 92, SSW-AJHS; "The Mockery at Bermuda" address by Dr. Israel Goldstein, April 28, 1943, IGP, A364/235; Shlomo Grodzensky, "In Days of Darkness," Furrows, November 1943, 11. "From Hitler to Bermuda" (editorial), New Republic 108 (May 10, 1943), 620.

43. "Congressman Sol Bloom Declares Bermuda Refugee Conference Was a Success," JTA, May 23, 1943; "Rumor Behind the News," HaMigdal, June 1943, 10; Hillel Kook interview with M.J. Nurenberger, 55, transcript in possession of the author.

44. "Failure in Bermuda," Opinion, May 1943, 4; Celler to Wise, May 14, 1943, SSW, Box 106.

45. Wise et al. to Welles, June 1, 1943; Joint Emergency Committee for European Jewish Affairs minutes, July 15, 1943, 1, AJCA, Box 8, File: Joint Emergency Committee for European Jewish Affairs.

46. "Confidential Memorandum of Rabbi Meyer Berlin," February 23, 1943, CZA, Z6/292. Two years later, in an ironic fulfillment of Rabbi Berlin's dire prediction, U.S. general George Patton diverted U.S. troops to rescue 150 prized Lippizzaner dancing horses, which were caught between Allied and Axis forces along the German-Czech border. See D'Este, *Patton*, 742–43.

47. "Confidential Memorandum of Rabbi Meyer Berlin," 9–12, February 23, 1943, CZA, Z6/292. Later that day, Wallace mentioned his conversation with Rabbi Berlin to Congressman Sol Bloom, who, Wallace recounted, told him that "the Zionists were troublemakers; if I had any more trouble with fellows like Rabbi Berlin to send them over to him." See Blum, *The Price of Vision*, 193–94.

48. "Confidential Memorandum of Rabbi Meyer Berlin," 6–8, February 23, 1943, CZA, Z6/292.

49. Joint Emergency Committee on European Jewish Affairs minutes, July 15, 1943, 2, AJCA, Box 8, File: Joint Emergency Committee for European Jewish Affairs; American Emergency Committee for Zionist Affairs minutes, May 3, 1943, 1, SSW-AJHS.

50. Berlin to Wise, April 30, 1943, SSW-AJHS, Box 109; "Dr. Weizmann's Remarks at Meeting of American Emergency Committee for Zionist Affairs, Tuesday, Dec. 8, 1942," 12, CWP; American Emergency Committee for Zionist Affairs minutes, May 3, 1943, 3–4, SSW-AJHS.

51. Jaffe to Wise, June 2, 1943, LJP; American Jewish Congress Executive Committee minutes, June 8, 1943, AJcong; Shultz to Wise et al., June 3, 1943, SSW-AJHS, Box 92; Minutes of the Administrative Committee Meeting, June 22, 1943, AJcong, Box 3, File 4: Administrative Committee Minutes, 1943–1944. Regarding Al Domi, see Porat, "Al-domi."

52. Jaffe's account of how he was permitted to attend the meeting is described in Jaffe to Keren HaYesod, August 19, 1943, LJP.

53. Jaffe to Hantke, in Jaffe, 205–7; Jaffe to Wise, July 1943, in Jaffe, *Leib Yaffe*, 203–4; Wise to Proskauer, July 11, 1943, SSW-AJHS, Box 118.

54. Jaffe to Goldmann, July 22, 1943, CZA, S5/733.

55. In 1943 the Kremlin sent Solomon Mikhoels and Itzik Feffer, chairman and deputy chairman of the Soviet Jewish Anti-Fascist Committee, to the United States to encourage American Jewish support for the Soviet war effort and to offset negative publicity the USSR had suffered as a result of its executions of Henryk Ehrlich and Viktor Alter, two prominent Polish Bundists with close ties to American Jewish and labor leaders. See Baron, *The Russian Jew*, 261–63.

56. Jaffe to Keren HaYesod, August 19, 1943, CZA, S5/773.

57. *New York Times*, November 24, 1943; *New York Times*, December 17, 1943; Wyman and Medoff, *A Race Against Death*, 74, 139. "My Uncle Abraham Reports"

(advertisement), *Washington Post*, November 9, 1943, 9; Ben-Ami, *Years of Wrath*, 292; Hecht, *Child of the Century*, 581.

58. "Unity in Crisis," *Opinion*, April 1943, 7; Wyman and Medoff, *A Race Against Death*, 65–67; Hecht, *Child of the Century*, 565; *New York Times*, September 14, 1943.

59. Jaffe to Keren HaYesod, August 19, 1943, CZA, S5/773.

60. Jaffe to Keren HaYesod, August 19, 1943, CZA, S5/773.

61. Jaffe to Keren HaYesod, August 19, 1943, CZA, S5/773. "The Jews of Europe: How to Help Them—A Special Section," *New Republic* 109 (August 30, 1943), 297–316; "Help for the Jews" (editorial), *New Republic* 109 (September 6, 1943), 319; "Another *New Republic* Supplement in Great Demand" (advertisement), *New Republic* 109 (September 13, 1943), 371; "A *New Republic* Supplement—The Jews of Europe: How to Help Them" (advertisement), *New Republic* 109 (September 20, 1943), 403.

62. Wise to Montor, July 5, 1936, Wise to Montor, June 13, 1941, and Wise to Montor, February 19, 1943, SSW-AJHS, Box 116; "Editorial," Independent Jewish Press Service, March 12, 1943; "The Emergency Conference," Independent Jewish Press Service, July 30, 1943; "Only Victory," Independent Jewish Press Service, August 6, 1943; Shultz to Wise et al., July 30, 1943, and Shultz to Montor, July 30, 1943, SSW-AJHS, Box 92; "Henry Montor is Dead at 76; UJA and Israel Bond Leader," *New York Times*, April 16, 1982; Minutes of the Joint Emergency Committee on European Jewish Affairs, April 10, 1943, 2, and April 18, 1943, 2, AJCA. For the American Jewish Committee's use of the JTA as a means of combating "the nationalist group" in the American Jewish leadership, see Friedman to Younker, June 23, 1944, AJCP, Box 13, File: Seven Arts Feature Syndicate, 1937–1939, 1944. Regarding the AJC's subsidy to the JTA and its close relationship with JTA publisher Jacob Landau, see Cohen, *Not Free to Desist*, 33, 178.

63. Goldmann to Kaplan, December 21, 1942, and January 28, 1943, AZEC.

64. Goldmann to Kaplan, December 21, 1942, and January 28, 1943, AZEC; Waldman to Prosauker, February 7, 1943, AJCA, File: American Jewish Congress-American Jewish Committee '32–'42.

65. Goldmann to Kaplan, December 21, 1942, and January 28, 1943, AZEC; Neustadt-Noy, "The Unending Task," 177–78.

66. Lewin, "Indeed, Your Blood," 31; "National Assembly to Fix Jewish Attitude on War and Peace," Independent Jewish Press Service, January 25, 1943; "Call for the American Jewish Conference," *Congress Weekly*, April 23, 1943, 24; "Platform of the Delegates of the American Jewish Congress to the American Jewish Conference," *Congress Weekly*, June 4, 1943, 20; Stephen S. Wise, "The American Jewish Conference: A Forecast," *Opinion*, August 1943, 5.

67. Neustadt-Noy, "The Unending Task," 181–82.

68. Neustadt-Noy, "The Unending Task," 463–68.

69. Wyman, *The Abandonment of the Jews*, 162; American Jewish Conference Executive Committee minutes, July 14–15, 1943, 9, SSW-AJHS, File: American Jewish Conference 1943–1948; Grossman to Goldstein, May 26, 1943,

and "Statement on the American Jewish Conference by Dr. Israel Goldstein," 364/1951, I, IGP.

70. Philip Rubin, "Will Zionists Rise To Their Responsibility?," *National Jewish Ledger*, August 12, 1943, 3; A.S. Lyrique, "Trust the Common Man," *Congress Weekly*, June 18, 1943, 5; Welles to Wise, August 6, 1943, SSW-AJHS, Box 66.

71. Baerwald to Wise, Monsky, and Goldstein, December 7, 1943, IGP, 364/1952; "Rumor Washington Urging Delay in American Jewish Conference," Independent Jewish Press Service, August 16, 1943. The JTS student activists, anxious to ensure the rescue issue was given adequate attention, stood outside the opening session and distributed a leaflet quoting the bitter "favorite restaurant" message from the Warsaw Ghetto. "How can the Conference discuss the rights and status of Jews in the postwar world—we are sure the Jews of Poland would ask—when there may not be any postwar Jews?," the leaflet asked. "The spokesman from Warsaw must be proven wrong! American Jewry cannot be out to lunch in the hour of crisis! The American Jewish Conference must see to that!" Leaflet, "Pardon Our Intruding," in possession of the author.

72. The first, and still the definitive, scholarly essay on the subject is Monty N. Penkower's "The 1943 Joint Anglo-American Statement on Palestine."

73. Ibn Saud to FDR, April 30, 1943, and FDR to Ibn Saud, undated [apparently May 26, 1943], SD, 890F.00/89.

74. State Department to U.S. Ambassador, London, June 8, 1943, FDRL, PPF 700; Wise to Weizmann, July 23, 1943, SSW-AJHS, Box 121; Penkower, "The 1943 Joint Anglo-American," 222; Wise to Goldmann, July 27, 1943, SSW-AJHS, Box 109.

75. Diary entry for March 10, 1944, in Blum, *The Price of Vision*, 313; Berlin to Foreign Office, August 9, 1943, PRO, FO371/35037.

76. Wise to Frankfurter, August 2, 1943, and Wise to Atkinson, August 2, 1943, SSW-AJHS, Box 109; Berlin to Malcolm, August 25, 1943, PRO, FO371/35037; Berlin to Foreign Office, August 9, 1943, PRO, FO371/35037.

77. Berlin to Foreign Office, August 9, 1943, PRO, FO371/35037; C. L. Sulzberger, "Palestine Fears 'Deeds of Despair,'" *New York Times*, July 30, 1943; "Mr. Churchill, Drop the Mandate!" (advertisement), *New York Times*, May 18, 1943.

78. Wise to Goldmann, August 4, 1943, SSW-AJHS, Box 109; ECZA minutes, August 12, 1943, SSW-AJHS; Kaufman, *Ambiguous Partnership*, 132–33; Waldman, *Nor By Power*, 262.

79. State Department to U.S. Ambassador, London, June 8, 1943, FDRL, PPF 700.

80. Wise to Weizmann, July 23, 1943, and Wise to Weiss, November 10, 1943, SSW-AJHS, Box 121; "Celler Sees Palestine Hopes Dashed," *PM*, August 13, 1943; Penkower, "The 1943 Joint Anglo-American Statement on Palestine," 230–31.

81. Wise to Rosenman, August 24, 1943, SSW-AJHS, Box 78.

82. Wise to Weizmann, February 10, 1943, SSW-AJHS, Box 122. Wise to Mack, August 3, 1937, SSW-AJHS, Box 115.

83. Waldman, *Nor By Power*, 258; Leff, *Buried by* The Times, 214–15. Zionist groups used the terms "commonwealth" and "state" interchangeably. At an American Emergency Council for Zionist Affairs meeting earlier that year, Goldmann noted that in planning their agenda, the council had decided: "For all practical purposes the term 'Commonwealth' is identical with 'State.' We will ask for a Jewish Commonwealth with the same kind of sovereignty as will be given to all states after the war. 'Commonwealth' had been chosen rather than 'state' because it had more liberal and democratic connotations, but it implies the setting up of a Jewish State in Palestine as and when there is a Jewish majority." See American Emergency Council for Zionist Affairs Minutes, January 7, 1943, SSW-AJHS.

84. Berlin to Foreign Office, August 9, 1943, PRO, FO371/35037; Wise to Rosenman, August 24, 1943, SSW-AJHS, Box 78.

85. Joint Emergency Committee for European Jewish Affairs minutes, August 10, 1943, AJCA, Box 8, File: Joint Emergency Committee for European Jewish Affairs.

86. Stephen S. Wise, "As I See It: 'The Jewish Vote,'" *Opinion*, November 1932, 15; "Rabbi Stephen S. Wise Sees No 'Jewish Vote,'" *New York Times*, November 2, 1936; "No Jewish Issue," *Opinion*, September 1937, 9.

87. Halperin, *The Political World*, 327; Joint Emergency Committee for European Jewish Affairs minutes, September 24, 1943, 2, AJCA, Box 8, File: Joint Emergency Committee for European Jewish Affairs; Joint Emergency Committee for European Jewish Affairs minutes, November 5, 1943, 1–2, AJCA, Box 8, File: Joint Emergency Committee for European Jewish Affairs.

88. Wyman and Medoff, *A Race Against Death*, 65, 111.

89. Lamm to Shulman, August 28, 1944, CZA, Z5/3480; "Statement by American Emergency Council on League for a Free Palestine," October 1, 1943, S/1540, CZA.

90. Wise to Goldmann, August 4, 1943, Box 109, SSW-AJHS; Wise to Tobin, February 5, 1945, Box 102, SSW-AJHS; Morgenthau Diaries, May 24, 1944, 31, FDRL.

5. The Politics of Rescue

1. "Oil & the Rabbis," *Time*, October 18, 1943, 21.

2. There were some pockets of sympathy for such tactics within the Jewish leadership. For example, when the Bergsonites encountered difficulties in arranging transportation for the rabbis who were coming to Washington, veteran Hadassah leader Denise Tourover provided logistical advice. See Eri Jabotinsky to Mrs. Raphael Tourover, October 8, 1943, BGC, File: 2/11/11-chet, The March of 500 Rabbis, Correspondence, Invitations, Speeches, Reports, Clippings.

3. "Only Invasion of Europe and Allied Victory Can Save Jews, Berle Tells Boston Meeting," JTA, May 3, 1943; "Refugee Aid Linked to Victory in War," *New York Times*, April 20, 1943. Princeton University president Harold W. Dodds, chairman of the U.S. delegation to the 1943 Bermuda refugee conference, went

so far as to assert that questioning the "rescue through victory" concept "would not only be foolish; it would be criminal." Feingold, *Politics of Rescue*, 198.

4. Wyman, *The Abandonment of the Jews*, 97–99.

5. Long to Welles, May 15, 1943, with fifteen-page enclosure, BLP, Box 203, File: Refugee Movement and National Groups, 1943.

6. Long to Travers, May 4, 1943, Alexander to Long, May 7, 1943, and Bucknell to Long, May 17, 1943, BLP, Box 203, File: Refugee Movement and National Groups, 1943.

7. Eri Jabotinsky to Mirelman et al., October 12, 1943, BGC, File: 2/11/11-chet, The March of 500 Rabbis, Correspondence, Invitations, Speeches, Reports, Clippings.

8. "Oil & the Rabbis," *Time*, October 18, 1943, 21.

9. Efraim Zuroff, "The Evolution of American Orthodox Relief and Rescue Efforts During the Holocaust: Two Documents," 450–56; Hertzberg, "The Day the Rabbis Marched," introduction.

10. Bergson and van Paassen to Roosevelt, August 20, 1943; Bergson and van Paassen to Roosevelt, September 4, 1943; Bergson to Early, September 20, 1943; Levovitz to McIntyre, October 3, 1943; Bergson to Cox, October 4, 1943; and Watson to Levovitz, October 5, 1943, all in BGC, File: 2/11/11-chet, The March of 500 Rabbis, Correspondence, Invitations, Speeches, Reports, Clippings.

11. Hertzberg, "The Day the Rabbis Marched," introduction.

12. "Rabbis Report 'Cold Welcome' At White House," *Washington Times-Herald*, October 7, 1943; "A Report of Failure and a Call to Action" (advertisement), *New York Times*, October 5, 1943; and *Washington Post*, October 6, 1943.

13. "Strictly Confidential" summary by Goldman of his conversation with Rosenman, CZA Z5/388; Berlin to Hayter, November 11, 1943, PRO, FO371/35041; "Transcript of Proceedings at Conference of American Zionist Emergency Council," Cleveland, December 11–12, 1943, 180, CZA, Z5/388. Goldmann also repeated his account at a Jewish Agency Executive meeting in Jerusalem a year later. Jewish Agency Executive Minutes, September 28, 1944, 10, CZA.

14. Hassett, *Off the Record*, 209; "Propaganda by Stunts," *Opinion*, November 1943, 4. Wise actually called Weisgal the "chiefest of stuntists." See Wise to Mack, April 10, 1933, CZA, A243/148.

15. Press coverage of the march, in BGC, File: 2/11/11-chet, The March of 500 Rabbis, Correspondence, Invitations, Speeches, Reports, Clippings; Eri Jabotinsky, untitled memorandum, December 9, 1943, BGC, File: 8/10/11, File: Serial-Jabotinsky, Eri, 1943–1945.

16. I. F. Stone, "U.S. Ambassador Fought Easing Visa Rules on Refugees," *PM*, October 3, 1943, 6; I. F. Stone, "State Dept. Blocks Plan to Rescue European Jews," *PM*, October 17, 1943, 6; Melvin J. Lasky, "No Voice Was Heard: The Shame of a World," *The New Leader*, October 23, 1943, 2.

17. Thomas to Long, October 1, 1943, and Long to Thomas, October 27, 1943, NA, File 840.48 Refugees.

18. Memorandum of Conversation, "Saving the Jews from Germany, and the care of Refugees-Mr. Peter H. Bergson, Mr. Henry Pringle, and Mr. Long," October 15, 1943, NA, File 840.48 Refugees.

19. Eri Jabotinsky to Arieh Ben-Eliezer, November 26, 1943, BGC, File: 8/10–11 chet, Jabotinsky, Eri, Correspondence; Harper to Gillette, November 1, 1943, with drafts, BGC, File: 1/7/1–11 chet-Resolutions.

20. Wyman and Medoff, *A Race Against Death*, 43–44.

21. Wyman and Medoff, *A Race Against Death*, 41–42.

22. Wyman, *The Abandonment of the Jews*, 194.

23. Bennet to Morgenthau, undated (1944), reprinted in Emergency Committee to Save the Jewish People of Europe, *The Work is Still Ahead*, 21; Wise to Tobin, February 5, 1945, SSW-AJHS, Box 102. The resolution, authored by Sen. W. Warren Barbour (D-NJ), called for the admission of 100,000 Jewish refugees.

24. Merlin, *Millions of Jews*, 101.

25. Wise to Rosenblatt, September 13, 1938, SSW-CZA, File A243/133; Wise to McDonald, December 8, 1938, SSW-AJHS, Box 109.

26. Wyman and Medoff, *A Race Against Death*, 142.

27. "Committee to Save Jews of Europe Files Charges Against Dr. Wise Before Rabbinical Body," JTA, January 21, 1944; "Executive Committee Meeting-American Jewish Conference, Biltmore Hotel, New York, November 6, 1943," 2, SSW-AJHS; American Jewish Conference news release, December 2, 1943, AJconf.

28. Committee on International Relations, *Problems of World War II*, 171; Alexander to Long, May 7, 1943, BLP, File: Refugee Movement and National Groups, 1943, Box 203; Wyman, *The Abandonment of the Jews*, 197.

29. Alexander to Long, May 7, 1943, BLP, File: Refugee Movement and National Groups, 1943, Box 203.

30. Committee on International Relations, *Problems of World War II*, 15–249 (La Guardia's testimony is on 147–56; Wise's is on 217–43); Rogers to Goldstein, Monsky, and Wise, February 8, 1944, IGP, A364/1954; "Congressional Committee Suspends Hearing of Resolution to Rescue Jews from Europe," JTA, December 19, 1943.

31. *Congressional Record-Senate*, 78th Congress, 1st Session, 9305; Detzer, *Appointment*, 242.

32. Wise to Tucker, June 17, 1943, AJCA, File: Emergency Conference 1943.

33. "Memorandum-issued by the Interim Committee of the American Jewish Conference," December 29, 1943, AJconf.

34. Perlzweig to Wise, Goldmann, Miller, and Shultz, June 17, 1943, AJcong; Lourie to Cohen, December 11, 1942, PSGC, 1:7; "Annual Report to the Zionist Organization of America-47th Annual Convention, October 14–17, 1944, Atlantic City, New Jersey," 59, 1753, CZA; American Zionist Emergency Council Executive Committee Minutes, April 17, 1944, CZA, Z5/1208; Wise to Thurman, November 20, 1944, SSW-AJHS, Box 102.

35. Wise to Ickes, December 23, 1943, and Ickes to Wise, January 5, 1944, PSGC, 1:10; Shultz to Weisgal, August 16, 1944, CZA, Z5/868; Feuer to Silver,

May 10, 1944, HMP, File II-6; American Zionist Emergency Council Executive Committee Minutes, May 15, 1944, CZA, Z5/1208.

36. Morgenthau Diaries, 735/60–61, FDRL.

37. Memorandum of Conversation with Nahum Goldmann, May 19, 1944, SD, 867N.01/2347PS/LC; Goldmann to Murray, May 24, 1944, CZA, Z5/395; Goldmann to Klotz, May 18, 1944, CZA, Z5/395; "Withdrawals from League and/or Hebrew Committee of National Liberation," ALFP; "Minutes of Conversation with Mr. Oscar Cox-Washington DC, March 31, 1944," CZA, Z6/281; Shapiro to Aaron, "Third Follow-Up to Sponsors of American League for a Free Palestine," October 24, 1944, CZA, F39/26.

Ironically, in 1942 Wise complained to Maurice Perlzweig of a rumor that a Jewish opponent of Wise's had remarked, "Stephen Wise is a greater enemy of the Jewish people than Hitler." See Wise to Perlzweig, October 23, 1942, SSW-AJHS, Box 92.

38. Alden to Ladd, March 24, 1945, FBI; Halifax to Foreign Office, May 24, 1944, PRO, FO 371/40131; Chancery (British Embassy, Washington DC) to Eastern Department, Foreign Office, August 6, 1945, PRO, FO 371/45599; Memorandum of Conversation with Nahum Goldmann, May 19, 1944, SD, 867N.0123/47/PS/LC.

Morris Waldman, executive director of the AJ committee, urged the State Department to undertake similar action against Bergson. Ironically, however, Waldman regarded Goldmann with almost equal hostility. He told the State Department that Goldmann was "an alien" whose organization was involved in "dangerous" activities. See "Department of State-Memorandum of Conversation (Waldman, Murray, Alling, Wilson), January 10, 1944," PSGPC, 3:67.

39. FBI New York to FBI Washington, "HCNL Registration Act," September 11, 1950, 2, FBI.

40. FBI New York to FBI Washington, "HCNL Registration Act," September 11, 1950, 2, FBI.

41. FBI New York to FBI Washington, "HCNL Registration Act," September 11, 1950, 2, FBI; Wyman and Medoff, A Race Against Death, 94–95.

42. Wyman, The Abandonment of the Jews, 180–81.

43. Medoff, Blowing the Whistle, 20–22.

44. Medoff, Blowing the Whistle, 22–24.

45. Penkower, The Jews Were Expendable, 130; "Rabbi Wise Sees FDR on Plan to Avert Jews' Extermination," PM, July 23, 1943; Wise to Roosevelt, July 23, 1943, SSW-AJHS, Box 68; Voss, Rabbi, 316; Roosevelt to Wise, August 16, 1943, FDRL, Office File 76-C; Morgenthau to Hull, November 24, 1943, SD, 862.4016/2297 PS/FP.

46. Morgenthau Diaries, 688II/61, FDRL; Morgenthau Diaries, 694/48, FDRL; Morgenthau Diaries, 688II/82–89, FDRL.

47. Medoff, Blowing the Whistle, 33.

48. Josiah E. DuBois Jr. interview with Henry Morgenthau III, February 26, 1981, Pitman NJ, transcript in the possession of the present author.

49. Morgenthau Diaries, 693/188–211, FDRL.

50. Morgenthau Diaries, 694/88–90, 94–97, FDRL.

51. Morgenthau Diaries 688, Morgenthau-Rosenman conversation, January 15, 1944, 148–50. A year later, when Rosenman belatedly suggested to FDR that it might be helpful to his re-election to encourage the British to permit more immigration to Palestine, he emphasized that the refugees should be "Christian and Jewish alike." That was consistent with Rosenman's philosophy of never appearing to favor Jews, even if in this instance it made no sense, since there was no clamor by Christian refugees to enter Palestine. (Rosenman to Roosevelt, September 16, 1944, Samuel I. Rosenman Papers, FDRL.) Exasperated, Morgenthau complained to his staff: "My God! Sam Rosenman: 'Would there be any publicity? Would there be any leaks?'. . . . I said, 'Do you realize how serious it is?' . . . . Take it from me, it adds to our difficulty to have a meeting with him present, [but] if this went to the president, and he didn't know about it, he could very well block it, just the way he has started to block it already . . . I mean, you have got to carry with you the people that the president may turn to." Assistant Treasury Secretary Harry Dexter White agreed that having Rosenman in the meeting would give them the opportunity "to work on him." Facing an entire group of rescue advocates, Rosenman could be "pushed and shamed" into supporting the Treasury's initiative. "Otherwise he will oppose it when you are not in a position to meet his arguments; whereas, you have either got to render him on your side, or at least weaken his opposition." (Morgenthau Diaries 693, 209–10). Having been tipped off as to Morgenthau's intentions, it is likely that Rosenman discussed the rescue agency issue with the president at some point during the three days between Morgenthau's January 13 phone call and his meeting with FDR. Considering the tumult on Capitol Hill and Morgenthau's insistence on pressing ahead, Rosenman would have realized the agency was going to come about one way or another, and it would be better for Roosevelt if its agenda seemed ecumenical and if the president received credit for a humanitarian gesture. Roosevelt may have consulted other aides, as well. Bernard Baruch privately indicated to his longtime acquaintance, Hollywood producer and Bergson supporter Billy Rose, that he (Baruch) had spoken favorably about the proposal to the president. Afterward, Rose relayed to Ben Hecht the good news that Baruch "has evidently gotten part of his job done with the boss" with regard to "the boss's appointment of a Refugee Commission." Apparently, Rose added, "he's finally in a position [in the president's inner circle] where he can ask for certain things." (Rose to Hecht, January 30, 1944, File: Billy Rose, Ben Hecht Papers, Newberry Library, Chicago.)

52. John Pehle, "Memorandum for the Secretary's Files, January 16, 1944, in Morgenthau Diaries, 692/289, FDRL.

53. Morgenthau Diaries, 707/220–21, FDRL.

54. Morgenthau Diaries, 710/194, FDRL; Morgenthau Diaries, 735/224–26, FDRL; Josiah E. DuBois Jr. interview with Richard Breitman and Alan Kraut, Camden NJ, October 12, 1982; the interviewers provided a tape to the present

author. Writing in the *Journal of American History* in 2014, David B. Woolner, the resident historian at the Franklin and Eleanor Roosevelt Institute, claimed that Rabbi Wise played a role in the creation of the War Refugee Board. When privately questioned about that statement by this author, Woolner backtracked, saying he did not mean to credit either Roosevelt or Wise for the creation of the board. While Woolner acknowledged these significant errors in private correspondence, he did not publish a correction in the *Journal of American History*. See *Journal of American History*, June 2014, 300–301; Medoff to Woolner, September 29, 2014, Medoff to Woolner, October 3, 2014, and Woolner to Medoff, November 12, 2014, in possession of the author.

55. Morgenthau Diaries, 696/183–92, FDRL.

56. Samuel Grafton, "I'd Rather Be Right," *New York Post*, July 22, 1943, 26.

57. Stember et al., *Jews in the Mind of America*, 148–49; Wyman, *Paper Walls*, 47, 210.

58. Press Conference #952, May 30, 1944, 14, FDRL: Press Conference #955, June 9, 1944, 1.

59. "American Jewish Conference Hails Roosevelt's Order Admitting 1,000 Refugees," JTA, June 12, 1944; "Symbols and Their Uses" (editorial), *Congress Weekly*, June 23, 1944; Marie Syrkin, "Free Port," *Jewish Frontier*, July 1944, 6; "Polish-Jewish Relations" (editorial), *National Jewish Ledger*, June 23, 1944, 6; "What They Are Saying: 'Token Rescue'," Independent Jewish Press Service, June 23, 1944.

60. Wyman, *The Abandonment of the Jews*, 66, 285. The Washington DC correspondent for the Independent Jewish Press Service had a somewhat similar take on the implications of the president's action: "The President's order creating the War Refugee Board showed that the President did not share Mr. Long's opinion on the [issue of rescue]," he contended. See Arnold Levin, "Heard in the Lobbies: Capitol Line," Independent Jewish Press Service, May 19, 1944.

6. FDR, Wise, and Palestine

1. Frankfurter to Roosevelt, April 23, 1934, in Freedman, *Roosevelt and Frankfurter*, 212.

2. "Palestine Aim Gets Praise of Roosevelt," JTA, January 20, 1935; Penkower, *Palestine in Turmoil*, 214:33.

3. Penkower, *Palestine in Turmoil*, 243–44.

4. Wise to Brandeis, April 28, 1937, CZA, A243/83; "Report of Meeting of S.S.W. with F.D.R., Saturday morning, Jan. 22, 1938," 1–2, CZA, A243/83; Penkower, *Palestine in Turmoil*, 504.

5. Penkower, *Palestine in Turmoil*, 574–75, 590; Blum, *From the Morgenthau Diaries*, 208.

6. Freedman, *Roosevelt and Frankfurter*, 212; Martin, *Isaiah Bowman*, 126; Smith, *American Empire*, 249, 302.

7. Penkower, *The Holocaust and Israel Reborn*, 208–9, 214; Lash, *Eleanor*, 111–12.

8. Walko, "Isolationism," 42; Gal, *David Ben-Gurion*, 56.

9. Gal, *David Ben-Gurion*, 50–52; Wise to Goldman, December 5, 1940, SSW-CZA, A243/126.

10. Wise to Rosenblatt, May 9, 1938, SSW-AJHS, Box 121; Wise to Neuman, December 6, 1938, SSW-AJHS, Box 117; Wise to Gottheil, September 20, 1938, SSW-AJHS, Box 109.

11. Brandeis to Roosevelt, May 4, 1939, FDRL, Office File 700; Roosevelt's notations on memo of Isadore Breslau telephone message, May 18, 1939, FDRL, Office File 700; Urofsky, *American Zionism*, 414; Wise to Goldman, May 23, 1939, SSW-CZA, A243/125.

12. Wise to Goldman, May 23, 1939, SSW-CZA, A243/125.

13. Wise to Frankfurter, May 19, 1943, SSW-AJHS, Box 109.

14. Wise to Berman, July 10, 1939, SSW-CZA, A243/143.

15. Wise to Frankfurter, October 17, 1939, SSW-AJHS, Box 109; Wise to Brandeis, October 17, 1939, SSW-AJHS, Box 106.

16. Wise to Goldman, February 27, 1940, SSW-AJHS, Box 109.

17. Wise to Frankfurter, November 27, 1940, SSW-AJHS, Box 109; "Zionist Delegation Sees Embassy Officials," JTA, November 28, 1940.

18. "1,584 Refugees Deported," JTA, December 20, 1940; Pitot, *The Mauritian Shekel*, 110–11; Ofer, *Escaping the Holocaust*, 36, 142; Emergency Committee for Zionist Affairs Minutes, March 14, 1941, 2, CZA, F39/381; "McMichael Must Go," *Hashomer Hatzair*, March 1941, 7–8; Wise to Frankfurter, March 17, 1941, SSW-AJHS, Box 109.

19. Wyman, *The Abandonment of the Jews*, 117; Hull to Roosevelt, December 29, 1942, FDRL, President's Personal File 700.

20. Smith, *American Empire*, 249, 302, 305–8, 310.

21. Wise to Weizmann, July 23, 1943, SSW-AJHS, Box 121.

22. "Conversation with Congressman Sol Bloom-Washington, DC, September 2, 1943," CZA, Z6/282.

23. Emergency Committee for Zionist Affairs Minutes, September 28, 1943, CZA, F39/381.

24. "Sons of King Ibn Saud Welcomed to Washington as Guests of U.S. Government," JTA, October 4, 1943; "Emir Feisal Advocates Inclusion of Palestine in United States of Arabia," JTA, October 5, 1943; "Solution of Palestine Question Must Precede Pan-Arab Union, Says Ibn Saud," JTA, October 6, 1943; "Sol Bloom Swaps Autographs with One of the King of Arabia's 31 Sons," PM, October 7, 1943.

25. Blum, *The Price of Vision*, 313; "Arabs Open News Agency in London, Protest Willkie Message," JTA, November 14, 1943; Eri Jabotinsky, untitled memorandum, December 9, 1943, BGC, File: 8/10/11, Jabotinsky, Eri, 1943–1945.

26. Blum, *The Price of Vision*, 300.

27. "Resolution on Jewish Immigration to Palestine Introduced in Senate," JTA, February 2, 1944; Wise to Niles, March 13, 1944, SSW-CZA, A243/83.

28. Blum, *The Price of Vision*, 313.

29. Hull, *Memoirs*, 1535–36; Perkins et al., eds., *Foreign Relations of the United States*, 1944, 5:591.

30. Morgenthau Diaries, FDRL, 707/223. Wise to Weiss, November 10, 1943, SSW-AJHS, Box 121; Blum, *The Price of Vision*, 265; Wise to Niles, April 11, 1944, CZA, A243/83.

31. Celler to McIntyre, undated "Confidential Memo," ECP, File: Israel (Palestine) Correspondence 1930–1946. The context indicates it was written in early October 1943.

32. Goldmann interview with Melvin Urofsky, April 21, 1975, 10, Hebrew University interviews; Weisgal to Weizmann, November 9, 1943, 2–3, CWP.

33. Silver to Neumann, August 16, 1944, CZA, A123/315; Wise to Mrs. Gottheil, January 16, 1945, SSW-AJHS, Box 109.

34. Raphael, *Abba Hillel Silver*, 110.

35. Medoff, *Militant Zionism*, 108–9.

36. "Palestine Plank of Republicans Lauded by Silver, Hopes Democrats Will Follow Suit," JTA, June 29, 1944.

37. Wise to Roosevelt, July 7, 1944, FDRL, President's Personal File 3292; Raphael, *Abba Hillel Silver*, 110–11.

38. Wise to Frankfurter, June 28, 1944, CZA, A243/137; Silver to Wise, July 1, 1944, CZA, A364/1656-B.

39. Wise to Niles, June 29, 1944, CZA, A243/83.

40. Wise to Frankfurter, July 26, 1944, CZA, A243/137; Wise to Szold, July 26, 1944, CZA, A243/157.

41. American Zionist Emergency Council minutes, July 24, 1944, CZA, F39/378. Not long afterward, Wise wrote to Roosevelt that a partition of Palestine "would be in every sense disastrous." See Wise to Roosevelt, September 14, 1944, FDRL, President's Personal File 601; Wise to Rosenblatt, July 26, 1944, CZA, A243/133.

42. Littell, *My Roosevelt Years*, 268–69.

43. Wise to Rosenblatt, July 26, 1944, CZA, A243/133.

44. Hull to Roosevelt, August 30, 1944, FDRL, Office File 700.

45. Wise to Roosevelt, September 16, 1944, SSW-AJHS, Box 68.

46. S.I.R. to the President, September 16, 1944, SRP, File: Palestine; F.D.R. to S.I.R., September 16, 1944, SRP, File: Palestine.

47. Wise to Rosenman, September 26, 1944, SRP, Box 4, File: Wise, Stephen S.

48. Minutes of the Jewish Agency Executive meeting, September 28, 1944, 5, CZA; Wise to Weiss, November 10, 1943, SSW-AJHS, Box 121.

49. Wise and Silver to Roosevelt, September 26, 1944, FDRL, Office File 700; Wagner to Roosevelt, September 29, 1944, FDRL, Office File 700.

50. AZEC Minutes, October 12, 1944, 4–9, CZA, F39/382.

51. "Dewey Supports Establishment of Jewish Commonwealth on Basis of Balfour Declaration," JTA, October 15, 1944.

52. "Dewey Supports Establishment of Jewish Commonwealth on Basis of Balfour Declaration," JTA, October 15, 1944.

53. S.I.R. to the President, October 12, 1944, SRP, Box 4, File: Wise, Stephen S.; "Draft of Letter to Senator Wagner," CZA, Z5/388; "Draft of Letter to Senator Wagner"; Wagner to Roosevelt (telegram), October 13, 1944; Roosevelt to Wagner, October 13, 1944; and Roosevelt to Wagner, October 14, 1944, all in FDRL, President's Personal File 601. Of the four changes cited herein, the latter two were first revealed in Penkower, *Decision on Palestine*, 314–15.

54. Neuman to Netanyahu, December 14, 1944, A123/307, ENP; Wallace, *The Price of Vision*, 300.

55. Telegram, Wise to Stettinius, December 3, 1944, SSW-AJHS, Box 66; Penkower, *Decision on Palestine*, 314–19; Wise to Van Paassen, December 28, 1944, SSW-AJHS, Box 121.

56. Ganin, "Activism versus Moderation"; Wise to Stettinius, December 12, 1944, SSW-AJHS, Box 66.

57. Sherwood, *Roosevelt and Hopkins*, 871; Meacham, *Franklin and Winston*, 125.

58. "Memorandum of Conversation between His Majesty Abdul Aziz al Saud, King of Saudi Arabia, and President Roosevelt, February 14, 1945, aboard the *U.S.S. Quincy*," in Fine et al., *Foreign Relations of the United States 1945, Vol. VIII*, 2–3, 691, 698. Curiously, the exchange regarding Poland is not mentioned in Woolner, *The Last 100 Days*, although he devotes an entire chapter to Roosevelt's meeting with Ibn Saud (153–66); nor does it appear in Breitman and Lichtman, *FDR and the Jews*, where the meeting is discussed in some detail (302–3).

59. Penkower, *Decision on Palestine*, 333–34.

60. "Roosevelt Says His Position on Zionism Unchanged; Reiterates Support of Commonwealth," JTA, March 18, 1945; Wise to McDonald, April 9, 1945, SSW-AJHS, Box 66.

61. Wise, "The following is an account of the meeting of SSW with FDR on Friday, March 16, 1945, at 11:45 A.M.-White House, Washington DC," CZA, Z6/296; Kaufman, *Ambiguous Partnership*, 177–78; Hoskins to Alling, March 5, 1945, in Fine et al., *Foreign Relations of the United States 1945, Vol. VIII*, 690–91; Cohen, *Not Free to Desist*, 295–96; Proskauer, *A Segment*, 69–70.

62. Edward Pinsky, "The American Jewish Committee and the Joint Distribution Committee," in Finger, ed., *American Jewry during the Holocaust*, 9; Urofsky, *We Are One!*, 63; Neumann to Silver, April 16, 1947, ENP, A123/223; Weil to Wise, October 19, 1945, ENP, A243/83; Wise to Weil, October 22, 1945, ENP, A243/83; Proskauer to Rosenblatt, November 13, 1945, SSW-AJHS, Reel 001; Rosenblatt to Proskauer, November 14, 1945, SSW-AJHS, Reel 001; Rosenblatt to Wise, November 13, 1945, SSW-AJHS, Reel 001; Proskauer to Wise, November 13, 1945, SSW-AJHS, Reel 001; Proskauer to Wise, November 15, 1945, SSW-AJHS, Reel 001; Proskauer to Wise, November 21, 1945, SSW-AJHS, Reel 001; Wise to Proskauer, November 23, 1945, SSW-AJHS, Reel 001; Wise to Frankfurter, November 26, 1945, SSW-AJHS, Reel 001; Wise to Rosenblatt, November

27, 1945, SSW-AJHS, Reel 001; Proskauer to Wise, December 5, 1945, SSW-AJHS, Reel 001; Epstein to Wise, December 6, 1945, SSW-AJHS, Reel 001; Wise to Epstein, December 21, 1945, SSW-AJHS, Reel 001; Wise to Shulman, December 24, 1945, SSW-AJHS, Reel 001.

63. Wise to Frankfurter, November 26, 1945, SSW-AJHS, Reel 001.

64. Wise to Akzin, May 20, 1946, SSW-AJHS, Box 66; Wise to Welles, May 20, 1946, SSW-AJHS, Box 66; Welles to Wise, May 23, 1946, SSW-AJHS, Box 66.

65. Van Paassen to Silver, January 6, 1945, CZA, A123/103.

66. Fine et al., *Foreign Relations of the United States 1945, Volume 8*, 710–12.

67. "Dr. Silver Takes Issue with Dr. Wise; Charges Him with Resenting New Leadership," JTA, January 2, 1945; Wise to Gottheil, January 16, 1945, SSW-AJHS, Box 109.

68. Emergency Committee for Zionist Affairs minutes, March 14, 1941, 2, CZA, F39/381; Wise to Mrs. Roosevelt, April 1, 1942, SSW-AJHS, Box 68; "20,000 at Garden in Appeal for Jews Under Heel of Nazi," *Boston Herald*, May 3, 1943.

7. The Failure to Bomb Auschwitz

1. Israel, *War Diary*, 353.

2. Vrba and Bestic, *I Cannot Forgive*, 229.

3. Wyman, *The Abandonment of the Jews*, 289–90, 298.

4. Wyman, *The Abandonment of the Jews*, 289.

5. "Polish Pressure Campaign Takes Form," *Foreign Nationality Groups in the United States*, No. 179, 6–7, Office of Strategic Services, FDRL, President's Secretary's File 66.

6. "Polish Pressure Campaign Takes Form," *Foreign Nationality Groups in the United States*, No. 179, 1–2, Office of Strategic Services, FDRL, President's Secretary's File 66; Jonathan Daniels memorandum to The President, June 2, 1944, FDRL, President's Secretary's File 66.

7. Israel, *War Diary*, 354.

8. Loewenheim et al., *Roosevelt and Churchill*, 396, 406.

9. Wise to MacDonald, May 19, 1939, Box 5, File 165, JMP.

10. "Saving the Last Million," *Congress Weekly*, May 19, 1944, 3–4; Gilbert, *Auschwitz and the Allies*, 210; "Hungary's Jews," *Opinion*, May 1944, 4.

11. "Saving the Last Million," *Congress Weekly*, May 19, 1944, 3–4.

12. "We and Hungarian Jewry," Independent Jewish Press Service, July 7, 1944; "Protests Register," Independent Jewish Press Service, July 21, 1944; "Devil's Barter," Independent Jewish Press Service, July 28, 1944.

13. Schwartz, "G. George Fox"; Fox, "From the Watch Tower," *The Sentinel*, August 3, 1944.

14. Wyman, *The Abandonment of the Jews*, 298–99.

15. *Moreinu Rosenheim's Diary During Wartime-Covering the Years 1941–1945*, entry for June 20, 1944, 240–41, AIA; John W. Pehle, "Memorandum for the Files," June 24, 1944, WRB.

16. Wyman, *The Abandonment of the Jews*, 291–94, 298–300.

17. Wiesel, *Night*, 71–72.

18. "Blows at Nazi Oil Reach New Zones," *New York Times*, August 21, 1944; Gruson, "2 Reich Cities Hit by 600,000 Bombs," *New York Times*, September 14, 1944.

19. Gilbert, *Auschwitz and the Allies*, 321.

20. Minutes of the Jewish Agency Executive meeting, June 11, 1944, 4–7, CZA; Lichtheim to Gruenbaum, June 19, 1944, YGP, A127/1856; Gruenbaum to Barlas, June 20, 1944, CZA, A127/544; Lichtheim to the Jewish Agency, June 26, 1944, CZA, L22/56; Krausz to JAE, June 27, 1944, CZA, S26/1251A; Chief Secretary to Ben-Gurion, July 12, 1944, CZA, S25/5209; Epstein to Ben-Gurion, September 3, 1944, CZA, S25/486; Minutes of the Smaller Zionist Actions Committee, September 5, 1944, 4663, CZA; Protocols of Jewish Agency Rescue Committee meeting, October 3, 1944, 4, CZA, S26/1240. For a detailed account of the Jewish Agency's stance, see Medoff, "The Roosevelt Administration."

21. Goldmann to Masaryk, July 3, 1944, WJC; Masaryk to Goldmann, July 17, 1944, WJC; Perlzweig to Pehle, July 21, 1944, WJC.

22. Theodore N. Lewis, "Men and Events," *Opinion*, September 1944, 33–34; Theodore N. Lewis interview with Rafael Medoff, May 20, 1996; Gruenbaum to Shertok and "Weiss [sic]-Goldmann," July 25, 1944, CZA, A127/1856; Gruenbaum to Wise, Goldmann (New York), Shertok, and Brodet[s]ky (London), August 31, 1944, CZA, A127/544; Gruenbaum to Shertok (London), Wise, and Goldmann (New York), September 3, 1944, A127/544, CZA.

23. Smertenko to Roosevelt, July 24, 1944, PSGC, File: Emergency Committee to Save the Jewish People of Europe; "Last Chance for Rescue," *Jewish Frontier*, August 1944, 4.

24. Fishman, "From Day to Day," *Morgen Zhurnal*, June 27, 1944; "We and Hungarian Jewry," Independent Jewish Press Service, July 7, 1944; "Germans Reported Willing to Exchange Hungarian Jews for Supplies," JTA, July 20, 1944.

25. Kubowitzki to Pehle, July 1, 1944, WRB, Box 29; Kubowitzki to Pehle, July 5, 1944, WRB, Box 22; Kubowitzki to Frischer, August 2, 1944, WRB, Box 29; Pehle to Kubowitzki, August 3, 1944, WRB, Box 29; Kubowitzki to McCloy, August 9, 1944, WRB; Kubowitzki to Pehle, August 29, 1944, WRB, Box 29; McCloy to Kubowitzki, August 14, 1944, and September 3, 1944, WJC, D/107; Kubowitzki to Pehle, WRB, August 29, 1944; Kubowitzki to McCloy, August 30, 1944, WJC, D109/1.

26. "Huge Open-Air Demonstration in New York Demands Rescue of Jews from Europe," JTA, August 1, 1944; "40,000 Here Seek Way to Save Jews," *New York Times*, August 1, 1944; "Jewish Congress Submits Rescue Program to Intergovernmental Committee Session," JTA, August 15, 1944.

27. Erdheim, "The U.S. Holocaust Museum," 61–62.

28. See "Report of Meeting with John W. Pehle, executive director, and Messrs Lesser and Friedman of the War Refugee Board, August 16, 1944," AJCA, Box 6, File: Hungary, 1944, 1949–1950.

29. Wyman, *The Abandonment of the Jews*, 291.

30. Wyman, *The Abandonment of the Jews*, 306–7.

31. Friedman, "Election of 1944," 3023, 3037; Sherwood, *Roosevelt and Hopkins*, 822.

32. Gordon to Early, June 2, 1944, Glenn to Niles, October 2, 1944, and W.D.H. to Daniels, undated, all in FDRL, Official File 300: Democratic National Committee; Levering, *American Opinion*, 171.

33. Winant to Hopkins, September 1, 1944, HH, Box 337, File: Growing Crisis in Poland.

34. Wyman, *The Abandonment of the Jews*, 238–39.

35. Feingold, *Bearing Witness*, 155; "Hungary to Set Up Camps for Jews Near Bombing Objectives," Independent Jewish Press Service, May 5, 1944.

8. Antisemitism in the White House

1. Zucker, *In Search of Refuge*, 42, 90; Breitman and Kraut, *American Refugee Policy*, 15, 32; Diary of Breckinridge Long, entries for October 3, 1940, and October 10, 1940, BLP.

2. Zucker, *In Search of Refuge*, 81–82, 93.

3. Eleanor Roosevelt, too, made antisemitic remarks in her early years, although she appears to have shed that prejudice under the impact of later experiences. See Lash, *Eleanor and Franklin*, 53, 198, 295, 379, 750; Cook, *Eleanor Roosevelt-Volume One*, 299, 388; Collier with Horowitz, 281; Cook, *Eleanor Roosevelt-Volume Two*, 316–17; Penkower, *The Holocaust and Israel Reborn*, 271–72.

4. Morgan, FDR, 298; Lash, *Eleanor and Franklin*, 295; Roosevelt and Roosevelt, eds., *F.D.R.*

In their 1987 book, *American Refugee Policy*, Breitman and Kraut wrote: "The president's mother was anti-Semitic, his brother even more so" (245). However in his 2013 book, *FDR and the Jews* (coauthored with Allan Lichtman), Breitman claimed Sara influenced her son to *reject* antisemitism. Breitman has never responded to multiple inquiries from this author asking what additional evidence he uncovered that led him to reverse his 1987 judgment.

5. Freidel, *The Apprenticeship*, 5–6; Cook, *Eleanor Roosevelt-Volume 1*, 144–45.

6. Cited in Robinson, *By Order of the President*, 271–72:86.

7. Robinson, *By Order of the President*, 35. In an interview on the eve of the 1932 presidential election, Roosevelt alluded to his belief that dispersing Jews, in small groups, to rural communities would lead to the disappearance of prejudice. In "small communities," he said, "there is little discrimination because everybody knows everybody else." See "'Human' Alien Laws Urged by Governor," *New York Times*, October 24, 1932, 9.

8. Robinson, *By Order of the President*, 38.

9. Robinson, *By Order of the President*, 38, 40–41.

10. Robinson, *By Order of the President*, 105.

11. "Confidential-Memo on conference at the White House with the President—August 4, 1939," Burton K. Wheeler Papers, Box 11: File 18, Montana State University, Bozeman MT. The historian Arthur Schlesinger Jr. learned of FDR's remark about "Jewish blood" in 1959, while he was working on *The Politics of Upheaval*, the final installment of his three-volume history of the New Deal. Schlesinger never quoted FDR's statement in any of the books and articles he wrote about Roosevelt and his era—including a 1994 essay in *Newsweek* defending FDR against suspicions of antisemitism. In an exchange of correspondence with this author in 2005, Schlesinger insisted that he had done nothing wrong in withholding the "Jewish blood" document from publication, because, in his view, Roosevelt's statement was not antisemitic. "It appears to me a neutral comment about people of mixed ancestry," he wrote. See Schlesinger to Wheeler, November 30, 1959, and December 22, 1959, Burton K. Wheeler Papers, Box 11: File 18, Montana State University, Bozeman MT; Arthur Schlesinger Jr., "Did FDR Betray the Jews?," *Newsweek*, April 18, 1994, 14; Schlesinger to Medoff, September 4, 2005, copy in the possession of the author. As for Mrs. Hull, her father was a Jewish immigrant from Austria, her mother was Christian, and she was raised as an Episcopalian. See Gellman, *Secret Affairs*, 25.

12. Lash, *Dealers and Dreamers*, 338; Lasser, *Benjamin V. Cohen*, 105–7, 182, 201; Cook, *Eleanor Roosevelt-Volume 2*, 317. Leonard Dinnerstein has pointed out: "The number of Jews employed [by FDR] in policymaking positions in the Departments of State, War, Navy, and Commerce, the Federal Reserve Board, the Federal Trade Commission, the U.S. Tariff Commission, and the Board of Tax Appeals could probably be counted on one's fingers and toes." See Dinnerstein, "Jews and the New Deal," 475.

13. As Breitman and Kraut put it (*American Refugee Policy*, 245): "Some of FDR's best friends were anti-Semites."

14. Morgan, *FDR*, 445.

15. Blum, *The Price of Vision*, 189.

16. Penkower, *The Holocaust and Israel Reborn*, 208–9, 213–14.

17. The "Chosen Race" remark first appeared in Cook, *Eleanor Roosevelt-Volume 1*, 192; see also Freidel, *Launching the New Deal*, 390–95.

18. Ward, *A First-Class Temperament*, 661, 676.

19. Ward, *A First-Class Temperament*, 253:45. Breitman and Lichtman (*FDR and the Jews*, 9:4) cited Ward's book as their source for a point about Roosevelt's adolescence, but made no mention of Ward's revelation concerning the president's jokes about Jews—an odd omission, considering the title and subject of their book.

20. Harry Schwartz, "Stalin Called Himself a Zionist but Cited Soviet Jewish 'Problem,'" *New York Times*, March 17, 1955; "Doctored History Again," *Washington Post and Times-Herald*, March 19, 1955; "Roosevelt's Alleged Yalta Remarks

on Jews Doubted in Washington," JTA, March 23, 1955. According to Schneiderman and Maller, *American Jewish Year Book 5707* (599), there were actually approximately five million, not six million, Jews in the United States in 1945.

For the details of the State Department's several-decades suppression of FDR's statement, see "'Out of the Frying Pan Into the Fire': The Politics of the Yalta FRUS," remarks by Joshua Botts, Office of the Historian, U.S. Department of State, delivered at the June 2011 conference of the Society of Historians of American Foreign Relations in Alexandria VA and posted at https://history.state .gov/historicaldocuments/frus-history/research/politics-of-the-yalta-frus; and Bohlen, *Witness to History*, 203. FDR's most ardent defenders have regarded this comment as not merely innocuous but actually a good thing: Breitman and Lichtman contended that Roosevelt "was using anti-Semitism as an ice-breaker with Stalin." Who could object to breaking the ice and thereby, perhaps, advancing the cause of world peace? The problem is that an "ice-breaker" is, by definition, something that is done at the beginning of a conversation, in order to facilitate a more open discussion. Yet Roosevelt did not make his joke about Jews until the next-to-last day of the week-long Yalta conference. Breitman and Lichtman did not explain this inconsistency (*FDR and the Jews*, 301).

21. Lelyveld, *His Final Battle*, 292.

22. *Foreign Relations of the United States-Diplomatic Papers 1942*, 570–71. In *FDR and the Jews*, Breitman and Lichtman acknowledged the Molotov exchange (citing Frank Costigliola), but explained it away as another example of Roosevelt using antisemitism as an "ice-breaker." Once again, however, the "ice-breaker" theory was contradicted by the timeline of events. The *Foreign Relations* transcript described one discussion about various topics held when Molotov arrived at the White House; another detailed conversation that took place before dinner; yet another during dinner; and then a final one after dinner, in the president's study. Only in this very last segment (and just before the conclusion of that segment), many hours after the ice was broken, did the exchange about Jews take place. (Costigliola, *Roosevelt's Lost Alliances*, 168–69; Breitman and Lichtman, *FDR and the Jews*, 301.)

23. Tifft and Jones, *The Trust*, 171.

24. "Report of Meeting of S.S.W. with F.D.R., Saturday morning, Jan. 22, 1938," 4, SSW-CZA, A243/83, Jerusalem. Henry Feingold has recounted an uncorroborated incident in which "a German delegation came to see [President Roosevelt] in 1937 to complain that German culture was being transmitted to the German people through Jewish hands and Jewish eyes, that the four redactors of Goethe were Jewish, so were too many symphony orchestra conductors, and so on. Roosevelt shook his head in understanding and advised that a quota system was in order." ("FDR and the Holocaust: Did the President Do All He Could to Save European Jewry?" Harvard Club, NYC, May 1997, published in Leo Baeck Institute Occasional Paper No. 2, 18–19.) Breitman and Lichtman had access to the January 1938 memo, but chose only to quote from the part in which Wise

described his discussion with Roosevelt about the potential for development of Palestine. (*FDR and the Jews*, 100.) In an email on November 11, 2013, this author asked Professor Breitman why he and his coauthor withheld the unflattering part from publication. He did not respond.

25. Freidel, *Rendezvous*, 295–96; Morgenthau Diaries, November 26, 1941, FDRL.

26. Ward, *First Class*, 255:48 (quoting an abbreviated version); Morgenthau Diaries, January 27, 1942, FDRL.

27. *Foreign Relations of the United States-The Conferences*, 608. The actual statistics were quite different. Jews comprised only about 16 percent of Germany's lawyers, 11 percent of the doctors, less than 3 percent of college professors, and less than 1 percent of the schoolteachers (Wyman, *The Abandonment of the Jews*, 313). FDR may have derived his wildly inflated numbers from his old friend Samuel R. Fuller, president of the American Bemberg Corporation, who had known Roosevelt since World War I, when he was a commander in the Naval Reserve and Roosevelt was assistant secretary of the navy. Fuller visited Europe frequently in the 1930s and sent the president memos outlining his impressions. After a visit to Germany in May 1933, for example, Fuller reported to FDR: "The appointed judges of the Courts were largely Jewish. The ministry of Education was filled with Jews. The Chief of Police of Berlin was a Jew. 2600 out of the 3200 Berlin lawyers were Jews. In the University of Berlin 3 per cent to 4 per cent of the student body were Jews, and 40 per cent of the professors were Jews. Germany felt that this was wrong; and they put them out and filled their places, or places where necessary, with Gentiles." Fuller's information came from Reichsbank president Hjalmar Schacht. (Fuller to Roosevelt, May 11, 1933, FDRL, President's Personal File 2616.)

28. Blum, *The Price of Vision*, 210–11; Breitman and Lichtman, *FDR and the Jews*, 249. Wallace actually wrote "Marietta County," but there is no such county in Georgia; the president must have meant Meriwether County, where Warm Springs was located. The German ambassador to the United States, Hans Luther, cited similar numbers when he spoke in May 1933 at an orphanage established by German Americans in Mount Vernon NY. Luther said "the legal and medical professions in Berlin, Frankfurt, and other large cities were almost monopolized" by Jews, "and nearly fifty percent of the government officials have been Jewish, although the total Jewish population was only one percent." See "Nazi Jewish Policies Political, Not Religious, Dr. Luther Asserts," JTA, May 26, 1933.

29. Press Conference #982, November 21, 1944, FDRL.

30. In letters written while serving in the military in 1918, Truman characterized New York City as a "kike town." In 1935 he wrote to his wife Bess that a participant in a poker game "screamed like a Jewish merchant." (Ferrell, *Dear Bess*, 242, 248, 254, 366.) As president, too, Truman gave vent to such sentiments. When Truman's mother forwarded him a note "from a Jewish friend of a friend" urging U.S. support of Jewish statehood, the president responded: "These people are the usual European conspirators and they try to approach

the President from every angle." (Truman, *Harry S. Truman*, 299.) When Secretary of War Stimson complained about Henry Morgenthau Jr. being included in the U.S. delegation to Potsdam, Truman assured him, according to Stimson's diary: "Don't worry, neither Morgenthau nor [Bernard] Baruch nor any of the Jew boys will be going to Pottsdam' [*sic*]." During a 1946 cabinet discussion about Jewish protests over Palestine, Truman declared: "Jesus Christ couldn't please them when he was here on earth, so how could anyone expect that I would have any luck?" (Transcript of Henry Morgenthau III interview with John M. Blum, New Haven CT, March 15, 1984, 5, copy in the possession of the author. Morgenthau III quoted in Morgenthau III, *Mostly Morgenthaus*, 435; Michael Cohen, *Truman and Israel*, 7, 133.) In a 1947 diary entry, Truman had this to say about Jewish protests over the refugee issue: "The Jews have no sense of proportion nor do they have any judgement on world affairs. . . . The Jews, I find are very, very selfish. They care not how many Estonians, Latvians, Finns, Poles, Yugoslavs or Greeks get murdered or mistreated as D[isplaced] P[ersons] as long as the Jews get special treatment. Yet when they have power, physical, financial or political neither Hitler nor Stalin has anything on them for cruelty or mistreatment to the under dog." Other accounts quote Truman as complaining about "the fanaticism of our New York Jews" and accusing "the New York Jews" of being "disloyal to their country." See Wadsworth to Henderson, February 4, 1948, in United States Department of State, *Foreign Relations of the United States, 1948*, 593; "Truman Says 'Lie;' Reporter Says 'No'; President Denies Remark on Jews," United Press dispatch in the *Pittsburgh Post-Gazette*, March 12, 1948; "Truman Denies Angrily Press Report That He Said New York Jews Were Disloyal to U.S.," JTA, March 12, 1948.

Richard Nixon referred to some of his critics as "Jew boys," complained about "those Jews" in the U.S. Attorney's Office, and charged that Jews in the government were leaking damaging information about him to "Jewish liberals" in the news media. Nixon quizzed aides about which antiwar activists were Jewish, and asked an adviser to draw up a list of Jewish employees of the Bureau of Labor Statistics, suspecting they were part of a "Jewish cabal" that was reporting inflated unemployment statistics in order to harm him. He believed in the "total Jewish domination of the media." He complained that Jews were "aggressive, abrasive and obnoxious" and "untrustworthy." He told aides to "do a little persecuting" of "rich Jews" who were contributing to the Democrats. In one pseudo-historical diatribe that echoed attempts by Franklin Roosevelt and others to intimidate Jewish leaders into keeping quiet, Nixon once asserted to his aides: "It happened in Spain, it happened in Germany, it's happening—and now it's going to happen in America if these people don't start behaving." See "Nixon Wanted His Daughters to Stay Away from 'the Arts' Because 'They're Jews, They're Left-Wing,'" JTA, August 7, 1974; "Times, CBS-TV Claim Nixon Used Epithet 'Jew Boy' Several Times in Taped Conversations with Dean," May 13, 1974; "Tapes Reveal Nixon Complained That He Was Surrounded by Jews,"

JTA, May 2, 1977; Nixon Blamed Jews for Anti-War Activity," JTA, June 7, 1991; "Haldeman Diaries Attribute Anti-Semitic Comments to Nixon," JTA, May 19, 1994; "Tapes: Nixon Targeted Jews in His Anti-Democrat Campaign," JTA, December 10, 1996; "News Brief," JTA, March 10, 1999; "News Brief," JTA, October 7, 1999; "News Brief," JTA, March 4, 2002; Eric Fingerhut, "Nixon, Graham Talk on Tape of American Anti-Semitism," JTA, June 24, 2009.

Conclusion

1. Dallek, *A Political Life*, 233; Franklin D. Roosevelt radio address, April 7, 1932, http://www.presidency.ucsb.edu/ws/?pid=88408; Meacham, *Franklin and Winston*, xv.

2. Press Conferences of Franklin D. Roosevelt, November 5, 1943, 196–97, FDRL.

3. Committee on International Relations, *Problems of World War II*, 169; Zucker, *Cecilia Razovsky*, 112–13; Penkower, *Decision on Palestine*, 75; Herzog to Roosevelt, May 14, 1941, FDRL, Presidential File 7520; Laurence Jarvik interview with Emanuel Celler, 1978, 7–8, transcript in the possession of the author. Celler, *You Never Leave Brooklyn*, 92; Wyman, *The Abandonment of the Jews*, 154, 336.

4. Shipping For Refugees," *Baltimore Jewish Times*, May 14, 1943; "How to Continue Our Traditional Foreign Policy: Radio Address to be Delivered by Congressman Samuel Dickstein—April 17, 1944, 11:30 P.M., Station WOL, Washington, D.C.," 4, CZA, F39/54; Penkower, *Decision on Palestine*, 363; "To Honor British Rubble," *New York Times*, June 28, 1942; "Mill of the Gods" (editorial), *The Answer*, May 1943, 4; Protocols of the Jewish Agency Executive, April 27, 1943 (Volume 38), CZA, 24; Lubin to Hassett, March 8, 1945, FDRL, OF 700.

5. Zucker, *Cecelia Razovsky*, 112-13; Penkower, *Decision on Palestine*, 75; Herzog to Roosevelt, May 14, 1941, FDRL I, Presidential File 7520; Laurence Jarvik interview with Emanuel Celler, 1978, 7-8, transcript in the possession of the author.

6. American Jewish Congress Administrative Committee minutes, March 13, 1934, 4, 1–77, AJCP. Nonetheless, B'nai B'rith did not change its position regarding public protests. See Moore, *B'nai B'rith and the Challenge of Ethnic Leadership*, 170–77.

7. "Democratic and Republican Parties Urge Congress to Admit European Jews," JTA, September 10, 1943; "Asylum in America," *Congress Weekly*, September 24, 1943, 4; Wyman, *The Abandonment of the Jews*, 264.

8. Urofsky, "American Jewish Leadership," 413.

9. Elath, *Zionism at the UN*, 83.

10. Eliahu Elath interview with Melvin Urofsky, June 5, 1975, 4–5, Oral History Division, Hebrew University.

11. Nahum Goldmann interview with Melvin Urofsky, April 21, 1975, 10, Oral History Division, Hebrew University.

12. Nahum Goldmann interview with Laurence Jarvik, February 11, 1979, 65–66, transcript in the possession of the author.

13. Arthur Lourie interview with Melvin Urofsky, June 9, 1975, 7–8, Oral History Division, Hebrew University.

14. Carl Hermann Voss interview with Melvin Urofsky, September 9, 1975, 28–30, Oral History Division, Hebrew University.

15. Israel Goldstein interview with Melvin Urofsky, September 12, 1973, 13–14, Oral History Division, Hebrew University; Israel Goldstein interview with Geoffrey Wigoder and Menahem Kaufman, May 29, 1977, 3, Oral History Division, Hebrew University.

16. Israel Goldstein, "The Holocaust and American Jewry," *Jerusalem Post*, April 10, 1983.

17. Undated draft of chapter 17 of *Challenging Years*, CZA, A243/117.

18. Wise, *Challenging Years*, 230–32.

19. Minutes of Jewish Agency Executive meeting, September 28, 1944, 1, CZA.

20. Wise to B. A. Hoover, September 8, 1936, SSW-AJHS, Box 109.

21. Wise to Frankfurter, January 22, 1937, SSW-AJHS, Box 109.

22. Memorandum, Harry Schneiderman to Morris Waldman, "Subject: Proposed Immigration Legislation, April 5, 1935," AJCA, Box 6, File: Immigration, 1936–39; Celler to Wise, May 14, 1943, SSW-AJHS, Box 109; "Conversation with Congressman Sol Bloom, Washington DC, September 22, 1943," AHS; "Oil & the Rabbis, *Time*, October 18, 1943; "Sons of King Ibn Saud Welcomed to Washington As Guests of U.S. Government," JTA, October 4, 1943; "King Ibn Saud Declares Opposition to Jewish Claims on Palestine," JTA, May 31, 1943; Feuer to Silver, May 10, 1944, and June 12, 1944, AZEC, F39/24.

23. MD 735/83.

24. Wise to Gordon, December 21, 1936, SSW-AJHS, Box 45; Wise to Goldman, January 8, 1937, SSW-AJHS, Box 45; Brandeis to Szold, July 4, 1937, SSW-AJHS, Box 106; Wise to Ettlinger, September 1, 1938, SSW-AJHS, Box 44; Wise to Brandeis, January 10, 1939, SSW-AJHS, Box 106; Wise to Easterman, June 29, 1939, SSW-AJHS, Box 90; Wise to Brandeis, October 17, 1939, SSW-AJHS, Box 106; Wise to MacDonald, December 18, 1939, SSW-AJHS, Box 66; Wise to Hirsch, January 10, 1940, SSW-AJHS, Box 45; Wise to Neumann, July 29, 1941, CZA, A243/737.

25. Wise to Niles, March 7, 1935, SSW-AJHS, Box 118; Wise to Chipkin, December 25, 1936, SSW-AJHS, Box 43; Wise to Berman, July 19, 1939, CZA, A243/143; Wise to MacDonald, March 12, 1940, SSW-AJHS, Box 66.

26. For the "Jewish blood" remark, see "Confidential-Memo on conference at the White House with the President—August 4, 1939," Burton K. Wheeler Papers, Box 11: File 18, Montana State University, Bozeman MT. For "mingling of Asiatic blood," see Robinson, *By Order of the President*, 38. Regarding Jews' innate characteristics, note his "dirty Jewish trick" remark in 1937 (Tifft and Jones, *The Trust*, 171.) Concerning the danger of having too many Jews in a university, note his role in imposing a quota on the admission of Jews to Harvard in the 1920s, about which he still boasted as late as 1941 (Morgenthau Diaries, January 27, 1942, FDRL). Regarding Jews in professions, he insisted at the 1943

Casablanca conference that Jews not be permitted to "overcrowd" various professions in North Africa (Aandahl, Franklin, and Slant, eds., *Foreign Relations of the United States—The Conferences*, 608). Concerning "spreading the Jews thin," see his 1943 proposal to Churchill to that effect (Blum, *The Price of Vision*, 210–11), and his remarks about "scattering" Japanese Americans around the country (Press Conference #982, November 21, 1944, FDRL). Concerning the ability to assimilate, Roosevelt referred to Japanese as "non-assimilable immigrants" (in his 1923 Asia magazine essay; cited in Robinson, *By Order of the President*, 38) and as being "not capable of assimilation" (in his April 30, 1925, column in the *Macon Daily Telegraph*; cited in Robinson, *By Order of the President*, 40). With regard to Jews, he asserted in 1920 that "the foreign population of the City of New York"—obviously including Jews—should be "distributed to different localities upstate" (Robinson, *By Order of the President*, 35) and made similar comments in his April 23, 1925, column in the *Macon Daily Telegraph* (Robinson, *By Order of the President*, 38). Roosevelt made the "sufferance" statement in a private conversation with Leo Crowley and Henry Morgenthau Jr., which Morgenthau noted at the time in Morgenthau Diaries, January 27, 1942, FDRL.

BIBLIOGRAPHY

Aandahl, Frederick, William M. Franklin, and William Slant, eds. *Foreign Relations of the United States—The Conferences at Washington, 1941–1942 and Casablanca Conference, 1943.* Washington DC: Government Printing Office, 1958.

Abitbol, Michael. *The Jews of North Africa During the Second World War.* Detroit: Wayne State University Press, 1989.

Abzug, Robert H. *America Views the Holocaust 1933–1945: A Brief Documentary History.* Boston and New York: Bedford/St. Martin's, 1999.

Adler, Cyrus, and Aaron M. Margalith. *With Firmness in the Right: American Diplomatic Action Affecting Jews, 1840–1945.* New York: The American Jewish Committee, 1946.

Adler, Selig. "The Roosevelt Administration and Zionism: The Pre-War Years, 1933–1939." In *Essays in American Zionism, 1917–1948, The Herzl Year Book, Volume VIII,* edited by Melvin I. Urofsky, 132–48. New York: Herzl Press, 1978.

Anthes, Louis. "Publicly Deliberative Drama: The 1934 Mock Trial of Adolf Hitler for 'Crimes against Civilization.'" *American Journal of Legal History* 42, no. 4 (October 1998): 391–410.

Ashton, Dianne. *Hanukkah in America: A History.* New York: New York University Press, 2013.

Baron, Salo W. *The Russian Jew Under Tsars and Soviets.* New York: Macmillan, 1964.

Bartrop, Paul R. *The Evian Conference of 1938 and the Jewish Refugee Crisis.* London: Palgrave Macmillan, 2018.

Berman, Gerald S. "Reaction to the Resettlement of World War II Refugees in Alaska." *Jewish Social Studies* 61, no. 3–4 (Summer–Fall 1982): 271–82.

Best, Gary Dean. "The Jewish 'Center of Gravity' and Secretary Hay's Roumanian Notes." *American Jewish Archives* 32:1 (April 1980): 5, 23–34.

Blum, John Morton, ed. *The Price of Vision: The Diary of Henry A. Wallace 1942–1946.* New York: Houghton Mifflin, 1973.

———, ed. *From the Morgenthau Diaries: Years of War 1941–1945.* Boston: Houghton Mifflin, 1967.

Bohlen, Charles E. *Witness to History, 1929–1969.* New York: W.W. Norton, 1973.

Breitman, Richard. *Official Secrets: What the Nazis Planned, What the British and Americans Knew.* New York: Hill and Wang, 1998.

———. "The Allied War Effort and the Jews, 1942–1943." *Journal of Contemporary History* 20, no. 1 (January 1985): 135–56.

Breitman, Richard, and Alan M. Kraut. *American Refugee Policy and European Jewry, 1933–1945.* Bloomington: Indiana University Press, 1988.

Breitman, Richard, and Allan J. Lichtman. *FDR and the Jews.* Cambridge MA: Harvard University Press, 2014.

Breitman, Richard, Barbara McDonald Stewart, and Severin Hochberg, eds. *Advocate for the Doomed, Volume 1: The Diaries and Papers of James G. McDonald 1932–1935.* Bloomington and Indianapolis: Indiana University Press, 2007.

———. *Refugees and Rescue, Volume 2: The Diaries and Papers of James G. McDonald 1935–1945.* Bloomington and Indianapolis: Indiana University Press, 2009.

Bryant, Elizabeth. "Rabbi Stephen S. Wise's Actions Upon Receipt of the Riegner Telegram: What More Could He Have Done?" *Studia Historyczne* 56 (2013): 185–202.

Burns, James MacGregor. *Roosevelt: The Lion and the Fox.* New York: Harcourt Brace, 1956.

Celler, Emanuel. *You Never Leave Brooklyn: The Autobiography of Emanuel Celler.* New York: John Day, 1953.

Cohen, Michael A. *Truman and Israel.* Berkeley: University of California Press, 1990.

Cohen, Naomi W. *Not Free to Desist: The American Jewish Committee, 1906–66.* Philadelphia: Jewish Publication Society, 1972.

———. "The Abrogation of the Russo-American Treaty of 1832." *Jewish Social Studies* 25, no. 1 (January 1963): 3–41.

Collier, Peter, with David Horowitz. *The Roosevelts: An American Saga.* New York: Simon & Schuster, 1994.

Committee on International Relations. *Problems of World War II and Its Aftermath, Part 2: The Palestine Question, Problems of Postwar Europe.* Washington DC: Government Printing Office, 1976.

Cook, Blanche Wiesen. *Eleanor Roosevelt, Volume 1: The Early Years, 1884–1933.* New York: Viking Press, 1992.

———. *Eleanor Roosevelt, Volume 2: The Defining Years, 1933–1938.* New York: Viking Press, 1999.

Costigliola, Frank. *Roosevelt's Lost Alliances.* Princeton NJ: Princeton University Press, 2012.

Dallek, Robert. *Franklin D. Roosevelt: A Political Life*. New York: Viking, 2017.

———. *Franklin D. Roosevelt and American Foreign Policy, 1932–1945*. New York: Oxford University Press, 1979.

D'Este, Carlo. *Patton: A Genius for War*. New York: HarperCollins, 1990.

Detzer, Dorothy. *Appointment on the Hill*. New York: Henry Holt, 1948.

Dinnerstein, Leonard. "Jews and the New Deal." *American Jewish History* 72, no. 4 (June 1983): 461–76.

Dodd, William E., Jr., and Martha Dodd, eds. *Ambassador Dodd's Diary, 1933–1938*. New York: Harcourt Brace, 1941.

Elath, Eliahu. *Zionism at the UN: A Diary of the First Days*. Philadelphia: Jewish Publication Society of America, 1976.

Emergency Committee to Save the Jewish People of Europe. *The Work Is Still Ahead*. New York: Emergency Committee to Save the Jewish People of Europe, 1944.

Erdheim, Stuart. "The U.S. Holocaust Museum, and the Failure to Bomb Auschwitz." In *Distorting America's Response to the Holocaust*, 61–63. Washington DC: David S. Wyman Institute for Holocaust Studies, 2018.

Feingold, Henry L. *Bearing Witness: How America and its Jews Responded to the Holocaust*. Syracuse NY: Syracuse University Press, 1995.

———. *The Politics of Rescue: The Roosevelt Administration and the Holocaust, 1938–1945*. New Brunswick NJ: Rutgers University Press, 1970.

Feis, Herbert. *1933: Characters in Crisis*. Boston: Little, Brown, 1966.

Ferrell, Robert H., ed. *Dear Bess: The Letters from Harry to Bess Truman, 1910–1959*. New York: W. W. Norton, 1983.

Fine, Herbert A., and David H. Stauffer, eds. *Foreign Relations of the United States, 1948, The Near East, South Asia, and Africa, Volume V, Part 1*. Washington DC: Government Printing Office, 1975.

Fine, Herbert A., Ralph R. Goodwin, and John P. Glennon, eds. *Foreign Relations of the United States: Diplomatic Papers, 1945, The Near East and Africa, Vol. VIII*. Washington DC: Government Printing Office, 1969.

Finger, Seymour Maxwell, ed. *American Jewry During the Holocaust*. New York: Holmes and Meier, 1984.

Freedman, Max. *Roosevelt and Frankfurter: Their Correspondence 1928–1945*. Boston: Little, Brown, 1967.

Freidel, Frank. *Franklin D. Roosevelt: A Rendezvous with Destiny*. Boston: Little, Brown, 1990.

———. *Franklin D. Roosevelt: Launching the New Deal*. Boston: Little Brown, 1973.

———. *Franklin D. Roosevelt: The Apprenticeship*. Boston: Little, Brown, 1952.

Friedman, Leon. "Election of 1944." In *History of American Presidential Elections, 1784–1968, Vol. 4, 1940–1968*, edited by Arthur M. Schlesinger Jr., 3023–28. New York: McGraw Hill, 1971.

Fromer, Morris. "The American Jewish Congress: A History, 1914–1950." PhD diss., Ohio State University, 1978.

Frommer, Myrna, and Harvey Frommer, eds. *Growing Up Jewish in America: An Oral History.* New York: Houghton Mifflin Harcourt, 1995.

Gal, Allon. *David Ben-Gurion and the American Alignment for a Jewish State.* Bloomington and Indianapolis: Indiana University Press, 1985.

Ganin, Zvi. "Activism versus Moderation: The Conflict between Abba Hillel Silver and Stephen Wise during the 1940s." *Studies in Zionism* 5, no. 1 (Spring 1984): 71–95.

Gartner, Lloyd P. "Roumania, America, and World Jewry: Consul Peixotto in Bucharest, 1870–1876." *American Jewish Historical Quarterly* 58, no. 1 (September 1968): 25–117.

———. "The Two Continuities of Antisemitism in the United States." In *Antisemitism through the Ages,* edited by Shmuel Almog, 311–20. Oxford UK: Pergamon Press, 1998.

Gelb, Saadia. *The Chase is the Game: The Journeys of an American-Israeli Pioneer.* Englewood Cliffs NJ: M. Dworkin, 2001.

Gellman, Irwin F. *Secret Affairs: Franklin Roosevelt, Cordell Hull, and Sumner Welles.* Baltimore: Johns Hopkins University Press, 1995.

Gilbert, Martin. *Auschwitz and the Allies.* New York: Holt, Rinehart & Winston, 1980.

Gleizer, Daniela. *Unwelcome Exiles: Mexico and the Jewish Refugees from Nazism, 1933–1945.* Leiden, The Netherlands: Brill, 2014.

Gottlieb, Moshe R. *American Anti-Nazi Resistance: An Historical Analysis, 1933–1941.* New York: Ktav, 1982.

———. "The American Controversy Over the Olympic Games." *American Jewish Historical Quarterly* 61, no. 3 (March 1972): 181–213.

———. "The Anti-Nazi Boycott Movement in the American Jewish Community, 1933–1941." PhD diss., Brandeis University, 1967.

———. "The Anti-Nazi Boycott Movement in the United States: An Ideological and Sociological Appreciation." *Jewish Social Studies* 35, no. 3 (July–October 1973), 198–99.

Greenberg, Evelyn Levow. "An 1869 Petition on Behalf of Russian Jews." *American Jewish Historical Quarterly* 54, no. 3 (March 1965): 278–95.

Greenberg, Hayim. *Yiddishe Kemfer.* February 12, 1943, translated and reprinted in Midstream, March 1964, 5–10.

Halperin, Samuel. *The Political World of American Zionism.* Detroit: Wayne State University Press, 1961.

Hassett, William D. *Off the Record with F.D.R. 1942–1945.* New Brunswick NJ: Rutgers University Press, 1958.

Hawkins, Richard A. "Samuel Untermyer and the Boycott of Nazi Germany, 1933–1938." *American Jewish History* 93, no. 1 (March 2007): 21–50.

Hecht, Ben. *A Child of the Century.* New York: Simon and Schuster, 1954.

Hertzberg, Arthur. Introduction to "The Day the Rabbis Marched." www.Wyman Institute.org, 2004.

Hull, Cordell. *The Memoirs of Cordell Hull, Volume II.* New York: MacMillan, 1948.

Ickes, Harold L. *The Secret Diary of Harold L. Ickes, Volume 2: The Inside Struggle 1936–1939*. New York: Simon and Schuster, 1954.

———. *The Secret Diary of Harold L. Ickes, Volume 3: The Lowering Clouds 1939–1941*. New York: Simon and Schuster, 1954.

Israel, Fred L., ed. *The War Diary of Breckinridge Long*. Lincoln: University of Nebraska Press, 1966.

Jaffe, Binyamin, ed. *Leib Yaffe: B'Shlihut Am: Mikhtavim v'Teudot 1892–1948*. Jerusalem: Zionist Library, 1968.

Jonas, Manfred. *The United States and Germany: A Diplomatic History*. Ithaca NY: Cornell University Press, 1984.

Kaplan, Marion A. *Dominican Haven: The Jewish Refugee Settlement in Sosua, 1940–1945*. New York: Museum of Jewish Heritage, 2008.

Kaufman, Menahem. *An Ambiguous Partnership: Non Zionists and Zionists in America, 1939–1948*. Detroit: Wayne State University Press, 1991.

Kinsella, William E., Jr. "The Prescience of a Statesman: FDR's Assessment of Adolf Hitler before the World War, 1933–1941." In *Franklin D. Roosevelt: The Man, the Myth, the Era, 1882–1945*, edited by Herbert D. Rosenbaum and Elizabeth Bartelme, 73–84. Westport CT: Greenwood Press, 1987.

Klieman, Aharon, and Adrian Klieman, eds. *American Zionism: A Documentary Series of American Jewish & Zionist History from the Nineteenth Century to 1968, Volume 8*. New York: Routledge, 1992.

Kraut, Alan M., Richard Breitman, and Thomas W. Inhoof. "The State Department, the Labor Department, and German Jewish Immigration, 1930–1940." *Journal of American Ethnic History* 3, no. 2 (Spring 1984): 5–38.

Kupsky, Gregory. "Germanness and Jewishness: Samuel Untermyer, Felix Warburg, and National Socialism, 1914–1938." *American Jewish Archives Journal* 62, no. 2 (2011): 24–42.

Laffer, Dennis R. "The Jewish Trail of Tears: The Evian Conference of 1938." PhD diss., University of South Florida, 2011.

Laqueur, Walter. *The Terrible Secret: Suppression of the Truth About Hitler's "Final Solution."* Boston: Little, Brown, 1980.

Laqueur, Walter, and Richard Breitman. *Breaking the Silence*. New York: Simon and Schuster, 1986.

Larson, Erik. *In the Garden of Beasts: Love, Terror, and an American Family in Hitler's Berlin*. New York: Crown, 2011.

Lash, Joseph P. *Dealers and Dreamers: A New Look at the New Deal*. Garden City NY: Doubleday, 1988.

———. *Eleanor and Franklin*. New York: W. W. Norton, 1971.

———. *Eleanor: The Years Alone*. New York: W. W. Norton, 1972.

Lasser, William. *Benjamin V. Cohen, Architect of the New Deal*. New Haven CT: Yale University Press, 2002.

Lazin, Frederick A. "The Response of the American Jewish Committee to the Crisis of German Jewry, 1933–1939." *American Jewish Archives* 68, no. 1 (March 1979): 284–304.

Leff, Laurel. *Buried by The Times: The Holocaust and America's Most Important Newspaper.* New York: Cambridge University Press, 2005.

Lelyveld, Joseph. *His Final Battle: The Last Months of Franklin Roosevelt.* New York: Alfred A. Knopf, 2016.

Levering, Ralph B. *American Opinion and the Russian Alliance, 1939–1945.* Chapel Hill: University of North Carolina Press, 1976.

Lewin, Isaac. "Indeed, Your Blood, of Your Souls, I Shall Seek" (Hebrew). *HaPardes* 17 (1943): 31–33.

Lipstadt, Deborah E. *Beyond Belief: The American Press & the Coming of the Holocaust 1933–1945.* New York: The Free Press, 1986.

Littell, Norman M. *My Roosevelt Years.* Seattle: University of Washington Press, 1987.

Loewenheim, Francis L., Harold D. Langley, and Manfred Jonas. *Roosevelt and Churchill: Their Secret Wartime Correspondence.* New York: E. P. Dutton, 1975.

Lookstein, Haskel. *Were We Our Brothers' Keepers?: The Public Response of American Jews to the Holocaust, 1938–1944.* New York: Hartmore House, 1985.

Marino, Andy. *A Quiet American: The Secret War of Varian Fry.* New York: St. Martin's, 1999.

Martin, Geoffrey J. *The Life and Thought of Isaiah Bowman.* Hamden CT: Archon Books, 1980.

Mashberg, Michael. "The West and the Holocaust." *Patterns of Prejudice* 12, no. 3 (May–June 1978): 19–32.

Meacham, Jon. *Franklin and Winston: An Intimate Portrait of an Epic Friendship.* New York: Random House, 2003.

Medoff, Rafael. "American Jewish Leaders and the North Africa Controversy of 1943: Applying the Gurock Principle," *American Jewish History* 101, no. 3 (July 2017): 297–310.

———. "Revisiting the Voyage of the Damned," *Prism* 6 (Spring 2014): 63–69.

———. *FDR and the Holocaust: A Breach of Faith.* Washington DC: David S. Wyman Institute for Holocaust Studies, 2013.

———. "The Roosevelt Administration, David Ben-Gurion, and the Failure to Bomb Auschwitz: A Mystery Solved." Washington DC: David S. Wyman Institute for Holocaust Studies, 2013.

———. *Blowing the Whistle on Genocide: Josiah E. DuBois, Jr. and the Struggle for a U.S. Response to the Holocaust.* West Lafayette IN: Purdue University Press, 2009.

Medoff, Rafael, and David Golinkin. *The Student Struggle Against the Holocaust.* New York and Jerusalem: Jewish Theological Seminary of America, Schecter Institute of Jewish Studies, and David S. Wyman Institute for Holocaust Studies, and Targum Shlishi, 2010.

————. "'Retribution Is Not Enough': The 1943 Campaign by Jewish Students to Raise American Public Awareness of the Nazi Genocide." *Holocaust and Genocide Studies* 11, no. 2 (Fall 1997): 171–89.

Meir, Golda. *My Life.* New York: G. P. Putnam's Sons, 1975.

Merkley, Paul C. *The Politics of Christian Zionism 1891–1948.* London: Frank Cass, 1998.

Merlin, Samuel. *Millions of Jews to Rescue.* Edited by Rafael Medoff. Washington DC: David S. Wyman Institute for Holocaust Studies, 2011.

Meyer, Michael A. "The Refugee Scholars Project of the Hebrew Union College." In *A Bicentennial Festschrift for Jacob Rader Marcus,* edited by Bertram Wallace Korn, 359–75. New York: Ktav, 1976.

Moore, Deborah Dash. *B'nai B'rith and the Challenge of Ethnic Leadership.* Albany: State University of New York Press, 1981.

Morgan, Ted. *FDR: A Biography.* New York: Simon and Schuster, 1985.

Morgenthau, Henry III. *Mostly Morgenthaus: A Family History.* New York: Tickson and Fields, 1992.

Morewitz, Stephen J., and Lieberman, Susan B. "The Saving of the S.S. Quanza in Hampton Roads, Virginia, on September 14, 1940: A Prelude to the Nazi Holocaust," unpublished manuscript.

Morse, Arthur D. *While Six Million Died: A Chronicle of American Apathy.* New York: Random House, 1968.

Murphy, Robert. *Diplomat Among Warriors.* New York: Doubleday, 1964.

Neu, Charles E. *Colonel House: A Biography of Woodrow Wilson's Silent Partner.* New York: Oxford University Press, 2014.

Neumann, Emanuel. *In the Arena.* New York: Herzl Press, 1976.

Neuringer, Sheldon. "American Jewry and United States Immigration Policy, 1881–1953." PhD diss., University of Wisconsin, 1969.

Neustadt-Noy, Isaac. "The Unending Task: Efforts to Unite American Jewry from the American Jewish Congress to the American Jewish Conference." PhD diss., Brandeis University, 1976.

Noack, Thorsten. "William L. Shirer and International Awareness of the Nazi 'Euthanasia' Program." *Holocaust and Genocide Studies* 30, no. 3 (Winter 2016): 433–57.

Noble, G. Bernard, and E. R. Perkins, eds. *Foreign Relations of the United States: Diplomatic Papers, 1942, Europe, Volume III.* Washington DC: Government Printing Office, 1961.

Norwood, Stephen H. "Entertaining Nazi Warriors in America, 1934–1936." In *From Antisemitism to Anti-Zionism: The Past and Present of a Lethal Ideology,* edited by Eunice G. Pollack, 148–84. Boston: Academic Studies Press, 2017.

————. *The Third Reich in the Ivory Tower: Complicity and Conflict on American Campuses.* New York: Cambridge University Press, 2009.

Ofer, Dalia. *Escaping the Holocaust: Illegal Immigration to the Land of Israel, 1939–1944.* New York: Oxford University Press, 1990.

Olitzky, Kerry M. "The Sunday-Sabbath Movement in American Reform Judaism: Strategy or Evolution." *American Jewish Archives* 34 (April 1982): 75–88.

Penkower, Monty Noam. *Decision on Palestine Deferred: America, Britain and Wartime Diplomacy 1939–1945*. London: Frank Cass, 2002.

———. *The Holocaust and Israel Reborn: From Catastrophe to Sovereignty*. Urbana and Chicago: University of Illinois Press, 1994.

———. *The Jews Were Expendable: Free World Diplomacy and the Holocaust*. Urbana and Chicago: University of Illinois Press, 1983.

———. *Palestine in Turmoil: The Struggle for Sovereignty, 1933–1939, Volume I: Prelude to Revolt, 1933–1936*. New York: Touro College Press and Academic Studies Press, 2014.

Perkins, E. Ralph, S. Everett Gleason, John G. Reid, John P. Glennon, N. O. Sappington, William Slant, Velma Hastings Cassidy, and Warren H. Reynolds, eds. *Foreign Relations of the United States: Diplomatic Papers, 1944, The British Commonwealth and Europe, Volume 3*. Washington DC: Government Printing Office, 1965.

Pitot, Geneviève. *The Mauritian Shekel: The Story of the Jewish Detainees in Mauritius, 1940–1945*. Lanham MD: Rowman & Littlefield, 2000.

Porat, Dina. "Al-domi: Palestinian Intellectuals and the Holocaust, 1943–1945." *Studies in Zionism* 5, no. 1 (Spring 1984): 97–124.

Proskauer, Joseph M. *A Segment of My Times*. New York: Farrar, Strauss, 1950.

Raphael, Marc Lee. *Abba Hillel Silver*. New York: Holmes and Meier, 1989.

Rescue of the Jewish and Other Peoples in Nazi-Occupied Territory, Extract from Hearings before the Committee on Foreign Affairs House of Representatives, Seventy-Eighth Congress, First Session, on H. Res. 350 and H. Res. 352, November 26, 1943. Washington DC: Government Printing Office, 1943.

Robinson, Greg. *By Order of the President: FDR and the Internment of Japanese Americans*. Cambridge MA: Harvard University Press, 2001.

Robinson, Ira, ed. *Cyrus Adler: Selected Letters*, 2 vols. Philadelphia: Jewish Publication Society of America, 1985.

Roosevelt, Elliot, and Eleanor Roosevelt, eds. *FDR: His Personal Letters, Vol. 1, Early Years (1887–1905)*. New York: Duell, Sloan, and Pearce, 1947.

Rudin, A. James. *Pillar of Fire: A Biography of Rabbi Stephen S. Wise*. Lubbock: Texas Tech University, 2015.

Salmon, Milka. "Forced Emigration of the Jews of Burgenland: Test Case," Shoah Resource Center, yadvashem.org.il.

Sappington, Newton O., Kieran J. Carroll, and Francis C. Prescott, eds. *Foreign Relations of the United States Diplomatic Papers, 1934, Europe, Near East and Africa, Volume II*. Washington DC: Government Printing Office, 1951.

Schneiderman, Harry, and Julius B. Maller, eds. *American Jewish Year Book 5707 (1946–47), Volume 48*. Philadelphia: Jewish Publication Society of America, 1946.

Schwartz, Samuel. "G. George Fox." In *Central Conference of American Rabbis Year-book 1960*, 201–2. New York: Central Conference of American Rabbis, 1961.

Shafir, Shlomo. "American Jewish Leaders and the Emerging Nazi Threat (1928–January, 1933)." *American Jewish Archives* 31, no. 2 (November 1979): 150–83.

———. "The Impact of the Jewish Crisis on American-German Relations." PhD diss., Georgetown University, 1971.

Shapiro, Edward S. "The Approach of War: Congressional Isolationism and Anti-Semitism, 1939–1941." *American Jewish History* 74, no. 1 (September 1984): 45–64.

Shapiro, Robert D. "A Reform Rabbi in the Progressive Era: The Early Career of Stephen S. Wise." PhD diss., Harvard University, 1984.

Sheramy, Rona. "'There Are Times When Silence Is a Sin': The Women's Division of the American Jewish Congress and the Anti-Nazi Boycott." *American Jewish History* 89, no. 1 (March 2001): 105–21.

Sherwood, Robert E. *Roosevelt and Hopkins: An Intimate History.* New York: Harper & Brothers, 1948.

Shirer, William L. *The Rise and Fall of the Third Reich: A History of Nazi Germany.* New York: Simon and Schuster, 1960.

Smith, Gene. *The Shattered Dream: Herbert Hoover and the Great Depression.* New York: William Morrow, 1970.

Smith, Neil. *American Empire: Roosevelt's Geographer and the Prelude to Globalization.* Berkeley: University of California Press, 2003.

Stember, Charles H. et al., eds. *Jews in the Mind of America.* New York: Basic Books, 1966.

Stewart, Barbara McDonald. *United States Government Policy on Refugees from Nazism, 1933–1940.* New York: Garland, 1982.

Tenenbaum, Joseph. "The Anti-Nazi Boycott Movement in the United States." *Yad Vashem Studies* 3 (1959): 141–59.

Tifft, Susan E., and Alex S. Jones, *The Trust: The Private and Powerful Family Behind The New York Times.* New York: Little, Brown, 2000.

Tomaszewski, Jerzy. "Stephen S. Wise's Meeting with the Polish Ambassador in Washington, 1 April 1938." *Gal-Ed* 11 (1989): 103–15.

Truman, Margaret. *Harry S. Truman.* New York: HarperCollins, 1973.

Urofsky, Melvin I. *A Voice That Spoke for Justice: The Life and Times of Stephen S. Wise.* Albany: State University of New York Press, 1982.

———. "American Jewish Leadership." *American Jewish History* 70, no. 4 (June 1981): 401–19.

———. *American Zionism from Herzl to the Holocaust.* Garden City NY: Doubleday, 1975.

———. *We Are One! American Jewry and Israel.* Garden City NY: Anchor Press/Doubleday, 1978.

Voss, Carl Hermann. "Let Stephen Wise Speak for Himself." *Dimensions in American Judaism* (Fall 1968): 37-39.

———. *Rabbi and Minister: The Friendship of Stephen S. Wise and John Haynes Holmes.* Cleveland and New York: World Publishing, 1964.

Vrba, Rudolf, and Alan Bestic. *I Cannot Forgive.* New York: Grove Press, 1964.

Waldman, Morris D. "Effects of Hitlerism in America." *Proceedings of the Rabbinical Assembly of America.* New York: Ap Press, 1934.

———. *Nor By Power.* New York: International Universities Press, 1953.

Walko, John. "Isolationism: How Would We Know If We Saw It? Reopening the Case of the 1930s." *The Public Perspective* (August–September 1997): 41–42.

Walsh, James A. "The Helium Controversy of 1938," MA thesis, University of Arizona, 1964.

Ward, Geoffrey C. *A First-Class Temperament: The Emergence of Franklin Roosevelt.* New York: Harper and Row, 1989.

Wasserstein, Bernard. *Britain and the Jews of Europe 1939–1945.* New York: Oxford University Press, 1979.

Wells, Allen. *Tropical Zion: General Trujillo, FDR, and the Jews of Sosua.* Durham NC: Duke University Press, 2009.

Wells, Leon Weliczker. *Who Speaks for the Vanquished? American Jewish Leaders and the Holocaust.* New York: Peter Lang, 1987.

Wenn, Stephen R. "A Tale of Two Diplomats: George S. Messersmith and Charles H. Sherrill on Proposed American Participation in the 1936 Olympics." *Journal of Sport History* 16, no. 1 (Spring 1989): 27–43.

Wiesel, Elie. *Night.* New York: Avon, 1960.

Wise, Stephen S. *Challenging Years: The Autobiography of Stephen S. Wise.* New York: G. P. Putnam's Sons, 1949.

Woolner, David B. *The Last 100 Days: FDR at War and Peace.* New York: Basic Books, 2017.

Wyman, David S. *The Abandonment of the Jews: America and the Holocaust 1941–1945.* New York: Pantheon, 1984.

———. *Paper Walls: America and the Refugee Crisis 1938–1941.* Amherst: University of Massachusetts Press, 1968.

Wyman, David S., and Rafael Medoff. *A Race Against Death: Peter Bergson, America, and the Holocaust.* New York: The New Press, 2002.

Zuccotti, Susan. *Under His Very Windows: The Vatican and the Holocaust in Italy.* New Haven CT: Yale University Press, 2000.

Zucker, Bat-Ami. *Cecilia Razovsky and the American-Jewish Women's Rescue Operations in the Second World War.* London: Vallentine Mitchell, 2008.

———. "Frances Perkins and the German-Jewish Refugees, 1933–1940." *American Jewish History* 89, no. 1 (March 2001): 35–59.

———. *In Search of Refuge: Jews and U.S. Consuls in Nazi Germany, 1933–1941.* London: Vallentine Mitchell, 2001.

INDEX

Acheson, Dean, 109–10
Adler, Cyrus, 10
Adler, Stella, 148
Agudath Israel, 107, 176, 177, 271, 273
Alaska immigration proposal, 94–95, 143, 232
Al Domi, 165
Alexander, Robert, 193–94, 204
Alfange, Dean, 201
Allied declaration on mass murder, xi, 128, 148, 149
Alski, Victor, 267
America First, xiii
American Civil Liberties Union, 2
American Council for Judaism, 174, 247
American Federation of Labor, 26, 201, 221, 323n57
American Friends of a Jewish Palestine, 147
American Friends Service Committee, 15, 95
American Jewish Assembly. *See* American Jewish Conference
American Jewish Committee, 12, 13, 29, 114, 121, 122, 170, 257; and American Jewish Conference, 175–77, 185; anti-Nazi demonstrations, 6, 7, 8, 10, 157; boycott of German goods, 10, 22;

Brooklyn Jewish Democracy, 39; criticism of Breckinridge Long, 205; Hitler's rise to power, 5; immigration proposals, 77; North Africa policy, 137; on plebiscite plan (1938), 57; relationship with American Jewish Congress, 1, 10, 88; relationship with Jewish Telegraphic Agency, 172; response to news of the Holocaust, 126, 129; and Zionism, 173–74
American Jewish Conference, 183–85, 204, 259, 262; absorbs Joint Emergency Committee on European Jewish Affairs, 187; and Bergson Group, 207–8; and bombing of Auschwitz, 276; controversy over putting rescue on agenda, 177–78, 344n71; and "free ports" proposal, 222; genesis of, 173–74; opposed by Roosevelt administration, 181–82; rally for rescue (1944), 276; and unfilled quotas, 69
American Jewish Congress, 1, 12, 21, 43, 118, 119, 122, 127, 128, 157, 178, 208, 222, 309, 312; and American Jewish Conference, 175, 176; anti-Nazi demonstrations, 9, 10, 15, 17, 24–25, 35, 37, 51, 102, 149, 154, 167, 194, 300; and Bergson Group, 149–51, 208, 217; boycott

CPSIA information can be obtained
at www.ICGtesting.com
Printed in the USA
LVHW090302250320
651106LV00001B/1/J